THE ANCIENT CITY

THE ANCIENT CITY

A Study on the Religion, Laws,
and Institutions of Greece and Rome

NUMA DENIS
FUSTEL DE COULANGES

with a new foreword by
ARNALDO MOMIGLIANO AND S. C. HUMPHREYS

The Johns Hopkins University Press
Baltimore and London

Published in 1956 as a Doubleday Anchor Book

The Johns Hopkins University Press, Baltimore, Maryland 21218
The Johns Hopkins Press Ltd., London

Library of Congress Cataloging in Publication Data

Fustel de Coulanges, Numa Denis, 1830–1889.
  The ancient city.

  Translation of La cité antique.
  Includes bibliographical references.
  1. Cities and towns, Ancient. 2. Rome—Politics and
government. 3. Greece—Politics and government. I. Title.
JC51.F95 1980   938   79-3703
ISBN 0-8018-2304-8

CONTENTS

BOOK THIRD

THE CITY

BOOK FOURTH

THE REVOLUTIONS

BOOK FIFTH

THE MUNICIPAL REGIME DISAPPEARS

FOREWORD

Part I.

IN THE SIXTIES and seventies of the nineteenth century scholars working in different countries and in different fields produced radically new interpretations of ancient societies. H. S. Maine and J. J. Bachofen perhaps opened the series in 1861 with, respectively, *Ancient Law* and *Das Mutterrecht*. Numa D. Fustel de Coulanges followed up with *La Cité antique* in 1864, J. F. McLennan with *Primitive Marriage* in 1865. Bachofen's *Die Sage von Tanaquil* was published in 1870, E. B. Tylor's *Primitive Culture* in 1871, and L. H. Morgan's *Ancient Society* in 1877. To these we must add two books by W. Robertson Smith, *Kinship and Marriage in Early Arabia* and *The Religion of the Semites*, which successively appeared in 1885 and 1889. All these authors were of course aware of the recent achievements of comparative philology and mythology. They accepted the existence of an Indo-European civilization unconnected with Semitic civilization, but only Maine and Robertson Smith worked out their own models of ancient social life within the framework of these great prehistoric units characterized by common language and common political and religious institutions. The others—even Fustel de Coulanges, who gladly used the Indians for comparison with Greeks and Romans—elaborated evolutionary schemes that were essentially unrelated to the notions of Aryans and Semites. Each of the scholars mentioned seems to have worked independently of the others, although (for instance) Morgan quotes Fustel and was on friendly personal terms with McLennan; the only clear exception is Robertson Smith's avowed debt to McLennan on totemism.

Fustel de Coulanges was born in 1830 and educated at the Ecole Normale Supérieure of Paris, where one of his teachers was J. D. Guigniaut, who translated and vulgarized F. Creuzer's ideas about ancient religion. Fustel started with a history of the island of Chios (1856), notable for its sweep from the origins to the nineteenth century. He obtained his doctorate in 1858 with two theses, one on Polybius (*Polybe, ou la Grèce conquise*) and one on the cult of Vesta (*Quid Vestae cultus in institutis veterum privatis publicisque valuerit*), in which some of the interests and theories of the *Cité antique* are anticipated. *The Ancient City—La Cité antique*—was written at Strasbourg, where Fustel became a professor. It was very much the work of a scholar who lived on the borders of German culture and had a poor opinion of it. Fustel was acquainted with what G. B. Niebuhr and A. Schwegler and young Theodor Mommsen had written about early Roman history. He was probably also well informed about the books of K. O. Müller, A. Boeckh, F. G. Welcker, and G. F. Schoemann on Greek mythology, religion, and institutions. Furthermore, he was necessarily dependent on German scholars for his notions about Indo-Europeans (or Aryans) because they had done most of the spadework in this field. But he intentionally disregarded modern authorities in his *Ancient City* and, though he involved French and English writers in his provocative silence, there is no doubt that they were not his main target. In a posthumous fragment by him one reads: "I would rather be mistaken in the manner of Livy than that of Niebuhr." In 1864 Fustel was still mainly a classical scholar with an extraordinary familiarity with classical texts. His knowledge of other Aryan groups was as yet superficial and in the case of Indian civilization always remained so. The main attraction of the Aryan idea for him was that it freed him from having to include the Semites—and therefore the Jews and the dangerous Bible—in his discourse.

After publishing *The Ancient City* Fustel became increasingly involved in the question of whether medieval French institutions were mainly German or Celtic or Roman in origin. He embraced the Roman thesis. As his main work on the subject, the *Histoire des institutions politiques de l'Ancienne France*, began to appear after the great crisis of the Franco-Prussian War of 1870–71 (more precisely in 1875), it became symptomatic of the revulsion against Germany that then prevailed in France. After 1871 Fustel did indeed stand up as the leader of the new nationalistic historiography. But he is not responsible for the extravagant notions about the Gauls produced by his pupil C. Jullian and even less for the use Ch. Maurras and other extreme rightists of the Action Française made of him. Moreover, the main outlines of his ideas about the origins of French civilization were expressed by Fustel before the war, early in 1870, in lectures he had been invited to deliver in the presence of the Empress Eugénie as soon as he had left the University of Strasbourg to become a teacher at the Ecole Normale. Though it would be wrong to play down the emotional impact of the events of 1870–71 on the later development of Fustel (who died prematurely in 1889), his transition from classical interests to a concern with problems of French history should be dated about 1865.

There are, however, traits that remained constant in his activity. One of these, which we have already noticed, is his distrust of German scholarship. This goes together with a certain uncritical attitude towards his sources, because source criticism had been perfected by the schools of Niebuhr and Pertz (the latter in the context of the *Monumenta Germaniae*). The reader of *The Ancient City* must be on guard at every step about what Fustel states as given in his sources. For instance, the notion—essential for the validity of Fustel's theories and presented by him as a fact—that the Greeks and Latins buried their dead in family tombs within their own estates is simply not supported by the evidence he produces (or by any evidence discovered subsequently). Secondly, throughout his career Fustel was involved in a polemic against socialist and generally egalitarian ideas. He defended the institution of private property against French and German socialists by making private property one of the original institutions of mankind (and, as we shall soon see, connecting it with the cult of the dead). He maintained with equal firmness that the revolutionaries of 1789 had deceived their followers by presenting the ancient republics of Athens, Sparta, and Rome (more especially Sparta) as models of liberty. In agreement with B. Constant and indeed with a whole line of anti-Jacobin thinkers Fustel believed that there was no respect for individual liberty in ancient Greece and Rome (not even in Athens). Individual liberty was to him the product of Christi-

anity, which in its turn he considered unthinkable without
the universality of the Roman Empire. Here is the root of
Fustel's ambiguity about ancient values. On the one hand he
admires, and feels nostalgia for, the ancestral traditions that
ensured private property and family solidarity in the days of
old. On the other hand he feels that without Christianity there
would be no respect for the individual or even separation
between state and religion; therefore, though a confessed un-
believer, he chooses to remain within the Catholic Church and
avoids discussing the Bible.

Fustel's ambiguous attitude towards the historical materials
and the values inherent in them goes beyond the subjects of
private property and individual freedom and seems to pervade
his whole historical outlook in *The Ancient City*. Paradox-
ically, this gives the volume both its superficial appearance of
compact argument and its ultimate reality of self-contradictory
historical construction. We are introduced to a simple world
where people claiming to have the same ancestors live together
on privately owned ground sanctified by the tombs of the
ancestors themselves and by the hearth in which the spirits
of the ancestors are supposed to live perennially as gods: "the
religion of the dead is the oldest in man." Keeping the fire
alive means keeping the ancestors alive. Because the dead
expect to be kept alive by their descendants, celibacy is a
crime. The tomb establishes an indissoluble union between
the land and the extended family living on it (let us call it
the *gens*, in Roman terminology). Thus the dead are at the
root of both religion and property. The father is the priest of
the family cult and also king over his family; land is inalienable; daughters do not inherit because they marry outside the
family and join the ancestor cult of their husbands. But the
sons are not all on an equal footing. The first-born inherits
the priestly and sovereign rights of the father. If the evidence
about primitive Rome does not show any trace of the right
of primogeniture (unlike that about India and, according to
Fustel, Greece), we must postulate its existence. Indians,
Greeks, and Romans (and the other Aryans) must have passed
through this stage, in which the extended family ruled by the
eldest living member was the only political and religious
corporation.

But how could this coherent society disintegrate and give place to cities in which different families without common ancestors lived together, in which religion was no longer limited to the household, and in which property rights in land became alienable? Fustel admires such a society just because it appears immutable. The internal contradictions revealed by Marxist analysis did not yet exist for him. For an explanation he relies on what I have called his ambiguity and would now call more precisely his dualistic attitude towards historical developments. He has one or two trump cards up his sleeve. Somewhere, somehow, another religion developed that had nothing to do with ancestors. It was the cult of natural phenomena, the worship of sun, moon, stars, etc. Besides, Fustel unexpectedly adds, it was not quite true that everyone lived happily inside the family structure so far outlined. Somewhere, somehow, the original family had been complicated by the admission of clients who in exchange for help had agreed to worship the ancestors of their patrons and had been admitted into the extended family in a subordinate position. Furthermore, somewhere, somehow, there existed families unable either to create a religion of their own or to accept the religion of others. These unfortunate families remained outside the original civilization of the Aryan *gentes* in a near-beastly condition. The religion of natural phenomena and the existence of clients inside the *gentes* and of plebeians outside them were the driving factors in the dissolution of the old order.

When the original *gentes* recognized the narrowness of their ancestral groups, the common cult of physical objects like the sun helped them to combine in the greater unit we call the city. In the city each family group preserved its own ancestral cult, but shared these "physical" gods (for instance, Jupiter) with other families. In addition, certain features of family worship were extended to the city; hence, the common hearth for the city personified in Rome by the goddess Vesta. At first the cities preserved the monarchic government each family had had in isolation. But it was soon recognized that a confederation of families, as the city was, would be better governed by a council made of family heads, that is, by an aristocracy. The transition from monarchy to aristocracy in the young cities did not represent a revolution, but rather a revival of a traditional institution, and therefore involved no bloodshed. The real revolutions came from clients and plebeians. As soon as the city had been founded by the association of various families, the combined strength of their clients began to exercise pressure on the ruling class. In their turn the outsiders or plebeians tried to penetrate into the city and obtain recognition in it. Clients and plebeians were natural allies. The changes, or real "revolutions," in the social and economic structure of the ancient cities—the abolition of clientship, the parification of patricians and plebeians, the liberalization of land tenure and of inheritance rules—are all deduced by Fustel from the unstable position of the *gentes* within the cities, where the clients became ungovernable and the outsiders claimed political rights. Shrewdly enough, Fustel saw the point of real weakness in the patricians, that is, the need they had of the military co-operation of clients and plebeians in war.

It is superfluous to go into the details of the various revolutions. Even in explaining the last revolution of the ancient world—the substitution of a universal empire for the city states—Fustel produces a historical factor he had not mentioned before. He had previously presented Rome as an ordinary city beset by all the problems characteristic of the other ancient cities. Now, suddenly, Rome becomes an exceptional city. We are told that from its very beginnings Rome collected different nationalities, even different cities, within its own territory. Consequently, Rome was prepared to transcend the limitations of the ordinary city state and to pave the way for a universal state and a universal church. Fustel explains all the transformations of ancient society, before and after the creation of the city, by introducing new elements whose presence he cannot properly account for. We must conclude that the earthly paradise of the *gentes* worshiping their ancestors on the land they had inherited from them cannot have existed, because the very notion of this paradise is incompatible with the existence of the hostile forces that allegedly destroyed it.

University of Chicago   ARNALDO MOMIGLIANO

Bibliographical Note

The preceding pages try to carry the analysis of the *Cité antique* beyond the point I had reached in my paper of 1970, originally written in Italian and now translated into English and republished in *Essays in Ancient and Modern Historiography* (Middletown, Conn., 1977, pp. 325–43: "The Ancient City of Fustel de Coulanges"). The reader is referred to this essay for further information and bibliography. Three important contributions have since appeared: Ch.-O. Carbonell, *Histoire et historiens, une mutation idéologique des historiens français, 1865–1885* (Toulouse, 1976); P. Grossi, *Un altro modo di possedere* (Milan, 1977), pp. 125–90; and M. I. Finley, "The Ancient City: From Fustel de Coulanges to Max Weber and Beyond," *Comparative Studies in Society and History* 19 (1977): 305–27. For the development of the discussion on the difference between ancient and modern liberty there is now a good book by L. Guerci, *Libertà degli Antichi e Libertà dei Moderni* (Naples, 1979). The old biography of Fustel by his pupil P. Guiraud (Paris, 1896), is still indispensable. Jane Herrick's *The Historical Thought of Fustel de Coulanges* (Washington, D.C., 1954), is a useful general introduction. The penetrating little book by T. O. Beidelman, *W. Robertson Smith and the Sociological Study of Religion* (Chicago, 1974), is very relevant.

Part II.

Fustel's conception of the earthly paradise of primitive society was very much the product of his own times. His model of the evolution of society is vitiated at the outset by two basic inconsistencies: although he stresses the importance and cohesion of the *gens* as a *group*, he is trying to use its primordial role in human history to defend the primordial character of *individual* private property, which he derives from the burial of *individuals* on their own land by their heirs.

Tombs, in antiquity, were usually placed beside roads, and although land used for burial became private property and might in various ways be safeguarded from abuse or alienation, I know of no evidence that it was regarded as particularly desirable to be buried in land that formed part of a larger family holding. On the contrary, the most desirable sites were those on main roads leading out of the city, where the tomb would be most in the public eye. Exceptionally, those who merited heroic honors might be buried inside the city, perhaps even in the public square. Fustel's thesis, therefore, is not an obvious or even a natural inference from the ancient sources. In fact, many antiquarian writers had discussed the funeral rites and tombs of the ancients before him, without laying any particular stress on the relation of burial to private estates or the religious duties of the heir. The features of ancient practice selected for attention varied, predictably, with the writer's interests and culture. In the sixteenth and early seventeenth centuries it was the magnificence of the funerals of great men, attended by crowds of supporters and hangers-on, that attracted the most attention. Toward the end of the seventeenth century other interests begin to appear: for example, embalming is discussed in detail and recommended to contemporaries by the doctor Thomas Greenhill in *Nekrokedeia; or, The art of embalming, wherein is shewn the right of burial, the funeral ceremonies, and the several ways of preserving dead bodies in most nations of the world* . . . (London, 1705)— it was used particularly by doctors in preserving bodies for dissection. Protestants, from about 1730 onward, concerned themselves especially with the ancient prohibition of burial inside cities and with demonstrating that burial in and beside churches was not a practice going back to the earliest days of Christianity; such discussions belong to the contemporary campaign against burial in churches and city churchyards as an unhygienic practice. Protestants were prominent in this campaign, no doubt, partly because in many cases the new religion had had to set up its own new burial grounds on sites unhallowed by tradition. But even those who resisted the proposals for change were defending a complex of ritual and material commemorative practices without singling out for particular attention either the right of sons to be buried with their fathers or the obligation of the son to protect and venerate his father's mortal remains. According to Philippe Ariès, whose researches in *L'Homme devant la mort* (Paris, 1977) provide the essential basis for this reassessment of Fustel's views, the removal of more than 20,000 corpses from the cemetery of Les Innocents in Paris in 1785–87 did not give rise to any public concern for the rights of those disinterred; wealthy as well as poor Parisians were buried in Les Innocents, yet the relatives of the dead showed no interest in visiting them in the new "catacombs" to which they were transported.

It seems that one can analytically distinguish three separate elements in the commemoration of the dead: the regular celebration of commemorative rites in church, the setting up of a monument proclaiming the status and virtues of the dead where it could be seen by contemporaries and by posterity, and continued contact with the physical remains in the tomb. While the custom of burying the dead in churches or their associated churchyards persisted, the third of these elements could be taken for granted as a logical consequence of the others, without being singled out for special attention. The new practice of burying the dead in suburban cemeteries remote from the parish churches of the city dissolved the unity of these three elements and produced an abundant crop of pamphlets and reform proposals, studied by Ariès, in which a variety of new combinations are suggested; it is in this context that the theme of burial in private property emerges.

The change in cemetery location had come at the time of the profound general upheaval of society in the French Revolution; the tombs of the upper classes, notably the royal tombs of St Denis, had suffered in the violence directed against the symbols of wealth and status. This thorough shaking-up of customary behavior and ideas allowed new configurations of sentiment, anxiety, and ambition to emerge, and the essay competition organized by the Institut de France in 1801 on the subject of the proper ritual to be performed at funerals and the organization of cemeteries gave full scope for their expression. There are several points to note in Ariès's report of these proposals. The organization of cemeteries seems to receive far more attention than that of funerary rites, except insofar as the latter take on a commemorative character through a focus on speeches praising the achievements of the dead. It seems to be taken for granted that the funerary monument will be transferred, with the physical remains of the dead, from the church or its associated graveyard to the suburban cemetery. This in itself implies that the cemetery is thought of as a place that will be regularly visited. The idea that the dead should be buried at home is less prominent, but occurs several times in different contexts. Pierre Giraud, who in 1796 had already submitted a cemetery project to the Department of the Seine, proposed to vitrify the remains of the dead by a special cremation process and use the resulting material to make two portrait medallions, one of which was to remain on display in the cemetery while the other would become a family heirloom. He had directed in his will that his heirs "should use me as an example by arranging with a soapmaker or surgeon to have my bones separated from the rest of my corpse, should burn my flesh and bodily liquids, and should collect the ashes of these, with my skeleton, in the tomb which I have constructed for this very purpose in my garden, until such time as my descendants can convert my bones into glass" (Ariès, pp. 506–9). The tomb in the garden for Giraud himself is in part merely a way of facilitating exhumation, but his portrait medallions are themselves a form of home burial, which can also be seen as a development of the fashion represented in eighteenth and nineteenth century mourning pictures to use part of the body (the hair) as a memento of the dead (Ariès, pp. 454–55).

The desire to retain some part of the loved dead at home had been growing in strength for some time, and in rare cases mummification had been used to preserve the whole corpse in the house or in a mausoleum on private property (ibid., p. 379). But now burial on private land seemed to offer advantages of a less private character as well. J. Girard, in his competition essay, frankly rejects the traditional church rituals of commemoration and is equally hostile to the "materialism" of the ostentatious tomb monument. The essential relation for him is that between the survivors and the physical remains of the dead; and the best place for the latter is on the dead man's own land. Attachment to the land will be increased by the presence on it of ancestral tombs; patriotism will be solidly grounded in a chain of loyalties spreading outward from the tomb to property, locality, province, and nation; land will be less frequently alienated, and society will be more stable (ibid., pp. 503–4). Here we have not only the recommendation of burial in private property, which can also be amply documented from many other sources of the period, but the precise tie between such burials and attachment to land-ownership that was to become central to Fustel's argument sixty years later— although, by the time *The Ancient City* was written, the practice of private burial was on the decline, largely because

the frequency with which land changed hands made burial in
the public cemetery seem a better guarantee of the continued
respect and cult of the tomb.

Fustel's concern with the extended family also reflects contemporary ideas. Frédéric Le Play's monumental study, *Les
ouvriers européens*, published in 1855, related three main
structural types—patriarchal extended family, stem family, and
nuclear family—to ecological and occupational variables. In
La réforme sociale en France, published, like *The Ancient
City*, in 1864, Le Play recommended laws on inheritance that
would strengthen the stem family, in which a single heir has
control over the whole parental estate (with obligations to
maintain siblings if they continue to live and work with him),
as a remedy against the subdivision of land-holdings. Fustel
failed to distinguish clearly between extended and stem families
—indeed, part of the ambiguity of his argument lies here. His
view of the gradual growth of the *gens* implied an expanding
extended family. But his emphasis on primogeniture points to
the stem family as his preferred model.

The main achievement for which Fustel will be remembered,
at least among anthropologists, is not his inconsistent picture
of the earliest stages of human evolution but his account of
the *gens* as a fully developed institution and his awareness
of the evolutionary problems it raised. Together with Sir Henry
Maine, he introduced into evolutionary theory a body of
material that was already familiar to classicists, but one that
was also capable of illuminating the new discoveries anthropologists were to make in Australia, Africa, and North America.
It was Fustel's insistence on the *rules* governing agnation and
the composition and activities of the *gens* that was to prove
important, rather than his attempt to find a plausible psycho-
logical origin for these rules in the cult of the dead. Both
Fustel and Maine clearly emphasized that kinship was a cultural rather than a natural phenomenon: cultural rules determined who was and who was not a kinsman in different
societies; kinship could be created or destroyed by social rites.
The *gens* was not a casual agglomeration of families: Fustel
specifies that it had a name, rules of recruitment, its own
religious cults, a common tomb (*sic*), its leader, its assemblies,

and its own body of regulations governing members' behavior (*The Ancient City,* pp. 94–97). These two key ideas of kinship as a set of social rules and the descent group as a corporation, together with the general notion of a stage of social evolution in which kinship forms the basis of the structure of social relationships, provided the foundation for the social anthropology of kinship systems. Fustel's views on the decisive role of religion in social evolution also had their influence in sociology and social anthropology, particularly in stimulating Durkheim, Lévy-Bruhl, and later, Evans-Pritchard to ask why religious obligations and beliefs should be so much more imperative and unquestioned in simple societies than in complex ones. Durkheim "stood Fustel on his head" by arguing that it was not religious beliefs that shaped social structure, but social experience that gave religious beliefs their force.

Among classicists, Fustel currently holds a much less prominent position in the gallery of famous ancestors. This a partly because it has never been universally accepted that the Roman *gens,* or Greek *genos,* was an institution common in early times to all strata of society. For Rome, those who believed that the division between patricians and plebeians went back to the earliest settlement of the city tended also to believe that the organization in *gentes* was confined to the patricians. The belief that patricians and plebeians were in origin two separate groups with distinct ethnic origins, culture, and institutions was particularly prevalent in the later nineteenth century, as historians of early Rome grappled with new data on the interrelations of the Italic languages and with the evidence for population môvements produced by archaeology; while those who rejected the "ethnic" model tended to concentrate on trying to reconstruct the immediate bases for the class conflict that broke out in the fifth century B.C., rather than dwell on a possible earlier stage of greater homogeneity. More recently, the growing acceptance of the view that the distinction between patricians and plebeians hardened into a fundamental social cleavage only after the expulsion of the kings implicitly favors the view that the *gens* could have been an institution common to both groups; but the latest discussion of the origins of the plebs (J.-C. Richard, *Les origines de la plèbe romaine,*

Rome, 1978) devotes only a few pages to the *gens*. Students
of Roman law, too, are increasingly feeling discouraged by
paucity of evidence from attempts to reconstruct a "gentile"
stage of society. Alan Watson, in *Rome of the Twelve Tables*
(Princeton, 1975), has only this to say: "It may well be that
at an earlier stage the *gens* was a political unit, but if so its
importance was gone before the XII tables. There is no evidence that in historical times a *gens* had any formal organization or a leader." (G. Franciosi, *Clan gentilizio e strutture
monogamiche. Contributo alla storia della famiglia romana*,
2d ed., Naples, 1978, is confused and very imperfectly acquainted with modern anthropological theory.) The most useful
contribution to the problem from this quarter has been J. M.
Crook's suggestion that the Roman doctrine of *patria potestas*
and agnation, on which Fustel and Maine based such a large
part of their theories, should be recognized as an anomaly
among Indo-European institutions and regarded as a product
of Roman interest in precise legal formulation, rather than
as an Indo-European "survival" ("Patria Potestas," *Classical
Quarterly* 17 (1967): 113–22).

It may be worth pointing out here that the problem of
distinguishing a kernel of genuinely early institutions from
the archaic-looking products of later legal thought was one
that already preoccupied Maine, especially in the very important *Dissertations on Early Law and Custom* (London, 1883),
in which he revised his earlier views in relation to subsequent
research on Indian law and on the structure of Indian and
Slavonic extended families. Modern research seems to confirm
the point that Maine already recognized here, that extended
and nuclear families, rather than representing successive evolutionary forms, should be seen as stages in a single cyclical
process of growth and dispersal. Neither the joint Hindu
family nor the south Slav *zadruga* supply evidence for a stage
of evolution in which nuclear family units were unknown.
(Cf. G.-D. Sontheimer, *The Joint Hindu Family: Its Evolution
as a Legal Institution*, New Delhi, 1977; Robert F. Byrnes,
Communal Families in the Balkans: The Zadruga, South Bend,
Ind., 1976.) However, the importance of ancestor-worship remains much greater in Indian studies of the history of the
family than in recent accounts of Greece and Rome. But it

should also be noted that the major twentieth-century attempt
to trace Roman institutions back to their Indo-European origins through comparison with Indian and other sources, that
of Georges Dumézil, takes a totally different line from Fustel's
and regards the three original Roman tribes as quite possibly
in origin occupational castes (most recently, "Les trois tribus
primitives," *Idées romaines*, Paris, 1969, pp. 209–23).

The situation with regard to ancient Greece is somewhat
different. Fustel's main follower here, G. Glotz (*La solidarité
de la famille dans la Grèce ancienne*, 1904; *La cité grecque*,
1928) accentuated Fustel's tendency to confuse two meanings
of *genos*, which may denote either a corporate, named group
holding rights to priestly office or the bilateral network of
kin on whom a particular individual can call for support.
The latter group, of course, is different for each individual
and does not give rise to any permanent corporate descent
group; and the evidence for "solidarity" and combined action
cited by Fustel and Glotz belongs to the *genos* in the latter
and not the former sense. The view that the *genos* as a for-
malized corporate descent group is confined to the aristocracy
has, on the whole, been the majority opinion throughout the
history of the question, and is reiterated by the latest specialist
studies (F. Bourriot, *Recherches sur la nature du genos*, Lille,
1976; cf. also Momigliano and Humphreys, "The social structure of the ancient city," *Annali della Scuola Normale, Pisa*,
ser. 3, 4 [1974]: 329–67, reprinted in Humphreys, *Anthropology
and the Greeks*, London, 1978, pp. 177–208).

Furthermore, study of family burials in ancient Attica lends
little support to Fustel's thesis. It is true that collective burials
in chamber tombs are common in Bronze Age Greece, but no
continuity can be demonstrated between these tombs and the
burials of the historical period. The most prominent funerary
monuments in archaic Attica (7th–6th century B.C.) were set
up by parents for children, not by pious sons for their fathers;
tombs that can be interpreted as family groupings are unusual
in this period and almost unknown in the preceding Dark
Ages; and tomb-groupings that ostentatiously proclaim family
unity are a phenomenon of the fourth century B.C. and later,
rather than of early times—although they always remain in a
minority (Humphreys, "Family Tombs and Tomb Cult in

Ancient Attica: Tradition or Traditionalism?" *Journal of Hellenic Studies,* in press).

Yet, however much of Fustel's argument we may reject, the task he proposed retains its attraction, despite its difficulty. There is no reason to reject a priori the idea that something may be learnt by comparing the kinship systems of the different Indo-European societies. The task becomes steadily more difficult to attempt, because of the need to combine familiarity with the original sources in each culture and the historical circumstances that produced them, command of modern anthropological theory, and a critical awareness of the way in which research and theory may be influenced by the interests and problems of the researchers' own culture. What we have tried to show here is that the weaknesses in Fustel's argument are intimately connected with the vitality of his reactions to the beliefs and problems of his own society; yet it is also this vitality, as well as the validity of his structural insights, that gives his work its enduring value.

University College, London   S. C. HUMPHREYS

THE ANCIENT CITY

Introduction

IT is proposed here to show upon what principles and by what
rules Greek and Roman society was governed. We unite in the
same study both the Greeks and the Romans, because these two
peoples, who were two branches of a single race, and who
spoke two idioms of a single language, also had the same institutions and the same principles of government, and passed
through a series of similar revolutions.

We shall attempt to set in a clear light the radical and
essential differences which at all times distinguished these
ancient peoples from modern societies. In our system of education, we live from infancy in the midst of the Greeks and
Romans, and become accustomed continually to compare them
with ourselves, to judge of their history by our own, and to
explain our revolutions by theirs. What we have received from
them leads us to believe that we resemble them. We have some
difficulty in considering them as foreign nations; it is almost
always ourselves that we see in them. Hence spring many
errors. We rarely fail to deceive ourselves regarding these
ancient nations when we see them through the opinions and
facts of our own time.

Now, errors of this kind are not without danger. The ideas
which the moderns have had of Greece and Rome have often
been in their way. Having imperfectly observed the institutions
of the ancient city, men have dreamed of reviving them among
us. They have deceived themselves about the liberty of the
ancients, and on this very account liberty among the moderns
has been put in peril. The last eighty years have clearly shown
that one of the great difficulties which impede the march of
modern society is the habit which it has of always keeping
Greek and Roman antiquity before its eyes.

To understand the truth about the Greeks and Romans, it is
wise to study them without thinking of ourselves, as if they

were entirely foreign to us; with the same disinterestedness, and with the mind as free, as if we were studying ancient India or Arabia.

Thus observed, Greece and Rome appear to us in a character absolutely inimitable; nothing in modern times resembles them; nothing in the future can resemble them. We shall attempt to show by what rules these societies were regulated, and it will be freely admitted that the same rules can never govern humanity again.

Whence comes this? Why are the conditions of human government no longer the same as in earlier times? The great changes which appear from time to time in the constitution of society can be the effect neither of chance nor of force alone.

The cause which produces them must be powerful, and must be found in man himself. If the laws of human association are no longer the same as in antiquity, it is because there has been a change in man. There is, in fact, a part of our being which is modified from age to age; this is our intelligence. It is always in movement; almost always progressing; and on this account, our institutions and our laws are subject to change. Man has not, in our day, the way of thinking that he had twenty-five centuries ago; and this is why he is no longer governed as he was governed then.

The history of Greece and Rome is a witness and an example of the intimate relation which always exists between men's ideas and their social state. Examine the institutions of the ancients without thinking of their religious notions, and you find them obscure, whimsical, and inexplicable. Why were there patricians and plebeians, patrons and clients, eupatrids and thetes; and whence came the native and ineffaceable differences which we find between these classes? What was the meaning of those Lacedæmonian institutions which appear to us so contrary to nature? How are we to explain those unjust caprices of ancient private law; at Corinth and at Thebes, the sale of land prohibited; at Athens and at Rome, an inequality in the succession between brother and sister? What did the jurists understand by *agnation,* and by *gens?* Why those revolutions in the laws, those political revolutions? What was that singular patriotism which sometimes effaced every natural sentiment? What did they understand by that liberty of which they were always talking? How did it happen that institutions so very different from anything of which we have an idea to-day, could become established and reign for so long a time? What is the superior principle which gave them authority over the minds of men?

But by the side of these institutions and laws place the religious ideas of those times, and the facts at once become clear, and their explanation is no longer doubtful. If, on going back to the first ages of this race—that is to say, to the time when its institutions were founded—we observe the idea which it had of human existence, of life, of death, of a second life, of the divine principle, we perceive a close relation between these opinions and the ancient rules of private law; between the rites which spring from these opinions and their political institutions.

A comparison of beliefs and laws shows that a primitive religion constituted the Greek and Roman family, established marriage and paternal authority, fixed the order of relationship, and consecrated the right of property, and the right of inheritance. This same religion, after having enlarged and extended the family, formed a still larger association, the city, and reigned in that as it had reigned in the family. From it came all the institutions, as well as all the private law, of the ancients. It was from this that the city received all its principles, its rules, its usages, and its magistracies. But, in the course of time, this ancient religion became modified or effaced, and private law and political institutions were modified with it. Then came a series of revolutions, and social changes regularly followed the development of knowledge.

It is of the first importance, therefore, to study the religious ideas of these peoples, and the oldest are the most important for us to know. For the institutions and beliefs which we find at the flourishing periods of Greece and Rome are only the development of those of an earlier age; we must seek the roots of them in the very distant past. The Greek and Italian populations are many centuries older than Romulus and Homer. It was at an epoch more ancient, in an antiquity without date, that their beliefs were formed, and that their institutions were either established or prepared.

But what hope is there of arriving at a knowledge of this

distant past? Who can tell us what men thought ten or fifteen centuries before our era? Can we recover what is so intangible and fugitive — beliefs and opinions? We know what the Aryas of the East thought thirty-five centuries ago: we learn this from the hymns of the Vedas, which are certainly very ancient, and from the laws of Manu, in which we can distinguish passages that are of an extremely early date. But where are the hymns of the ancient Hellenes? They, as well as the Italians, had ancient hymns, and old sacred books; but nothing of these has come down to us. What tradition can remain to us of those generations that have not left us a single written line?

Fortunately, the past never completely dies for man. Man may forget it, but he always preserves it within him. For, take him at any epoch, and he is the product, the epitome, of all the earlier epochs. Let him look into his own soul, and he can find and distinguish these different epochs by what each of them has left within him.

Let us observe the Greeks of the age of Pericles, and the Romans of Cicero's time; they carry within them the authentic marks and the unmistakable vestiges of the most remote ages. The contemporary of Cicero (I speak especially of the man of the people) has an imagination full of legends; these legends come to him from a very early time, and they bear witness to the manner of thinking of that time. The contemporary of Cicero speaks a language whose roots are very ancient; this language, in expressing the thoughts of ancient ages, has been modelled upon them, and it has kept the impression, and transmits it from century to century. The primary sense of a root will sometimes reveal an ancient opinion or an ancient usage; ideas have been transformed, and the recollections of them have vanished; but the words have remained, immutable witnesses of beliefs that have disappeared.

The contemporary of Cicero practised rites in the sacrifices, at funerals, and in the ceremony of marriage; these rites were older than his time, and what proves it is that they did not correspond to his religious belief. But if we examine the rites which he observed, or the formulas which he recited, we find the marks of what men believed fifteen or twenty centuries earlier.

BOOK FIRST

ANCIENT BELIEFS

Chapter I

NOTIONS ABOUT THE SOUL AND DEATH

Down to the latest times in the history of Greece and Rome we find the common people clinging to thoughts and usages which certainly dated from a very distant past, and which enable us to discover what notions man entertained at first regarding his own nature, his soul, and the mystery of death.

Go back far as we may in the history of the Indo-European race, of which the Greeks and Italians are branches, and we do not find that this race has ever thought that after this short life all was finished for man. The most ancient generations, long before there were philosophers, believed in a second existence after the present. They looked upon death not as a dissolution of our being, but simply as a change of life.

But in what place, and in what manner, was this second existence passed? Did they believe that the immortal spirit, once escaped from a body, went to animate another? No; the doctrine of metempsychosis was never able to take root in the minds of the Greco-Italians; nor was it the most ancient belief of the Aryas of the East; since the hymns of the Vedas teach another doctrine. Did they believe that the spirit ascended towards the sky, towards the region of light? Not at all; the thought that departed souls entered a celestial home is relatively recent in the West; we find it expressed for the first time by the poet Phocylides. The celestial abode was never regarded as anything more than the recompense of a few great men, and of the benefactors of mankind. According to the oldest belief of the Italians and Greeks, the soul did not go into a foreign world to pass its second existence; it remained near men, and continued to live under ground.[1]

[1] *Sub terra censebant reliquam vitam agi mortuorum.* Cicero, *Tusc.,* I. 16. Euripides, *Alc.,* 163; *Hec.,* passim.

They even believed for a very long time that, in this second existence, the soul remained associated with the body; born together, they were not separated by death, and were buried together in the grave.

Old as this belief is, authentic evidences of it still remain to us. These evidences are the rites of sepulture, which have long survived this primitive belief, but which certainly began with it, and which enable us to understand it.

The rites of sepulture show clearly that when a body was buried, those ancient peoples believed that they buried something that was living. Virgil, who always describes religious ceremonies with so much care and precision, concludes the account of the funeral of Polydorus in these words: "We enclose the soul in the grave." The same expression is found in Ovid, and in Pliny the Younger; this did not correspond to the ideas which these writers had of the soul, but from time immemorial it had been perpetuated in the language, attesting an ancient and common belief.[2]

It was a custom, at the close of a funeral ceremony, to call the soul of the deceased three times by the name he had borne. They wished that he might live happy under ground. Three times they said to him, Fare thee well. They added, May the earth rest lightly upon thee.[3] Thus firmly did they believe that the person would continue to live under ground, and that he would still preserve a sense of enjoyment and suffering. They wrote upon the tomb that the man rested there — an expression which survived this belief, and which has come down through so many centuries to our time. We still employ it, though surely no one to-day thinks that an immortal being rests in a tomb. But in those ancient days they believed so

[2] Ovid, *Fast.*, V. 451. Pliny, *Letters,* VII. 27. Virg., *Æn.*, III. 67. Virgil's description relates to the employment of cenotaphs; it was admitted that when the body of a relative could not be found, they might perform a ceremony which exactly reproduced all the rites of sepulture; and it was believed that in this way, in the absence of the body, they enclosed the soul in the tomb. Eurip., *Helen.*, 1061, 1240. Scholiast, *ad Pind. Pyth.*, IV. 284. Virg., VI. 505; XII. 214.

[3] *Iliad*, XXIII. 221. Pausanias, II. 7, 2. Eurip., *Alc.*, 463. Virg., *Æn.*, III. 68. Catul., 98, 10. Ovid, *Trist.*, III. 3, 43; *Fast.*, IV. 852; *Metam.*, X. 62. Juvenal, VII. 207. Martial, I. 89; V. 35; IV. 30. Servius, *ad Æn.*, II. 644; III. 68; XI. 97. Tacit., *Agric.*, 46.

firmly that a man lived there that they never failed to bury
with him the objects of which they supposed he had need —
clothing, utensils, and arms. They poured wine upon his tomb
to quench his thirst, and placed food there to satisfy his
hunger. They slaughtered horses and slaves with the idea that
these beings, buried with the dead, would serve him in the
tomb, as they had done during his life. After the taking of
Troy, the Greeks are about to return to their country; each
takes with him his beautiful captive; but Achilles, who is under
the earth, claims his captive also, and they give him Polyxena.[4]

A verse of Pindar has preserved to us a curious vestige of the
thoughts of those ancient generations. Phrixus had been
compelled to quit Greece, and had fled as far as Colchis. He
had died in that country; but, dead though he was, he wished
to return to Greece. He appeared, therefore, to Pelias, and
directed him to go to Colchis and bring away his soul. Doubtless this soul regretted the soil of its native country, and the
tomb of its family; but being attached to its corporeal remains,
it could not quit Colchis without them.[5]

From this primitive belief came the necessity of burial. In
order that the soul might be confined to this subterranean
abode, which was suited to its second life, it was necessary that
the body to which it remained attached should be covered with
earth. The soul that had no tomb had no dwelling-place. It was
a wandering spirit. In vain it sought the repose which it would
naturally desire after the agitations and labor of this life; it
must wander forever under the form of a *larva*, or phantom,
without ever stopping, without ever receiving the offerings and
the food which it had need of. Unfortunately, it soon became
a malevolent spirit; it tormented the living; it brought diseases
upon them, ravaged their harvests, and frightened them by
gloomy apparitions, to warn them to give sepulture to its body
and to itself. From this came the belief in ghosts. All antiquity
was persuaded that without burial the soul was miserable, and
that by burial it became forever happy. It was not to display

---

[4] Eurip., *Hec.*, passim; *Alc., Iphig.*, 162. *Iliad*, XXIII. 166. Virg.,
Æn., V. 77; VI. 221; XI. 81. Pliny, *N. H.*, VIII. 40 Suet., *Cæsar*, 84.
Lucian, *De Luctu*, 14.

[5] Pind., *Pythic.*, IV. 284, ed. Heyne; see the Scholiast.

their grief that they performed the funeral ceremony, it was for the rest and happiness of the dead.[6]

We must remark, however, that to place the body in the ground was not enough. Certain traditional rites had also to be observed, and certain established formulas to be pronounced. We find in Plautus an account of a ghost;[7] it was a soul that was compelled to wander because its body had been placed in the ground without due attention to the rites. Suetonius relates that when the body of Caligula was placed in the earth without a due observation of the funeral ceremonies, his soul was not at rest, and continued to appear to the living until it was determined to disinter the body and give it a burial according to the rules. These two examples show clearly what effects were attributed to the rites and formulas of the funeral ceremony. Since without them souls continued to wander and appear to the living, it must have been by them that souls became fixed and enclosed in their tombs; and just as there were formulas which had this virtue, there were others which had a contrary virtue — that of evoking souls, and making them come out for a time from the sepulchre.

We can see in ancient writers how man was tormented by the fear that after his death the rites would not be observed for him. It was a source of constant inquietude. Men feared death less than the privation of burial; for rest and eternal happiness were at stake. We ought not to be too much surprised at seeing the Athenians put generals to death, who, after a naval victory, had neglected to bury the dead. These generals, disciples of philosophers, distinguished clearly between the soul and the body, and as they did not believe that the fate of the one was connected with the fate of the other, it appeared to them of very little consequence whether a body was decomposed in the earth or in the water. Therefore they did not brave the tempest for the vain formality of collecting and burying their dead. But the multitude, who, even at Athens, still clung to the ancient doctrines, accused these generals of impiety, and had them put to death. By their victory they had

[6] *Odyssey*, XI. 72. Eurip., *Troad.*, 1085. Hdts., V. 92. Virg., VI. 371, 379. Horace, *Odes*, I. 23. Ovid, *Fast.*, V. 483. Pliny, *Epist.*, VII. 27. Suetonius, *Calig.*, 59. Servius, *ad Æn.*, III. 68.

[7] Plautus, *Mostellaria*.

saved Athens; but by their impiety they had lost thousands of souls. The relatives of the dead, thinking of the long-suffering which these souls must bear, came to the tribunal clothed in mourning, and asked for vengeance. In the ancient cities the law condemned those guilty of great crimes to a terrible punishment — the privation of burial. In this manner they punished the soul itself, and inflicted upon it a punishment almost eternal.

We must observe that there was among the ancients another opinion concerning the abode of the dead. They pictured to themselves a region, also subterranean, but infinitely more vast than the tomb, where all souls, far from their bodies, lived together, and where rewards and punishments were distributed according to the lives men had led in this world. But the rites of burial, such as we have described them, manifestly disagree with this belief — a certain proof that, at the epoch when these rites were established, men did not yet believe in Tartarus and the Elysian Fields. The earliest opinion of these ancient generations was, that man lived in the tomb, that the soul did not leave the body, and that it remained fixed to that portion of ground where the bones lay buried. Besides, man had no account to render of his past life. Once placed in the tomb, he had neither rewards nor punishments to expect. This is a very crude opinion surely, but it is the beginning of the notion of a future life.

The being who lived under ground was not sufficiently free from human frailties to have no need of food; and, therefore, on certain days of the year, a meal was carried to every tomb. Ovid and Virgil have given us a description of this ceremony. The observance continued unchanged even to their time, although religious beliefs had already undergone great changes. According to these writers, the tomb was surrounded with large wreaths of grasses and flowers, and cakes, fruits, and flowers were placed upon it; milk, wine, and sometimes even the blood of a victim were added.[8]

We should greatly deceive ourselves if we thought that these funeral repasts were nothing more than a sort of commemoration. The food that the family brought was really for the dead — exclusively for him. What proves this is, that the milk

8 Virgil, Æn., III. 300 et seq.; V. 77. Ovid, Fast., II. 535–542.

and wine were poured out upon the earth of the tomb; that the earth was hollowed out so that the solid food might reach the dead; that if they sacrificed a victim, all its flesh was burnt, so that none of the living could have any part of it; that they pronounced certain consecrated formulas to invite the dead to eat and drink; that if the entire family were present at the meal, no one touched the food; that, in fine, when they went away, they took great care to leave a little milk and a few cakes in vases; and that it was considered gross impiety for any living person to touch this scant provision destined for the needs of the dead.[9]

These usages are attested in the most formal manner. "I pour upon the earth of the tomb," says Iphigenia in Euripides, "milk, honey, and wine; for it is with these that we rejoice the dead."[10] Among the Greeks there was in front of every tomb a place destined for the immolation of the victim and the cooking of its flesh.[11] The Roman tomb also had its *culina,* a species of kitchen, of a particular kind, and entirely for the use of the dead.[12] Plutarch relates that after the battle of Platæa, the slain having been buried upon the field of battle, the Platæans engaged to offer them the funeral repast every year. Consequently, on each anniversary, they went in grand procession, conducted by their first magistrates to the mound under which the dead lay. They offered the departed milk, wine, oil, and perfumes, and sacrificed a victim. When the provisions had been placed upon the tomb, the Platæans pronounced a formula by which they called the dead to come and partake of this repast. This ceremony was still performed in the time of Plutarch, who was enabled to witness the six hundredth anniversary of it.[13] A little later, Lucian, ridiculing these opinions and usages, shows how deeply rooted they were in the common mind. "The dead," says he, "are nourished by the provisions which we place upon their tomb, and drink the wine which we pour out there; so that one of the dead to whom nothing is offered is condemned to perpetual hunger.[14]

---

[9] Hdts., II. 40. Eurip., *Hec.,* 536. Pausanias, II. 10. Virgil, V. 98. Ovid, *Fast.,* II. 566. Lucian, *Charon.*

[10] Æsch., *Choeph.,* 476. Eurip., *Iph.,* 162.

[11] Euripides, *Electra,* 513.   [13] Plutarch, *Aristides,* 21.

[12] Festus, v. *Culina.*   [14] Lucian, *De Luctu.*

These are very old forms of belief, and are quite groundless and ridiculous; and yet they exercised empire over man during a great number of generations. They governed men's minds; we shall soon see that they governed societies even, and that the greater part of the domestic and social institutions of the ancients was derived from this source.

Chapter II

THE WORSHIP OF THE DEAD

THIS belief very soon gave rise to certain rules of conduct. Since the dead had need of food and drink, it appeared to be a duty of the living to satisfy this need. The care of supplying the dead with sustenance was not left to the caprice or to the variable sentiments of men; it was obligatory. Thus a complete religion of the dead was established, whose dogmas might soon be effaced, but whose rites endured until the triumph of Christianity. The dead were held to be sacred beings. To them the ancients applied the most respectful epithets that could be thought of; they called them good, holy, happy. For them they had all the veneration that man can have for the divinity whom he loves or fears. In their thoughts the dead were gods.[1]

This sort of apotheosis was not the privilege of great men; no distinction was made among the dead. Cicero says, "Our ancestors desired that the men who had quitted this life should be counted in the number of the gods." It was not necessary to have been even a virtuous man: the wicked man, as well as the good man, became a god; but he retained in the second life all the bad inclinations which had tormented him in the first.[2]

The Greeks gave to the dead the name of subterranean gods. In Æschylus, a son thus invokes his deceased father: "O thou who art a god beneath the earth." Euripides says, speaking of Alcestis, "Near her tomb the passer by will stop and say, 'This is now a thrice happy divinity.' "[3]

The Romans gave to the dead the name of *Manes*. "Render to the manes what is due them," says Cicero; "they are men

[1] Æsch., *Choeph.*, 469. Sophocles, *Antig.*, 451. Plutarch, *Solon*, 21; *Rom. Quest.*, 52; *Gr. Quest.*, 5. Virgil, V. 47; V. 80.
[2] Cicero, *De Legib.*, 22. St. Augustine, *City of God*, IX. 11; VIII. 26.
[3] Eurip., *Alc.*, 1003, 1015.

who have quitted this life; consider them as divine beings."[4]

The tombs were the temples of these divinities, and they bore the sacramental inscription, *Dis Manibus,* and in Greek, ϑεοις χθονιοις. There the god lived beneath the soil, *manesque sepulti,* says Virgil. Before the tomb there was an altar for the sacrifices, as before the temples of the gods.[5]

We find this worship of the dead among the Hellenes, among the Latins, among the Sabines,[6] among the Etruscans; we also find it among the Aryas of India. Mention is made of it in the hymns of the Reg-Veda. It is spoken of in the Laws of Manu as the most ancient worship among men. We see in this book that the idea of metempsychosis had already passed over this ancient belief, even before the religion of Brahma was established; and still beneath the worship of Brahma, beneath the doctrine of metempsychosis, the religion of the souls of ancestors still subsists, living and indestructible, and compels the author of the Laws of Manu to take it into account, and to admit its rules into the sacred book. Not the least singular thing about this strange book is, that it has preserved the rules relative to this ancient belief, whilst it was evidently prepared in an age when a belief entirely different had gained the ascendency. This proves that much time is required to transform a human belief, and still more to modify its exterior forms, and the laws based upon it. At the present day, even, after so many ages of revolutions, the Hindus continue to make offerings to their ancestors. This belief and these rites are the oldest and the most persistent of anything pertaining to the Indo-European race. This worship was the same in India as in Greece and Italy. The Hindu had to supply the manes with the repast, which was called *sraddha.* "Let the master of the house make the sraddha with rice, milk, roots, and fruits, in order to procure for himself the good-will of the manes."

The Hindu believed that at the moment when he offered this funeral repast, the manes of his ancestors came to seat themselves beside him, and took the nourishment which was

[4] Cicero, *De Legib.,* II. 9 Varro, in St. Augustine, *City of God,* VIII. 26.

[5] Virgil, *Æn.,* IV. 34. Aulus Gellius, X. 18. Plutarch, *Rom. Quest.,* 14. Eurip., *Troades,* 96; *Electra,* 513. Suetonius, *Nero,* 50.

[6] Varro, *De Ling. Lat.,* V. 74.

offered them. He also believed that this repast afforded the
dead great enjoyment. "When the sraddha is made according
to the rites, the ancestors of the one who offers it experience
unbounded satisfaction."[7]

Thus the Aryas of the East had, in the beginning, the same
notions as those of the West, relative to man's destiny after
death. Before believing in metempsychosis, which supposes an
absolute distinction between the soul and the body, they
believed in the vague and indefinite existence of man, invisible,
but not immaterial, and requiring of mortals nourishment and
offerings.

The Hindu, like the Greek, regarded the dead as divine
beings, who enjoyed a happy existence; but their happiness
depended on the condition that the offerings made by the
living should be carried to them regularly. If the sraddha for a
dead person was not offered regularly, his soul left its peaceful
dwelling, and became a wandering spirit, who tormented the
living; so that, if the dead were really gods, this was only whilst
the living honored them with their worship.

The Greeks and Romans had exactly the same belief. If the
funeral repast ceased to be offered to the dead, they immediately left their tombs, and became wandering shades, that were
heard in the silence of the night. They reproached the living
with their negligence; or they sought to punish them by afflicting them with diseases, or cursing their soil with sterility. In a
word, they left the living no rest till the funeral feasts were
re-established. The sacrifice, the offering of nourishment, and
the libation restored them to the tomb, and gave them back
their rest and their divine attributes. Man was then at peace
with them.[8]

If a deceased person, on being neglected, became a malignant
spirit, one who was honored became, on the other hand, a
tutelary diety. He loved those who brought him nourishment.
To protect them he continued to take part in human affairs,
and frequently played an important part there. Dead though
he was, he knew how to be strong and active. The living

[7] *Laws of Manu*, I. 95; III. 82, 122, 127, 146, 189, 274.

[8] Ovid, *Fast.*, II. 549–556. Thus in Æschylus: Clytemnestra, warned
by a dream that the manes of Agamemnon are irritated against her,
hastens to send offerings to his tomb.

prayed to him, and asked his support and his favors. When any one came near a tomb, he stopped, and said, "Subterranean god, be propitious to me."[9]

We can judge of the power which the ancients attributed to the dead by this prayer, which Electra addresses to the manes of her father: "Take pity on me, and on my brother Orestes; make him return to this country; hear my prayer, O my father; grant my wishes, receiving my libations." These powerful gods did not give material aid only; for Electra adds, "Give me a heart more chaste than my mother's, and purer hands."[10] Thus the Hindu asks of the manes "that in his family the number of good men may increase, and that he may have much to give."

These human souls deified by death were what the Greeks called *demons,* or *heroes.*[11] The Latins gave them the name of *Lares, Manes, Genii.* "Our ancestors believed," says Apuleius, "that the Manes, when they were malignant, were to be called *larvæ;* they called them *Lares* when they were benevolent and propitious."[12] Elsewhere we read, "Genius and Lar is the same being; so our ancestors believed."[13] And in Cicero, "Those that the Greeks called demons we call Lares."[14]

This religion of the dead appears to be the oldest that has existed among this race of men. Before men had any notion of Indra or of Zeus, they adored the dead; they feared them, and addressed them prayers. It seems that the religious senti-

---

[9] Eurip., *Alc.,* 1004 (1016): "They believe that if we have no care for these dead, and if we neglect their worship, they will do us harm, and that, on the contrary, they do us good if we render them propitious to us by offerings." Porphyry, *De Abstin.,* II. 37. See Horace, *Odes,* II. 23; Plato, *Laws,* IX. p. 926, 927.

[10] Æsch., *Choeph.,* 122–135.

[11] The primitive sense of this last word appears to have been that of dead men. The language of the inscriptions, which is that of the common people among the Greeks, often employs it in this sense. Boeckh, *Corp. inscript.,* Nos. 1629, 1723, 1781, 1784, 1786, 1789, 3398. Ph. Lebas, *Monum. de Morée,* p. 205. Vide Theognis, ed. Welcker, V. 513. The Greeks also gave to one dead the name of δαιμων. Eurip. *Alc.,* 1140, et Schol. Æsch., *Pers.,* 620. Pausanias, VI. 6.

[12] Servius, *ad Æn.,* III. 63.

[13] Censorinus, 3.

[14] Cicero, *Timæus,* 11. Dionysius Halicarnasseus translates *Lar familiaris* by 'ο κατ' οικιαν 'ηρως. (*Antiq. Rom.,* IV. 2.)

ment commenced in this way. It was perhaps while looking upon the dead that man first conceived the idea of the supernatural, and began to have a hope beyond what he saw. Death was the first mystery, and it placed man on the track of other mysteries. It raised his thoughts from the visible to the invisible, from the transitory to the eternal, from the human to the divine.

Chapter III

THE SACRED FIRE

In the house of every Greek and Roman was an altar; on this altar there had always to be a small quantity of ashes, and a few lighted coals.[1] It was a sacred obligation for the master of every house to keep the fire up night and day. Woe to the house where it was extinguished. Every evening they covered the coals with ashes to prevent them from being entirely consumed. In the morning the first care was to revive this fire with a few twigs. The fire ceased to glow upon the altar only when the entire family had perished; an extinguished hearth, an extinguished family, were synonymous expressions among the ancients.[2]

It is evident that this usage of keeping fire always upon an altar was connected with an ancient belief. The rules and the rites which they observed in regard to it, show that it was not an insignificant custom. It was not permitted to feed this fire with every sort of wood; religion distinguished among the trees those that could be employed for this use from those it was impiety to make use of.[3]

1 The Greeks called this altar by various names, βωμος, εσχαρα, εστια; this last finally prevailed in use, and was the name by which they afterwards designated the goddess Vesta. The Latins called the same altar *ara* or *focus*.

2 *Homeric Hymns*, XXIX. *Orphic Hymns*, LXXXIV. Hesiod, *Opera*, 732. Æsch., *Agam.*, 1056. Eurip., *Herc. Fur.*, 503, 599. Thuc., I. 136. Aristoph., *Plut.*, 795. Cato, *De Re Rust.*, 143. Cicero, *Pro Domo*, 40. Tibullus, I. 1, 4. Horace, *Epod.*, II. 43. Ovid, *A. A.*, I. 637. Virgil, II. 512.

3 Virgil, VII. 71. Festus, v. *Felicis*. Plutarch, *Numa*, 9.

It was also a religious precept that this fire must always remain pure;[4] which meant, literally, that no filthy object ought to be cast into it, and figuratively, that no blameworthy deed ought to be committed in its presence. There was one day in the year — among the Romans it was the first of March — when it was the duty of every family to put out its sacred fire, and light another immediately.[5] But to procure this new fire, certain rites had to be scrupulously observed. Especially must they avoid using flint and steel for this purpose. The only processes allowed were to concentrate the solar rays into a focus, or to rub together rapidly two pieces of wood of a given sort.[6] These different rules sufficiently prove that, in the opinion of the ancients, it was not a question of procuring an element useful and agreeable; these men saw something else in the fire that burnt upon their altars.

This fire was something divine; they adored it, and offered it a real worship. They made offerings to it of whatever they believed to be agreeable to a god — flowers, fruits, incense, wine, and victims. They believed it to have power, and asked for its protection. They addressed fervent prayers to it, to obtain those eternal objects of human desire — health, wealth, and happiness. One of these prayers, which has been preserved to us in the collection of Orphic Hymns, runs thus: "Render us always prosperous, always happy, O fire; thou who art eternal, beautiful, ever young; thou who nourishest, thou who art rich, receive favorably these our offerings, and in return give us happiness and sweet health."[7]

Thus they saw in the fire a beneficent god, who maintained the life of man; a rich god, who nourished him with gifts; a powerful god, who protected his house and family. In presence of danger they sought refuge near this fire. When the palace of Priam is destroyed, Hecuba draws the old man near the hearth. "Thy arms cannot protect thee," she says; "but this altar will protect us all."[8]

[4] Eurip., *Herc. Fur.*, 715. Cato, *De Re Rust.*, 143. Ovid, *Fast.*, III. 698.

[5] Macrob. *Saturn.*, I. 12.

[6] Ovid, *Fast.*, III. 143. Festus, v. *Felicis.* Julian, *Speech on the Sun.*

[7] *Orphic Hymns*, 84. Plaut., *Captiv.*, II. 2. Tibull., I. 9, 74. Ovid, *A. A.*, I. 637. Plin., *Nat. Hist.*, XVIII. 8.

[8] Virgil, *Æn.*, II. 523. Horace, *Epist.*, I. 5. Ovid, *Trist.*, IV. 8, 22.

See Alcestis, who is about to die, giving her life to save her husband. She approaches the fire, and invokes it in these terms: "O divinity, mistress of this house, for the last time I fall before thee, and address thee my prayers, for I am going to descend among the dead. Watch over my children, who will have no mother; give to my boy a tender wife, and to my girl a noble husband. Let them not, like me, die before the time; but let them enjoy a long life in the midst of happiness."[9]

In misfortune man betook himself to his sacred fire, and heaped reproaches upon it; in good fortune he returned it thanks. The soldier who returned from war thanked it for having enabled him to escape the perils. Æschylus represents Agamemnon returning from Troy, happy, and covered with glory. His first act is not to thank Jupiter; he does not go to a temple to pour out his joy and gratitude, but makes a sacrifice of thank-offerings to the fire in his own house.[10] A man never went out of his dwelling without addressing a prayer to the fire; on his return, before seeing his wife or embracing his children, he must fall before the fire, and invoke it.[11]

The sacred fire was the Providence of the family. The worship was very simple. The first rule was, that there should always be upon the altar a few live coals; for if this fire was extinguished a god ceased to exist. At certain moments of the day they placed upon the fire dry herbs and wood; then the god manifested himself in a bright flame. They offered sacrifices to him; and the essence of every sacrifice was to sustain and reanimate the sacred fire, to nourish and develop the body of the god. This was the reason why they gave him wood before everything else; for the same reason they afterwards poured out wine upon the altar, — the inflammable wine of Greece, — oil, incense, and the fat of victims. The god received these offerings, and devoured them; radiant with satisfaction, he rose above the altar, and lighted up the worshipper with his brightness. Then was the moment to invoke him; and the hymn of prayer went out from the heart of man.

Especially were the meals of the family religious acts. The god presided there. He had cooked the bread, and prepared the

9 Eurip., *Alc.*, 162–168.
10 Æsch., *Agam.*, 1015.
11 Cato, *De Re Rust.*, 2. Eurip., *Herc. Fur.*, 523.

food;[12] a prayer, therefore, was due at the beginning and end of the repast. Before eating, they placed upon the altar the first fruits of the food; before drinking, they poured out a libation of wine. This was the god's portion. No one doubted that he was present, that he ate and drank; for did they not see the flame increase as if it had been nourished by the provisions offered? Thus the meal was divided between the man and the god. It was a sacred ceremony, by which they held communion with each other.[13] This is an old belief, which, in the course of time, faded from the minds of men, but which left behind it, for many an age, rites, usages, and forms of language of which even the incredulous could not free themselves. Horace, Ovid, and Petronius still supped before their fires, and poured out libations, and addressed prayers to them.[14]

This worship of the sacred fire did not belong exclusively to the populations of Greece and Italy. We find it in the East. The Laws of Manu, as they have come to us, show us the religion of Brahma completely established, and even verging towards its decline; but they have preserved vestiges and remains of a religion still more ancient, — that of the sacred fire, — which the worship of Brahma had reduced to a secondary rank, but could not destroy. The Brahmin has his fire to keep night and day; every morning and every evening he feeds it with wood; but, as with the Greeks, this must be the wood of certain trees. As the Greeks and Italians offer it wine, the Hindu pours upon it a fermented liquor, which he calls *soma*. Meals, too, are religious acts, and the rites are scrupulously described in the Laws of Manu. They address prayers to the fire, as in Greece; they offer it the first fruits of rice, butter, and honey. We read that "the Brahmin should not eat the rice of the new harvest without having offered the first fruits of it to the hearth-fire; for the sacred fire is greedy of grain, and when it is not honored, it will devour the existence of the negligent Brahmin." The Hindus, like the Greeks and the Romans, pictured the gods to themselves as greedy not only of honors and respect, but of food and drink. Man believed

[12] Ovid, *Fast.*, VI. 315.
[13] Plutarch, *Rom. Quest.*, 64; *Comm. on Hesiod*, 44. *Homeric Hymns*, 29.
[14] Horace, *Sat.*, II. 6, 66. Ovid, *Fast.*, II. 631. Petronius, 60.

himself compelled to satisfy their hunger and thirst, if he wished to avoid their wrath.

Among the Hindus this divinity of the fire is called *Agni*. The Rig-Veda contains a great number of hymns addressed to this god. In one it is said, "O Agni, thou art the life, thou art the protector of man. . . . In return for our praises, bestow upon the father of the family who implores thee glory and riches. . . . Agni, thou art a prudent defender and a father; to thee we owe life; we are thy family." Thus the fire of the hearth is, as in Greece, a tutelary power. Man asks abundance of it: "Make the earth ever liberal towards us." He asked health of it: "Grant that I may enjoy long life, and that I may arrive at old age, like the sun at his setting." He even asks wisdom of it: "O Agni, thou placest upon the good way the man who has wandered into the bad. . . . If we have committed a fault, if we have gone far from thee, pardon us." This fire of the hearth was, as in Greece, essentially pure: the Brahmin was forbidden to throw anything filthy into it, or even to warm his feet by it. As in Greece, the guilty man could not approach his hearth before he had purified himself.

It is a strong proof of the antiquity of this belief, and of these practices, to find them at the same time among men on the shores of the Mediterranean and among those of the peninsula of India. Assuredly the Greeks did not borrow this religion from the Hindus, nor the Hindus from the Greeks. But the Greeks, the Italians, and the Hindus belonged to the same race; their ancestors, in a very distant past, lived together in Central Asia. There this creed originated and these rites were established. The religion of the sacred fire dates, therefore, from the distant and dim epoch when there were yet no Greeks, no Italians, no Hindus; when there were only Aryas. When the tribes separated, they carried this worship with them, some to the banks of the Ganges, others to the shores of the Mediterranean. Later, when these tribes had no intercourse with each other, some adored Brahma, others Zeus, and still others Janus; each group chose its own gods; but all preserved, as an ancient legacy, the first religion which they had known and practised in the common cradle of their race.

If the existence of this worship among all the Indo-European nations did not sufficiently demonstrate its high antiquity, we might find other proofs of it in the religious rites of the Greeks and Romans. In all sacrifices, even in those offered to Zeus or to Athene, the first invocation was always addressed to the fire.[15] Every prayer to any god whatever must commence and end with a prayer to the fire.[16] At Olympia, the first sacrifice that assembled Greece offered was to the hearth-fire, the second was to Zeus.[17] So, too, at Rome, the first adoration was always addressed to Vesta, who was no other than the hearth-fire. Ovid says of this goddess, that she occupied the first place in the religious practices of men. We also read in the hymns of the Rig-Veda, "Agni must be invoked before all the other gods. We pronounce his venerable name before that of all the other immortals. O Agni, whatever other god we honor with our sacrifices, the holocaust is always offered to thee."[18] It is certain, therefore, that at Rome in Ovid's time, and in India in the time of the Brahmins, the fire of the hearth took precedence of all other gods; not that Jupiter and Brahma had not acquired a greater importance in the religion of men, but it was remembered that the hearth-fire was much older than those gods. For many centuries he had held the first place in the religious worship, and the newer and greater gods could not dispossess him of this place.

The symbols of this religion became modified in the course of ages. When the people of Greece and Italy began to represent their gods as persons, and to give each one a proper name and a human form, the old worship of the hearth-fire submitted to the common law which human intelligence, in that period, imposed upon every religion. The altar of the sacred fire was personified. They called it εστια, Vesta; the name was the same in Latin and in Greek, and was the same that in the common and primitive language designated an altar. By a process frequent enough, a common noun had become a proper name. By degrees a legend was formed. They pictured this divinity to themselves as wearing a female form, because the word used for altar was of the feminine gender. They even went so far as to

---

[15] Porphyry, *De Abstin.*, II. p. 106. Plutarch *De Frigido.*

[16] *Homeric Hymns*, 29; *Ibid.*, 3, v. 33. Plato, *Cratylus*, 18. Hesychius, αφ' στιας. Diodorus, VI. 2. Aristoph., *Birds*, 865.

[17] Pausanias, V. 14.

[18] Cicero, *De Nat. Deorum*, II. 27. Ovid, *Fast.*, VI. 304.

represent this goddess in statues. Still they could never efface the primitive belief, according to which this divinity was simply the fire upon the altar; and Ovid himself was forced to admit that Vesta was nothing else than a "living flame."[19]

If we compare this worship of the sacred fire with the worship of the dead, of which we have already spoken, we shall perceive a close relation between them.

Let us remark, in the first place, that this fire, which was kept burning upon the hearth, was not, in the thoughts of men, the fire of material nature. What they saw in it was not the purely physical element that warms and burns, that transforms bodies, melts metals, and becomes the powerful instrument of human industry. The fire of the hearth is of quite another nature. It is a pure fire, which can be produced only by the aid of certain rites, and can be kept up only with certain kinds of wood. It is a chaste fire; the union of the sexes must be removed far from its presence.[20] They pray to it not only for riches and health, but also for purity of heart, temperance, and wisdom. "Render us rich and flourishing," says an Orphic hymn; "make us also wise and chaste." Thus the hearth-fire is a sort of a moral being; it shines, and warms, and cooks the sacred food; but at the same time it thinks, and has a conscience; it knows men's duties, and sees that they are fulfilled. One might call it human, for it has the double nature of man; physically, it blazes up, it moves, it lives, it procures abundance, it prepares the repast, it nourishes the body; morally, it has sentiments and affections, it gives man purity, it enjoins the beautiful and the good, it nourishes the soul. One might say that it supports human life in the double series of its manifestations. It is at the same time the source of wealth, of health, of virtue. It is truly the god of human nature. Later, when this worship had been assigned to a second place by Brahma or by Zeus, there still remained in the hearth-fire whatever of divine was most accessible to man. It became his mediator with the gods of physical nature; it undertook to carry to heaven the prayer and the offering of man, and to bring the divine favors back to him. Still later, when they made the great Vesta of this myth of the sacred fire, Vesta was the

19 Ovid, *Fast.*, VI. 291.
20 Hesiod, *Opera*, 731. Plutarch, *Comm. on Hes.*, frag. 43.

virgin goddess. She represented in the world neither fecundity nor power; she was order, but not rigorous, abstract, mathematical order, the imperious and unchangeable law, αναγχη, which was early perceived in physical nature. She was moral order. They imagined her as a sort of universal soul, which regulated the different movements of worlds, as the human soul keeps order in the human system.

Thus are we permitted to look into the way of thinking of primitive generations. The principle of this worship is outside of physical nature, and is found in this little mysterious world, this microcosm — man.

This brings us back to the worship of the dead. Both are of the same antiquity. They were so closely associated that the belief of the ancients made but one religion of both. Hearth-fire demons, heroes, Lares, all were confounded.[21] We see, from two passages of Plautus and Columella, that, in the common language, they said, indifferently, hearth or domestic Lares; and we know that, in Cicero's time, they did not distinguish the hearth-fire from the Penates, nor the Penates from the Lares.[22] In Servius we read, "By hearth the ancients understood the Lares;" and Virgil has written, indifferently, hearth for Penates and Penates for hearth.[23] In a famous passage of the Æneid, Hector tells Æneas that he is going to intrust to him the Trojan Penates, and it is the hearth-fire that he commits to his care. In another passage Æneas, invoking these same gods, calls them at the same time Penates, Lares, and Vesta.[24]

We have already seen that those whom the ancients called Lares, or heroes, were no other than the souls of the dead, to which men attributed a superhuman and divine power. The recollection of one of these sacred dead was always attached to the hearth-fire. In adoring one, the worshipper could not forget the other. They were associated in the respect of men, and in their prayers. The descendants, when they spoke of the

[21] Tibulus, II. 2. Horace, Odes, IV. 11. Ovid., Trist., III. 13; V. 5. The Greeks gave to their domestic gods or heroes the epithet of ἐφεστιοι or ἑστιουχοι.

[22] Plaut., Aulul., II. 7, 16 — In foco nostro Lari. Columella, XI. 1, 19 — Larem focumque familiarem. Cicero, Pro Domo, 41; Pro Quintio, 27, 28.

[23] Servius, in Æn., III. 134

[24] Virgil, IX. 259; V. 744.

hearth-fire, recalled the name of the ancestor: "Leave this place," says Orestes to his sister, "and advance towards the ancient hearth of Pelops, to hear my words."[25] So, too, Æneas, speaking of the sacred fire which he transports across the waters, designates it by the name of the Lar of Assaracus, as if he saw in this fire the soul of his ancestor.

The grammarian Servius, who was very learned in Greek and Roman antiquities (which were studied much more in his time than in the time of Cicero), says it was a very ancient usage to bury the dead in the houses; and he adds, "As a result of this custom, they honor the Lares and Penates in their houses.[26] This expression establishes clearly an ancient relation between the worship of the dead and the hearth-fire. We may suppose, therefore, that the domestic fire was in the beginning only the symbol of the worship of the dead; that under the stone of the hearth an ancestor reposed; that the fire was lighted there to honor him, and that this fire seemed to preserve life in him, or represented his soul as always vigilant.

This is merely a conjecture, and we have no proof of it. Still it is certain that the oldest generations of the race from which the Greeks and Romans sprang worshipped both the dead and the hearth-fire — an ancient religion that did not find its gods in physical nature, but in man himself, and that has for its object the adoration of the invisible being which is in us, the moral and thinking power which animates and governs our bodies.

This religion, after a time, began to lose its power over the soul; it became enfeebled by degrees, but it did not disappear. Contemporary with the first ages of the Aryan race, it became rooted so deeply in the minds of this race that the brilliant religion of the Greek Olympus could not extirpate it; only Christianity could do this. We shall see presently what a powerful influence this religion exercised upon the domestic and social institutions of the ancients. It was conceived and established in that distant age when this race was just forming its institutions, and determined the direction of their progress.

[25] Euripides, *Orestes*, 1140–1142.
[26] Servius, in *Æn.*, V. 84; VI. 152. See Plato, *Minos*, p. 315.

Chapter IV

THE DOMESTIC RELIGION

WE are not to suppose that this ancient religion resembled those founded when men became more enlightened. For a great number of centuries the human race has admitted no religious doctrine except on two conditions: first, that it proclaimed but one god; and, second, that it was addressed to all men, and was accessible to all, systematically rejecting no class or race. But this primitive religion fulfilled neither of these conditions. Not only did it not offer one only god to the adoration of men, but its gods did not accept the adoration of all men. They did not offer themselves as the gods of the human race. They did not even resemble Brahma, who was at least the god of one whole great caste, nor the Panhellenian Zeus, who was the god of an entire nation. In this primitive religion each god could be adored only by one family. Religion was purely domestic.

We must illustrate this important point; otherwise the intimate relation that existed between this ancient religion and the constitution of the Greek and Roman family may not be fully understood.

The worship of the dead in no way resembled the Christian worship of the saints. One of the first rules of this worship was, that it could be offered by each family only to those deceased persons who belonged to it by blood. The funeral obsequies could be religiously performed only by the nearest relative. As to the funeral meal, which was renewed at stated seasons, the family alone had a right to take part in it, and every stranger was strictly excluded.[1] They believed that the dead ancestor accepted no offerings save from his own family; he desired no worship save from his own descendants. The presence of one who was not of the family disturbed the rest of the manes. The

[1] Cicero, *De Legib.*, II. 26. Varro, *L. L.*, VI. 13 — *Ferunt epulas ad sepulcrum quibus jus ibi parentare.* Gaius, II. 5, 6 — *Si modo mortui funus ad nos pertineat.* Plutarch, *Solon.*

law, therefore, forbade a stranger to approach a tomb.[2] To touch a tomb with the foot, even by chance, was an impious act, after which the guilty one was expected to pacify the dead and purify himself. The word by which the ancients designated the worship of the dead is significant; the Greeks said πατριαζειν, the Romans said *parentare*. The reason of this was because the prayer and offering were addressed by each one only to his fathers. The worship of the dead was nothing more than the worship of ancestors.[3] Lucian, while ridiculing common beliefs, explains them clearly to us when he says the man who has died without leaving a son, receives no offerings, and is exposed to perpetual hunger.[4]

In India, as in Greece, an offering could be made to a dead person only by one who had descended from him. The law of the Hindus, like Athenian law, forbade a stranger, even if he were a friend, to be invited to the funeral banquet. It was so necessary that these banquets should be offered by the descendants of the dead, and not by others, that the manes, in their resting-place, were supposed often to pronounce this wish: "May there be successively born of our line sons who, in all coming time, may offer us rice, boiled in milk, honey, and clarified butter."[5]

Hence it was, that, in Greece and Rome, as in India, it was the son's duty to make the libations and the sacrifices to the manes of his father and of all his ancestors. To fail in this duty was to commit the grossest act of impiety possible, since the interruption of this worship caused the dead to fall from their happy state. This negligence was nothing less than the crime of parricide, multiplied as many times as there were ancestors in the family.

If, on the contrary, the sacrifices were always accomplished according to the rites, if the provisions were carried to the tomb on the appointed days, then the ancestor became a pro-

---

2 *Pittacus omnino accedere quemquam vetat in funus aliorum.* Cicero, *De Legib.*, II. 26. Plutarch, *Solon,* 21. Demosthenes, in *timocr.* Isæus, I.

3 In the beginning at least; for later the cities had their local and national heroes, as we shall see.

4 Lucian, *De Luctu.*

5 *Laws of Manu,* III. 138; III. 274.

tecting god. Hostile to all who had not descended from him, driving them from his tomb, inflicting diseases upon them if they approached, he was good and provident to his own family.

There was a perpetual interchange of good offices between the living and the dead of each family. The ancestor received from his descendants a series of funeral banquets, that is to say, the only enjoyment that was left to him in his second life. The descendant received from the ancestor the aid and strength of which he had need in this. The living could not do without the dead, nor the dead without the living. Thus a powerful bond was established among all the generations of the same family, which made of it a body forever inseparable.

Every family had its tomb, where its dead went to repose, one after another, always together. This tomb was generally near the house, nor far from the door, "in order," says one of the ancients, "that the sons, in entering and leaving their dwelling, might always meet their fathers, and might always address them an invocation."[6] Thus the ancestor remained in the midst of his relatives; invisible, but always present, he continued to make a part of the family, and to be its father. Immortal, happy, divine, he was still interested in all of his whom he had left upon the earth. He knew their needs, and sustained their feebleness; and he who still lived, who labored, who, according to the ancient expression, had not yet discharged the debt of existence, he had near him his guides and his supports — his forefathers. In the midst of difficulties, he invoked their ancient wisdom; in grief, he asked consolation of them; in danger, he asked their support, and after a fault, their pardon.

Certainly we cannot easily comprehend how a man could adore his father or his ancestor. To make of man a god appears to us the reverse of religion. It is almost as difficult for us to comprehend the ancient creeds of these men as it would have been for them to understand ours. But, if we reflect that the ancients had no idea of creation, we shall see that the mystery of generation was for them what the mystery of creation is for us. The generator appeared to them to be a divine being; and they adored their ancestor. This sentiment must have been very natural and very strong, for it appears as a principle of religion in the origin of almost all human societies. We find it

6 Euripides, *Helena*, 1163–1168.

among the Chinese as well as among the ancient Getæ and Scythians, among the tribes of Africa as well as among those of the new world.[7]

The sacred fire, which was so intimately associated with the worship of the dead, belonged, in its essential character, properly to each family. It represented the ancestors; it was the providence of a family, and had nothing in common with the fire of a neighboring family, which was another providence.[8] Every fire protected its own and repulsed the stranger. The whole of this religion was enclosed within the walls of each house. The worship was not public. All the ceremonies, on the contrary, were kept strictly secret.[9] Performed in the midst of the family alone, they were concealed from every stranger. The hearth was never placed either outside the house or even near the outer door, where it would have been too easy to see. The Greeks always placed it in an enclosure,[10] which protected it from the contact, or even the gaze, of the profane. The Romans concealed it in the interior of the house. All these gods, the sacred fire, the Lares, and the Manes, were called the consecrated gods, or gods of the interior.[11] To all the acts of this religion secrecy was necessary.[12] If a ceremony was looked upon by a stranger, it was disturbed, defiled, made unfortunate simply by this look.

There were neither uniform rules nor a common ritual for this domestic religion. Each family was most completely independent. No external power had the right to regulate either the ceremony or the creed. There was no other priest than the father: as a priest, he knew no hierarchy. The pontifex of Rome, or the archon of Athens, might, indeed, ascertain if the father of a family performed all his religious ceremonies; but he had no right to order the least modification

---

[7] Among the Etruscans and the Romans it was a custom for every religious family to keep the images of its ancestors ranged around the atrium. Were these images simple family portraits, or were they idols?

[8] ‘Εοτια πατρωα, focus patrius. So in the Vedas Agni is sometimes invoked as a domestic god.

[9] Isæus, VIII. 17, 18.

[10] This enclosure was called ερκος.

[11] θεοι μυχιοι, dii Penates.

[12] Cicero, De Arusp. Resp., 17.

of them. *Suo quisque ritu sacrificia faciat* — such was the absolute rule.[13] Every family had its ceremonies, which were peculiar to itself, its particular celebrations, its formulas of prayer, its hymns.[14] The father, sole interpreter and sole priest of his religion, alone had the right to teach it, and could teach it only to his son. The rites, the forms of prayer, the chants, which formed an essential part of this domestic religion, were a patrimony, a sacred property, which the family shared with no one, and which they were even forbidden to reveal to strangers. It was the same in India. "I am strong against my enemies," says the Brahmin, "from the songs which I receive from my family, and which my father has transmitted to me."[15]

Thus religion dwelt not in temples, but in the house; each house had its gods; each god protected one family only, and was a god only in one house. We cannot reasonably suppose that a religion of this character was revealed to man by the powerful imagination of one among them, or that it was taught to them by a priestly caste. It grew up spontaneously in the human mind; its cradle was the family; each family created its own gods.

This religion could be propagated only by generation. The father, in giving life to his son, gave him at the same time his creed, his worship, the right to continue the sacred fire, to offer the funeral meal, to pronounce the formulas of prayer. Generation established a mysterious bond between the infant, who was born to life, and all the gods of the family. Indeed, these gods were his family — θεοι εγγενεις; they were of his blood — θεοι συναιμοι.[16] The child, therefore, received at his birth the right to adore them, and to offer them sacrifices; and later, when death should have deified him, he also would be counted, in his turn, among these gods of the family.

But we must notice this peculiarity — that the domestic religion was transmitted only from male to male.

---

[13] Varro, *De Ling. Lat.*, VII. 88.

[14] Hesiod, *Opera,* 753. Macrobius, *Sat.*, I. 10. Cic., *De Legib.*, II. 11.

[15] *Rig-Veda*, Langlois' trans., v. i. p. 113. The Laws of Manu often mention rites peculiar to each family. VII. 3; IX. 7.

[16] Sophocles, *Antig.*, 199; *Ibid.*, 659. Comp. πατρωοι θεοι in Aristophanes, *Wasps*, 388; Æschylus, *Pers.*, 404; Sophocles, *Electra*, 411; θεοι γενεθλιοι, Plato, *Laws*, V. p. 729; *Di Generis*, Ovid, *Fast.*, II.

This was owing, no doubt, to the idea that generation was due entirely to the males.[17] The belief of primitive ages, as we find it in the Vedas, and as we find vestiges of it in all Greek and Roman law, was that the reproductive power resided exclusively in the father. The father alone possessed the mysterious principle of existence, and transmitted the spark of life. From this old notion it followed that the domestic worship always passed from male to male; that a woman participated in it only through her father or her husband; and, finally, that after death women had not the same part as men in the worship and the ceremonies of the funeral meal. Still other important consequences in private law and in the constitution of the family resulted from this: we shall see them as we proceed.

[17] The Vedas call the sacred fire the cause of male posterity. See the *Mitakchara,* Oriannes' trans., p. 139.

BOOK SECOND

THE FAMILY

Chapter I

RELIGION WAS THE CONSTITUENT PRINCIPLE OF THE ANCIENT FAMILY

IF we transport ourselves in thought to those ancient generations of men, we find in each house an altar, and around this altar the family assembled. The family meets every morning to address its first prayers to the sacred fire, and in the evening to invoke it for a last time. In the course of the day the members are once more assembled near the fire for the meal, of which they partake piously after prayer and libation. In all these religious acts, hymns, which their fathers have handed down, are sung in common by the family.

Outside the house, near at hand, in a neighboring field, there is a tomb — the second home of this family. There several generations of ancestors repose together; death has not separated them. They remain grouped in this second existence, and continue to form an indissoluble family.[1]

Between the living part and the dead part of the family there is only this distance of a few steps which separates the house from the tomb. On certain days, which are determined for each one by his domestic religion, the living assemble near

---

[1] The use of family tombs by the ancients in incontestable; it disappeared only when the beliefs relative to the worship of the dead became obscured. The words ταφος πατρωος, ταφος των προγονων, appear continually in Greek writers, as *tumulus patrius* or *avitus, sepulcrum gentis,* are found in Roman writers. See Demosthenes, *in Eubul.,* 28; *in Macart.,* 79. Lycurgus, *in Leocr.,* 25. Cicero, *De Offic.,* I. 17. *De Legib.,* II. 22 — *Mortuum extra gentem inferri fas negant.* Ovid, *Trist.,* IV. 3, 45. Velleius, II. 119. Suetonius, *Nero,* 50; *Tiberius,* 1. *Digest,* XI. 5; XVIII. 1, 6. There is an old anecdote that shows how necessary it was thought to be that every one should be buried in the tomb of his family. It is related that the Lacedæmonians, when about to join battle with the Messenians, attached to their right arms their

their ancestors; they offer them the funeral meal, pour out milk and wine to them, lay out cakes and fruits, or burn the flesh of a victim to them. In exchange for these offerings they ask protection; they call these ancestors their gods, and ask them to render the fields fertile, the house prosperous, and their hearts virtuous.

Generation alone was not the foundation of the ancient family. What proves this is, that the sister did not bear the same relation to the family as the brother; that the emancipated son and the married daughter ceased completely to form a part of the family; and, in fine, several other important provisions of the Greek and Roman laws, that we shall have occasion to examine farther along.

Nor is the family principle natural affection. For Greek and Roman law makes no account of this sentiment. The sentiment may exist in the heart, but it is not in the law. The father may have affection for his daughter, but he cannot will her his property. The laws of succession — that is to say, those laws which most faithfully reflect the ideas that men had of the family — are in open contradiction both with the order of birth and with natural affection.[2]

The historians of Roman laws, having very justly remarked that neither birth nor affection was the foundation of the Roman family, have concluded that this foundation must be found in the power of the father or husband. They make a sort of primordial institution of this power; but they do not explain how this power was established, unless it was by the superiority of strength of the husband over the wife, and of the father over the children. Now, we deceive ourselves sadly when we thus place force as the origin of law. We shall see farther on that the authority of the father or husband, far from having

name, and those of their fathers, in order that, in case of death, each body might be recognized on the field of battle, and transported to the paternal tomb. Justin, III. 5. See Æschylus, *Sept.*, 889 (914), τάφων πατρῳον λαχαι. The Greek orators frequently refer to this custom: Isæus, Lysias, or Demosthenes, when he wishes to prove that such a man belongs to a certain family, and has the right to inherit its property, rarely fails to say that this man's father is buried in the tomb of this family.

2 It must be understood that we here speak of the most ancient law. We shall soon see that, at a later date, these early laws were modified.

been a first cause, was itself an effect; it was derived from religion, and was established by religion. Superior strength, therefore, was not the principle that established the family.

The members of the ancient family were united by something more powerful than birth, affection, or physical strength; this was the religion of the sacred fire, and of dead ancestors. This caused the family to form a single body, both in this life and in the next. The ancient family was a religious rather than a natural association; and we shall see presently that the wife was counted in the family only after the sacred ceremony of marriage had initiated her into the worship; that the son was no longer counted in it when he had renounced the worship, or had been emancipated; that, on the other hand, an adopted son was counted a real son, because, though he had not the ties of blood, he had something better — a community of worship; that the heir who refused to adopt the worship of this family had no right to the succession; and, finally, that relationship and the right of inheritance were governed not by birth, but by the rights of participation in the worship, such as religion had established them. Religion, it is true, did not create the family; but certainly it gave the family its rules; and hence it comes that the constitution of the ancient family was so different from what it would have been if it had owed its foundation to natural affection.

The ancient Greek language has a very significant word to designate a family. It is ἐπίστιον, a word which signifies, literally, *that which is near a hearth.* A family was a group of persons whom religion permitted to invoke the same sacred fire, and to offer the funeral repast to the same ancestors.

Chapter II

MARRIAGE

THE first institution that the domestic religion established, probably, was marriage.

We must remark that this worship of the sacred fire and of ancestors, which was transmitted from male to male, did not belong, after all, exclusively to man; woman had a part in it.

As a daughter, she took part in the religious acts of her father; as a wife, in those of her husband.

From this alone we see the essential character of the conjugal union among the ancients. Two families live side by side; but they have different gods. In one, a young daughter takes a part, from her infancy, in the religion of her father; she invokes his sacred fire; every day she offers it libations. She surrounds it with flowers and garlands on festal days. She asks its protection, and returns thanks for its favors. This paternal fire is her god. Let a young man of the neighboring family ask her in marriage, and something more is at stake than to pass from one house to the other. She must abandon the paternal fire, and henceforth invoke that of the husband. She must abandon her religion, practise other rites, and pronounce other prayers. She must give up the god of her infancy, and put herself under the protection of a god whom she knows not. Let her not hope to remain faithful to the one while honoring the other; for in this religion it is an immutable principle that the same person cannot invoke two sacred fires or two series of ancestors. "From the hour of marriage," says one of the ancients, "the wife has no longer anything in common with the domestic religion of her fathers; she sacrifices at the hearth of her husband."[1]

Marriage is, therefore, a grave step for the young girl, and not less grave for the husband; for this religion requires that one shall have been born near the sacred fire, in order to have the right to sacrifice to it. And yet he is now about to bring a stranger to this hearth; with her he will perform the mysterious ceremonies of his worship; he will reveal the rites and formulas which are the patrimony of his family. There is nothing more precious than this heritage; these gods, these rites, these hymns which he has received from his fathers, are what protect him in this life, and promise him riches, happiness, and virtue. And yet, instead of keeping to himself this tutelary power, as the savage keeps his idol or his amulet, he is going to admit a woman to share it with him.

Thus, when we penetrate the thoughts of these ancient men, we see of how great importance to them was the conjugal union, and how necessary to it was the intervention of religion.

[1] Stephen of Byzantium, πατρα.

Was it not quite necessary that the young girl should be initiated into the religion that she was henceforth to follow by some sacred ceremony? Was not a sort of ordination or adoption necessary for her to become a priestess of this sacred fire, to which she was not attached by birth?

Marriage was this sacred ceremony, which was to produce these important effects. The Greek and Roman writers habitually designate marriage by a word indicative of a religious act.[2] Pollux, who lived in the time of the Antonines, but who was well instructed in the ancient usages of his language, says, that in ancient times, instead of designating marriage by its particular name, γαμος, they designated it simply by the word τελος, which signifies sacred ceremony,[3] as if marriage had been, in those ancient times, the ceremony sacred above all others.

Now, the religion that created marriage was not that of Jupiter, of Juno, or of the other gods of Olympus. The ceremony did not take place in a temple; it was performed in a house, and the domestic god presided. When the religion of the gods of the sky became preponderant, men could not help invoking them also in the prayers of marriage, it is true; it even became habitual to go to the temple before the marriage, and offer sacrifices to these gods. These sacrifices were called the preludes of marriage;[4] but the principal and essential part of the ceremony always took place before the domestic hearth.

Among the Greeks the marriage ceremony consisted, so to speak, of three acts. The first took place before the hearth of the father, εγγυησις; the third before the hearth of the husband, τελος; the second was the passage from the one to the other, πομπη.[5]

1. In the paternal dwelling, in the presence of the future bridegroom, the father, surrounded ordinarily by his family, offers a sacrifice. The sacrifice concluded, he declares — pro-

---

[2] θυειν γαμον, sacrum nuptiale.   [3] Pollux, III. 3, 38.

[4] Προτελεια, προγαμια, Pollux, III. 38.

[5] Homer, Ill., XVIII. 391. Hesiod, Scutum, v. 275. Herodotus, VI. 129, 130. Plutarch, Theseus, 10; Lycurg., passim. Solon, 20; Aristides, 20; Gr. Quest., 27. Demosthenes, in Stephanum, II. Isæus, III. 39. Euripides, Helena, 722–725; Phen., 345. Harpocration, v. γαμηλια. Pollux, III. c. 3. The same usage among the Macedonians. Quintus Curtius, VIII. 16.

nouncing a sacramental formula — that he gives his daughter to the young man. This declaration is absolutely indispensable to the marriage; for the young girl would not be able to go at once to worship at the hearth of her husband, if her father had not already separated her from the paternal hearth. To enable her to adopt her new religion, she must be freed from every bond that attaches her to her first religion.

2. The young girl is carried to the house of the husband. Sometimes the husband himself conducts her. In certain cities the duty of bringing her belongs to one of those men who, among the Greeks, were clothed with a sacerdotal character, and who were called heralds. The bride was usually placed upon a car; her face was covered with a veil, and on her head was a crown. The crown, as we shall often have occasion to see, was used in all the ceremonies of this worship. She was dressed in white. White was the color of the vestments in all the religious acts. She was preceded by a torch — the nuptial torch. For the whole distance they sang around her religious hymns, whose refrain was ω 'υμην, ω 'υμεναιε. This hymn they called the *hymeneal,* and the importance of this sacred chant was so great that they gave its name to the whole ceremony.

The bride dares not go of her own accord into her new dwelling. Her husband must take her, and simulate a seizure by force. She must cry out, and the women that accompany her must pretend to defend her. Why this rite? Is it a symbol of the modesty of the bride? This is hardly probable: the moment for shame has not yet come; for what is now to take place is a religious ceremony. Was it not to mark more strongly that the wife, who was now to sacrifice to this fire, had herself no right there, that she did not approach it of her own free will, and that the master of the place and of the god introduced her by an act of his power? However this may be, after a feigned struggle, the husband raises her in his arms, and carries her through the doorway, taking great care, however, that her feet do not touch the sill.

What precedes is only a preparation, a prelude to the ceremony. The sacred act now commences in the house.

3. They approach the hearth; the wife is brought into the presence of the domestic divinity. She is sprinkled with the lustral water. She touches the sacred fire. Prayers are repeated.

Finally, the husband and wife share between themselves a cake or a loaf.

This sort of light meal, which commences and ends with a libation and a prayer, this sharing of nourishment in presence of the fire, puts the husband and wife in religious communion with each other, and in communion with the domestic gods.

The Roman marriage closely resembled that of Greece, and, like it, comprised three acts — *traditio, deductio in domum, confarreatio*.[6]

1. The young girl quits the paternal hearth. As she is not attached to this hearth by her own right, but through the father of the family, the authority of the father only can detach her from it. The *tradition* is, therefore, an indispensable ceremony.

2. The young girl is conducted to the house of the husband. As in Greece, she is veiled. She wears a crown, and a nuptial torch precedes the cortege. Those about her sing an ancient religious hymn. The words of this hymn changed doubtless with time, accommodating themselves to the variations of belief, or to those of the language; but the sacramental refrain continued from age to age without change. It was the word *Talassie*, a word whose sense the Romans of Horace's time no more understood than the Greeks understood the word υμεναιε, and which was, probably, the sacred and inviolable remains of an ancient formula.

The cortege stops before the house of the husband. There the bride is presented with fire and water. The fire is the emblem of the domestic divinity; the water is the lustral water, that serves the family for all religious acts. To introduce the bride into the house, violence must be pretended, as in Greece. The husband must take her in his arms, and carry her over the sill, without allowing her feet to touch it.

3. The bride is then led before the hearth, where the

---

[6] Varro, *L. L.*, 61. Dionysius of Halicarnassus, II. 25, 26. Ovid, *Fast.*, II. 558. Plutarch, *Rom. Quest.*, I. 29; *Romul.*, 15; Plin., *N. H.*, XVIII. 3. Tacit. *Ann.*, IV. 16; XI. 27. Juvenal, *Sat.* X. 329-336. Gaius, *Inst.*, I. 112. Ulpian, IX. *Digest*, XXIII. 2, 1. Festus, v. *Rapi*. Macrobius, *Sat.*, I. 15. Servius, *ad Æn.*, IV. 168. The same custom among the Etruscans, Varro, *De Re Rust.*, II. 4. The same custom among the ancient Hindus, *Laws of Manu*, III. 27-30, 172; V. 152; VIII. 227; IX. 194. *Mitakchara*, Orianne's trans., p. 166, 167, 236.

Penates, and all the domestic gods, and the images of ancestors, are grouped around the sacred fire. As in Greece, the husband and wife offer a sacrifice, pouring out a libation, pronouncing prayers, and eating a cake of wheaten flour (*panis farreus*).[7]

This cake, eaten during the recitation of prayers, in the presence and under the very eyes of the domestic divinities, makes the union of the husband and wife sacred. Henceforth they are associated in the same worship. The wife has the same gods, the same rites, the same prayers, the same festivals as her husband. Hence this old definition of marriage, which the jurists have preserved to us: *Nuptiæ sunt divini juris et humani communicatio;* and this other: *Uxor socia humanæ rei atque divinæ.*[8] This is because the wife participates in the worship of the husband; this wife whom, according to the expression of Plato, the gods themselves have introduced into the house.

The wife, thus married, also worships the dead; but it is not to her own ancestors that she carries the funeral repast. She no longer has this right. Marriage has completely detached her from the family, and has interrupted all the religious relations that she had with it. Her offerings she carries to the ancestors of her husband; she is of their family; they have become her ancestors. Marriage has been for her a second birth; she is henceforth the daughter of her husband; *filiæ loco,* say the jurists. One could not belong to two families, or to two domestic religions; the wife belongs entirely to her husband's family, and to his religion. We shall see the consequences of this rule in the right of succession.

The institution of sacred marriage must be as old in the Indo-European race as the domestic religion; for the one could not exist without the other. This religion taught man that the conjugal union was something more than a relation of the sexes and a fleeting affection, and united man and wife by the powerful bond of the same worship and the same belief. The

---

[7] We shall speak presently of other forms of marriage in use among the Romans, in which religion had no part. Let it suffice to say here, that the sacred marriage appears to us to be the oldest; for it corresponds to the most ancient beliefs, and disappeared only as those beliefs died out.

[8] *Digest,* XXIII. title 2. *Code,* IX. 32, 4. Dionysius of Halicarnassus, II. 25: Κοινωνος χρηματων και 'ιερων. Stephen of Byzantium, πατρα.

marriage ceremony, too, was so solemn, and produced effects so grave, that it is not surprising that these men did not think it permitted or possible to have more than one wife in each house. Such a religion could not admit of polygamy.

We can understand, too, that such a marriage was indissoluble, and that divorce was almost impossible. The Roman law did indeed permit the dissolution of the marriage by *coemptio*, or by *usus*. But the dissolution of the religious marriage was very difficult. For that, a new sacred ceremony was necessary, as religion alone could separate what religion had united. The effect of the *confarreatio* could be destroyed only by the *diffarreatio*. The husband and wife who wished to separate appeared for the last time before the common hearth; a priest and witnesses were present. As on the day of marriage, a cake of wheaten flour was presented to the husband and wife.[9] But, instead of sharing it between them, they rejected it. Then, instead of prayers, they pronounced formulas of a strange, severe, spiteful, frightful character,[10] a sort of malediction, by which the wife renounced the worship and gods of the husband. From that moment the religious bond was broken. The community of worship having ceased, every other common interest ceased to exist, and the marriage was dissolved.

Chapter III

CONTINUITY OF THE FAMILY. CELIBACY FORBIDDEN. DIVORCE IN CASE OF STERILITY. INEQUALITY BETWEEN THE SON AND DAUGHTER

THE belief relative to the dead, and to the worship that was due them, founded the ancient family, and gave it the greater part of its rules. We have seen above that man, after death, was reputed a happy and divine being, but on the condition that the living continued to offer him the funeral repasts. If these

---

[9] Festus, v. *Diffarreatio*. Pollux, III. c. 3: ἀποπομπή. We read, in an inscription, *Sacerdos confarreationum et diffarreationum*. Orelli, No. 2648.

[10] φρικωδη, αλλοκοτα, σκυθρωπα. Plutarch, *Rom. Quest.*, 50.

offerings ceased, the dead ancestor fell to the rank of an unhappy and malevolent demon. For when these ancient generations began to picture a future life to themselves, they had not dreamed of rewards and punishments; they imagined that the happiness of the dead depended not upon the life led in this state of existence, but upon the way in which their descendants treated them. Every father, therefore, expected of his posterity that series of funeral repasts which was to assure to his manes repose and happiness.

This opinion was the fundamental principle of domestic law among the ancients. From it followed, in the first place, this rule, that every family must perpetuate itself forever. It was necessary to the dead that the descendants should not die out. In the tomb where they lived this was the only inquietude which they experienced. Their only thought, their only interest, was, that there should be a man of their blood to carry them offerings at the tomb. The Hindu, too, believed that the dead repeated continually, "May there be born in our line sons who shall bring us rice, milk, and honey." The Hindu also had this saying: "The extinction of a family causes the ruin of the religion of this family; the ancestors, deprived of the offering of cakes, fall into the abode of the unhappy."[1] The men of Italy and Greece long held to the same notions. If they have not left us in their writings an opinion so clearly expressed as in the old books of the East, their laws, at least, remain to attest their ancient opinions. At Athens the law made it the duty of the first magistrate of the city to see that no family should become extinct.[2] In the same way, the Roman law made provision that no family should fail and become extinct.[3] We read in the discourse of an Athenian orator, "There is no man who, knowing that he must die, is so careless about himself as to wish to leave his family without descendants; for then there would be no one to render him that worship that is due to the dead."[4] Every one, therefore, had an interest in leaving a son after him, convinced that his immortal happiness depended upon it. It was even a duty towards those ancestors whose happiness could last no longer than the family lasted. The Laws of Manu call the oldest son "the one who is begotten for the accomplishment of a duty."

1 Bhagavad-Gita, I. 40.   2 Cicero, De Legib., II. 19.
3 Isæus, VII. 30–32.   4 Isæus, VII. 30.

Here we touch upon one of the most remarkable characteristics of the ancient family. The religion that had founded it
required that it should never perish.

When a family becomes extinct, a worship dies out. We must
take these families at a time before the belief had yet been
altered. Each one of them possessed a religion and gods, a
precious trust, over which it was required to watch. The
greatest misfortune that its piety had to fear, was that its line
of descendants might cease and come to an end; for then its
religion would disappear from the earth, its fire would be
extinguished, and the whole series of its dead would fall into
oblivion and eternal misery. The great interest of human life
was to continue the descent, in order to continue the worship.

In view of these opinions, celibacy was a grave impiety and
a misfortune; an impiety, because one who did not marry put
the happiness of the manes of the family in peril; a misfortune,
because he himself would receive no worship after his death,
and could not know "what the manes enjoyed." Both for himself and for his ancestors it was a sort of damnation.

We can easily believe that in the absence of laws such a
belief would long be sufficient to prevent celibacy. But it
appears, moreover, that, as soon as there were laws, they pronounced celibacy to be wrong, and a punishable offense.
Dionysius of Halicarnassus, who had searched the ancient
annals of Rome, asserts that he had seen an old law which
required young people to marry.[5] Cicero's treatise on the laws —
a treatise which almost always reproduces, under a philosophic
form, the ancient laws of Rome — contains a law which forbids
celibacy.[6] At Sparta, the legislation of Lycurgus deprived the
man who did not marry of all the rights of citizenship.[7] We
know from many anecdotes, that when celibacy ceased to be
forbidden by laws, usage still forbade it. Finally, it appears
from a passage of Pollux, that in many Greek cities the law
punished celibacy as a crime.[8] This was in accordance with the
ancient belief: man did not belong to himself; he belonged to
the family. He was one member in a series, and the series

[5] Dionysius of Halicarnassus, IX. 22.
[6] Cicero, De Legib., III. 2.
[7] Plutarch, Lycurg., Apoth. of the Lacedæmonians.
[8] Pollux, III. 48.

must not stop with him. He was not born by chance; he had been introduced into life that he might continue a worship; he must not give up life till he is sure that this worship will be continued after him.

But to beget a son is not sufficient. The son who is to perpetuate the domestic religion must be the fruit of a religious marriage. The bastard, the natural son, he whom the Greeks called νοθος, and the Romans *spurius*, could not perform the part which religion assigned to the son. In fact, the tie of blood did not of itself alone constitute the family; the tie of a common worship had to be added. Now, the son born of a woman who had not been associated in the worship of the husband by the ceremony of marriage could not himself take any part in the worship.[9] He had no right to offer the funeral repast, and the family was not perpetuated for him. We shall see, farther on, that for the same reason he had not the right of inheritance.

Marriage, then, was obligatory. Its aim was not pleasure; its principal object was not the union of two beings who were pleased with each other, and who wished to go united through the pleasures and the trials of life. The effect of marriage, in the eyes of religion and of the laws, was the union of two beings in the same domestic worship, in order to produce from them a third who would be qualified to continue the worship. We see this plainly by the sacramental formula that was pronounced in the act of marriage. *Ducere uxorem liberum quærendorum causa* was the Roman expression; παιδων επ᾽ υροτω γνησιων was the Greek.[10]

This marriage having been contracted only to perpetuate the family, it seemed just that it should be broken if the wife was sterile. The right of divorce, in this case, always existed among the ancients; it is even possible that divorce was an obligation. In India religion proscribed that the sterile woman should be replaced by another at the end of eight years.[11] That the duty was the same in Greece and Rome, there is no formal text to prove. Still Herodotus mentions two kings of Sparta who were

[9] Isæus, VII. Demosthenes, *in Macart.*
[10] Menander, *fr.* 185, ed. Didot. Alciphron, I. 16. Æsch., *Agam.*, 1166, ed. Hermann.
[11] *Laws of Manu*, IX. 81.

constrained to repudiate their wives on account of sterility.[12] As to Rome, every one knows the history of Carvilius Ruga, whose divorce is the first of which the Roman annals make mention. "Carvilius Ruga," says Aulus Gellius, "a man of rank, separated from his wife by divorce because he could not have children by her. He loved her tenderly, and had no reason to complain of her conduct; but he sacrificed his love to the sanctity of his oath, because he had sworn (in the formula of marriage) that he took her to wife in order to have children."[13]

Religion demanded that the family should never become extinct; all affection and all natural right had to give way before this absolute rule. If the sterility of a marriage was due to the husband, it was no less necessary that the family should be continued. In that case, a brother or some other relative of the husband had to be substituted in his place. The child born of such a connection was held to be the son of the husband, and continued his worship. Such were the rules among the ancient Hindus. We find them again in the laws of Athens, and in those of Sparta.[14] So powerful was the empire of this religion! So much did religious duty surpass all others!

For a still stronger reason, ancient laws prescribed the marriage of the widow, when she had had no children, with the nearest relative of her husband. The son born of such a union was reputed to be the son of the deceased.[15] The birth of a daughter did not fulfil the object of the marriage; indeed, the daughter could not continue the worship, for the reason that on the day of her marriage she renounced the family and worship of her father, and belonged to the family and religion of her husband. The family, like the worship, was continued only by the males — a capital fact, the consequences of which we shall see farther on.

It was, therefore, the son who was looked for, and who was necessary; he it was whom the family, the ancestors, and the sacred fire demanded. "Through him," according to the old

---

[12] Herodotus, V. 39; VI. 61.

[13] Aulus Gellius, IV. 3. Valerius Maximus, II. 1, 4. Dionys., II. 25.

[14] Xenophon, *Gov. of the Laced.* Plutarch, *Solon,* 20. *Laws of Manu,* IX. 121.

[15] *Laws of Manu,* IX. 69, 146. The same is true of the Hebrews. Deuteron., 25.

laws of the Hindus, "a father pays the debt due to the manes of his ancestors, and assures immortality to himself." This son was not less precious in the eyes of the Greeks; for later he was to perform the sacrifices, offer the funeral repast, and preserve by his worship the domestic religion. In accordance with this idea, old Æschylus calls the son the savior of the paternal hearth.[16]

The entrance of this son into the family was signalized by a religious act. First, he had to be accepted by the father, who, as master and guardian of the hearth, and as a representative of his ancestors, had to decide whether the new comer was or was not of the family. Birth formed only the physical bond; the declaration of the father formed the religious and moral bond. This formality was equally obligatory in Greece, in Rome, and in India.

A sort of initiation was also required for the son, as we have seen it was for the daughter. This took place a short time after birth — the ninth day at Rome, the tenth in Greece, the tenth or twelfth in India.[17] On that day the father assembled the family, assembled witnesses, and offered a sacrifice to his fire. The child was presented to the domestic gods; a female carried him in her arms, and ran, carrying him, several times round the sacred fire.[18] This ceremony had a double object; first, to purify the infant — that is to say, to free him from the stain which the ancients supposed he had contracted by the mere fact of gestation; and, second, to initiate him into the domestic worship. From this moment the infant was admitted into this sort of sacred society or small church that was called the family. He possessed its religion, he practised its rites, he was qualified to repeat its prayers; he honored its ancestors, and at a later period he would himself become an honored ancestor.

16 Æsch., Choeph., 264 (262).

17 Aristophanes, Birds, 922. Demosthenes. in Bœot., p. 1016. Macrobius, Sat., I. 17. Laws of Manu, II. 30.

18 Plato, Theætetus. Lysias, in Harpocration, v. Ἀμφιδρομι α.

Chapter IV

ADOPTION AND EMANCIPATION

THE duty of perpetuating the domestic worship was the foundation of the law of adoption among the ancients. The same religion which obliged a man to marry, which pronounced a divorce in case of sterility, which, in case of impotence or of premature death, substituted a relative in place of the husband, still offered to a family one final resource to escape the so much dreaded misfortune of extinction; this resource was the right of adoption. "He to whom nature has denied a son can adopt one, so that the funeral ceremonies may not cease." Thus speaks the old legislator of the Hindus.[1] We have a curious plea of an Athenian orator in a case where the legitimacy of a son's adoption was contested. The defendant shows us first the motive for which one adopted a son. "Menecles," he says, "did not wish to die without children; he was desirous of leaving behind him some one to bury him, and in after time to perform the ceremonies of the funeral worship." He then goes on to show what will happen if the tribunal annuls his adoption; what will happen, not only to himself, but to the one who has adopted him. Menecles is dead, and still it is the interest of Menecles that is at stake. "If you annul my adoption, you will leave Menecles, who is dead, without a son; and consequently no one will perform the sacrifices in his honor, no one will offer him the funeral repast, and thus he will be without worship."[2]

To adopt a son, was then, to watch over the perpetuity of the domestic religion, the safety of the sacred fire, the continuation of the funeral offerings, and the repose of the manes of the ancestors. There being no reason for adoption, except the necessity of preventing the extinction of a worship, it was permitted only to one who had no son. The law of the Hindus is formal on this point.[3] That of the Athenians is not less so;

---

[1] *Laws of Manu,* IX. 10.   [2] Isæus, II. 10–46.

[3] *Laws of Manu,* X. 168, 174. *Dattaca-Sandrica,* Orianne's trans., p. 260.

all the orations of Demosthenes against Leochares are proof of
this.[4] No particular passage proves that this was the case in
the old Roman law, and we know that in the time of Gaius a
man might have at the same time sons by nature and sons by
adoption. It appears, however, that this point was not admitted
as legal in Cicero's time; for in one of his orations the orator
expresses himself thus: "What is the law concerning adoption?
Why, that he may adopt children who is no longer able to
have children himself, and who failed of having them when he
was of an age to expect it. To adopt is to seek, by regular and
sacerdotal law, that which by the ordinary process of nature he
is no longer able to obtain."[5] Cicero attacks the adoption of
Clodius, taking the ground that the man who has adopted him
already has a son, and he declares that this adoption is contrary
to sacerdotal law.

When a son was adopted, it was necessary, first of all, that
he should be initiated into a form of worship, "introduced into
a domestic religion, brought into the presence of new
Penates."[6] Adoption, therefore, was accompanied by a ceremony very like that which took place at the birth of a son. In
this way the new comer was admitted to the hearth, and associated in the new religion. Gods, sacred objects, rites, prayers,
all became common between him and his adopted father. They
said of him, *In sacra transiit* — He has passed to the worship
of the new family.[7]

By this very ceremony he renounced the worship of the old
one.[8] We have seen, indeed, that according to this ancient
belief, the same man could not sacrifice at two hearths, or
honor two series of ancestors. Admitted to a new house, the
old became foreign to him. He no longer had anything in
common with the hearth near which he was born, and could
no longer offer the funeral repast to his own ancestors. The ties
of birth were broken; the new tie of a common worship took
the ascendency. The man became so completely a stranger to

---

4 See also Isæus, II. 11-14.

5 Cicero, *Pro Domo,* 13, 14. Aulus Gellius, V. 19.

6 Επι τα ʻιερα αγειν. Isæus, VII. *Venire in Sacra,* Cicero, *Pro, Domo,*
13; *in Penates adsciscere,* Tacitus, *Hist.,* I. 15.

7 Valerius Maximus, VII. 7.

8 *Amissis sacris paternis,* Cicero, *ibid.*

his own family, that, if he happened to die, his natural father had no right to take charge of the funeral, or to conduct the procession. The adopted son could not return again to the old family; or, at most, the law permitted this only when, having a son, he left that son to take his place in the adoptive family. They considered that, the perpetuity of this family being thus assured, he might leave it; but, in this case, he severed all the ties that bound him to his own son.[9]

Emancipation corresponded, as a correlative, to adoption. In order that a son might enter a new family, it was necessary that he should be able to leave the old; that is to say, that he should be emancipated from its religion.[10] The principal effect of emancipation was the renunciation of the worship of the family in which one was born. The Romans designated this act by the very significant name of *sacrorum detestatio*.[11]

Chapter V

KINSHIP. WHAT THE ROMANS CALLED AGNATION

PLATO says that kinship is the community of the same domestic gods.[1] When Demosthenes wishes to prove that two men are relatives, he shows that they practise the same religious rites, and offer the funeral repast at the same tomb. Indeed, it was the domestic religion that constituted relationship. Two men could call themselves relatives when they had the same gods, the same sacred fire, and the same funeral repast.

Now, we have already observed that the right to offer sacrifices to the sacred fire was transmitted only from male to male, and that the worship of the dead was addressed to the ascendants in the male line only. It followed from this rule that one could not be related through females. In the opinion of those ancient generations, a female transmitted neither being nor worship.

---

[9] Isæus, VI. 44; X. 11. Demosthenes, *against Leochares*. Antiphon., *Frag.*, 15. Comp. *Laws of Manu*, IX. 142.

[10] *Consuetudo apud antiquos fuit ut qui in familiam transiret prius se abdicaret ab ea in qua natus fuerat.* Servius, ad Æn., II. 156.

[11] Aulus Gellius, XV. 27.

[1] Plato, *Laws*, V. p. 729.

The son owed all to the father. Besides, one could not belong to two families, or invoke two fires; the son, therefore, had no other religion or other family than that of the father.[2] How could there have been a maternal family? His mother herself, the day on which the sacred rites of marriage were performed, had absolutely renounced her own family; from that time she had offered the funeral repast to her husband's ancestors, as if she had become their daughter, and she had no longer offered it to her own ancestors, because she was no longer considered as descended from them. She had preserved neither religious nor legal connection with the family in which she was born. For a still stronger reason her son had nothing in common with this family.

The foundation of relationship was not birth; it was worship. This is seen clearly in India. There the chief of the family, twice each month, offers the funeral repast; he presents a cake to the manes of his father, another to his paternal grandfather, a third to his great-grandfather; never to those from whom he is descended on the mother's side, neither to his mother, nor to his mother's father. Afterwards, ascending still higher, but always in the same line, he makes an offering to fourth, fifth, and sixth ascendant. The offering to these last is lighter; it is a libation of water and a few grains of rice. Such is the funeral repast; and it is according to the accomplishment of these rites that relationship is reckoned. When two men, who offer their funeral repasts separately, can, each one, by ascending through a series of six ancestors, find one who is common to both, they are akin. They are called *samanodacas,* if the common ancestor is one of those to whom they offer only the libation of water; *sapindas,* if he is of those to whom the cake is presented.[3] Counting according to our usage, the relation of the *sapindas* would go to the seventh degree, and that of the *samanodacas* to the fourteenth. In both cases the relationship is shown by the fact that both make an offering to the same ancestor; and we see that in this system the relationship through females cannot be admitted.

The case was the same in the West. There has been much discussion as to what the Roman jurists understood by *agna-*

2 *Patris, non matris, familiam sequitur. Digest,* 50, tit. 16, § 196.
3 *Laws of Manu,* V. 60; *Mitakchara,* Orianne's trans., p. 213.

tion. But the problem is of easy solution as soon as we bring agnation and the domestic religion together. Just as this religion was transmitted only from male to male, so it is attested by all the ancient jurists, that two men can be "agnates" only when, ascending from male to male, they were found to have common ancestors.[4] The rule for agnation was, then, the same as that for worship. There was between these two things a manifest relation. Agnation was nothing more than relationship such as religion had originally established it.

To render this truth clearer, let us trace the genealogical table of a Roman family.

L. Cornelius Scipio, died about 250 B. C.

Publius Scipio.   Cn. Scipio

Luc. Scipio Asiaticus.   P. Scipio Africanus.   P. Scipio Nasica.

Luc. Scipio Asiaticus.   P. Scipio.   Cornelia.   P. Scip. Nasica.
                                              wife of Sempr. Gracchus.
Scipio Asiaticus.   Scip. Æmilianus.   Scip. Serapio.
                            Tib. Sempr. Gracchus.

In this table, the fifth generation, which lived towards the year 140 B. C., is represented by four personages. Were they all akin? According to our modern ideas on this subject, they were; in the opinion of the Romans, all were not. Now, let us inquire if they all had the same domestic worship; that is to say, if they all made offerings to the same ancestors. Let us suppose the third Scipio Asiaticus, who alone remains of his branch, offering the funeral repast on a particular day; ascending from male to male, he finds for the third ancestor Publius Scipio. Again, Scipio Æmilianus, offering his sacrifice, will meet in the series of his ascendants this same Publius Scipio. Scipio Asiaticus and Scipio Æmilianus are, therefore, related to each other. Among the Hindus they would be called *sapindas.* On the other hand, Scipio Serapio has for a fourth ancestor L. Cornelius Scipio, who is also the fourth ancestor of Scipio Æmilianus. They are, therefore, akin. Among the Hindus they would be called *samanodacas.* In the judicial and religious

[4] Gaius, I. 156; III. 10. Ulpian, 26. *Institutes of Justinian,* III. 2; III. 5.

language of the Romans, these three Scipios are agnates — the two first are agnates in the sixth degree, the third is their agnate in the eighth degree.

The case is not the same with Tiberius Gracchus. This man, who, according to our modern customs, would be nearest related to Scipio Æmilianus, was not related to him in the remotest degree. It was of small account, indeed, for Tiberius that he was the son of Cornelia, the daughter of the Scipios. Neither he nor Cornelia herself belonged to that family, in a religious point of view. He has no other ancestors than the Sempronii; it is to them that he offers the funeral repast; in ascending the series of his ancestors he never comes to a Scipio. Scipio Æmilianus and Tiberius Gracchus, therefore, are not agnates. The tie of blood does not suffice to establish this relationship; a common worship is necessary.

We can now understand why, in the eyes of the Roman law, two consanguineous brothers were agnates, while two uterine brothers were not. Still we cannot say that descent by males was the immutable principle on which relationship was founded. It was not by birth, it was by worship alone, that the agnates were recognized. The son whom emancipation had detached from the worship was no longer the agnate of his father. The stranger who had been adopted, that is to say, who had been admitted to the worship, became the agnate of the one adopting him, and even of the whole family. So true is it that it was religion that established relationship.

There came a time, indeed, for India and Greece, as well as for Rome, when relationship of worship was no longer the only kind admitted. By degrees, as this old religion lost its hold, the voice of blood spoke louder, and the relationship of birth was recognized in law. The Romans gave the name of *cognatio* to this sort of relationship, which was absolutely independent of the rules of the domestic religion. When we read the jurists from Cicero to Justinian, we see the two systems as rivals of each other, and contending in the domain of law. But in the time of the Twelve Tables, agnation was the only relationship known, and this alone conferred the right of inheritance. We shall see, farther on, that the case was the same among the Greeks.

Chapter VI

THE RIGHT OF PROPERTY

HERE is an institution of the ancients of which we must not form an idea from anything that we see around us. The ancients founded the right of property on principles different from those of the present generation; as a result, the laws by which they guaranteed it are sensibly different from ours.

We know that there are races who have never succeeded in establishing among themselves the right of private property, while others have reached this stage only after long and painful experience. It is not, indeed, an easy problem, in the origin of society, to decide whether the individual may appropriate the soil, and establish such a bond between his being and a portion of the earth, that he can say, This land is mine, this is the same as a part of me. The Tartars have an idea of the right of property in a case of flocks or herds, but they cannot understand it when it is a question of land. Among the ancient Germans the earth belonged to no one; every year the tribe assigned to each one of its members a lot to cultivate, and the lot was changed the following year. The German was proprietor of the harvest, but not of the land. The case is still the same among a part of the Semitic race, and among some of the Slavic nations.

On the other hand, the nations of Greece and Italy, from the earliest antiquity, always held to the idea of private property. We do not find an age when the soil was common among them;[1] nor do we find anything that resembles the annual allotment of land which was in vogue among the Germans.

---

[1] Some historians have expressed the opinion that at Rome property was at first public, and did not become private till Numa's reign. This error comes from a false interpretation of three passages of Plutarch (Numa, 16), Cicero (Republic, II. 14), and Dionysius of Halicarnassus (II. 74). These three authors say, it is true, that Numa distributed lands to the citizens, but they indicate very clearly that these lands were conquests of his predecessor, *agri quos bello Romulus ceperat.* As to the Roman soil itself — *ager Romanus* — it was private property from the origin of the city.

And here we note a remarkable fact. While the races that do not accord to the individual a property in the soil, allow him at least a right to the fruits of his labor, — that is to say, to his harvest, — precisely the contrary custom prevailed among the Greeks. In many cities the citizens were required to store their crops in common, or at least the greater part, and to consume them in common. The individual, therefore, was not the master of the corn which he had gathered; but, at the same time, by a singular contradiction, he had an absolute property in the soil. To him the land was more than the harvest. It appears that among the Greeks the conception of priviate property was developed exactly contrary to what appears to be the natural order. It was not applied to the harvest first, and to the soil afterwards, but followed the inverse order.

There are three things which, from the most ancient times, we find founded and solidly established in these Greek and Italian societies: the domestic religion; the family; and the right of property — three things which had in the beginning a manifest relation, and which appear to have been inseparable. The idea of private property existed in the religion itself. Every family had its hearth and its ancestors. These gods could be adored only by this family, and protected it alone. They were its property.

Now, between these gods and the soil, men of the early ages saw a mysterious relation. Let us first take the hearth. This altar is the symbol of a sedentary life; its name indicates this.[2] It must be placed upon the ground; once established, it cannot be moved. The god of the family wishes to have a fixed abode; materially, it is difficult to transport the stone on which he shines; religiously, this is more difficult still, and is permitted to a man only when hard necessity presses him, when an enemy is pursuing him, or when the soil cannot support him. When they establish the hearth, it is with the thought and hope that it will always remain in the same spot. The god is installed there not for a day, not for the life of one man merely, but for as long a time as this family shall endure, and there remains any one to support its fire by sacrifices. Thus

[2] 'Εστια, 'ιστημι, stare. See Plutarch, De primo frigido, 21; Macrob., I. 23; Ovid, Fast., VI. 299.

the sacred fire takes possession of the soil, and makes it its own. It is the god's property.

And the family, which through duty and religion remains grouped around its altar, is as much fixed to the soil as the altar itself. The idea of domicile follows naturally. The family is attached to the altar, the altar is attached to the soil; an intimate relation, therefore, is established between the soil and the family. There must be his permanent home, which he will not dream of quitting, unless an unforeseen necessity constrains him to it. Like the hearth, it will always occupy this spot. This spot belongs to it, is its property, the property not simply of a man, but of a family, whose different members must, one after another, be born and die here.

Let us follow the idea of the ancients. Two sacred fires represent two distinct divinities, who are never united or confounded; this is so true, that even intermarriage between two families does not establish an alliance between their gods. The sacred fire must be isolated — that is to say, completely separated from all that is not of itself; the stranger must not approach it at the moment when the ceremonies of the worship are performed, or even be in sight of it. It is for this reason that these gods are called the concealed gods, μυχιοι, or the interior gods, *Penates*. In order that this religious rule may be well observed, there must be an enclosure around this hearth at a certain distance. It did not matter whether this enclosure was a hedge, a wall of wood, or one of stone. Whatever it was, it marked the limit which separated the domain of one sacred fire from that of another. This enclosure was deemed sacred.[3] It was an impious act to pass it. The god watched over it, and kept it under his care. They, therefore, applied to this god the epithet of 'ιρχειος.[4] This enclosure, traced and protected by

---

[3] 'Ερκος 'ιερσυ. Sophocles, *Trachin.*, 606.

[4] At an epoch when this ancient worship was almost effaced by the younger religion of Zeus, and when they associated him with the fire-god, the new god assumed the title of 'ερκειος. It is not less true that, in the beginning, the real protector of the enclosure was the domestic god. Dionysius of Halicarnassus asserts this (I. 68), when he says that the θεοι 'ερκειοι are the same as the Penates. This follows, moreover, from a comparison of a passage of Pausanias (IV. 17) with a passage of Euripides (*Troad.*, 17), and one of Virgil (*Æn.*, II. 514); the three passages relate to the same fact, and show that Zευς 'ερκειος was no other than the domestic fire.

religion, was the most certain emblem, the most undoubted mark of the right of property.

Let us return to the primitive ages of the Aryan race. The sacred enclosure, which the Greeks call 'εοχος, and the Latins *herctum*, was the somewhat spacious enclosure in which the family had its house, its flocks, and the small field that it cultivated. In the midst rose the protecting fire-god. Let us descend to the succeeding ages. The tribes have reached Greece and Italy, and have built cities. The dwellings are brought nearer together: they are not, however, contiguous. The sacred enclosure still exists, but is of smaller proportions; oftenest it is reduced to a low wall, a ditch, a furrow, or to a mere open space, a few feet wide. But in no case could two houses be joined to each other; a party wall was supposed to be an impossible thing. The same wall could not be common to two houses; for then the sacred enclosure of the gods would have disappeared. At Rome the law fixed two feet and a half as the width of the free space, which was always to separate two houses, and this space was consecrated to "the god of the enclosure."[5]

A result of these old religious rules was, that a community of property was never established among the ancients. A phalanstery was never known among them. Even Pythagoras did not succeed in establishing institutions which the most intimate religion of men resisted. Neither do we find, at any epoch in the life of the ancients, anything that resembled that multitude of villages so general in France during the twelfth century. Every family, having its gods and its worship, was required to have its particular place on the soil, its isolated domicile, its property.

According to the Greeks, the sacred fire taught men to build houses;[6] and, indeed, men who were fixed by their religion to one spot, which they believed it their duty not to quit, would soon begin to think of raising in that place some solid structure. The tent covers the Arab, the wagon the Tartar; but a family that has a domestic hearth has need of a permanent dwelling. The stone house soon succeeds the mud cabin or the wooden hut. The family did not build for the life of a single man, but for generations that were to succeed each other in the same dwelling.

[5] Festus, v. *Ambitus.* Varro, *L. L.,* V. 22. Servius, *ad Æn.,* II. 469.
[6] Diodorus, V. 68.

The house was always placed in the sacred enclosure. Among the Greeks, the square which composed the enclosure was divided into two parts; the first part was the court; the house occupied the second. The hearth, placed near the middle of the whole enclosure, was thus at the bottom of the court, and near the entrance of the house. At Rome the disposition was different, but the principle was the same. The hearth remained in the middle of the enclosure, but the buildings rose round it on four sides, so as to enclose it within a little court.

We can easily understand the idea that inspired this system of construction. The walls are raised around the hearth to isolate and defend it, and we may say, as the Greeks said, that religion taught men to build houses. In this house the family is master and proprietor; its domestic divinity assures it this right. The house is consecrated by the perpetual presence of gods; it is a temple which preserves them.

"What is there more holy," says Cicero, "what is there more carefully fenced round with every description of religious respect, than the house of each individual citizen? Here is his altar, here is his hearth, here are his household gods; here all his sacred rights, all his religious ceremonies, are preserved."[7] To enter this house with any malevolent intention was a sacrilege. The domicile was inviolable. According to a Roman tradition, the domestic god repulsed the robber, and kept off the enemy.[8]

Let us pass to another object of worship — the tomb; and we shall see that the same ideas were attached to this. The tomb held a very important place in the religion of the ancients; for, on one hand, worship was due to the ancestors, and on the other, the principal ceremony of this worship — the funeral repast — was to be performed on the very spot where the ancestors rested.[9] The family, therefore, had a common tomb, where its members, one after another, must come to sleep. For this tomb the rule was the same as for the hearth. It was no more permitted to unite two families in the same tomb than it was to establish two domestic hearths in the same house. To bury one out of the family tomb, or to place a

---

[7] Cicero, *Pro Domo*, 41.   [8] Ovid, *Fast.*, V. 141.
[9] Such, at least, was the ancient rule, since they believed that the funeral repast served as food for the dead. Eurip., *Troad.*, 381.

stranger in this tomb, was equally impious.[10] The domestic
religion, both in life and in death, separated every family from
all others, and strictly rejected all appearance of community.
Just as the houses could not be contiguous, so the tombs could
not touch each other; each one of them, like the house, had a
sort of isolating enclosure.

How manifest is the character of private property in all this!
The dead are gods, who belong to a particular family, which
alone has a right to invoke them. These gods have taken possession of the soil; they live under this little mound, and no one,
except one of the family, can think of meddling with them.
Furthermore, no one has the right to dispossess them of the soil
which they occupy; a tomb among the ancients could never
be destroyed or displaced;[11] this was forbidden by the severest
laws. Here, therefore, was a portion of the soil which, in the
name of religion, became an object of perpetual property for
each family. The family appropriated to itself this soil by
placing its dead here; it was established here for all time. The
living scion of this family could rightly say, This land is mine.
It was so completely his, that it was inseparable from him, and
he had not the right to dispose of it. The soil where the dead
rested was inalienable and imprescriptible. The Roman law
required that, if a family sold the field where the tomb was
situated, it should still retain the ownership of this tomb, and
should always preserve the right to cross the field, in order to
perform the ceremonies of its worship.[12]

The ancient usage was to inter the dead, not in cemeteries
or by the road-side, but in the field belonging to the family.
This custom of ancient times is attested by a law of Solon, and
by several passages in Plutarch. We learn from an oration of
Demosthenes, that even in his time, each family buried its dead

[10] Cicero, *De Legib.*, II. 22; II. 26. Gaius, *Instit.*, II. 6. *Digest*,
XLVII. tit. 12. We must note that the slave and the client, as we shall
see, farther on were a part of the family, and were buried in the common tomb. The rule which prescribed that every man should be
buried in the tomb of his family, admitted of an exception in the case
where the city itself granted a public funeral.

[11] Lycurgus, *against Leocrates*, 25. At Rome, before a burial-place
could be changed, the permission of the pontiffs was required. Pliny,
Letters, X. 73.

[12] Cicero, *De Legib.*, II. 24. *Digest*, XVIII. tit. 1. 6.

in its own field, and that when a domain was bought in Attica, the burial-place of the old proprietors was found there.[13] As for Italy, this same custom is proved to have existed by the laws of the Twelve Tables, by passages from two jurisconsults, and by this sentence of Siculus Flaccus: "Anciently there were two ways of placing the tomb; some placed it on one side of the field, others towards the middle."[14]

From this custom we can see that the idea of property was easily extended from the small mound to the field that surrounded this mound. In the works of the elder Cato there is a formula according to which the Italian laborer prayed the manes to watch over his field, to take good care against the thief, and to bless him with a good harvest. Thus these souls of the dead extended tutelary action, and with it their right of property, even to the boundaries of the domain. Through them the family was sole master in this field. The tomb had established an indissoluble union of the family with the land — that of ownership.

In the greater number of primitive societies the right of property was established by religion. In the Bible, the Lord said to Abraham, "I am the Lord, that brought thee out of Ur of the Chaldees, to give thee this land, to inherit it;" and to Moses, "Go up hence, . . . into the land which I sware unto Abraham, to Isaac, and to Jacob, saying, Unto thee will I give it."

Thus God, the primitive proprietor, by right of creation, delegates to man his ownership over a part of the soil.[15] There was something analogous among the ancient Græco-Italian peoples. It was not the religion of Jupiter that founded this right, it is true; perhaps because this religion did not yet exist. The gods who conferred upon every family its right to a portion of the soil, were the domestic gods, the sacred fire, and the manes.

[13] *Laws of Solon,* cited by Gaius in *Digest,* X. tit. 1. 13. Demosthenes, *against Callicles.* Plutarch, *Aristides,* 1.

[14] Siculus Flaccus, edit. Goez, p. 4. See *Fragm. terminalia,* edit. Goez, p. 147. Pomponius, *in Digest,* XLVII. tit. 12. 5. Paul, *in Digest,* VIII. 1, 14.

[15] Same tradition among the Etruscans: "*Quum Jupiter terram Etruriæ sibi vindicavit, constituit jussitque metiri campos signarique agros.*" *Auctores Rei Agrariæ,* in the fragment entitled *Idem Vegoiæ Arrunti,* edit. Goez.

The first religion that exercised its empire on their minds was also the one that established the right of property among them.

It is clearly evident that private property was an institution that the domestic religion had need of. This religion required that both dwellings and burying-places should be separate from each other; living in common was, therefore, impossible. The same religion required that the hearth should be fixed to the soil, that the tomb should neither be destroyed nor displaced. Suppress the right of property, and the sacred fire would be without a fixed place, the families would become confounded, and the dead would be abandoned and without worship. By the stationary hearth and the permanent burial-place, the family took possession of the soil; the earth was in some sort imbued and penetrated by the religion of the hearth and of ancestors. Thus the men of the early ages were saved the trouble of resolving too difficult a problem. Without discussion, without labor, without a shadow of hesitation, they arrived, at a single step, and merely by virtue of their belief, at the conception of the right of property; this right from which all civilization springs, since by it man improves the soil, and becomes improved himself.

Religion, and not laws, first guaranteed the right of property. Every domain was under the eyes of household divinities, who watched over it.[16] Every field had to be surrounded, as we have seen for the house, by an enclosure, which separated it completely from the domains of other families. This enclosure was not a wall of stone; it was a band of soil, a few feet wide, which remained uncultivated, and which the plough could never touch. This space was sacred; the Roman law declared it indefeasible;[17] it belonged to the religion. On certain appointed days of each month and year, the father of the family went round his field, following this line; he drove victims before him, sang hymns, and offered sacrifices.[18] By this ceremony he believed he had awakened the benevolence of his gods towards his field and his house; above all, he had marked

---

[16] *Lares agri custodes,* Tibullus, I. 1, 23. *Religio Larum posita in fundi villæque conspectu.* Cicero, *De Legib.,* II. 11.

[17] Cicero, *De Legib.,* I. 21.

[18] Cato, *De Re Rust.,* 141. *Script. Rei Agrar.,* edit. Goez, p. 308. Dionysius of Halicarnassus, II. 74. Ovid, *Fast.,* II. 639. Strabo, V. 3.

his right of property by proceeding round his field with his domestic worship. The path which the victims and prayers had followed was the inviolable limit of the domain.

On this line, at certain points, the men placed large stones or trunks of trees, which they called *Termini*. We can form a good idea as to what these bounds were, and what ideas were connected with them, by the manner in which the piety of men established them. "This," says Seculus Flaccus, "was the manner in which our ancestors proceeded: They commenced by digging a small hole, and placing the Terminus upright near it; next they crowned the Terminus with garlands of grasses and flowers; then they offered a sacrifice. The victim being immolated, they made the blood flow into the hole; they threw in live coals (kindled, probably, at the sacred fire of the hearth), grain, cakes, fruits, a little wine, and some honey. When all this was consumed in the hole, they thrust down the stone or piece of wood upon the ashes while they were still warm."[19] It is easy to see that the object of the ceremony was to make of this Terminus a sort of sacred representation of the domestic worship. To continue this character for it, they renewed the sacred act every year, by pouring out libations and reciting prayers. The Terminus, once placed in the earth, became in some sort the domestic religion implanted in the soil, to indicate that this soil was forever the property of the family. Later, poetry lending its aid, the Terminus was considered as a distinct god.

The employment of Termini, or sacred bounds for fields, appears to have been universal among the Indo-European race. It existed among the Hindus at a very early date, and the sacred ceremonies of the boundaries had among them a great analogy with those which Siculus Flaccus has described for Italy.[20] Before the foundation of Rome, we find the Terminus among the Sabines;[21] we also find it among the Etruscans. The Hellenes, too, had sacred landmarks, which they called ὅροι, θεοὶ ὅριοι.[22]

The Terminus once established according to the required

[19] Siculus Flaccus, edit. Goez, p. 5.
[20] *Laws of Manu,* VIII. 245. Vrihaspati, cited by Sicé, *Hindu Legislation,* p. 159.
[21] Varro, *L. L.,* V. 74.
[22] Pollux, IX. 9. Hesychius, ὅρος. Plato, *Laws,* p. 842.

rites, there was no power on earth that could displace it. It was to remain in the same place through all ages. This religious principle was expressed at Rome by a legend: Jupiter, having wished to prepare himself a site on the Capitoline hill for a temple, could not displace the god Terminus. This old tradition shows how sacred property had become; for the immovable Terminus signified nothing less than inviolable property.

In fact, the Terminus guarded the limit of the field, and watched over it. A neighbor dared not approach too near it: "For then," says Ovid, "the god, who felt himself struck by the ploughshare, or mattock, cried, 'Stop: this is my field; there is yours.' "[23] To encroach upon the field of a family, it was necessary to overturn or displace a boundary mark, and this boundary mark was a god. The sacrilege was horrible, and the chastisement severe. According to the old Roman law, the man and the oxen who touched a Terminus were devoted[24] — that is to say, both man and oxen were immolated in expiation. The Etruscan law, speaking in the name of religion, says, "He who shall have touched or displaced a bound shall be condemned by the gods; his house shall disappear; his race shall be extinguished; his land shall no longer produce fruits; hail, rust, and the fires of the dog-star shall destroy his harvests; the limbs of the guilty one shall become covered with ulcers, and shall waste away."[25] We do not possess the text of the Athenian law on this subject; there remain of it only three words, which signify, "Do not pass the boundaries." But Plato appears to complete the thought of the legislator when he says, "Our first law ought to be this: Let no person touch the bounds which separate his field from that of his neighbor, for this ought to remain immovable. . . . Let no one attempt to disturb the small stone which separates friendship from enmity, and which the land-owners have bound themselves by an oath to leave in its place."[26]

From all these beliefs, from all these usages, from all these laws, it clearly follows that the domestic religion taught man to appropriate the soil, and assured him his right to it.

There is no difficulty in understanding that the right of property, having been thus conceived and established, was

---

[23] Ovid, *Fast.*, II. 677.   [24] Festus, v. *Terminus*.
[25] *Script. Rei Agrar.*, ed. Goez, p. 258.
[26] Plato, *Laws*, VIII. p. 842.

much more complete and absolute in its effects than it can be in our modern societies, where it is founded upon other principles. Property was so inherent in the domestic religion that a family could not renounce one without renouncing the other. The house and the field were — so to speak — incorporated in it, and it could neither lose them nor dispose of them. Plato, in his treatise on the Laws, did not pretend to advance a new idea when he forbade the proprietor to sell his field; he did no more than to recall an old law. Everything leads us to believe that in the ancient ages property was inalienable. It is well known that at Sparta the citizen was formally forbidden to sell his lot of land.[27] There was the same interdiction in the laws of Locri and of Leucadia.[28] Pheidon of Corinth, a legislator of the ninth century B. C., prescribed that the number of families and of estates should remain unchangeable.[29] Now, this prescription could be observed only when it was forbidden to sell an estate, or even to divide it.

The law of Solon, later by seven or eight generations than that of Pheidon of Corinth, no longer forbade a man to sell his land, but punished the vender by a severe fine, and the loss of the rights of citizenship.[30] Finally, Aristotle mentions, in a general manner, that in many cities the ancient laws forbade the sale of land.[31]

Such laws ought not to surprise us. Found property on the right of labor, and man may dispose of it. Found it on religion, and he can no longer do this; a tie stronger than the will of man binds the land to him. Besides, this field where the tomb is situated, where the divine ancestors live, where the family is forever to perform its worship, is not simply the property of a man, but of a family. It is not the individual actually living who has established his right over this soil, it is the domestic god. The individual has it in trust only; it belongs to those who are dead, and to those who are yet to be born. It is a part of the body of this family, and cannot be separated from it. To detach one from the other is to alter a worship, and to offend

---

[27] Plutarch, *Lycurg., Agis.* Aristotle, *Polit.,* II. 6, 10 (II. 7).
[28] Aristotle, *Polit.,* II. 4, 4 (II. 5).
[29] Id., *Ibid.,* II. 3, 7.
[30] Æschines, *against Timarchus.* Diogenes Laertius, I. 55.
[31] Aristotle, *Polit.,* VII. 2.

a religion. Among the Hindus, property, also founded upon religion, was also inalienable.[32]

We know nothing of Roman law previous to the laws of the Twelve Tables. It is certain that at that time the sale of property was permitted; but there are reasons for thinking that, in the earlier days of Rome, and in Italy before the existence of Rome, land was inalienable, as in Greece. Though there remains no evidence of this old law, there remain to us at least the modifications which were made in it by degrees. The law of the Twelve Tables, though attaching to the tomb the character of inalienability, has freed the soil from it. Afterwards it was permitted to divide property, if there were several brothers, but on condition that a new religious ceremony should be performed, and that the new partition should be made by a priest;[33] religion only could divide what had before been proclaimed indivisible. Finally, it was permitted to sell the domain; but for that formalities of a religious character were also necessary. This sale could take place only in the presence of a priest, whom they called *libripens,* and with the sacred formality which they called *mancipation.* Something analogous is seen in Greece; the sale of a house or of land was always accompanied with a sacrifice to the gods.[34] Every transfer of property needed to be authorized by religion. If a man could not, or could only with difficulty, dispose of land, for a still stronger reason he could not be deprived of it against his will.

The appropriation of land for public utility was unknown among the ancients. Confiscation was resorted to only in case of condemnation to exile[35] — that is to say, when a man, deprived of his right to citizenship, could no longer exercise any right over the soil of the city. Nor was the taking of property for debt known in the ancient laws of cities.[36] The laws of the Twelve Tables assuredly do not spare the debtor; still they

[32] *Mitakchara,* Orianne's trans., p. 50. This rule disappeared by degrees after Brahminism became dominant.

[33] This priest was called *agrimensor.* See *Scriptores Rei Agrariæ.*

[34] Stobæus, 42.

[35] This rule disappeared in the democratic age of the cities.

[36] A law of the Elæans forbade the mortgaging of land. Aristot., *Polit.,* VII. 2. Mortgages were unknown in ancient Roman law. What is said of mortgages in the Athenian law before Solon is based on a doubtful passage of Plutarch.

do not permit his property to be sold for the benefit of the creditor. The body of the debtor is held for the debt, not his land, for the land is inseparable from the family. It is easier to subject a man to servitude than to take his property from him. The debtor is placed in the hands of the creditor; his land follows him, in some sort, into slavery. The master who uses the physical strength of a man for his own profit, enjoys at the same time the fruits of his land, but does not become the proprietor of it. So inviolable above all else is the right of property.[37]

Chapter VII

THE RIGHT OF SUCCESSION

1. Nature and Principle of the Right of Succession among the Ancients.

THE right of property having been established for the accomplishment of an hereditary worship, it was not possible that this right should fail after the short life of an individual. The man dies, the worship remains; the fire must not be extinguished, nor the tomb abandoned. So long as the domestic religion continued, the right of property had to continue with it.

Two things are closely allied in the creeds as well as in the laws of the ancients — the family worship and its property. It was therefore a rule without exception, in both Greek and Roman law, that a property could not be acquired without the

[37] In the article of the law of the Twelve Tables which relates to insolvent debtors, we read, *Si volet suo vivito;* then the debtor, having become almost a slave, still retains something for himself; his land, if he has any, is not taken from him. The arrangements known in Roman law under the names of *fiduciary mancipation,* and of *pignus,* were, before the introduction of the Servian action, the means employed to insure to the creditor the payment of the debt; these prove indirectly that the seizure of property for debt was not practised. Later, when they suppressed corporal servitude, it was necessary that there should be some claim on the property of a debtor. The change was not without difficulty; but the distinction which was made between *property* and *possession* offered a resource. The creditor obtained of the prætor the right to sell, not the property, *dominium,* but the goods of the debtor, bona. Then only, by a disguised seizure, the debtor lost the enjoyment of his property.

worship, or the worship without the property. "Religion prescribes," says Cicero, "that the property and the worship of a
family shall be inseparable, and that the care of the sacrifices
shall always devolve upon the one who receives the inheritance."[1] At Athens an orator claims a succession in these terms:
"Weigh it well, O judges, and say whether my adversary or I
ought to inherit the estate of Philoctemon, and offer the sacrifices upon his tomb."[2] Could one say more directly that the
care of the worship was inseparable from the succession? It was
the same in India: "He who inherits, whoever he may be, is
bound to make the offerings upon the tomb."[3]

From this principle were derived all the rules regarding the
right of succession among the ancients. The first is that, the
domestic religion being, as we have seen, hereditary from male
to male, property is the same. As the son is the natural continuator of the religion, he also inherits the estate. Thus the
rule of inheritance is found; it is not the result of a simple
agreement made between men; it is derived from their belief,
from their religion, from that which has the greatest power
over their minds. It is not the personal will of the father that
causes the son to inherit. The father need not make a will; the
son inherits of full right, — *ipso jure heres exsistit,* — says the
jurisconsult. He is even a necessary successor — *heres necessarius.*[4] He has neither to accept nor to reject the inheritance.
The continuation of the property, like that of the worship, is
for him an obligation as well as a right. Whether he wishes it or
not, the inheritance falls to him, whatever it may be, even with
its encumbrances and its debts. The right to inherit without
the debts, and to reject an inheritance, was not allowed to the
son in Greek legislation, and was not introduced until a later
period into Roman law.

The judicial language of Rome calls the son *heres suus,* as if
one should say, *heres sui ipsius.* In fact, he inherits only of
himself. Between his father and him there is neither donation,
nor legacy, nor change of property. There is simply a continuation — *morte parentis continuatur dominium.* Already,
during the life of the father, the son was co-proprietor of the

---

1 Cicero, *De Legib.,* II. 19, 20. Festus, v. *Everriator.*
2 Isæus, VI. 51. Plato calls the heir διαδοχος θεων. Laws, V. 740.
3 *Laws of Manu,* IX. 186.   4 *Digest,* XXXVIII. tit. 16, 14.

field and house — *vivo quoque patre dominus existimatur.*[5]

To form an idea of inheritance among the ancients, we must not figure to ourselves a fortune which passes from the hands of one to those of another. The fortune is immovable, like the hearth, and the tomb to which it is attached. It is the man who passes away. It is the man who, as the family unrolls its generations, arrives at his hour appointed to continue the worship, and to take care of the domain.

2.   *The Son, not the Daughter, inherits.*

It is here that ancient laws, at first sight, appear whimsical and unjust. We experience some surprise when we see in the Roman law that the daughter does not inherit if she is married, and that, according to the Greek law, she does not inherit in any case. What concerns the collateral branches appears, at first sight, still farther removed from nature and justice. This is because all these laws flow, according to a very rigorous logic, from the creed and religion that we have described above.

The rule for the worship is, that it shall be transmitted from male to male; the rule for the inheritance is, that it shall follow the worship. The daughter is not qualified to continue the paternal religion, since she may marry, and thus renounce the religion of her father to adopt that of her husband; she has, therefore, no right to the inheritance. If a father should happen to leave his property to a daughter, this property would be separated from the worship, which would be inadmissible. The daughter could not even fulfil the first duty of an heir, which was to continue the series of funeral repasts; since she would offer the sacrifices to the ancestors of her husband. Religion forbade her, therefore, to inherit from her father.

Such is the ancient principle; it influenced equally the legislators of the Hindus and those of Greece and Rome. The three peoples had the same laws; not that they had borrowed from each other, but because they had derived their laws from the same belief.

"After the death of the father," says the Code of Manu, "let the brothers divide the patrimony among them;" and the legislator adds, that he recommends the brothers to endow their sisters, which proves that the latter have not of themselves any right to the paternal succession.

[5] *Institutes*, III. 1, 3; III. 9, 7; III. 19, 2.

This was the case, too, at Athens. Demosthenes, in his orations, often has occasion to show that daughters cannot inherit.[6] He is himself an example of the application of this rule; for he had a sister, and we know, from his own writings, that he was the sole heir to the estate; his father had reserved only the seventh part to endow the daughter.

As to Rome, the provisions of primitive law which excluded the daughters from the inheritance are not known to us from any formal and precise text; but they have left profound traces in the laws of later ages. The Institutes of Justinian still excluded the daughter from the number of natural heirs, if she was no longer under the power of the father; and she was no longer under the power of the father after she had been married according to the religious rites.[7] From this it follows that, if the daughter before marriage could share the inheritance with her brother, she had not this right after marriage had attached her to another religion and another family. And, if this was still the case in the time of Justinian, we may suppose that in primitive law, this principle was applied in all its rigor, and that the daughter not yet married, but who would one day marry, had no right to inherit the estate. The Institutes also mention the old principle, then obsolete, but not forgotten, which prescribed that an inheritance always descended to the males.[8] It was clearly as a vestige of this old rule, that, according to the civil law, a woman could never be constituted an heiress. The farther we ascend from the Institutes of Justinian towards earlier times, the nearer we approach the rule that woman could not inherit. In Cicero's time, if a father left a son and a daughter, he could will to his daughter only one third of his fortune; if there was only a daughter, she could still have but half. We must also note that, to enable this daughter to receive a third or half of this patrimony, it was necessary that the father should make a will in her favor; the daughter had nothing of full right.[9] Finally, a century and a half before Cicero, Cato, wishing to revive ancient manners, proposed and carried the Voconian law, which forbade, — 1. Making a woman an heiress, even if she was an only child,

6 Demosthenes, in Bœotum. Isæus, X. 4. Lysias, in Mantith., 10.
7 Institutes, II. 9, 2.   8 Ibid., III. 1, 15; III. 2, 3.
9 Cicero, De Rep., III. 7.

married or unmarried. 2. The willing to a woman of more than a fourth part of the patrimony.[10] The Voconian law merely renewed laws of an earlier date; for we cannot suppose it would have been accepted by the contemporaries of the Scipios if it had not been supported upon old principles which they still respected. It re-established what time had changed. Let us add that it contained nothing regarding heirship, *ab intestat,* probably because on this point the old law was still in force, and there was nothing to repair on the subject. At Rome, as in Greece, the primitive law excluded the daughter from the heritage; and this was only a natural and inevitable consequence of the principles which religion had established.

It is true men soon found out a way of reconciling the religious prescription which forbade the daughter to inherit with the natural sentiment which would have her enjoy the fortune of her father. The law decided that the daughter should marry the heir.

Athenian legislation carried this principle to its ultimate consequences. If the deceased left a son and a daughter, the son alone inherited and endowed his sister; if they were not both children of the same mother, he had his choice to marry her or to endow her.[11] If the deceased left only a daughter, his nearest of kind was his heir; but this relative, who was of course also a near relative of the daughter, was required, nevertheless, to marry her. More than this, if this daughter was already married, she was required to abandon her husband in order to marry her father's heir. The heir himself might be already married; in this case, he obtained a divorce, in order to marry his relative.[12] We see here how completely ancient law ignored nature to conform to religion.

[10] Cicero, *in Verr.,* I. 42. Livy, XLI. 4. St. Augustine, *City of God,* III. 21.

[11] Demosthenes, *in Eubul.,* 21. Plutarch, *Themist.,* 32. Isæus, X. 4. Corn. Nepos, *Cimon.* It must be noted that the law did not permit marrying a uterine brother, or an emancipated brother; it could be only a brother by the father's side, because the latter alone could inherit of the father.

[12] Isæus, III. 64; X. 5. Demosthenes, *in Eubul.,* 41. The only daughter was called επικληρος, wrongly translated *heiress;* it signifies the daughter who goes with the inheritance. In fact, the daughter was never an heiress.

The necessity of satisfying the requirements of religion, combined with the desire of saving the interests of an only daughter, gave rise to another subterfuge. On this point Hindu law and Athenian law correspond marvellously. We read in the Laws of Manu, "He who has no male child may require his daughter to give him a son, who shall become his, and who may perform the funeral ceremonies in his honor." In this case the father was required to admonish the husband to whom he gave his daughter, by pronouncing this formula: "I give you this daughter, adorned with jewels, who has no brother; the son born of her shall be my son, and shall celebrate my obsequies."[13] The custom was the same at Athens; the father could continue his descent through his daughter, by giving her a husband on this special condition. The son who was born of such a union was reputed the son of the wife's father; followed his worship; assisted at his religious ceremonies; and, later guarded his tomb.[14] In Hindu law this child inherited from his grandfather, as if he had been his son; it was exactly the same at Athens. When the father had married his daughter in the manner we have described, his heir was neither his daughter nor his son-in-law; it was *the daughter's son*.[15] As soon as the latter had attained his majority, he took possession of the patrimony of his maternal grandfather, though his father and mother were still living.[16]

This singular tolerance of religion and law confirms the rule which we have already pointed out. The daughter was not qualified to inherit; but, by a very natural softening of the rigor of this principle, the only daughter was considered as an intermediary by whom the family might be continued. She did not inherit; but the worship and the inheritance were transmitted through her.

3. Of the Collateral Succession.

A man died without children; to know who the heir of his estate was, we have only to learn who was qualified to continue his worship.

[13] *Laws of Manu*, IX. 127, 136. Vasishta, XVII. 16.
[14] Isæus, VII.
[15] He was not called the grandson; they gave him the particular name of θυγατριδοῦς.
[16] Isæus, VIII. 31; X. 12. Demosthenes, *in Steph.*, II. 20.

Now, the domestic religion was transmitted by blood from male to male. The descent in the male line alone established between two men the religious relation which permitted one to continue the worship of the other. What is called relationship, as we have seen above, was nothing more than the expression of this relation. One was a relative because he had the same worship, the same original sacred fire, the same ancestors. But one was not a relative because he had the same mother; religion did not admit of kinship through women. The children of two sisters, or of a sister and a brother, had no bond of kinship between them, and belonged neither to the same domestic religion nor to the same family.

These principles regulated the order of succession. If a man, having lost his son and his daughter, left only grandchildren after him, his son's son inherited, but not his daughter's son. In default of descendants, he had as an heir his brother, not his sister, the son of his brother, not the son of his sister. In default of brothers and nephews, it was necessary to go up in the series of ascendants of the deceased, always in the male line, until a branch of the family was found that was detached through a male; then to re-descend in this branch from male to male, until a living man was found; this was the heir.

These rules were in force equally among the Hindus, the Greeks, and the Romans. In India "the inheritance belongs to the nearest sapinda; in default of a sapinda, to the samano-daca."[17] Now, we have seen that the relationship which these two words expressed was the religious relationship, or the relationship through the males, and corresponded to the Roman agnation.

Here, again, is the law of Athens: "If a man dies without children, the heir is the brother of the deceased, provided he is a consanguineous brother; in default of him, the son of the brother; *for the succession always passes to the males, and to the descendants of males.*"[18] They still cited this old law in the time of Demosthenes, although it had already been modified, and they had commenced at this epoch to admit relationship through women.

In the same way, the Twelve Tables ordained that, if a man

[17] *Laws of Manu,* IX, 186, 187.
[18] Demosthenes, *in Macart.; in Leoch.* Isæus, VII, 20.

died without *his heir,* the succession belonged to the nearest agnate. Now, we have seen that one was never an agnate through females. The ancient Roman law also specified that the nephew inherited from the *patruus,* — that is to say, from his father's brother, — and did not inherit from the *avunculus,* his mother's brother.[19]

By returning to the table which we have traced of the family of the Scipios, it will be seen that, Scipio Æmilianus, having died without children, his estate could not pass either to Cornelia, his aunt, or to C. Gracchus, who, according to our modern ideas, was his cousin-german, but to Scipio Asiaticus, who was really his nearest of kin.

In the time of Justinian, the legislator no longer understood these old laws; they appeared unjust to him, and he complained of the excessive rigor of the laws of the Twelve Tables, "which always accorded the preference to the masculine posterity, and excluded from the inheritance those who were related to the deceased only through females."[20] Unjust laws, if you will, for they made no account of natural affection; but singularly logical laws, for setting out from the principle that the inheritance was attached to the worship, they excluded from the inheritance those whom this religion did not authorize to continue the worship.

4. *Effects of Emancipation and Adoption.*

We have already seen that emancipation and adoption produced a change in a man's worship. The first separated him from the paternal worship, the second initiated him into the religion of another family. Here also the ancient law conformed to the rules of religion. The son who had been excluded from the paternal worship by emancipation was also excluded from the inheritance. On the other hand, the stranger who had been associated in the worship of a family by adoption became a son there; he continued its worship, and inherited the estate. In both cases ancient law made more account of the religious tie than of the tie of birth.

As it was contrary to religion that one man should have two domestic worships, so he could not inherit from two families.

19 *Institutes,* III. 2, 4.
20 *Ibid.,* III. 3.

Besides, the adopted son, who inherited of the adopting family, did not inherit from his natural family. Athenian law was very explicit on this point. The orations of Attic orators often show us men who have been adopted into a family, and who wished to inherit in the one in which they were born; but the law was against them. The adopted son could not inherit from his own family unless he re-entered it; he could not re-enter it except by renouncing the adopting family; and he could leave this latter only on two conditions: the one was, that he abandoned the patrimony of this family; the other was, that the domestic worship, for the continuation of which he had been adopted, did not cease by his abandonment; and, to make this certain, it was necessary for him to leave this family a son, who should replace him. This son took charge of the worship, and inherited the estate; the father could then return to the family of his birth, and inherit its property. But this father and son could no longer inherit from each other; they were not of the same family, they were not of kin.[21]

We can easily see what was the idea of the old legislator when he established these precise rules. He did not suppose it possible that two estates could fall to the same heir, because two domestic worships could not be kept up by the same person.

5. Wills Were Not Known Originally.

The right of willing — that is to say, of disposing of one's property after death, in order to make it pass to other than natural heirs — was in opposition to the religious creed that was at the foundation of the law of property and the law of succession. The property being inherent in the worship, and the worship being hereditary, could one think of a will? Besides, property did not belong to the individual, but to the family; for man had not acquired it by the right of labor, but through the domestic worship. Attached to the family, it was transmitted from the dead to the living, not according to the will and choice of the dead, but by virtue of superior rules which religion had established.

The will was not known in ancient Hindu law. Athenian

[21] Isæus, X. Demosthenes, *passim*. Gaius, III. 2. *Institutes*, III. 1, 2. It is hardly necessary to state that these rules were modified in the pretorian laws.

legislation, up to Solon's time, forbade it absolutely, and Solon himself permitted it only to those who left no children.[22] Wills were for a long time forbidden or unknown at Sparta, and were authorized only after the Peloponnesian war.[23] Aristotle speaks of a time when the case was the same at Corinth and at Thebes.[24] It is certain that the power of transmitting one's property arbitrarily by will was not recognized as a natural right; the constant principle of the ancient ages was, that all property should remain in the family to which religion had attached it.

Plato, in his treatise on the Laws, which is largely a commentary on the Athenian laws, explains very clearly the thought of ancient legislators. He supposes that a man on his death-bed demands the power to make a will, and that he cries, "O gods, is it not very hard that I am not able to dispose of my property as I may choose, and in favor of any one to whom I please to give it, leaving more to this one, less to that one, according to the attachment they have shown for me?" But the legislator replies to this man, "Thou who canst not promise thyself a single day, thou who art only a pilgrim here below, does it belong to thee to decide such affairs? Thou art the master neither of thy property nor of thyself: thou and thy estate, all these things, belong to thy family; that is to say, to thy ancestors and to thy posterity."[25]

For us the ancient laws of Rome are very obscure; they were obscure even to Cicero. What we know reaches little farther back than the Twelve Tables, which certainly are not the primitive legislation of Rome; and of these only fragments remain. This code authorizes the will; yet the fragment relating to the subject is too short, and too evidently incomplete to enable us to flatter ourselves that we know the exact provisions of the legislators in this matter. When they granted the power of devising property, we do not know what reserve and what conditions they placed upon it.[26] We have no legal text,

---

22 Plutarch, *Solon*, 21.   23 Id., *Agis*, 5.

24 Aristotle, *Polit.*, II. 3, 4.

25 Plato, *Laws*, XI.

26 *Uti legassit, ita jus esto.* If we had of Solon's law only the words διαθεσθαι 'οπως αν εθελη, we should also suppose that the will was permitted in all possible cases; but the law adds, α μη παιδες ωσι.

earlier than the Twelve Tables, that either forbids or permits a will; but the language preserved traces of a time when wills were not known; for it called the son the *self-successor and necessary — heres suus et necessarius.* This formula, which Gaius and Justinian still employed, but which was no longer in accord with the legislation of their time, came, without doubt, from a distant epoch, when the son could not be disinherited or refuse the heritage. The father had not then the free disposition of his fortune. In default of sons, and if the deceased had only collateral relatives, the will was not absolutely unknown, but was not easily made valid. Important formalities were necessary. First, secrecy was not allowed to the testator during life; the man who disinherited his family, and violated the law that religion had established, had to do this publicly, in broad daylight, and take upon himself, during his lifetime, all the odium attached to such an act. This was not all; it was also necessary that the will of the testator should receive the approbation of the sovereign authority — that is to say, of the people assembled by curies, under the presidency of the pontiff.[27] We must not imagine that this was an empty formality, particularly in the early ages. These *comitia* by curies were the most solemn assemblies of the Roman city; and it would be puerile to say that they convoked the people under the presidency of the religious chief, to act simply as witnesses at the reading of a will. We may suppose that the people voted, and we shall see, on reflection, that this was absolutely necessary. There was, in fact, a general law which regulated the order of succession in a rigorous manner; to modify this order in any particular, another law was necessary. This exceptional law was the will. The right of a man to devise by will was not, therefore, fully accorded, and could not be, so long as this society remained under the empire of the old religion. In the belief of these ancient ages, the living man was only the representative, for a few years, of a constant and immortal being — the family. He held the worship and the property only in trust; his right to them ceased with his life.

[27] Ulpian, XX. 2. Gaius, I. 102, 119. Aulus Gellius, XV. 27. The testament *calatis comitiis* was doubtless the oldest in use. It was no longer known in Cicero's time. (*De Orat., I.* 53.)

6. The Right of Primogeniture.

We must transport ourselves beyond the time of which history has preserved the recollection, to those distant ages during which domestic institutions were established, and social institutions were prepared. Of this epoch there does not remain, nor can there remain, any written monument; but the laws which then governed men have left some traces in the legislation of succeeding times.

In these distant days we distinguish one institution which must have survived a long time, which had a considerable influence upon the future constitution of societies, and without which this constitution could not be explained. This is the right of primogeniture.

The old religion established a difference between the older and the younger son. "The oldest," said the ancient Aryas, "was begotten for the accomplishment of the duty due the ancestors; the others are the fruit of love." In virtue of this original superiority, the oldest had the privilege, after the death of the father, of presiding at all the ceremonies of the domestic worship; he it was who offered the funeral repast, and pronounced the formulas of prayer; "for the right of pronouncing the prayers belongs to that son who came into the world first." The oldest was, therefore, heir to the hymns, the continuator of the worship, the religious chief of the family. From this creed flowed a rule of law: the oldest alone inherited property. Thus says an ancient passage, which the last editor of the Laws of Manu still inserted in the code: "The oldest takes possession of the whole patrimony, and the other brothers live under his authority as if they were under that of their father. The oldest son performs the duties towards the ancestors; he ought, therefore, to have all."[28]

Greek law is derived from the same religious beliefs as Hindu law; it is not astonishing, then, to find here also the right of primogeniture. Sparta preserved it longer than other Greek cities, because the Spartans were longer faithful to old institutions; among them the patrimony was indivisible,

[28] *Laws of Manu*, IX. 105–107, 126. This ancient rule was modified as the old religion became enfeebled. Even in the code of Manu we find articles that authorize a division of the inheritance.

and the younger brothers had no part of it.[29] It was the same
with many of the ancient codes that Aristotle had sudied. He
informs us, indeed, that the Theban code prescribed absolutely
that the number of lots of land should remain unchangeable,
which certainly excluded the division among brothers. An
ancient law of Corinth also provided that the number of
families should remain invariable, which could only be the case
where the right of the oldest prevented families from becoming
dismembered in each generation.[30]

Among the Athenians we need not expect to find this old
institution in full vigor in the time of Demosthenes; but there
still existed at this epoch what they called the privilege of the
elder.[31] It consisted in retaining, above his proportion, the
paternal dwelling — an advantage which was materially considerable, and which was still more considerable in a religious
point of view; for the paternal house contained the ancient
hearth of the family. While the younger sons, in the time of
Demosthenes, left home to light new fires, the oldest, the true
heir, remained in possession of the paternal hearth and of the
tomb of his ancestors. He alone also preserved the family
name.[32] These were the vestiges of a time when he alone received the patrimony.

We may remark, that the inequality of the law of primogeniture, besides the fact that it did not strike the minds of the
ancients, over whom religion was all-powerful, was corrected
by several of their customs. Sometimes the younger son was
adopted into a family, and inherited property there; sometimes
he married an only daughter; sometimes, in fine, he received
some extinct family's lot of land. When all these resources
failed, younger sons were sent out to join a colony.

As to Rome, we find no law that relates to the right of
primogeniture; but we are not to conclude from this that the
right was unknown in ancient Italy. It might have disappeared,
and even its traces have been effaced. What leads us to believe
that before the ages known to us it was in force is, that the
existence of the Roman and Sabine *gens* cannot be explained

[29] *Fragments of the Greek Historians,* Didot's Coll., t. II. p. 211.
[30] Aristotle, *Polit.,* II. 9; II. 3.
[31] πρεσβεια, Demosthenes, *Pro Phorm.,* 34.
[32] Demosthenes, *in Bœot. de nomine.*

without it. How could a family reach the number of several thousand free persons, like the Claudian family, or several hundred combatants, all patricians, like the Fabian family, if the right of primogeniture had not maintained its unity during a long series of generations, and had not increased its numbers from age to age by preventing its dismemberment? This ancient right of primogeniture is proved by its consequences, and, so to speak, by its works.[33]

Chapter VIII

AUTHORITY IN THE FAMILY

1. The Principle and Nature of the Paternal Power among the Ancients.

THE family did not receive its laws from the city. If the city had established private law, that law would probably have been different from what we have seen. It would have established the right of property and the right of succession on different principles; for it was not for the interest of the city that land should be inalienable and the patrimony indivisible. The law that permitted a father to sell or even to kill his son — a law that we find both in Greece and in Rome — was not established by a city. The city would rather have said to the father, "Your wife's and your son's life does not belong to you any more than their liberty does. I will protect them, even against you; you are not the one to judge them, or to kill them, if they have committed a crime; I will be their judge." If the city did not speak thus, it is evident that it could not. Private law existed before the city. When the city began to write its

---

[33] The old Latin language, moreover, has preserved a vestige which, feeble as it is, deserves to be pointed out. A lot of land, the domain of a family, was called *sors; sors patrimonium significat,* says Festus. The word *consortes* was applied then to those who had among them only a single lot of land, and lived on the same domain. Now, the old language designated by this word brothers, and even those quite distantly related. This bears witness to a time when the patrimony and the family were indivisible. (Festus, v. *Sors.* Cicero, *in Verrem,* II. 323. Livy, XLI. 27. Vellius, I. 10. Lucretius, III. 772; VI. 1280.)

laws, it found this law already established, living, rooted in the customs, strong by universal observance. The city accepted it, because it could not do otherwise, and dared not modify it, except by degrees. Ancient law was not the work of a legislator; it was, on the contrary, imposed upon the legislator. It had its birth in the family. It sprang up spontaneously from the ancient principles which gave it root. It flowed from the religious belief which was universally admitted in the primitive age of these peoples, which exercised its empire over their intelligence and their wills.

A family was composed of a father, a mother, children, and slaves. This group, small as it was, required discipline. To whom, then, belonged the chief authority? To the father? No. There is in every house something that is above the father himself. It is the domestic religion; it is that god whom the Greeks called the hearth-master, — 'εστια δεσποινα, — whom the Romans called *Lar familiaris*. This divinity of the interior, or, what amounts to the same thing, the belief that is in the human soul, is the least doubtful authority. This is what fixed rank in the family.

The father ranks first in presence of the sacred fire. He lights it, and supports it; he is its priest. In all religious acts his functions are the highest; he slays the victim, his mouth pronounces the formula of prayer which is to draw upon him and his the protection of the gods. The family and the worship are perpetuated through him; he represents, himself alone, the whole series of ancestors, and from him are to proceed the entire series of descendants. Upon him rests the domestic worship; he can almost say, like the Hindu, "I am the god." When death shall come, he will be a divine being whom his descendants will invoke.

This religion did not place woman in so high a rank. The wife takes part in the religious acts, indeed, but she is not the mistress of the hearth. She does not derive her religion from her birth. She was initiated into it at her marriage. She has learned from her husband the prayer that she pronounces. She does not represent the ancestors, since she is not descended from them. She herself will not become an ancestor; placed in the tomb, she will not receive a special worship. In death, as in life, she counts only as a part of her husband.

Greek law, Roman law, and Hindu law, all derived from this old religion, agree in considering the wife as always a minor. She could never have a hearth of her own; she was never the chief of a worship. At Rome she received the title of *mater familias;* but she lost this if her husband died.[1] Never having a sacred fire which belonged to her, she had nothing of what gave authority in the house. She never commanded; she was never even free, or mistress of herself. She was always near the hearth of another, repeating the prayer of another; for all the acts of religious life she needed a superior, and for all the acts of civil life a guardian.

The Laws of Manu says, "Woman, during her infancy, depends upon her father; during her youth, upon her husband; when her husband is dead, upon her sons; if she has no son, on the nearest relative of her husband; for a woman ought never to govern herself according to her own will."[2] The Greek laws and those of Rome are to the same effect. As a girl, she is under her father's control; if her father dies, she is governed by her brothers; married, she is under the guardianship of her husband; if the husband dies, she does not return to her own family, for she has renounced that forever by the sacred marriage;[3] the widow remains subject to the guardianship of her husband's agnates — that is to say, of her own sons, if she has any, or, in default of sons, of the nearest kindred.[4] So complete is her husband's authority over her, that he can, upon his death, designate a guardian for her, and even choose her a second husband.[5]

To indicate the power of the husband over the wife, the Romans had a very ancient expression, which their jurisconsults have preserved; it is the word *manus*. It is not easy to discover the primitive sense of this word. The commentators make it the expression of material force, as if the wife was placed under the brutal hand of the husband. It is quite

[1] Festus, v. *Mater familiæ.*
[2] *Laws of Manu,* V. 147, 148.
[3] She returned only in case of divorce. Demosthenes, *in Eubulid.,* 41.
[4] Demosthenes, *in Steph.,* II.; *in Aphob.* Plutarch, *Themist.,* 32. Dionysius of Halicarnassus, II. 25. Gaius, I. 149, 155. Aulus Gellius, III. 2. Macrobius, I. 3.
[5] Demosthenes, *in Aphobum; pro Phormione.*

probable that this is wrong. The power of the husband over
the wife results in no wise from his superior strength. It came,
like all private law, from the religious belief that placed man
above woman. What proves this is, that a woman who had not
been married according to the sacred rites, and who, consequently, had not been associated in the worship, was not
subject to the marital power.[6] It was marriage which created
this subordination, and at the same time the dignity of the
wife. So true is it that the right of the strongest did not constitute the family.

Let us pass to the infant. Here nature speaks for itself, loud
enough. It demands that the infant shall have a protector, a
guide, a master. This religion is in accord with nature; it says
that the father shall be the chief of the worship, and that the
son shall merely aid him in his sacred functions. But nature
requires this subordination only during a certain number of
years; religion requires more. Nature brings the son to his
majority; religion does not grant it to him, according to
ancient principles; the sacred fire is indivisible, and the same is
true of property. The brothers do not separate at the death of
their father; for a still stronger reason they could not separate
from him during his life. In the rigor of primitive law, the sons
remained attached to the father's hearth, and, consequently,
subject to his authority; while he lived they were minors.

We may suppose that this rule lasted only so long as the old
domestic religion remained in full vigor. This unlimited subjection of the son to the father disappeared at an early day at
Athens. It subsisted longer at Sparta where a patrimony was
always indivisible. At Rome the old rule was scrupulously
observed; a son could never establish a separate hearth during
his father's life; married even, and the father of children, he
was still under parental authority.[7]

[6] Cicero, *Topic.*, 14. Tacitus, *Ann.*, IV. 16. Aulus Gellius, XVIII.
6. It will be seen farther on; that, at a certain epoch, new modes
of marriage were instituted, and that they had the same legal
effects as the sacred marriage.

[7] When Gaius said of the paternal power, *Jus proprium est
civium Romanorum,* we must understand that in his time the
Roman law recognized this power only in the *Roman citizen:* this
does not mean that the power had not existed before in other
places, or that it had not been recognized by the law of other
cities.

Besides, it was the same with the paternal as with the marital authority; its principle and condition were the domestic worship. A son born of concubinage was not placed under the authority of the father. Between his father and himself there existed no community of religion; there was nothing, therefore, that conferred authority upon the one and commanded obedience of the other. Paternity, of itself, gave the father no rights.

Thanks to the domestic religion, the family was a small organized body; a little society, which had its chief and its government. Nothing in modern society can give us an idea of this paternal authority. In primitive antiquity the father is not alone the strong man, the protector who has power to command obedience; he is the priest, he is heir to the hearth, the continuator of the ancestors, the parent stock of the descendants, the depositary of the mysterious rites of the worship, and of the sacred formulas of prayer. The whole religion resides in him.

The very name by which he is called — *pater* — contains in itself some curious information. The word is the same in Greek, in Latin, and in Sanskrit; from which we may conclude that this word dates from a time when the Hellenes, the Italians, and the Hindus still lived together in Central Asia. What was its signification, and what idea did it then present to the minds of men? We can discover this; for the word has preserved its primary signification in the formulas of religious language and in those of judicial language. When the ancients, invoking Jupiter, called him *pater hominum deorumque*, they did not intend to say that Jupiter was the father of gods and men, for they never considered him as such; they believed, on the contrary, that the human race existed before him. The same title of *pater* was given to Neptune, to Apollo, to Bacchus, to Vulcan, and to Pluto. These, assuredly, men never considered as their fathers; so, too, the title of *mater* was applied to Minerva, Diana, and Vesta, who were reputed three virgin goddesses. In judicial language, moreover, the title of *pater*, or *pater familias*, might be given to a man who had no children, who was not married, and who was not even of age to contract marriage. The idea of paternity, therefore, was not attached to this word. The old language had another word which properly designated the father, and which, as ancient as *pater,* is likewise found in the language of the Greeks, of the Romans, and of the Hindus *(gánitar, γεννητηρ, genitor)*. The word *pater* had another sense. In religious language they applied it to the gods; in legal language to every man who had a worship and a domain. The poets show us that they applied it to every one whom they wished to honor. The slave and the client applied it to their master. It was synonymous with the words *rex, αναξ, βασιλευς.* It contained in itself not the idea of paternity, but that of power, authority, majestic dignity.

That such a word should have been applied to the father of a family until it became his most common appellation, is assuredly a very significant fact, and one whose importance will appear to all who wish to understand ancient institutions. The history of this word suffices to give us an idea of the power which the father exercised for a long time in the family, and of the sentiment of veneration which was due him as a pontiff and a sovereign.

2. *Enumeration of the Rights that composed Paternal Power.*

Greek and Roman laws recognized in the father this un-limited power with which religion had at first clothed him. The numerous and diverse rights which these laws conferred upon him may be divided into three classes, according as we consider the father of a family as a religious chief, as the master of the property, or as a judge.

I. The father is the supreme chief of the domestic religion; he regulates all the ceremonies of the worship, as he under-stands them, or, rather, as he has seen his father perform them. No one contests his sacerdotal supremacy. The city itself and its pontiffs can change nothing in his worship. As priest of the hearth he recognizes no superior.

As religious chief, he is responsible for the perpetuity of the worship, and, consequently, for that of the family. Whatever affects this perpetuity, which is his first care and his first duty, depends upon him alone. From this flows a whole series of rights: —

The right to recognize the child at its birth, or to reject it. This right is attributed to the father by the Greek laws,[8] as well as by those of Rome. Barbarous as this is, it is not contrary to

8 Herodotus, I. 59. Plutarch, *Alcib.,* 23; *Agesilaus,* 3.

the principles on which the family is founded. Even uncontested filiation is not sufficient to admit one into the sacred circle of the family; the consent of its chief, and an initiation into its worship, are necessary. So long as the child is not associated in the domestic religion, he is nothing to the father.

The right to repudiate the wife, either in case of sterility, because the family must not become extinct, or in case of adultery, because the family and the descendants ought to be free from all debasement.

The right to give his daughter in marriage — that is to say, to cede to another the power which he has over her. The right of marrying his son; the marriage of the son concerns the perpetuity of the family.

The right to emancipate — that is to say, to exclude a son from the family and the worship. The right to adopt — that is to say, to introduce a stranger to the domestic hearth.

The right, at his death, of naming a guardian for his wife and children.

It is necessary to remark that all these rights belonged to the father alone, to the exclusion of all the other members of the family. The wife had not the right of divorce, at least in primitive times. Even when a widow, she could neither emancipate nor adopt. She was never the guardian even of her own children. In case of divorce, the children remained with the father, — even the daughters. Her children were never in her power. Her consent was not asked for the marriage of her own daughter.[9]

II. We have seen above that property was not understood, originally, as an individual right, but as a family right. The fortune, as Plato says, formally, and as all the ancient legislators say, implicitly, belongs to the ancestors and the descendants. This property, by its very nature, could not be divided. There could be in each family but one proprietor, which was the family itself, and only one to enjoy the use of property — the father. This principle explains several peculiarities of ancient law.

The property not being capable of division, and resting entirely on the head of the father, neither wife nor children had the least part in it. The dotal system, and even the com-

[9] Demosthenes, *in Eubul.*, 40 and 43. Gaius, I. 155. Ulpian, VIII. 8. *Institutes*, I. 9. *Digest*, I. tit. 1, 11.

munity of goods, were then unknown. The dowry of the wife belonged, without reserve, to the husband, who exercised over her dowry not only the rights of an administrator, but of an owner. Whatever the wife might have acquired during her marriage fell into the hands of her husband. She did not even recover her dower on becoming a widow.[10]

The son was in the same condition as the wife; he owned nothing. No donation made by him was valid, since he had nothing of his own. He could acquire nothing; the fruits of his labor, the profits of his trade, were his father's. If a will was made in his favor by a stranger, his father, not himself, received the legacy. This explains the provision of the Roman law which forbade all contracts of sale between father and son. If the father sold to the son, he sold to himself, as the son acquired only for the father.[11]

We see in the Roman laws, and we find also in the laws of Athens, that a father could sell his son.[12] This was because the father might dispose of all the property of the family, and the son might be looked upon as property, since his labor was a source of income. The father might, therefore, according to choice, keep this instrument of labor, or resign it to another. To resign it was called selling the son. The texts of the Roman law that we have do not inform us clearly as to the nature of this contract of sale, nor on the reservations that might have been contained in it. It appears certain that the son thus sold did not become the slave of the purchaser. His liberty was not sold; only his labor. Even in this state the son remained subject to the paternal authority, which proves that he was not considered to have left the family. We may suppose that this sale had no other effect than to cede the possession of the son for a time by a sort of contract to hire. Later it was employed only as an indirect means of emancipating the son.

III. Plutarch informs us that at Rome women could not appear in court even as witnesses.[13] We read in the jurisconsult

---

[10] Gaius, II. 98. All these rules of primitive law were modified by the pretorian law.

[11] Cicero, De Legib., II. 20. Gaius, II. 87. Digest, XVIII. tit. 1, 2.

[12] Plutarch, Solon, 13. Dionys. of Halic., II. 26. Gaius, I. 117; I. 132; IV. 79. Ulpian, X. 1. Livy, XLI. 8. Festus, v. Deminutus.

[13] Plutarch, Publicola, 8.

Gaius, "It should be known that nothing can be granted in the way of justice to persons under power — that is to say, to wives, sons, and slaves. For it is reasonably concluded that, since these persons can own no property, neither can they reclaim anything in point of justice. If a son, subject to his father's will, has committed a crime, the action lies against the father; nor has the father himself any action against his son."[14]

From all this it is clear that the wife and the son could not be plaintiffs or defendants, or accusers, or accused, or witnesses. Of all the family the father alone could appear before the tribunal of the city; public justice existed only for him; and he alone was responsible for the crimes committed by his family.

Justice for wife and son was not in the city, because it was in the house. The chief of the family was their judge, placed upon a judgment seat in virtue of his marital and parental authority, in the name of the family and under the eyes of the domestic divinities.[15]

Livy relates that the senate, wishing to extirpate the worship of Bacchus from Rome, decreed the punishment of death against all who had taken part in it. The decree was easily executed upon the citizens, but when it came to the women, who were not the least guilty, a grave difficulty presented itself; the women were not answerable to the state; the family alone had the right to judge them. The senate respected this old principle, and left to the fathers and husbands the duty of pronouncing the sentence of death against the women.

This judicial authority, which the chief of the family exercised in his house, was complete and without appeal. He could condemn to death like the magistrate in the city, and no authority could modify his sentence. "The husband," says Cato the Elder, "is the judge of his wife; his power has no limit; he can do what he wishes. If she has committed a fault, he punishes her; if she has drank wine, he condemns her; if she has been guilty of adultery, he kills her." The right was the same in regard to children. Valerius Maximus cites a certain Atilius who killed his daughter as guilty of unchastity, and

---

14 Gaius, II. 96; IV. 77, 78.

15 There came a time when this jurisdiction was modified; the father consulted the whole family, and formed it into a tribunal, over which he presided. Tacit., XIII. 32. *Digest*, XXIII. tit. 4, 5. Plato, *Laws*, IX.

everybody will recall the father who put his son, an accomplice of Catiline, to death.

Facts of this nature are numerous in Roman history. It would be a false idea to suppose that the father had an absolute right to kill his wife and children. He was their judge. If he put them to death, it was only by virtue of his right as judge. As the father of the family was alone subject to the judgment of the city, the wife and the son could have no other judge than him. Within his family he was the only magistrate.

We must also remark that the paternal authority was not an arbitrary power, like that which would be derived from the right of the strongest. It had its foundation in a belief which all shared alike, and it found its limits in this same belief. For example: the father had the right to exclude his son from the family; but he well knew that if he did this the family ran a risk of becoming extinct, and the manes of his ancestors of falling into eternal oblivion. He had the right to adopt a stranger; but religion forbade him to do this if he had a son. He was sole proprietor of the goods; but he had not, at least originally, a right to alienate them. He could repudiate his wife; but to do this he had to break the religious bond which marriage had established. Thus religion imposed upon the father as many obligations as it conferred rights.

Such for a long time was the ancient family. The spiritual belief was sufficient without the need of the law of force, or of the authority of a social power to constitute it regularly, to give it a discipline, a government and justice, and to establish private law in all its details.

Chapter IX

MORALS OF THE ANCIENT FAMILY

HISTORY does not study material facts and institutions alone; its true object of study is the human mind: it should aspire to know what this mind has believed, thought, and felt in the different ages of the life of the human race.

We described, at the opening of this book, the ancient opinion which men held concerning their destiny after death.

We have shown how this creed produced domestic institutions and private law. It remains to discover what its action was upon morals in primitive societies. Without pretending that this old religion created moral sentiments in the heart of man, we may at least believe that it was associated with them to fortify them, to give them greater authority, to assure their supremacy and their right of direction over the conduct of men, sometimes also to give them a false bias.

The religion of these primitive ages was exclusively domestic; so also were morals. Religion did not say to a man, showing him another man, That is thy brother. It said to him, That is a stranger; he cannot participate in the religious acts of thy hearth; he cannot approach the tomb of thy family; he has other gods than thine, and cannot unite with thee in a common prayer; thy gods reject his adoration, and regard him as their enemy; he is thy foe also.

In this religion of the hearth man never supplicates the divinity in favor of other men; he invokes him only for himself and his. A Greek proverb has remained as a souvenir and a vestige of this ancient isolation of man in prayer. In Plutarch's time they still said to the egotist, You sacrifice to the hearth.[1] This signified, You separate yourself from other citizens; you have no friends; your fellow-men are nothing to you; you live solely for yourself and yours. This proverb pointed to a time when, all religion being around the hearth, the horizon of morals and of affection had not yet passed beyond the narrow circle of the family.

It is natural that moral ideas, like religious ideas, should have their commencement and progress, and the god of the primitive generations in this race was very small; by degrees men made him larger; so morals, very narrow and incomplete at first, became insensibly enlarged, until, from stage to stage, they reached the point of proclaiming the duty of love towards all mankind. The point of departure was the family, and it was under the influence of the domestic religion that duties first appeared to the eyes of man.

Let us picture to ourselves this religion of the fire and of the tomb in its flourishing period. Man sees a divinity near him. It is present, like conscience itself, to his minutest actions. This

[1] Ἑστίᾳ θύεις. Pseudo-Plutarch, ed. Dubner, V. 167.

fragile being finds himself under the eye of a witness who never leaves him. He never feels himself alone. At his side in the house, in the field, he has protectors to sustain him in the toils of life, and judges to punish his guilty actions. "The Lares," said the Romans, "are formidable divinities, whose duty it is to punish mankind, and to watch over all that passes in the interior of the house." The Penates they also describe as "gods who enable us to live; they nourish our bodies and regulate our minds."[2]

Men loved to apply to the holy fire the epithet of chaste, and they believed that it enjoined chastity upon mortals. No act materially or morally impure could be committed in its presence.

The first ideas of wrong, of chastisement, of expiation, seem to have come from this. The man who felt guilty no longer dared to approach his own hearth; his god repelled him. He who had shed blood was no longer allowed to sacrifice, or to offer libations, or prayer, or to offer the sacred repast. The god was so severe that he admitted no excuse; he did not distinguish between an involuntary murder and a premeditated crime. The hand stained with blood could no longer touch sacred objects.[3] To enable a man to renew his worship, and to regain possession of his god, he was required at least to purify himself by an expiatory ceremony.[4] This religion knew pity, and had rites to efface the stains of the soul. Narrow and material as it was, it still knew how to console man for his errors.

If it absolutely ignored the duties of charity, at any rate it traced for man with admirable precision his family duties. It rendered marriage obligatory; celibacy was a crime in the eyes of a religion that made the perpetuity of the family the first and most holy of duties. But the union which it prescribed could be accomplished only in the presence of the domestic divinities; it is the religious, sacred, indissoluble union of the husband and wife. No man could omit the rites, and make of marriage a simple contract by consent, as it became in the latest period of Greek and Roman society. This ancient

---

2 Plutarch, *Rom. Quest.*, 51. Macrobius, *Sat.*, III. 4.
3 Hdts., I. 35. Virgil, *Æn.*, II. 719. Plutarch, *Theseus*, 12.
4 Apollonius of Rhodes, IV. 704–707. Æsch., *Choeph.*, 96.

religion forbade it, and if one dared to offend in this particular, it punished him for it. For the son sprung from such a union was considered a bastard, that is to say, a being who had neither place nor sacred fire; he had no right to perform any sacred act; he could not pray.[5]

This same religion watched with care over the purity of the family. In its eyes the greatest of crimes was adultery. For the first rule of the worship was that the sacred fire should be transmitted from father to son, and adultery disturbed the order of birth. Another rule was, that the tomb should contain only members of the family; but the son born of adultery was a stranger. If he was buried in the tomb, all the principles of the religion were violated, the worship defiled, the sacred fire became impure; every offering at the tomb became an act of impiety. Worse still, by adultery the series of descendants was broken; the family, even though living men knew it not, became extinct, and there was no more divine happiness for the ancestors. The Hindu also says, "The son born of adultery annihilates in this world and in the next the offerings made to the manes."[6]

Here is the reason that the laws of Greece and Rome give the father the right to reject the child just born. Here, too, is the reason that they are so rigorous, so inexorable, against adultery. At Athens the husband is allowed to kill the guilty one. At Rome the husband, as the wife's judge, condemns her to death. This religion was so severe that a man had not even the right to pardon completely, and that he was forced at least to repudiate his wife.[7]

These, then, are the first moral and domestic laws discovered and sanctioned. Here is, besides the natural sentiment — an imperious religion, which tells the husband and wife that they are united forever, and that from this union flow rigorous

---

[5] Isæus, VII. Demosthenes, *in Macart.*

[6] *Laws of Manu*, III. 175.

[7] Demosthenes, *in Neær.*, 89. Though this primitive morality condemned adultery, it did not reprove incest; religion authorized it. The prohibitions relative to marriage were the reverse of ours. One might marry his sister (Demosthenes, *in Neær.*, 22; Corn. Nepos., *proœmium;* id., *Life of Cimon;* Minucius Felix, *in Octavio*), but it was forbidden, as a principle, to marry a woman of another city.

duties, the neglect of which brings with it the gravest consequences in this life and in the next. Hence came the serious and sacred character of the conjugal union among the ancients, and the purity which the family long preserved.

This domestic morality prescribed still other duties. It taught the wife that she ought to obey; the husband, that he ought to command. It instructed both to respect each other. The wife had rights, for she had her place at the sacred fire; it was her duty to see that it did not die out.[8] She too, then, has her priesthood. Where she is not found, the domestic worship is incomplete and insufficient. It was a great misfortune to a Greek to have a "hearth deprived of a wife."[9] Among the Romans the presence of the wife was so necessary in the sacrifices that the priest lost his office on becoming a widower.[10]

It was, doubtless, to this division of the domestic priesthood that the mother of the family owed the veneration with which they never ceased to surround her in Greek and Roman society; hence it came that the wife had the same title in the family as the husband. The Romans said *pater familias* and *mater familias;* the Greeks, οικοδεσποτης and οικοδεσποινα; the Hindus, *grihapati* and *grehapatni.* Hence also came this formula, which the wife pronounced in the Roman marriage: *ubi tu Caius, ego Caia* — a formula which tells us that, if in the house there was not equal authority, there was equal dignity.

As to the son, we have seen him subject to the authority of a father, who could sell him or condemn him to death. But this son had also his part in the worship; he filled a place in the religious ceremonies; his presence on certain days was so necessary that the Roman who had no son was forced to adopt a fictitious one for those days, in order that the rites might be performed.[11] And here religion established a very powerful bond between father and son. They believed in a second life in the tomb — a life happy and calm if the funeral repasts were regularly offered. Thus the father is convinced that his destiny after this life will depend upon the care that his son will take of his tomb, and the son, on his part, is convinced that his father

---

[8] Cato, 143. Dionys. of Halic., II. 22. *Laws of Manu,* III. 62; V. 151.

[9] Xenophon, *Govt. of the Lacedæmonians.*

[10] Plutarch, *Rom. Quest.,* 50. [11] Dionys. of Halic., II. 20, 22.

will become a god after death, whom he will have to invoke.

We can imagine how much respect and reciprocal affection this belief would establish in the family. The ancients gave to the domestic virtues the name of *piety* — the obedience of the son to his father, the love which he bore to his mother. This was piety — *pietas erga parentes*. The attachment of the father for the child, the tenderness of the mother, — these, too, were piety — *pietas erga liberos*. Everything in the family was divine. The sense of duty, natural affection, the religious idea, — all these were confounded, were considered as one, and were expressed by the same word.

It will, perhaps, appear strange to find love of home counted among the virtues; but it was so counted among the ancients. This sentiment had a deep and powerful hold upon their minds. Anchises, when he sees Troy in flames, is still unwilling to leave his old home. Ulysses, when countless treasures, and immortality itself, are offered him, wishes only again to see the flame of his own hearth-fire. Let us come down to Cicero's time; it is no longer a poet, but a statesman, who speaks: "Here is my religion, here is my race, here are the traces of my forefathers. I cannot express the charm which I find here, and which penetrates my heart and my senses."[12] We must place ourselves, in thought, in the midst of these primitive generations to understand how lively and powerful were these sentiments, which were already enfeebled in Cicero's day. For us the house is merely a domicile — a shelter; we leave it, and forget it with little trouble; or, if we are attached to it, this is merely by the force of habit and of recollections; because, for us, religion is not there; our God is the God of the universe, and we find him everywhere. It was entirely different among the ancients; they found their principal divinity within the house: this was their providence, which protected them individually, which heard their prayers, and granted their wishes. Out of the house, man no longer felt the presence of a god; the god of his neighbor was a hostile god. Then a man loved his house as he now loves his church.[13]

[12] Cicero, *De Legib.*, II. 1. *Pro Domo*, 41.
[13] Of the sanctity of the domicile, which the ancients always spoke of as inviolable, Demosthenes, *in Androt.*, 52; *in Evergum*, 60. *Digest, de in jus voc.*, II. 4.

Thus the religion of the primitive ages was not foreign to the moral development of this part of humanity. Their gods enjoined purity, and forbade the shedding of blood; the notion of justice, if it was not born of this belief, must at least have been fortified by it. These gods belonged in common to all the members of the same family; thus the family was united by a powerful tie, and all its members learned to love and respect each other. These gods lived in the interior of each house; a man loved his house, his home, fixed and durable, which he had received from his ancestors, and which he transmitted to his children as a sanctuary.

Ancient morality, governed by this belief, knew no charity; but it taught at least the domestic virtues. Among this race the isolation of the family was the commencement of morals. Duties, clear, precise, and imperious, appeared, but they were restricted within a narrow circle. This narrow character of primitive morals we must recollect as we proceed; for civil society, founded later on these same principles, put on the same character, and several singular traits of ancient politics are explained by this fact.[14]

Chapter X

THE GENS AT ROME AND IN GREECE

WE find in the writings of Roman jurists and in Greek writers the traces of an antique institution which appears to have had its flourishing period in the first ages of Greek and Italian societies, but which, becoming enfeebled by degrees, left vestiges that were hardly perceptible in the later portion of their history. We speak of what the Romans called *gens,* and the Greeks γενος.

As the nature and constitution of the *gens* have been much discussed, it may not be amiss here to point out what has constituted the difficulty of the problem.

[14] What is said of ancient morals in this chapter is intended to apply to those peoples that afterwards became Greeks and Romans. This morality was modified with time, especially among the Greeks. Already in the *Odyssey* we find new sentiments and other manners.

The *gens,* as we shall see presently, formed a body whose constitution was radically aristocratic. It was through their internal organization that the patricians of Rome and the Eupatrids of Athens were able to perpetuate their privileges for so long a time. No sooner had the popular party gained the upper hand, than they attacked this old institution with all their power. If they had been able completely to destroy it, they would probably not have left us the slightest memorial of it. But it was singularly endowed with vitality, and deeply rooted in their manners, and they could not entirely blot it out. They therefore contented themselves with modifying it. They took away its essential character, and left only its external features, which were not in the way of the new regime. Thus, at Rome, the plebeians undertook to form *gentes,* in imitation of the patricians; at Athens they attempted to overthrow the *gentes,* to blend them together, and to replace them by the *demes,* which were established in imitation of them. We shall have to return to the subject when we speak of the revolutions. Let it suffice here for us to remark, that this profound alteration which the democracy introduced into the regime of the *gens* is of a nature to mislead those who undertake to learn its primitive constitution. Indeed, almost all the information concerning it that has come down to us dates from the epoch when it had been thus transformed, and shows us only that part which the revolutions had allowed to subsist.

Let us suppose that, twenty centuries hence, all knowledge of the middle ages has perished; that there remain no documents relating to what passed before the revolution of 1789; and that, notwithstanding this, an historian of that time wishes to form an idea of institutions of an earlier date. The only documents that he would have at hand would show him the nobility of the nineteenth century — that is to say, something very different from that of feudalism; but he would suspect that a great revolution had taken place, and he would rightly conclude that this institution, like all the others, must have been modified. This nobility, which his authorities would describe to him, would no longer be for him anything but the shadow or the enfeebled and altered image of another nobility, incomparably more powerful. Finally, if he examined with attention the slight remains of ancient monuments, a few expressions preserved in the langauge, a few terms escaped from the law, vague souvenirs or sterile regrets, he would perhaps be able to conjecture something concerning the feudal system, and would obtain an idea of the institutions of the middle ages that would not be very far from the truth. The difficulty would assuredly be great; nor is it less for him who to-day desires to understand the antique *gens;* for he has no information regarding it except what dates from a time when it was no longer anything but a shadow of itself.

We will commence by analyzing all that the ancient writers tell us of the *gens;* that is to say, what remained of it at the epoch when it was already greatly changed. Then, by the aid of these remains, we shall attempt to catch a glimpse of the veritable system of the antique *gens.*

1.   What Ancient Writers tell us of the Gens.

If we open a Roman history at the time of the Punic wars we meet three personages, whose names are Claudius Pulcher, Claudius Nero, and Claudius Centho. All three belong to the same gens — the Claudian gens.

Demosthenes in one of his orations produces seven witnesses, who certify that they belong to the same γενος, that of the Brytidæ. What is remarkable in this example is, that the seven persons cited as members of the same γενος are inscribed in six different demes. This shows that the γενος did not correspond exactly with the deme, and was not, like it, a simple administrative division.[1]

Here is one fact established: there were *gentes* at Rome and at Athens. We might cite examples relative to many other cities of Greece and Italy, and conclude from them that, in all probability, this institution was universal among these ancient nations.

Every gens had a special worship; in Greece the members of the same gens were recognized "by the fact that they had performed sacrifices in common from a very early period."[2]

---

[1] Demosthenes, *in Neær.*, 71. Plutarch, *Themist.*, 1. Æschines, *De Falsa Legat.*, 147. Bœckh, *Corp. Insc.*, 385. Ross, *Demi Attici.* 24. The *gens* among the Greeks is often called πατρα. Pindar, *passim.*

[2] Hesychius, γεννηται. Pollux, III. 52, Harpocration, οργεωνες.

Plutarch speaks of the place where the Lycomedæ, and Æschines speaks of the altar of the gens of the Butadæ.[3]

At Rome, too, each gens had religious ceremonies to perform; the day, the place, and the rites were fixed by its particular religion.[4] When the capital is besieged by the Gauls, one of the Fabii, clothed in religious robes, and carrying sacred objects in his hands, is seen to go out and cross the enemy's lines; he goes to offer sacrifice on the altar of his gens, which is situated on the Quirinal. In the second Punic war, another Fabius, whom they called the Shield of Rome, is making head against Hannibal. Certainly it is of the first importance to the republic that he remains with his army; and yet he leaves it in the hands of the imprudent Minucius: this is because the anniversary of the sacrifice of his gens has arrived, and he must be at Rome to perform the sacred act.[5]

It was a duty to perpetuate this worship from generation to generation, and every man was required to leave sons after him to continue it. Claudius, a personal enemy of Cicero, abandoned his gens to enter a plebeian family, and Cicero says to him, "Why do you expose the religion of the Claudian gens to the risk of becoming extinct through your fault?"

The gods of the gens — Dii gentiles — protected no other gens, and did not desire to be invoked by another. No stranger could be admitted to the religious ceremonies. It was believed that if a stranger had a part of the victim, or even if he merely assisted at the sacrifice, the gods of the gens were offended. and all the members were guilty of grave impiety.

Just as every gens had its worship and its religious festivals, so also it had its common tomb. We read in an oration of Demosthenes, "This man, having lost his children, buried them in the tomb of his fathers, in that tomb that is common to all those of his gens." The rest of the oration shows that no stranger could be buried in this tomb. In another discourse, the same orator speaks of the tomb where the gens of the Buselidæ buried its members, and where every year it per-

[3] Plutarch, *Themist,* I. Æsch., *De Falsa Legat.,* 147.
[4] Cicero, *De Arusp. Resp.,* 15. Dion. Halic., XI. 14. Festus, *Propudi.*
[5] Livy, V. 46; XXII. 18. Valer. Max., I. 1, 11. Polybius, III. 94. Pliny, XXXIV. 13. Macrobius, III. 5.

formed its funeral sacrifices: "this burial-place is a large field, surrounded with an enclosure, according to the ancient custom."[6]

The same was the case among the Romans. Velleius Paterculus speaks of the tomb of the Quintilian gens, and Suetonius informs us that the Claudian gens had one on the slope of the Capitoline Hill.

The ancient low of Rome permits the members of a gens to inherit from each other. The Twelve Tables declare that, in default of sons and of agnates, the *gentilis* is the natural heir. According to this code, therefore, the *gentiles* are nearer akin than the cognates; that is to say, nearer than those related through females.

Nothing is more closely united than the members of a gens. United in the celebration of the same sacred ceremonies, they mutually aid each other in all the needs of life. The entire gens is responsible for the debt of one of its members; it redeems the prisoner and pays the fine of one condemned. If one of its members becomes a magistrate, it unites to pay the expenses incident to the magistracy.[7]

The accused was accompanied to the tribunal by all the members of his gens; this marks the close relation which the law established between a man and the body of which he formed a part. For a man to plead or bear witness against one of his own gens was an act contrary to religion. A certain Claudius, a man of some rank, was a personal enemy of Appius Claudius the Decemvir; yet when the latter was placed on trial, and was menaced with death, this Claudius appeared in his defence, and implored the people in his favor, but not without giving them notice that he took this step "not on account of any affection which he bore the accused, but as a duty."

If a member of a gens could not accuse another member before a tribunal of the city, this was because there was a tribunal in the gens itself. Each gens had its chief, who was at the same time its judge, its priest, and its military commander.[8] Every one knows that when the Sabine family of the Claudii established itself at Rome, the three thousand persons who

---

6 Demosthenes, *in Macart.*, 79; *in Eubul.*, 28.

7 Livy, V. 32. Dion. Halic., XIII. 5. Appian, *Annib.*, 28.

8 Dion. Halic., II. 7.

composed it obeyed a single chief. Later, when the Fabii took upon themselves the whole war against the Veientes, we see that this gens had its chief, who spoke in its name before the senate, and who led it against the enemy.[9]

In Greece, too, each gens had its chief; the inscriptions confirm this, and they show us that this chief generally bore the title of archon.[10] Finally, in Rome, as in Greece, the gens had its assemblies; it passed laws which its members were bound to obey, and which the city itself respected.[11]

Such are the usages and laws which we find still in force at an epoch when the gens was already enfeebled and almost destroyed. Such are the remains of this ancient institution.

2. An Examination of certain Opinions that have been put forth to explain the Roman Gens.

On this subject, which has long been the theme of learned controversy, several theories have been offered. Some say that the gens was nothing more than a similarity in name;[12] others, that the word *gens* designated a sort of factitious relationship. Still others hold that the gens was merely the expression of a relation between a family which acted as patrons and other families that were clients. But none of these explanations answer to the whole series of facts, laws, and usages which we have just enumerated.

Another opinion, more plausible, is, that the gens was a political association of several families who were originally strangers to each other; and that in default of ties of blood, the city established among them an imaginary union and a sort of religious relationship.

But a first objection presents itself: If the gens is only a factitious association, how are we to explain the fact that its members inherited from each other? Why is the *gentilis* preferred to the cognate? It has been seen above what the rules of succession were, and we have pointed out the close and

9 Ibid., IX. 5.

10 Bœckh, *Corp. Inscrip.*, 397, 399. Ross, *Demi Attici*, 24.

11 Livy, VI. 20. Suetonius, *Tiber.*, 1. Ross, *Demi Attici*, 24.

12 Two passages of Cicero, *Tuscul.*, I. 16, and *Topica*, 6, have tended to confuse the question. Cicero, like most of his contemporaries, appears not to have understood what the ancient gens really was.

necessary relation which religion had established between the right of inheritance and masculine kinship. Can we suppose that ancient law deviated so far from this principle as to accord the right of succession to the *gentiles* if they had been strangers to each other?

The best established and most prominent characteristic of the gens is, that, like the family, it had a worship. Now, if we inquire what god each adores, we find almost always that it is a deified ancestor, and that the altar where the sacrifice is offered is a tomb. At Athens the Eumolpidæ worshipped Eumolpus, the author of their race; the Phytalidæ adored the hero Phytalus; the Butadæ, Butes; the Buselidæ, Buselus; the Lakiadæ, Lakios; the Amynandridæ, Cecrops.[13] At Rome the Claudii are descended from a Clausus; the Cæculii honored as chief of their race the hero Cæculus; the Calpurnii, a Calpus; the Julii, a Julus, the Clœlii, a Clœlus.[14]

We may easily suppose, it is true, that many of these genealogies were an afterthought; but we must admit that this sort of imposture would have had no motive if it had not been a constant usage among the real gentes to recognize and to worship a common ancestor. Falsehood always seeks to imitate the truth. Besides, the imposture was not so easy as it might seem to us. This worship was not a vain formality for parade. One of the most rigorous rules of the religion was, that no one should honor as an ancestor any except those from whom he was really descended; to offer this worship to a stranger was a grave impiety. If, then, the members of a *gens* adored a common ancestor, it was because they really believed they were descended from him. To counterfeit a tomb, to establish anniversaries and an annual worship, would have been to carry falsehood into what they held most dear, and to trifle with religion. Such a fiction was possible in the time of Cæsar, when the old family religion was cherished by nobody. But if we go back to the time when this creed was in its vigor, we cannot imagine that several families, taking part in the same imposture, could say to each other, We will pretend to have a common ancestor; we will erect him a tomb; we will offer him

---

[13] Demosthenes, *in Macart.*, 79. Pausanias, I. 37. *Inscription of the Amynandridæ*, cited by Ross, p. 24.

[14] Festus, *Cæculus, Calpurnii, Clœlii.*

funeral repasts; and our descendants shall adore him in all future time. Such a thought could not have presented itself to their minds, or it would have been scouted as an impiety.

In the difficult problems often found in history, it is well to seek from the terms of language all the instruction which they can afford. An institution is sometimes explained by the word that designates it. Now, the word *gens* means exactly the same as the word *genus;* so completely alike are they that we can take the one for the other, and say, indifferently, *gens Fabia* and *genus Fabium;* both correspond to the verb *gignere* and to the substantive *genitor,* precisely as γενος corresponds to γενναν and to γονευς. All these words convey the same idea of filiation. The Greeks also designated the members of a γενος by the word 'ομογαλακτες, which signifies *nourished by the same milk.* Let these words be compared with those which we are accustomed to translate by *family* — the Latin *familia,* the Greek οικος. Neither of these last has the sense of generation or of kinship. The true signification of *familia* is property; it designates the field, the house, money, and slaves; and it is for this reason that the Twelve Tables say, in speaking of the heir, *familiam nancitor* — let him take the succession. As to οικος, it is clear that this word presents to the mind no other idea than that of property or of domicile. And yet these are the words that we habitually translate by family. Now, is it admissible that terms whose intrinsic meaning is that of domicile or property were often used to designate a family, and that other words whose primary sense is filiation, birth, paternity, have never designated anything but an artificial association? Certainly this would not be in conformity with the logic, so direct and clear, of the ancient languages. It is unquestionable that the Greeks and the Romans attached to the words gens and γενος the idea of a common origin. This idea might have become obscured after the gens was modified, but the word has remained to bear witness of it.

The theory that presents the gens as a factitious association has against it, therefore, 1st, the old legislation, which gives the *gentiles* the right of inheritance; 2d, the old religion, which allowed a common worship only where there was a common parentage; 3d, the terms of language, which attest in the gens a common origin. The theory has also this other defect, that it supposes human societies to have commenced by a convention and an artifice — a position which historical science cannot admit as true.

3. The Gens is the Family still holding its primitive Organization and its Unity.

All the evidence presents us the gens as united by the tie of birth. Let us again consult language: the names of the gentes, in Greece as well as in Rome, all have the form which was used in the two languages for patronymics. Claudius signifies the son of Clausus, and Butadæ, the sons of Butes.

Those who think they see in the gens an artificial association, set out from a false assumption. They suppose that a gens always consisted of several families having different names, and they cite the Cornelian gens, which did indeed include Scipios, Lentuli, Cossi, and Syllæ. But this is very far from having been a general rule. The Marcian gens appears never to have had more than a single line. We also find but one in the Lucretian gens, and but one in the Quintilian gens, for a long time. It would certainly be very difficult to tell what families composed the Fabian gens, for all the Fabii known in history belong manifestly to the same stock. At first they all bear the same surname of Vibulanus; they all change it afterwards for that of Ambustus, which they replace still later by Maximus or Dorso.

We know that it was customary at Rome for all patricians to have three names. One was called, for example, Publius Cornelius Scipio. It may be worth the while to inquire which of these three names was considered as the true name. Publius was merely a *name placed before — prænomen;* Scipio was a *name added — agnomen.* The true name was Cornelius; and this name was at the same time that of the whole gens. Had we only this single indication regarding the ancient gens, it would justify us in affirming that there were Cornelii before there were Scipios, and not, as it is often said, that the family of the Scipios associated with others to form the Cornelian gens.

History teaches us, in fact, that the Cornelian gens was for a long time undivided, and that all the members alike bore the surname of Maluginensis, and that of Cossus. It was not till the time of the dictator Camillus that one of its branches adopted the surname of Scipio. A little later another branch took the surname of Rufus, which it replaced afterwards by that of Sylla. The Lentuli do not appear till the time of the Samnite wars, the Cethegi not until the second Punic war. It is the same with the Claudian gens. The Claudii remained a long time united in a single family, and all bore the surname of Sabinus or of Regillensis, a sign of their origin. We follow them for seven generations without seeing any branches formed in this family, although it had become very numerous. It was only in the eighth, that is to say, in the time of the first Punic war, that we see three branches separate, and adopt three surnames which became hereditary with them. These were the Pulchri, who continued during two centuries; the Centhos, who soon became extinct, and the Neros, who continued to the time of the empire.

From all this it is clear that the gens was not an association of families, but that it was the family itself. It might either comprise only a single line, or produce several branches; it was always but one family.

Besides, it is easy to account for the formation of the antique gens and for its nature, if we but refer to the old belief and to the old institutions that we have already described. We shall see, even, that the gens is derived very naturally from the domestic religion and from the private law of the ancient ages. Indeed, what did this primitive religion prescribe? That the ancestor, that is to say, the man who was first buried in the tomb, should be perpetually honored as a god, and that his descendants, assembled every year near the sacred place where he reposed, should offer him the funeral repast.

This fire always kept burning, this tomb always honored with a worship, were the centre around which all later generations came to live, and by which all the branches of the family, however numerous they might be, remained grouped in a single body. What more does private law tell us of those ancient ages? While studying the nature of authority in the ancient family, we saw that the son did not separate from the father; while studying the rules for the transmission of the patrimony, we saw that, on account of the right of primogeniture, the younger brothers did not separate from the oldest. Hearth, tomb, patrimony, all these, in the beginning, were indivisible. The family, consequently, was also indivisible. Time did not dismember it. This indivisible family, which developed through ages, perpetuating its worship and its name from century to century, was really the antique gens. The gens was the family, but the family having preserved the unity which its religion enjoined, and having attained all the development which ancient private law permitted it to attain.[15]

This truth admitted, all that the ancient writers have told us of the gens becomes clear. The close unity which we have remarked among its members is no longer surprising; they are related by birth, and the worship which they practise in common is not a fiction; it comes to them from their ancestors. As they are a single family, they have a common tomb. For the same reason the law of the Twelve Tables declares them qualified to inherit each other's property. For the same reason, too, they bear the same name. As all had, in the beginning, a single undivided patrimony, it was a custom, and even a necessity, that the entire gens should be answerable for the debt of one of its members, and that they should pay the ransom of the prisoner and the fine of the convict. All these rules became established of themselves while the gens still retained its unity; when it was dismembered they could not disappear entirely. Of the ancient and sacred unity of this

[15] We need not repeat what we have already said of agnation (B. II., ch. v). We can see that *agnatio* and *gentilitas*—the relationship of the *gentiles*—flowed from the same principles, and were relationships of the same nature. The passage in the law of the Twelve Tables which assigns the inheritance to the *gentiles,* in default of *agnati,* embarrassed the jurisconsults, and led to the opinion that there was an essential difference between these two kinds of kinship. But this difference is nowhere found. One was *agnatus,* as one was *gentilis,* by masculine descent and the religious bond. There was only a difference of degree, which began when the branches of the same gens were separated. The *agnatus* was a member of the branch; the *gentilis* of the *gens.* There was therefore the same distinction between the terms *gentilis* and *agnatus* as between the words *gens* and *familia. Familiam dicimus omnium agnatorum,* says Ulpian in the *Digest,* L. tit., 16, § 195. One, when he was the agnate of a man, was, for a still stronger reason, his gentilis; but he could not be a gentilis without being an agnate. The law of the Twelve Tables gave the inheritance, in default of agnates, to those who were only gentiles of the deceased, that is to say, who were of his gens, without being of his branch or of his *familia.*

family there remain persistent traces in the annual sacrifices which assembled the scattered members; in the name that remained common to them; in the legislation which recognized the right of *gentiles* to inherit; in their customs which enjoined them to aid each other.[16]

[16] The use of patronymics dates from this high antiquity, and is connected with this old religion. Every gens transmitted the name of the ancestor from generation to generation with the same care as it perpetuated its worship. What the Romans called *nomen* was this name of the ancestor which all the members of the gens bore. A day came when each branch, becoming independent in certain respects, marked its individuality by adopting a surname (*cognomen*). Each person was, moreover, distinguished by a particular denomination, *agnomen*, as Caius, or Quintus. But the true name, the official name, the sacred name, was that of the gens; this, coming from the first known ancestor, was to last as long as the family and the gods lasted. It was the same in Greece. Every Greek, at least if he belonged to an ancient and regularly established family, had, like the Roman patrician, three names. One was his individual name; another was that of his father; and as these two generally alternated with each other, they were, together, equivalent to the hereditary *cognomen*, which at Rome designated a branch of the gens. Lastly, the third name was that of the entire gens. Examples: Μιλτιαδης Κιμωνος Λακιαδης, and in the following generation, Κιμων Μιλτιαδου Λακιαδης. The Lakiadæ formed a γενος, as the Cornelii formed a gens. It was the same with the Butadæ, the Phytalidæ, &c. Pindar never extols his heroes without recalling the name of their γενος. This name, in Greek, usually ended in ιδης or αδης, and thus had an adjective form, just as the name of the gens among the Romans invariably ended in *ius*. This was none the less the true name. In daily life a man might be called by his individual surname; but in the official language of politics or religion, his complete name, and above all the name of the γενος, was required. (Later the democracy substituted the name of the deme for that of the γενος.) The history of names followed a different course in ancient from what it has followed in modern times. In the middle ages, until the twelfth century, the true name was the individual or baptismal name. Patronymics came quite late, as names of estates or surnames. It was just the reverse among the ancients; and this difference is due to the difference of the two religions. For the old domestic religion, the family was the true body, of which the individual was but an inseparable member; the patronymic was, therefore, the first name in date and in importance. The new religion, on the contrary, recognized in the individual complete liberty and entire personal independence, and was not in the least opposed to separating him from the family. Baptismal names were, therefore, the first, and for a long time the only, names.

4. The Family (Gens) was at first the only Form of Society.

What we have seen of the family, its domestic religion, the gods which it had created for itself, the laws that it had established, the right of primogeniture on which it had been founded, its unity, its development from age to age until the formation of the gens, its justice, its priesthood, its internal government, — carries us forcibly, in thought, towards a primitive epoch, when the family was independent of all superior power, and when the city did not yet exist.

When we examine the domestic religion, those gods who belonged only to one family and exercised their providence only within the walls of one house, this worship which was secret, this religion which would not be propagated, this antique morality which prescribed the isolation of families, — it is clear that beliefs of this nature could not have taken root in the minds of men, except in an age when larger societies were not yet formed. If the religious sentiment was satisfied with so narrow a conception of the divine, it was because human associations were then narrow in proportion. The time when men believed only in the domestic gods was the time when there existed only families. It is quite true that this belief might have subsisted afterwards, and even for a long time, when cities and nations existed. Man does not easily free himself from opinions that have once exercised a strong influence over him. This belief might endure, therefore, even when it was in disaccord with the social state. What is there, indeed, more contradictory than to live in civil society and to have particular gods in each family? But it is clear that this contradiction did not always exist, and that at the epoch when this belief was established in the mind, and became powerful enough to form a religion, it corresponded exactly with the social state of man. Now, the only social state that is in accord with such a belief is that in which the family lives independent and isolated.

In such a state the whole Aryan race appears to have lived for a long time. The hymns of the Vedas confirm this for the branch from which the Hindus are descended, and the old beliefs and the old private laws attest it for those who finally became Greeks and Romans.

If we compare the political institutions of the Aryas of the East with those of the Aryas of the West, we find hardly any analogy between them. If, on the contrary, we compare the domestic institutions of these various nations, we perceive that the family was constituted upon the same principles in Greece and in India; besides, these principles were, as we have already shown, of so singular a nature that we cannot suppose this resemblance to have been the work of chance. Finally, not only do these institutions offer an evident analogy, but even the words that designate them are often the same in the different languages, which this race has spoken from the Ganges to the Tiber. From this fact we may draw a double conclusion: one is, that the origin of domestic institutions among the nations of this race is anterior to the period when its different branches separated; the other is, that the origin of political institutions is, on the contrary, later than this separation. The first were fixed from the time when the race still lived in its ancient cradle of Central Asia. The second were formed by degrees in the different countries to which its migrations conducted. We can catch a glimpse therefore of a long period, during which men knew no other form of society than the family. Then arose the domestic religion, which could not have taken root in a society otherwise constituted, and which must long have been an obstacle to social development. Then also was established ancient private law, which was found later to be in disaccord with the interests of a more extended social organization, but which was in perfect harmony with the state of society in which it arose.

Let us place ourselves, in thought, therefore, in the midst of those ancient generations whose traces have not been entirely effaced, and who delegated their beliefs and their laws to subsequent ages. Each family has its religion, its gods, its priesthood. Religious isolation is a law with it; its ceremonies are secret. In death even, or in the existence that follows it, families do not mingle; each one continues to live apart in the tomb, from which the stranger is excluded. Every family has also its property, that is to say, its lot of land, which is inseparably attached to it by its religion; its gods — Termini — guard the enclosure, and its Manes keep it in their care. Isolation of property is so obligatory that two domains cannot be contiguous, but a band of soil must be left between them, which must be neutral ground, and must remain inviolable. Finally, every family has its chief, as a nation would have its king. It has its laws, which, doubtless, are unwritten, but which religious faith engraves in the heart of every man. It has its court of justice, above which there is no other that one can appeal to. Whatever man really needs for his material or moral life the family possesses within itself. It needs nothing from without; it is an organized state, a society that suffices for itself.

But this family of the ancient ages is not reduced to the proportions of the modern family. In larger societies the family separates and decreases. But in the absence of every other social organization, it extends, develops, and ramifies without becoming divided. Several younger branches remain grouped around an older one, near the one sacred fire and the common tomb.

Still another element entered into the composition of this antique family. The reciprocal need which the poor has of the rich, and the rich has of the poor, makes servants. But in this sort of patriarchal regime servant and slave were one. We can see, indeed, that the principle of a free and voluntary service, ceasing at the will of the servant, would ill accord with a social state in which a family lived isolated. Besides, the domestic religion did not permit strangers to be admitted into a family. By some means, then, the servant must become a member and an integrant part of the family. This was effected by a sort of initiation of the new comer into the domestic worship.

A curious usage, that subsisted for a long time in Athenian houses, shows us how the slave entered the family. They made him approach the fire, placed him in the presence of the domestic divinity, and poured lustral water upon his head. He then shared with the family some cakes and fruit.[17] This ceremony bore a certain analogy to those of marriage and adoption. It doubtless signified that the new comer, a stranger the day before, should henceforth be a member of the family,

[17] Demosthenes, in Stephanum, I. 74. Aristophanes, Plutus, 768. These two writers clearly indicate a ceremony, but do not describe it. The scholiast of Aristophanes adds a few details.

and share in its religion. And thus the slave joined in the prayers, and took part in the festivals.[18] The fire protected him; the religion of the Lares belonged to him as well as to his master. This is why the slave was buried in the burial-place of the family.[19]

But by the very act of acquiring this worship, and the right to pray, he lost his liberty. Religion was a chain that held him. He was bound to the family for his whole life and after his death.

His master could raise him from his base servitude, and treat him as a free man. But the servant did not on this account quit the family. As he was bound to it by his worship, he could not, without impiety, separate from it. Under the name of *freedman*, or that of *client*, he continued to recognize the authority of the chief or patron, to be under obligations to him. He did not marry without the consent of the master, and his children continued to obey this master.

There was thus formed in the midst of the great family a certain number of small families of clients and subordinates. The Romans attributed the establishment of clientship to Romulus, as if an institution of this nature could have been the work of a man. Clientship is older than Romulus. Besides, it has existed in other countries, in Greece as well as in all Italy. It was not the cities that established and regulated it; they, on the contrary, as we shall presently see, weakened and destroyed it by degrees. Clientship is an institution of the domestic law, and existed in families before there were cities.

We are not to judge of the clientship of earlier ages from the clients that we see in Horace's time. The client, it is clear, was for a long time a servant attached to a patron. But there was then something to give him dignity; he had a part in the worship, and was associated in the religion of the family. He had the same sacred fire, the same festivals, the same *sacra* as his patron. At Rome, in sign of this religious community, he took the name of the family. He was considered as a member of it by adoption. Hence the close bond and reciprocity of

18 *Ferias in famulis habento*, Cicero, *De Legib.*, II. 8; II. 12.

19 *Quum dominis, tum famulis religio Larum.* Cicero, *De Legib.*, II. 11. Comp. Æsch., *Agam.*, 1035–1038. The slave could even perform a religious act in the name of his master. Cato, *De Re Rust.*, 83.

duties between the patron and the client. Listen to the old
Roman law: "If a patron has done his client wrong, let him
be accursed, *sacer esto*, — let him die." The patron was obliged
to protect his client by all the means and with all the power
of which he was master; by his prayers as a priest, by his lance
as a warrior, by his law as a judge. Later, when the client was
called before the city tribunal, it was the patron's duty to
defend him. It was his duty even to reveal to him the mysterious formulas of the law that would enable him to gain his
cause. One might testify in court against a cognate, but not
against a client; and men continued long to consider their
duties towards clients as far above those towards cognates.[20]
Why? Because a cognate, connected solely through women,
was not a relative, and had no part in the family religion. The
client, on the contrary, had a community of worship; he had,
inferior though he was, a real relationship, which consisted,
according to the expression of Plato, in adoring the same
domestic gods.

Clientship was a sacred bond which religion had formed,
and which nothing could break. Once the client of a family,
one could never be separated from it. Clientship was even
hereditary.

From all this we see that the family, in the earliest times,
with its oldest branch and its younger branches, its servants
and its clients, might comprise a very numerous body of men.
A family that by its religion maintained its unity, by its private
law rendered itself indivisible, and through the laws of clientship retained its servants, came to form, in the course of time,
a very extensive organization, having its hereditary chief. The
Aryan race appears to have been composed of an indefinite
number of societies of this nature, during a long succession of
ages. These thousands of little groups lived isolated, having
little to do with each other, having no need of one another,
united by no bond religious or political, having each its
domain, each its internal government, each its gods.

[20] Cato, in Aulus Gellius, V. 3; XXI. 1.

BOOK THIRD

THE CITY

Chapter I

THE PHRATRY AND THE CURY. THE TRIBE

As yet we have given no dates, nor can we now. In the history of these antique societies the epochs are more easily marked by the succession of ideas and of institutions than by that of years.

The study of the ancient rules of private law has enabled us to obtain a glimpse, beyond the times that are called historic, of a succession of centuries during which the family was the sole form of society. This family might then contain within its wide compass several thousand human beings. But in these limits human association was yet too narrow; too narrow for material needs, since this family hardly sufficed for all the chances of life; too narrow for the moral needs of our nature, for we have seen how incomplete was the knowledge of the divine, and how insufficient was the morality of this little world.

The smallness of this primitive society corresponded well with the narrowness of the idea then entertained of the divinity. Every family had its gods, and men neither conceived of nor adored any save the domestic divinities. But he could not have contented himself long with these gods so much below what his intelligence might attain. If many centuries were required for him to arrive at the idea of God as a being unique, incomparable, infinite, he must at any rate have insensibly approached this ideal, by enlarging his conception from age to age, and by extending little by little the horizon whose line separated for him the divine Being from the things of this world.

The religious idea and human society went on, therefore, expanding at the same time.

The domestic religion forbade two families to mingle and unite; but it was possible for several families, without sacrificing anything of their special religions, to join, at least, for the celebration of another worship which might have been common to all of them. And this is what happened. A certain number of families formed a group, called, in the Greek language, a phratria, in the Latin, a curia.[1] Did there exist the tie of birth between the families of the same group? This cannot be affirmed. It is clear, however, that this new association was not formed without a certain enlargement of religious ideas. Even at the moment when they united, these families conceived the idea of a divinity superior to that of the household, one who was common to all, and who watched over the entire group. They raised an altar to him, lighted a sacred fire, and founded a worship.

There was no cury or phratry that had not its altar and its protecting god. The religious act here was of the same nature as in the family. It consisted essentially of a repast, partaken of in common; the nourishment had been prepared upon the altar itself, and was consequently sacred; while eating it, the worshippers recited prayers; the divinity was present, and received his part of the food and drink.

These religious repasts of the cury lasted a long time at Rome; Cicero mentions them, and Ovid describes them.[2] In the time of Augustus they had still preserved all their antique forms. "I have seen, in those sacred dwellings," says a historian of this epoch, "the repast displayed before the god; the tables were of wood, according to ancestral usage, and the dishes were of earthen ware. The food was loaves, cakes of fine flour, and fruits. I saw the libations poured out; they did not fall from gold or silver cups, but from vessels of clay, and I admired the men of our day who remain so faithful to the rites and customs

---

[1] Homer, *Iliad*, II. 362. Demosthenes, *in Macart.* Isæus, III. 37; VI. 10; IX. 33. Phratries at Thebes, Pindar, *Isthm.*, VII. 18, and Scholiast. *Phratria* and *curia* are two terms that were translated the one by the other. Dion of Halic., II. 85; Dion Cassius, *fr.* 14.

[2] Cicero, *De Orat.*, I. 7. Ovid, *Fast.*, VI. 305. Dionysius, II. 65.

of their fathers."[3] At Athens these repasts took place during the festival called *Apaturia*.[4]

There were usages remaining in the latest period of Greek history which throw some light upon the nature of the ancient phratry. Thus we see that in the time of Demosthenes, to be a member of a phratry, one must have been born of a legitimate marriage in one of the families that composed it; for the religion of the phratry, like that of the family, was transmitted only by blood. The young Athenian was presented to the phratry by his father, who swore that this was his son. The admission took place with a religious ceremony. The phratry sacrificed a victim, and cooked the flesh upon the altar. All the members were present. If they refused to admit the new comer, as they had a right to do, if they doubted the legitimacy of his birth, they took away the flesh from the altar. If they did not do this, if, after cooking, they shared with the young man the flesh of the victim, then he was admitted, and became a member of the association.[5] The explanation of these practices is, that the ancients believed any nourishment prepared upon an altar, and shared between several persons, established among them an indissoluble bond and a sacred union that ceased only with life.

Every phratry or cury had a chief, a curion, or phratriarch, whose principal function was to preside at the sacrifices.[6] Perhaps his attributes were at first more extensive. The phratry had its assemblies and its tribunal, and could pass decrees. In it, as well as in the family, there were a god, a worship, a priesthood, a legal tribunal, and a government. It was a small society that was modelled exactly upon the family.

The association naturally continued to increase, and after

[3] Dionysius, II. 23. And yet some changes had been introduced. The feasts of the cury had become a vain formality. The members of the cury willingly neglected them, and the custom was introduced of replacing the common meal by a distribution of victuals and money. Plautus, *Aulularia*, V. 69 and 137.

[4] Aristophanes, *Acharn.*, 146. *Athenæus,* IV. p. 171. Suidas, Ἀπατουρια·

[5] Demosthenes, *in Eubul.; in Macart.* Isæus, VIII. 18.

[6] Dionysius, II. 64. Varro, V. 83. Demosthenes, *in Eubul.,* 23.

the same fashion; several phratries, or curies, were grouped together, and formed a tribe.

This new circle also had its religion; in each tribe there were an altar and a protecting divinity.

The god of the tribe was generally of the same nature as that of the phratry, or that of the family. It was a man deified, a *hero*. From him the tribe took its name. The Greeks called him the *eponymous hero*. He had his annual festal day. The principal part of the religious ceremony was a repast, of which the entire tribe partook.[7]

The tribe, like the phratry, held assemblies and passed decrees, to which all the members were obliged to submit. It had a chief, *tribunus*, φυλοβασιλευς.[8] From what remains to us of the tribe we see that, originally, it was constituted to be an independent society, and as if there had been no other social power above it.

Chapter II

NEW RELIGIOUS BELIEFS

1. The Gods of Physical Nature.

BEFORE passing from the formation of tribes to the establishment of cities, we must mention an important element in the intellectual life of those ancient peoples.

When we sought the most ancient beliefs of these men, we found a religion which had their dead ancestors for its object, and for its principal symbol the sacred fire. It was this religion

---

[7] Demosthenes, *in Theocrinem.* Æschines, III. 27. Isæus, VII. 36. Pausanias, I. 38. Schol., *in Demosth.*, 702. In the history of the ancients a distinction must be made between the religious tribes and the local tribes. We speak here only of the first: the second came long afterwards. There were tribes everywhere in Greece. *Iliad*, II. 362, 668; *Odyssey*, XIX. 177; Herodotus, IV. 161.

[8] Æschines, III. 30, 31. Aristotle, *Frag.*, cited by Photius, v. Ναυκραρια. Pollux, VIII. 111. Boeckh, *Corp. Inscr.*, 82, 85, 108. Few traces remain of the political and religious organization of the three primitive tribes of Rome. These tribes were too considerable bodies for the city not to attempt to weaken them and take away their independence. The plebeians, moreover labored to abolish them.

that founded the family and established the first laws. But this race has also had in all its branches another religion — the one whose principal figures were Zeus, Here, Athene, Juno, that of the Hellenic Olympus, and of the Roman Capitol.

Of these two religions, the first found its gods in the human soul; the second took them from physical nature. As the sentiment of living power, and of conscience, which he felt in himself, inspired man with the first idea of the divine, so the view of this immensity, which surrounded and overwhelmed him, traced out for his religious sentiment another course.

Man, in the early ages, was continually in the presence of nature; the habits of civilized life did not yet draw a line between it and him. His sight was charmed by its beauties, or dazzled by the grandeur. He enjoyed the light, he was terrified by the night; and when he saw the "holy light of heaven" return, he experienced a feeling of thankfulness. His life was in the hands of nature; he looked for the beneficent cloud on which his harvest depended; he feared the storm which might destroy the labor and hope of all the year. At every moment he felt his own feebleness and the incomparable power of what surrounded him. He experienced perpetually a mingled feeling of veneration, love, and terror for this power of nature.

This sentiment did not conduct him at once to the conception of an only God ruling the universe; for as yet he had no idea of the universe. He knew not that the earth, the sun, and the stars are parts of one same body; the thought did not occur to him that they might all be ruled by the same being. On first looking upon the external world, man pictured it to himself as a sort of confused republic, where rival forces made war upon each other. As he judged external objects from himself, and felt in himself a free person, he saw also in every part of creation, in the soil, in the tree, in the cloud, in the water of the river, in the sun, so many persons like himself. He endued them with thought, volition, and choice of acts. As he thought them powerful, and was subject to their empire, he avowed his dependence; he invoked them, and adored them; he made gods of them.

Thus in this race the religious idea presented itself under two different forms. On the one hand, man attached the divine attribute to the invisible principle, to the intelligence, to what he perceived of the soul, to what of the sacred he felt in himself. On the other hand, he applied his ideas of the divine to the external object which he saw, which he loved or feared; to physical agents that were the masters of his happiness and of his life.

These two orders of belief laid the foundation of two religions that lasted as long as Greek and Roman society. They did not make war upon each other; they even lived on very good terms, and shared the empire over man; but they never became confounded. Their dogmas were always entirely distinct, often contradictory; and their ceremonies and practices were absolutely different. The worship of the gods of Olympus and that of heroes and manes never had anything common between them. Which of these two religions was the earlier in date no one can tell. It is certain however, that one — that of the dead — having been fixed at a very early epoch, always remained unchangeable in its practices, while its dogmas faded away little by little; the other — that of physical nature — was more progressive, and developed freely from age to age, modifying its legends and doctrines by degrees, and continually augmenting its authority over men.

2.   *Relation of this Religion to the Development of Human Society.*

We can easily believe that the first rudiments of this religion of nature are very ancient, though not so old, perhaps, as the worship of ancestors. But as it corresponded with more general and higher conceptions, it required more time to become fixed into a precise doctrine.[1] It is quite certain that it was not brought into the world in a day, and that it did not spring in full perfection from the brain of man. We find at the origin of this religion neither a prophet nor a body of priests. It grew up in different minds by an effort of their natural powers. Each man created it for himself in his own fashion. Among all

[1] Need we recall all the Greek and Italian traditions that showed the religion of Jupiter to be a young and relatively recent religion? Greece and Italy had preserved the recollection of a time when social organizations already existed, and when this religion was not yet known. Ovid, *fast.*, II. 289; Virg., *Georg.*, I. 126. Æsch., *Eumen.* Pausanias, VIII. 8. It appears that among the Hindus the *Pitris* were anterior to the *Devas*.

these gods, sprung from different minds, there were resemblances, because ideas were formed in the minds of men after a nearly uniform manner. But there was also a great variety, because each mind was the author of its own gods. Hence it was that for a long time this religion was confused, and that its gods were innumerable.

Still the elements which could be deified were not very numerous. The sun which gives fecundity, the earth which nourishes, the clouds, by turns beneficent and destructive — such were the different powers of which they could make gods. But from each one of these elements thousands of gods were created; because the same physical agent, viewed under different aspects, received from men different names. The sun, for example, was called in one place Hercules (the glorious) ; in another, Phœbus (the shining) ; and still again Apollo (he who drives away night or evil) ; one called him Hyperion (the elevated Being) ; another, Alexicacos (the beneficent) ; and in the course of time groups of men, who had given these various names to the brilliant luminary, no longer saw that they had the same god.

Indeed, each man adored but a very small number of divinities; but the gods of one were not those of another. The names, it is true, might resemble each other; many men might separately have given their god the name of Apollo, or of Hercules; these words belonged to the common language, and were merely adjectives, and designated the divine Being by one or another of his most prominent attributes. But under this same name the different groups of men could not believe that there was but one god. They counted thousands of different Jupiters; they had a multitude of Minervas, Dianas, and Junos, who resembled each other very little. Each of these conceptions was formed by the free operation of each mind, and being in some sort its property, it happened that these gods were for a long time independent of each other, and that each one of them had his particular legend and his worship.[2]

As the first appearance of these beliefs was at a time when men still lived under family government, these new gods had

---

[2] The same name often conceals very different divinities. Poseidon Hippius, Poseidon Phytalmius, the Erechthean Poseidon, the Ægean Poseidon, the Heliconian Poseidon, were different gods, who had neither the same attributes nor the same worshippers.

at first, like the demons, the heroes, and the Lares, the character of domestic divinities. Each family made gods for itself, and each kept them for itself, as protectors, whose good offices it did not wish to share with strangers. This thought appears frequently in the hymns of the Vedas; and there is no doubt that it was the same in the minds of the Aryas of the West; for there are visible traces of it in their religion. As soon as a family, by personifying a physical agent, had created a god, it associated him with its sacred fire, counted him among its Penates, and added a few words for him in its formula of prayer. This explains why we often meet among the ancients with expressions like this: The gods who sit near my hearth; the Jupiter of my hearth; the Apollo of my fathers.[3] "I conjure you," said Tecmessa to Ajax, "in the name of the Jupiter who sits near your hearth." Medea, the enchantress, says, in Euripides, "I swear by Hecate, my protecting goddess, whom I venerate, and who inhabits this sanctuary of my hearth." When Virgil describes what is oldest in the religion of Rome, he shows Hercules associated with the sacred fire of Evander, and adored by him as a domestic divinity.

Hence came those thousands of forms of local worship among which no unity could ever be established. Hence those contests of the gods of which polytheism is full, and which represent struggles of families, cantons, or villages. Hence, too, that innumerable multitude of gods and goddesses of whom assuredly we know but the smallest part; for many have perished without even having left their names, simply because the families who adored them became extinct, or the cities that had adopted them were destroyed.

It must have been a long time before these gods left the bosom of the families with whom they had originated and who regarded them as their patrimony. We know even that many of them never became disengaged from this sort of domestic tie. The Demeter of Eleusis remained the special divinity of the family of the Eumolpidæ. The Athene of the Acropolis of Athens belonged to the family of the Butadæ. The Potitii of Rome had a Hercules, and the Nautii a Minerva.[4] It appears

---

[3] Ἑστιουχοι, εφεστιοι, πατρωοι. Ὁ εμος Ζευς, Eurip., Hecuba, 345; Medea, 395. Sophocles, Ajax, 492. Virgil, VIII. 543. Herodotus, I. 44.

[4] Livy, IX. 29. Dionysius, VI. 69.

highly probable that the worship of Venus was for a long time limited to the family of the Julii, and that this goddess had no public worship at Rome.

It happened, in the course of time, the divinity of a family having acquired a great prestige over the imaginations of men, and appearing powerful in proportion to the prosperity of this family, that a whole city wished to adopt him, and offer him public worship, to obtain his favors. This was the case with the Demeter of the Eumolpidæ, the Athene of the Butadæ, and the Hercules of the Potitii. But when a family consented thus to share its god, it retained at least the priesthood. We may remark that the dignity of priest, for each god, was during a long time hereditary, and could not go out of a certain family.[5] This is a vestige of a time when the god himself was the property of this family; when he protected it alone, and would be served only by it.

We are correct, therefore, in saying that this second religion was at first in unison with the social condition of men. It was cradled in each family, and remained long bounded by this narrow horizon. But it lent itself more easily than the worship of the dead to the future progress of human association. Indeed, the ancestors, heroes, and manes were gods, who by their very nature could be adored only by a very small number of men, and who thus established a perpetual and impassable line of demarcation between families. The religion of the gods of nature was more comprehensive. No rigorous laws opposed the propagation of the worship of any of these gods. There was nothing in their nature that required them to be adored by one family only, and to repel the stranger. Finally, men must have come insensibly to perceive that the Jupiter of one family was really the same being or the same conception as the Jupiter of another, which they could never believe of two Lares, two ancestors, or two sacred fires.

Let us add, that the morality of this new religion was different. It was not confined to teaching men family duties. Jupiter was the god of hospitality; in his name came strangers, sup-

---

[5] Herodotus, V. 64, 65; IX. 27. Pindar, *Isthm.*, VII. 18. Xenophon, *Hell.*, VI. 8. Plato, *Laws*, p. 759; *Banquet*, p. 40. *Cicero, De Divin.*, I. 41. Tacitus, *Ann.* II. 54. Plutarch, *Theseus*, 23. Strabo, IX. 421; XIV. 634. Callimachus, *Hymn to Apollo*, 84. Pausanias, I. 37; VI. 17; X. 1. Apollodorus, III. 13. Harpocration, v. Εὐνίδαι. Boeckh, *Corp. Inscript.*, 1340.

pliants, "the venerable poor," those who were to be treated "as brothers." All these gods often assumed the human form, and appeared among mortals; sometimes, indeed, to assist in their struggles and to take part in their combats; often, also, to enjoin concord, and to teach them to help each other.

As this second religion continued to develop, society must have enlarged. Now, it is quite evident that this religion, feeble at first, afterwards assumed large proportions. In the beginning it was, so to speak, sheltered under the protection of its elder sister, near the domestic hearth. There the god had obtained a small place, a narrow *cella,* near and opposite to the venerated altar, in order that a little of the respect which men had for the sacred fire might be shared by him. Little by little, the god, gaining more authority over the soul, renounced this sort of guardianship, and left the domestic hearth. He had a dwelling of his own, and his own sacrifices. This dwelling (ναος, from ναιω, to inhabit) was, moreover, built after the fashion of the ancient sanctuary; it was, as before, a *cella* opposite a hearth; but the *cella* was enlarged and embellished, and became a temple. The holy fire remained at the entrance of the god's house, but appeared very small by the side of this house. What had at first been the principal, had now become only an accessory. It ceased to be a god, and descended to the rank of the god's altar, an instrument for the sacrifice. Its office was to burn the flesh of the victim, and to carry the offering with men's prayers to the majestic divinity whose statue resided in the temple.

When we see these temples rise and open their doors to the multitude of worshippers, we may be assured that human associations have become enlarged.

Chapter III

THE CITY FORMED

THE tribe, like the family and the phratry, was established as an independent body, since it had a special worship from which the stranger was excluded. Once formed, no new family could be admitted to it. No more could two tribes be fused into one; their religion was opposed to this. But just as several phratries were united in a tribe, several tribes might associate together, on condition that the religion of each should be respected. The day on which this alliance took place the city existed.

It is of little account to seek the cause which determined several neighboring tribes to unite. Sometimes it was voluntary; sometimes it was imposed by the superior force of a tribe, or by the powerful will of a man. What is certain is, that the bond of the new association was still a religion. The tribes that united to form a city never failed to light a sacred fire, and to adopt a common religion.

Thus human society, in this race, did not enlarge like a circle, which increases on all sides, gaining little by little. There were, on the contrary, small groups, which, having been long established, were finally joined together in larger ones. Several families formed the phratry, several phratries the tribe, several tribes the city. Family, phratry, tribe, city, were, moreover, societies exactly similar to each other, which were formed one after the other by a series of federations.

We must remark, also, that when the different groups became thus associated, none of them lost its individuality, or its independence. Although several families were united in a phratry, each one of them remained constituted just as it had been when separate. Nothing was changed in it, neither worship nor priesthood, nor property nor internal justice. Curies afterwards became associated, but each retained its worship, its assemblies, its festivals, its chief. From the tribe men passed to the city; but the tribe was not dissolved on that account, and each of them continued to form a body, very much as if the city had not existed. In religion there subsisted a multitude of subordinate worships, above which was established one common to all; in politics, numerous little governments continued to act, while above them a common government was founded.

The city was a confederation. Hence it was obliged, at least for several centuries, to respect the religious and civil independence of the tribes, curies, and families, and had not the right, at first, to interfere in the private affairs of each of these little bodies. It had nothing to do in the inerior of a family; it was not the judge of what passed there; it left to the father the right and duty of judging his wife, his son, and his client. It is for this reason that private law, which had been fixed at the time when families were isolated, could subsist in the city, and was modified only at a very late period.

The mode of founding ancient cities is attested by usages which continued for a very long time.

If we examine the army of the city in primitive times, we find it distributed into tribes, curies, and families,[1] "in such a way," says one of the ancients, "that the warrior has for a neighbor in the combat one with whom, in time of peace, he has offered the libation and sacrifice at the same altar." If we look at the people when assembled, in the early ages of Rome, we see them voting by curies and by *gentes*.[2] If we look at the worship, we see at Rome six Vestals, two for each tribe. At Athens, the archon offers the sacrifice in the name of the entire city, but he has in the religious part of the ceremony as many assistants as there are tribes.

Thus the city was not an assemblage of individuals; it was a confederation of several groups, which were established before it, and which it permitted to remain. We see, in the Athenian orators, that every Athenian formed a portion of four distinct societies at the same time; he was a member of a family, of a phratry, of a tribe, and of a city. He did not enter at the same time and the same day into all these four, like a Frenchman, who at the moment of his birth belongs at once to a family, a commune, a department, and a country. The phratry and the tribe are not administrative divisions. A man enters at different times into these four societies, and ascends, so to speak, from one to the other. First, the child is admitted into the family by the religious ceremony, which takes place six days after his birth. Some years later he enters the phratry by a new ceremony, which we have already described. Finally, at the age of sixteen or eighteen, he is presented for admission into the city. On that day, in the presence of an altar, and before the smoking flesh of a victim, he pronounces an oath, by which he binds himself, among other things, always to respect the religion of the city. From that day he is initiated into the public worship, and becomes a

[1] Homer, *Iliad*, II. 362. Varro, *De Ling. Lat.*, V. 89. Isæus, II. 42.
[2] Aulus Gellius, XV. 27.

citizen.[3] If we observe this young Athenian rising, step by step, from worship to worship, we have a symbol of the degrees through which human association has passed. The course which this young man is constrained to follow is that which society first followed.

An example will make this truth clearer. There have remained to us in the antiquities of Athens traditions and traces enough to enable us to see quite clearly how the Athenian city was formed. At first, says Plutarch, Attica was divided by families.[4] Some of these families of the primitive period, like the Eumolpidæ, the Cecropidæ, the Gephyræi, the Phytalidæ, and the Lakiadæ, were perpetuated to the following ages. At that time the city did not exist; but every family, surrounded by its younger branches and its clients, occupied a canton, and lived there in absolute independence. Each had its own religion; the Eumolpidæ, fixed at Eleusis, adored Demeter; the Cecropidæ, who inhabited the rocks where Athens was afterwards built, had Poseidon and Athene for protecting divinities. Near by, on the little hill of the Areopagus, the protecting god was Ares. At Marathon it was Hercules; at Prasiæ an Apollo, another Apollo at Phlius, the Dioscuri at Cephalus, and thus of all the other cantons.[5]

Every family, as it had its god and its altar, had also its chief. When Pausanias visited Attica, he found in the little villages ancient traditions which had been perpetuated with the worship; and these traditions informed him that every little burgh had had its king before the time when Cecrops reigned at Athens. Was not this a memorial of a distant age, when the great patriarchal families, like the Celtic clans, had each its hereditary chief, who was at the same time priest and judge? Some hundred little societies then lived isolated in the country, recognizing no political or religious bond among them, having each its territory, often at war, and living so completely separated that marriage between them was not always permitted.[6]

---

[3] Demosthenes, *in Eubul.* Isæus, VII. IX. Lycurgus, I. 76. Schol., *in Demosth.,* p. 438. Pollux, VIII. 105. Stobæus, *De Repub.*
[4] κατα γενη, Plutarch, *Theseus,* 24, 13.
[5] Pausanias, I. 15; 31, 37, II. 18.
[6] Plutarch, *Theseus,* 13.

But their needs or their sentiments brought them together. Insensibly they joined in little groups of four, five, or six. Thus we find in the traditions that the four villages of Marathon united to adore the same Delphian Apollo; the men of the Piræus, Phalerum, and two neighboring burghs, united and built a temple to Hercules.[7] In the course of time these many little states were reduced to twelve confederations. This change, by which the people passed from the patriarchal family state to a society somewhat more extensive, was attributed by tradition to the efforts of Cecrops: we are merely to understand by this, that it was not accomplished until the time at which they place this personage — that is to say, towards the sixteenth century before our era. We see, moreover, that this Cecrops reigned over only one of these twelve associations, that which afterwards became Athens; the other eleven were completely independent; each had its tutelary deity, its altar, its sacred fire, and its chief.[8]

Several centuries passed, during which the Cecropidæ insensibly acquired greater importance. Of this period there remains the tradition of a bloody struggle sustained by them against the Eumolpidæ of Eleusis, the result of which was, that the latter submitted, with the single reservation that they should preserve the hereditary priesthood of their divinity.[9] There were doubtless other struggles and other conquests, of which no memorial has been preserved. The rock of the Cecropidæ, on which was developed, by degrees, the worship of Athene, and which finally adopted the name of their principal divinity, acquired the supremacy over the other eleven states. Then appeared Theseus, the heir of the Cecropidæ. All the traditions agree in declaring that he united the twelve groups into one city. He succeeded, indeed, in bringing all Attica to adopt the worship of Athene Polias, so that thenceforth the whole country celebrated the sacrifice of the Panathenæa in common. Before him, every burgh had its sacred fire and its prytany. He wished to make the prytany of Athens

[7] Id., *ibid.*, 14. Pollux, VI. 105. Stephen of Byzantium, εχελιδαι.

[8] Philochorus, quoted by Strabo, IX. Thucydides, II. 16. Pollux, VIII. 111.

[9] Pausanias, I. 38.

the religious centre of all Attica.[10] From that time Athenian unity was established. In religion every canton preserved its ancient worship, but adopted one that was common to all. Politically, each preserved its chiefs, its judges, its right of assembling; but above all these local governments, there was the central government of the city.[11]

From these precise memorials and traditions, which Athens preserved so religiously, there seem to us to be two truths equally manifest: the one is, that the city was a confederation of groups that had been established before it; and the other is, that society developed only so fast as religion enlarged its sphere. We cannot, indeed, say that religious progress brought social progress; but what is certain is, that they were both produced at the same time, and in remarkable accord.

We should not lose sight of the excessive difficulty which, in primitive times, opposed the foundation of regular societies.

---

[10] Thucydides, II. 15. Plutarch, *Theseus*, 24. Pausanias, I. 26; VIII. 2.

[11] According to Plutarch and Thucydides, Theseus destroyed the local prytanies, and abolished the magistracies of the burghs. If he attempted this, he certainly did not succeed; for a long while after him we still find the local worships, the assemblies, and the *kings of tribes*. Boeckh, *Corp. Inscrip.*, 82, 85. Demosthenes, *in Theocrinem*. Pollux, VIII. 111. We put aside the legend of Ion, to which several modern historians seem to us to have given too much importance, by presenting it as an indication of a foreign invasion of Attica. This invasion is indicated by no tradition. If Attica had been conquered by these Ionians of the Peloponnesus, it is not probable that the Athenians would have so religiously preserved their names of Cecropidæ, and Erechtheidæ, and that they would have been ashamed of the name of Ionians. (Hdts, I. 143.) We can also reply to those who believe in this invasion, and that the nobility of the Eupatrids is due to it, that most of the great families of Athens go back to a date much earlier than that given for the arrival of Ion in Attica. The Athenians certainly belong to the Ionic branch of the Hellenic race. Strabo tells us that, in the earliest times, Attica was called *Ionia* and *Ias*. But it is a mistake to make the son of Xuthus, the legendary hero of Euripides, the parent stock of these Ionians; they are long anterior to Ion, and their name is perhaps much more ancient than that of Hellenes. It is wrong to make all the Eupatrids descendants of this Ion, and to present this class of men as conquerors who oppressed a conquered people. There is no ancient testimony to support this opinion.

The social tie was not easy to establish between those human beings who were so diverse, so free, so inconstant. To bring them under the rules of a community, to institute commandments and insure obedience, to cause passion to give way to reason, and individual right to public right, there certainly was something necessary, stronger than material force, more respectable than interest, surer than a philosophical theory, more unchangeable than a convention; something that should dwell equally in all hearts, and should be all-powerful there.

This power was a belief. Nothing has more power over the soul. A belief is the work of our mind, but we are not on that account free to modify it at will. It is our own creation, but we do not know it. It is human, and we believe it a god. It is the effect of our power, and is stronger than we are. It is in us; it does not quit us: it speaks to us at every moment. If it tells us to obey, we obey; if it traces duties for us, we submit. Man may, indeed, subdue nature, but he is subdued by his own thoughts.

Now, an ancient belief commanded a man to honor his ancestor; the worship of the ancestor grouped a family around an altar. Thus arose the first religion, the first prayers, the first ideas of duty, and of morals. Thus, too, was the right of property established, and the order of succession fixed. Thus, in fine, arose all private law, and all the rules of domestic organization. Later the belief grew, and human society grew at the same time. When men begin to perceive that there are common divinities for them, they unite in larger groups. The same rules, invented and established for the family, are applied successively to the phratry, the tribe, and the city.

Let us take in at a glance the road over which man has passed. In the beginning the family lived isolated, and man knew only the domestic gods — θεοι πατρωοι, *dii gentiles.* Above the family was formed the phratry with its god — θεος φρατριος, *Juno curialis.* Then came the tribe, and the god of the tribe — θεος φυλιος. Finally came the city, and men conceived a god whose providence embraced this entire city — θεος πολιευς, *penates publici;* a hierarchy of creeds, and a hierarchy of association. The religious idea was, among the ancients, the inspiring breath and organizer of society.

The traditions of the Hindus, of the Greeks, and of the

Etruscans, relate that the gods revealed social laws to man.
Under this legendary form there is a truth. Social laws were
the work of the gods; but those gods, so powerful and beneficent, were nothing else than the beliefs of men.

Such was the origin of cities among the ancients. This study
was necessary to give us a correct idea of the nature and
institutions of the city. But here we must make a reservation.
If the first cities were formed of a confederation of little societies previously established, this is not saying that all the
cities known to us were formed in the same manner. The
municipal organization once discovered, it was not necessary
for each new city to pass over the same long and difficult route.
It might often happen that they followed the inverse order.
When a chief, quitting a city already organized, went to found
another, he took with him commonly only a small number of
his fellow-citizens. He associated with them a multitude of
other men who came from different parts, and might even
belong to different races. But this chief never failed to organize
the new state after the model of the one he had just quitted.
Consequently he divided his people into tribes and phratries.
Each of these little associations had an altar, sacrifices, and
festivals; each even invented an ancient hero, whom it honored
with its worship, and from whom, with the lapse of time, it
believed itself to have been descended.

It often happened, too, that the men of some country lived
without laws and without order, either because no one had
ever been able to establish a social organization there, as in
Arcadia, or because it had been corrupted and dissolved by too
rapid revolutions, as at Cyrene and Thurii. If a legislator
undertook to establish order among these men, he never failed
to commence by dividing them into tribes and phratries, as if
this were the only type of society. In each of these organizations he named an eponymous hero, established sacrifices, and
inaugurated traditions. This was always the manner of commencing, if he wished to found a regular society.[12] Thus Plato
did when he imagined a model city.

[12] Herodotus, IV. 161. Cf. Plato, *Laws*, V. 738; VI. 771.

Chapter IV

THE CITY

CIVITAS, and URBS, either of which we translate by the word *city,* were not synonymous words among the ancients. *Civitas* was the religious and political association of families and tribes; *Urbs* was the place of assembly, the dwelling-place, and, above all, the sanctuary of this association.

We are not to picture ancient cities to ourselves as anything like what we see in our day. We build a few houses; it is a village. Insensibly the number of houses increases, and it becomes a city; and finally, if there is occasion for it, we surround this with a wall.

With the ancients, a city was never formed by degrees, by the slow increase of the number of men and houses. They founded a city at once, all entire in a day; but the elements of the city needed to be first ready, and this was the most difficult, and ordinarily the largest work. As soon as the families, the phratries, and the tribes had agreed to unite and have the same worship, they immediately founded the city as a sanctuary for this common worship, and thus the foundation of a city was always a religious act.

As a first example, we will take Rome itself, notwithstanding the doubt that is attached to its early history. It has often been said that Romulus was chief of a band of adventurers, and that he formed a people by calling around him vagabonds and robbers, and that all these men, collected without distinction, built at hazard a few huts to shelter their booty; but ancient writers present the facts in quite another shape, and it seems to us that if we desire to understand antiquity, our first rule should be to support ourselves upon the evidence that comes from the ancients. Those writers do, indeed, mention an asylum — that is to say, a sacred enclosure, where Romulus admitted all who presented themselves; and in this he followed the example which many founders of cities had afforded him. But this asylum was not the city; it was not even opened till after the city had been founded and completely built. It was an appendage added to Rome, but was not Rome. It did not even form a part of the city of Romulus; for it was situated at the foot of the Capitoline hill, whilst the city occupied the Palatine. It is of the first importance to distinguish the double element of the Roman population. In the asylum are adventurers without land or religion; on the Palatine are men from Alba — that is to say, men already organized into a society, distributed into *gentes* and curies, having a domestic worship and laws. The asylum is merely a hamlet or suburb, where the huts are built at hazard, and without rule; on the Palatine rises a city, religious and holy.

As to the manner in which this city was founded, antiquity abounds in information; we find it in Dionysius of Halicarnassus, who collected it from authors older than his time; we find it in Plutarch, in the *Fasti* of Ovid, in Tacitus, in Cato the Elder, who had consulted the ancient annals; and in two other writers who ought above all to inspire us with great confidence, the learned Varro and the learned Verrius Flaccus, whom Festus has preserved in part for us, both men deeply versed in Roman antiquities, lovers of truth, in no wise credulous, and well acquainted with the rules of historical criticism. All these writers have transmitted to us the tradition of the religious ceremony which marked the foundation of Rome, and we are not prepared to reject so great a number of witnesses.

It is not a rare thing for the ancients to relate facts that surprise us; but is this a reason why we should pronounce them fables? above all, if these facts, though not in accord with modern ideas, agree perfectly with those of the ancients? We have seen in their private life a religion which regulated all their acts; later, we saw that this religion established them in communities: why does it astonish us, after this, that the foundation of a city was a sacred act, and that Romulus himself was obliged to perform rites which were observed everywhere? The first care of the founder was to choose the site for the new city. But this choice — a weighty question, on which they believed the destiny of the people depended — was always left to the decision of the gods. If Romulus had been a Greek, he would have consulted the oracle of Delphi; if a Samnite, he would have followed the sacred animal — the wolf, or the green woodpecker. Being a Latin, and a neighbor of the

Etruscans, initiated into the augurial science,[1] he asks the gods
to reveal their will to him by the flight of birds. The gods
point out the Palatine.

The day for the foundation having arrived, he first offers a
sacrifice. His companions are ranged around him; they light a
fire of brushwood, and each one leaps through the flame.[2] The
explanation of this rite is, that for the act about to take place,
it is necessary that the people be pure; and the ancients
believed they could purify themselves from all stain, physical
or moral, by leaping through a sacred flame.

When this preliminary ceremony had prepared the people
for the grand act of the foundation, Romulus dug a small
trench, of a circular form, and threw into it a clod of earth,
which he had brought from the city of Alba.[3] Then each of
his companions, approaching by turns, following his example,
threw in a little earth, which he had brought from the country
from which he had come. This rite is remarkable, and reveals
to us a notion of the ancients to which we must call attention.
Before coming to the Palatine, they had lived in Alba, or some
other neighboring city. There was their sacred fire; there their
fathers had lived and been buried. Now, their religion forbade
them to quit the land where the hearth had been established,
and where their divine ancestors reposed. It was necessary,
then, in order to be free from all impiety, that each of these
men should employ a fiction, and that he should carry with
him, under the symbol of a clod of earth, the sacred soil where
his ancestors were buried, and to which their manes were
attached. A man could not quit his dwelling-place without
taking with him his soil and his ancestors. This rite had to be
accomplished, so that he might say, pointing out the new place
which he had adopted, This is still the land of my fathers,
terra patrum, patria; here is my country, for here are the
manes of my family.

The trench into which each one had thrown a little earth
was called mundus. Now, this word designated in the ancient

---

[1] Cicero, De Divin., I. 17. Plutarch, Camillus, 32. Pliny, XIV. 2;
XVIII. 12.

[2] Dionysius, I. 88.

[3] Plutarch, Romulus, 11. Dion Cassius, Fragm., 12. Ovid, Fasti,
IV. 821. Festus, v. Quadrata.

language, the region of the manes.[4] From this place, according to tradition, the souls of the dead escaped three times a
year, desirous of again seeing the light for a moment. Do we
not see also, in this tradition, the real thought of these ancient
men? When placing in the trench a cod of earth from their
former country, they believed they had enclosed there the souls
of their ancestors. These souls, reunited there, required a
perpetual worship, and kept guard over their descendants. At
this same place Romulus set up an altar, and lighted a fire
upon it. This was the holy fire of the city.[5]

Around this hearth arose the city, as the house rises around
the domestic hearth; Romulus traced a furrow which marked
the enclosure. Here, too, the smallest details were fixed by a
ritual. The founder made use of a copper ploughshare; his
plough was drawn by a white bull and a white cow. Romulus,
with his head veiled, and in the priestly robes, himself held
the handle of the plough and directed it, while chanting
prayers. His companions followed him, observing a religious
silence. As the plough turned up clods of earth, they carefully
threw them within the enclosure, that no particle of this sacred
earth should be on the side of the stranger.[6] This enclosure,
traced by religion, was inviolable. Neither stranger nor citizen
had the right to cross over it. To leap over this little furrow
was an impious act; it is a Roman tradition that the founder's
brother committed this act of sacrilege, and paid for it with his
life.[7]

But, in order that men might enter and leave the city, the
furrow was interrupted in certain places.[8] To accomplish this,
Romulus raised the plough and carried it over; these intervals
were called *portæ;* these were the gates of the city.

Upon the sacred furrow, or a little inside of it, the walls

[4] Festus, v. *Mundus.* Servius, *ad Æn.,* III. 134. Plutarch, *Romulus,* 11.

[5] Ovid, *ibid.* Later the hearth was removed. When the three
cities, the Palatine, the Capitoline, and the Quirinal were united
in one, the common hearth, or temple of Vesta, was placed on
neutral ground between the three hills.

[6] Plutarch, *Romulus,* 11. Ovid, *Ibidem.* Varro, *De Ling. Lat.,*
V. 143. Festus, v. *Primigenius;* v. *Urvat.* Virgil, V. 755.

[7] See Plutarch, *Rom. Quest.,* 27.

[8] Cato, in *Servius,* V. 755.

afterwards arose; they also were sacred.[9] No one could touch them, even to repair them, without permission from the pontiffs. On both sides of this wall a space, a few paces wide, was given up to religion, and was called the *pomœrium;*[10] on this space no plough could be used, no building constructed.

Such, according to a multitude of ancient witnesses, was the ceremony of the foundation of Rome. If it is asked how this information was preserved down to the writers who have transmitted it to us, the answer is, that the ceremony was recalled to the memory of the people every year by an anniversary festival, which they called the birthday of Rome. This festival was celebrated through all antiquity, from year to year, and the Roman people still celebrate it to-day, at the same date as formerly — the 21st of April. So faithful are men to old usages through incessant changes.

We cannot reasonably suppose that such rites were observed for the first time by Romulus. It is certain, on the contrary, that many cities, before Rome, had been founded in the same manner. According to Varro, these rites were common to Latium and to Etruria. Cato the Elder, who, in order to write his *Origines,* had consulted the annals of all the Italian nations, informs us that analogous rites were practised by all founders of cities. The Etruscans possessed liturgical books in which were recorded the complete ritual of these ceremonies.[11]

The Greeks, like the Italians, believed that the site of a city should be chosen and revealed by the divinity. So, when they wished to found one, they consulted the oracle at Delphi.[12] Herodotus records, as an act of impiety or madness, that the Spartan Dorieus dared to build a city "without consulting the oracle, and without observing any of the customary usages;" and the pious historian is not surprised that a city thus constructed in despite of the rules lasted only three years.[13] Thucydides, recalling the day when Sparta was founded, mentions the pious chants, and the sacrifices of that

[9] Cicero, *De Nat. Deor.,* III. 40. *Digest,* 8, 8. Gaius, II. 8.

[10] Varro, V. 143. Livy, I. 44. Aulus Gellius XIII. 14.

[11] Cato, in Servius, V. 755. Varro, *L. L.,* V. 143. Festus, v. *Rituales.*

[12] Diodorus, XII. 12; Pausanias, VII. 2. Athenæus, VIII. 62.

[13] Herodotus, V. 42.

day. The same historian tells us that the Athenians had a particular ritual, and that they never founded a colony without conforming to it.[14] We may see it in a comedy of Aristophanes a sufficiently exact picture of the ceremony practised in such cases. When the poet represented the amusing foundation of the city of the birds, he certainly had in mind the customs which were observed in the foundation of the cities of men. Now he puts upon the scene a priest who lighted a fire while invoking the gods, a poet who sang hymns, and a divine who recited oracles.

Pausanias travelled in Greece about Adrian's time. In Messenia he had the priests describe to him the foundation of the city of Messene, and he has transmitted this account to us.[15] This event was not very ancient; it took place in the time of Epaminondas. Three centuries before, the Messenians had been driven from their country, and since that time they had lived dispersed among the other Greeks, without a country, but preserving their customs and their national religion with pious care. The Thebans wished to restore them to Peloponnesus, in order to place an enemy on the flank of the Spartans; but the most difficult thing was to persuade the Messenians. Epaminondas, having superstitious men to deal with, thought it his duty to circulate an oracle predicting for this people a return to their former country. Miraculous apparitions proved to them that their gods, who had betrayed them at the time of the conquest, had again become favorable. This timid people then decided to return to the Peloponnesus in the train of a Theban army. But the question was, where a city should be built; for it would not do to think of re-occupying the old cities of the country: they had been soiled by the conquest. To choose the place where they should establish themselves, they could not have recourse to the Delphian oracle, for at this time the Pythia was favorable to the Spartans. Fortunately, the gods had other methods of revealing their will. A Messenian priest had a dream, in which one of the gods of his nation appeared and directed him to take his station on Mount Ithome, and invite the people to follow him there. The site of the new city was thus indicated, but it was still necessary to

14 Thucydides, V. 16; III. 24.
15 Pausanias, IV. 27.

know the rites to be performed at the foundation, for the
Messenians had forgotten them. They could not adopt those of
the Thebans, or of any other people; and so they did not know
how to build the city. A dream, however, came very oppor-
tunely to another Messenian; the gods commanded him to
ascend Mount Ithome, and find a yew tree that stood near a
myrtle, and to dig into the earth in that place. He obeyed, and
discovered an urn, and in this urn were leaves of tin, on which
was found engraved the complete ritual of the sacred ceremony. The priests immediately copied it, and inscribed it in
their books. They did not doubt that the urn had been
deposited there by an ancient king of the Messenians, before
the conquest of the country.

As soon as they were in possession of the ritual the foundation commenced. First, the priests offered a sacrifice; they
invoked the ancient gods of the Messenians, the Dioscuri, the
Jupiter of Ithome, and the ancient heroes, ancestors known
and venerated. All these protectors of the country had apparently quitted it, according to the belief of the ancients, on the
day when the enemy became masters of it. They were entreated
to return. Formulas were pronounced, which, it was believed,
would determine them to inhabit the new city in common
with the citizens. This was the great object; to fix the residence
of the gods with themselves was what these men had the most
at heart, and we may be sure that the religious ceremony had
no other aim. Just as the companions of Romulus dug a trench
and thought to bury the manes of their ancestors there, so the
contemporaries of Epaminondas called to themselves their
heroes, their divine ancestors, and the gods of their country.
They thought that by rites and formulas they could attach
these sacred beings to the soil which they themselves were
going to occupy, and could shut them up within the enclosure
which themselves were about to trace, and they said to them,
"Come with us, O divine kings, and dwell with us in this city."
The first day was occupied with these sacrifices and these
prayers. The next day the boundaries were traced, whilst the
people sang religious hymns.

We are surprised, at first, when we see in the ancient
authors that there was no city, however ancient it might be,
which did not pretend to know the name of its founder and

the date of its foundation. This is because a city could not lose the recollection of the sacred ceremony which had marked its birth. For every year it celebrated the anniversary of this birthday with a sacrifice. Athens, as well as Rome, celebrated its birthday.

It often happened that colonists or conquerors established themselves in a city already built. They had not to build houses, for nothing opposed their occupying those of the vanquished; but they had to perform the ceremony of foundation — that is, to establish their sacred fires, and to fix their national gods in their new home. This explains the statements of Thucydides and Herodotus that the Dorians founded Lacedæmon, and the Ionians Miletus, though these two tribes found Lacedæmon and Miletus built and already very ancient.

These usages show clearly what a city was in the opinion of the ancients. Surrounded by a sacred enclosure, and extending around an altar, it was the religious abode of gods and citizens. Livy said of Rome, "There is not a place in this city which is not impregnated with religion, and which is not occupied by some divinity. The gods inhabit it." What Livy said of Rome any man might say of his own city; for if it had been founded according to the rites, it had received within its walls protecting gods who were, as we may say, implanted in its soil, and could never quit it. Every city was a sanctuary; every city might be called holy.[16]

As the gods were attached to a city forever, so the people could never again abandon a place where their gods were established. In this respect there was a reciprocal engagement, a sort of contract between gods and men. At one time the tribunes of the people proposed, as Rome, devastated by the Gauls, was no longer anything but a heap of ruins, and as, five leagues distant, there was a city all built, large, beautiful, well situated, and without inhabitants, — since the Romans had conquered it, — that the people should abandon the ruins of Rome, and remove to Veii. But the pious Camillus replied, "Our city was religiously founded; the gods themselves pointed out the place, and took up their abode here with our fathers.

---

16 Ἴλιος ἱρη, ἱεραὶ Ἀθηραι (Aristoph., *Knights*, 1319). Λακεδαιμονι διη (Theognis, v. 837); ἱεραν πολιν, says Theognis, speaking of Megara.

Ruined as it is, it still remains the dwelling of our national gods." And the Romans remained at Rome.

Something sacred and divine was naturally associated with these cities which the gods had founded,[17] and which they continued to fill with their presence. We know that Roman traditions promised that Rome should be eternal. Every city had similar traditions. The ancients built all their cities to be eternal.

Chapter V

WORSHIP OF THE FOUNDER. THE LEGEND OF ÆNEAS

THE founder was the man who accomplished the religious act without which a city could not exist. He established the hearth where the sacred fire was eternally to burn. He it was, who, by his prayers and his rites, called the gods, and fixed them forever in the new city.

We can understand how much respect would be felt for this holy man. During his life men saw in him the author of a religion and the father of a city; after death he became a common ancestor for all the generations that succeeded him. He was for the city what the first ancestor was for the family — a *Lar familiaris*. His memory was perpetuated like the hearth-fire which he had lighted. Men established a worship for him, and believed him to be a god; and the city adored him as its providence. Sacrifices and festivals were renewed every year over his tomb.[1]

It is well known that Romulus was worshipped, and that he had a temple and priests. The senators might, indeed, take his life; but they could not deprive him of the worship to which he had a right as the founder of a city. In the same manner every city worshipped the one who had founded it. Cecrops and Theseus, who were regarded as having been successive founders of Athens, had temples there. Abdera offered sacrifices to its founder, Timesius, Thera to Theras, Tenedos to Tenes,

---

[17] *Neptunia Troja, θεοδμητοι 'Αθηναι.* See Theognis, 755. (Welcker.)

[1] Pindar, *Pyth.*, V. 129. *Olymp.*, VII. 145. Cicero, *De Nat. Deor.*, III. 19. Catullus, VII. 6.

Delos to Anius, Cyrene to Battus, Miletus to Naleus, Amphi-
polis to Hagnon. In the time of Pisistratus, one Miltiades went
to found a colony in the Thracian Chersonesus; this colony
instituted a worship for him after his death, "according to the
ordinary usage." Hiero of Syracuse, having founded the town
of Ætna, enjoyed there, in the course of time, "the worship due
to founders of cities."[2]

A city had nothing more at heart than the memory of its
foundation. When Pausanias visited Greece, in the second
century of our era, every city could tell him the name of its
founder, with his genealogy and the principal facts of his life.
This name and these facts could not escape the memory, for
they were a part of the religion, and were recalled every year
in the sacred ceremonies.

The memory of a great number of Greek poems has been
preserved, whose subject was the foundation of a city. Philochorus sang that of Salamis, Ion that of Chios, Crito that of
Syracuse, Zopyrus that of Miletus; and Apollonius, Hermo-
genes, Hellanicus, and Diocles composed poems or histories on
the same subject. There was not, perhaps, a single city that
had not its poem, or at least its hymn, on the sacred act that
had given it birth.

Among all these ancient poems which had the sacred foundation of a city for their theme, there is one that has not been
allowed to perish, because its subject rendered it dear to a
city, and its beauties have rendered it precious to all nations
and all ages. We know that Æneas founded Lavinium, whence
sprang the Albans and the Romans, and that, consequently, he
was regarded as the first founder of Rome. There had been
clustered about him a multitude of traditions, which we find
already recorded in the verses of old Nævius, and in the
histories of Cato the Elder, when Virgil seized upon this subject and wrote the national poem of the Roman city.

The arrival of Æneas, or rather the removal of the gods of
Troy into Italy, is the subject of the Æneid. The poem sings
this man, who traversed the seas to found a city and transport
his gods to Latium: —

[2] Herodotus, I. 168; VI. 38. Pindar, *Pyth.*, IV. Thucydides, V. 11.
Strabo, XIV. 1. Plutarch, *Gr. Quest.*, 20. Pausanias, I. 34; III. 1.
Diodorus, XI. 78.

"Dum conderet urbem
Inferretque Deos Latio."

We must not judge the Æneid after our modern ideas. Men
often complain at not finding in Æneas bravery, dash, passion.
They tire of that epithet of *pious* which is continually repeated. They are astonished to see this warrior consulting his
Penates with a care so scrupulous, invoking some divinity at
every new turn of affairs, raising his arms to heaven when he
ought to be fighting, allowing himself to be tossed over all
seas by the oracles, and shedding tears at the sight of danger.
Nor do they fail to reproach him with coldness towards Dido;
and they are tempted to say, with the unhappy queen, —

"Nullis ille movetur
Fletibus, aut voces ullas tractabilis audit."

"But this is because there is no place here for a warrior,
or a hero of romance. The poet wishes to represent a priest.
Æneas is the chief of a worship, a holy man, the divine
founder, whose mission is to save the Penates of the city.

"Sum pius Æneas, raptos qui ex hoste Penates
Classe veho mecum."

His dominant quality ought to be piety, and the epithet
which the poet oftenest applies to him is that which becomes
him best. His virtue ought to be a cold and lofty impersonality,
making of him, not a man, but an instrument of the gods.
Why should we look for passion in him? He has no right to
the passions; or, at any rate, he should confine them in the
depths of his heart.

"Multa gemens multoque animum labefactus amore,
Jussa tamen Divum insequitur."

Already, in Homer, Æneas was a holy personage, a high
priest, whom the people venerated as a god, and whom Jupiter
preferred to Hector. In Virgil he is the guardian and savior of
the Trojan gods. During the night that completed the ruin of
the city, Hector appeared to him in a dream, and said to him,
"Troy confides its gods to thee; search out a new city for
them." At the same time he committed to him the sacred things,
the protecting statues, and the sacred fire that was never to

be extinguished. This dream is not simply an ornament placed there by the fancy of the poet. It is, on the contrary, the foundation on which the entire poem rests; for it is through this that Æneas becomes the depositary of the city gods, and that his holy mission is revealed to him.

The *urbs* of the Trojans, the material part of Troy, has perished, but not the Trojan *civitas;* thanks to Æneas, the sacred fire is not extinguished, and the gods have still a worship. The city and the gods are with Æneas; they cross the seas, and seek a country where it is permitted them to stop.

> "Considere Teucros
> Errantesque Deos agitataque numina Trojæ."

Æneas seeks a fixed home, small though it be, for his paternal gods,—

> "Dis sedem exiguam patriis."

But the choice of this home, to which the destiny of the city shall be forever bound, does not depend upon men; it belongs to the gods. Æneas consults the priest and interrogates the oracles. He does not himself determine his route or his object; he is directed by the divinity: —

> "Italiam non sponte sequor."

He would have stayed in Thrace, in Crete, in Sicily, at Carthage with Dido: *Fata obstant.* Between him and his desire of rest, between him and his love, there always comes the will of the gods, the revealed word — *fata.*

We must not deceive ourselves in this: the real hero of the poem is not Æneas; the gods of Troy take the place of a hero; the same gods that, one day, are to be those of Rome. The subject of the Æneid is the struggle of the Roman gods against a hostile divinity. Obstacles of every kind are placed in their way.

> "Tantæ molis erat Romanam condere gentem!"

The tempest comes near ingulfing them, the love of a woman almost enslaves them; but they triumph over everything, and arrive at the object sought.

> "Fata viam inveniunt."

Things like these would interest the Romans to a wonderful degree. In this poem they saw themselves, their founder, their city, their institutions, their religion, their empire. For without those gods the Roman city would not have existed.[8]

Chapter VI

THE GODS OF THE CITY

WE must not lose sight of the fact that, among the ancients, what formed the bond of every society was a worship. Just as a domestic altar held the members of a family grouped around it, so the city was the collective group of those who had the same protecting deities, and who performed the religious ceremony at the same altar.

This city altar was enclosed within a building which the Greeks called prytaneum, and which the Romans called temple of Vesta.[1]

There was nothing more sacred within the city than this altar, on which the sacred fire was always maintained.

This great veneration, it is true, became weakened in Greece, at a very early date, because the Greek imagination allowed itself to be turned aside by more splendid temples, richer legends, and more beautiful statues. But it never became enfeebled at Rome. The Romans never abandoned the convic-

---

[8] We need not inquire here if the legend of Æneas represents a real fact; that it was believed is enough for us. It shows us how the ancients looked upon the founder of a city, what idea they had of a *penatiger;* and for us this is the important point. We may add, that several cities in Thrace, in Crete, in Epirus, at Cythera, at Zacynthus, in Sicily, and in Italy looked upon Æneas as their founder, and worshipped him as such.

[1] The prytaneum contained the common hearth of the city: Dion of Halicarnassus, II. 23. Pollux, I. 7. Scholiast of Pindar, *Nem.,* XI. Scholiast of Thucydides, II. 15. There was a prytaneum in every Greek city: Herodotus III. 57; V. 67; VII. 197. Polyb., XXIX. 5. Appian, *Mithridatic War,* 23; *Punic War,* 84. Diodorus, XX. 101. Cicero, *De Signis,* 53. Dionysius, II. 65. Pausanias, I. 42; V. 25; VIII. 9. Athenæus, I. 58; X. 24. Boeckh, *Corp. Inscr.,* 1193. At Rome the temple of Vesta was nothing more than a hearth. Cicero, *De Legib.,* II. 8; II. 12. Ovid, *Fast.,* VI. 297. Florus, I. 2. Livy, XXVIII. 31.

tion that the destiny of the city was connected with this fire which represented their gods. The respect which they had for their vestals proves the importance of their priesthood. If a consul met one of them, he ordered his fasces to be lowered before her. On the other hand, if one of them allowed the fire to go out, or sullied the worship by failing in her duty of chastity, the city, which then believed itself threatened with the loss of its gods, took vengeance upon her by burying her alive.

One day the temple of Vesta came near being burned in a conflagration of the surrounding houses. Rome was in consternation, for it felt all its future to be in peril. When the danger had passed, the senate instructed the consul to search out the authors of the fire, and the consul made accusations against several inhabitants of Capua, who happened at that time to be in Rome. This was not because he had any proof against them, but he reasoned in this manner: "A conflagration has threatened the hearth of our city; this conflagration, which might have destroyed our grandeur and stopped our progress, could have been started only by the hands of our most cruel enemies. Now, we have no more determined enemies than the inhabitants of Capua, this city which is now the ally of Hannibal, and which aspires to take our place as the capital of Italy. These, therefore, are the men who have attempted to destroy our temple of Vesta, our eternal fire, this gage and guarantee of our future grandeur."[2] Thus a consul, under the influence of his religious ideas, believed that the enemies of Rome could find no surer means of conquering it than by destroying its sacred hearth. Here we see the belief of the ancients; the public fire was the sanctuary of the city, the cause of its being, and its constant preserver.

Just as the worship of the domestic hearth was secret, and the family alone had the right to take part in it, so the worship of the public fire was concealed from strangers. No one, unless he were a citizen, could take part at a sacrifice. Even the look of a stranger sullied the religious act.[3]

Every city had gods who belonged to it alone. These gods were generally of the same nature as those of the primitive

[2] Livy, XXVI. 27.
[3] Virgil, III. 408. Pausanias, V. 15. Appian, *Civil Wars*, I. 54.

religion of families. They were called Lares, Penates, Genii, Demons, Heroes;[4] under all these names were human souls deified. For we have seen that, in the Indo-European race, man had at first worshipped the invisible and immortal power which he felt in himself. These genii, or heroes, were, more generally, the ancestors of the people.[5]

The bodies were buried either in the city itself or upon its territory; and as, according to the belief which we have already described, the soul did not quit the body, it followed that these divine dead were attached to the soil where their bodies were buried. From their graves they watched over the city; they protected the country, and were, in some sort, its chiefs and masters. This expression of chiefs of the country, applied to the dead, is found in an oracle addressed by the Pythia to Solon: "Honor with a worship the chiefs of the country, the dead who live under the earth."[6] These notions came from the very great power which the ancient generations attributed to the human soul after death. Every man who had rendered a great service to the city, from the one who had founded it to the one who had given it a victory, or had improved its laws, became a god for that city. It was not even necessary for one to have been a great man or a benefactor; it was enough to have struck the imagination of his contemporaries, and to have rendered himself the subject of a popular tradition, to become a hero — that is to say, one of the powerful dead, whose protection was to be desired and whose anger was to be feared. The Thebans continued during ten centuries to offer sacrifices to Eteocles and Polynices. The inhabitants of Acanthus worshipped a Persian who had died among them during the expedition of Xerxes. Hippolytus was venerated as a god at Trœzene. Pyrrhus, son of Achilles, was a god at Delphi only because he died and was buried there. Crotona worshipped a hero for the sole reason that during his life he had been the handsomest man in the city.[7] Athens adored as one of its protectors Eurystheus, though he was an Argive; but Euripides

---

[4] Ovid, *Fast.*, II. 616.
[5] Plutarch, *Aristides*, 11.
[6] Plutarch, *Solon*, 9.
[7] Pausanias, IX. 18. Herodotus, VII. 117. Diodorus, IV. 62. Pausanias, X. 23. Pindar, *Nem.*, 65. Herodotus. V. 47.

explains the origin of this worship when he brings Eurystheus upon the stage, about to die, and makes him say to the Athenians, "Bury me in Attica. I will be propitious to you, and in the bosom of the ground I will be for your country a protecting guest."[8] The entire tragedy of *Œdipus Coloneus* rests upon this belief. Athens and Thebes contend over the body of a man who is about to die, and who will become a god.

It was a great piece of good fortune for a city to possess the bodies of men of some mark.[9] Mantinea spoke with pride of the bones of Arcas, Thebes of those of Geryon, Messene of those of Aristomenes.[10] To procure these precious relics, ruse was sometimes resorted to. Herodotus relates by what unfair means the Spartans carried off the bones of Orestes.[11] These bones, it is true, to which the soul of a hero was attached, gave the Spartans a victory immediately. As soon as Athens had acquired power, the first use she made of it was to seize upon the bones of Theseus, who had been buried in the Isle of Scyros, and to build a temple for them in the city, in order to increase the number of her protecting deities.

Besides these gods and heroes, men had gods of another species, like Jupiter, Juno, and Minerva, towards whom the aspect of nature had directed their thoughts; but we have seen that these creations of human intelligence had for a long time the character of domestic or local divinities. At first men did not conceive of these gods as watching over the whole human race. They believed that each one of them belonged in particular to a family or a city.

Thus it was customary for each city, without counting its heroes, to have a Jupiter, a Minerva, or some other divinity which it had associated with its first Penates and its sacred fire. Thus there were in Greece and in Italy a multitude of city-guarding divinities. Each city had its gods, who lived within its walls.[12]

---

[8] Eurip., *Heracl.* 1032.
[9] Pausanias, I. 43. Polyb., VIII. 30. Plautus, *Trin.*, II. 2, 14.
[10] Pausanias, IV. 32; VIII. 9.
[11] Herodotus, I. 68.
[12] Herodotus, V. 82. Sophocles, *Phil.*, 134. Thucyd, II. 71. Eurip., *Electra*, 674. Pausanias, I. 24; IV. 8; VIII. 47. Aristoph., *Birds*, 828; *Knights*, 577. *Virgil*, IX. 246. Pollux, IX. 40. Apollodorus, III. 14.

The names of many of these divinities are forgotten; it is by chance that there have remained the names of the god Satrapes, who belonged to the city of Elis, of the goddess Dindymene at Thebes, of Soteira at Ægium, of Britomartis in Crete, of Hyblæa at Hybla. The names of Zeus, Athene, Hera, Jupiter, Minerva, and Neptune are better known to us, and we know that they were often applied to these city-guarding divinities; but because two cities happened to apply the same name to their god, we are not to conclude that they adored the same god. There was an Athene at Athens, and there was one at Sparta; but they were two goddesses. A great number of cities had a Jupiter as a city-protecting divinity. There were as many Jupiters as there were cities. In the legend of the Trojan war we see a Pallas who fights for the Greeks, and there is among the Trojans another Pallas, who receives their worship and protects her worshippers.[13] Would any one say that it was the same divinity who figured in both armies? Certainly not; for the ancients did not attribute the gift of ubiquity to their gods. The cities of Argos and Samos had each a Here Polias, but it was not the same goddess, for she was represented in the two cities with very different attributes. There was at Rome a Juno; at a distance of five leagues, the city of Veii had another. So little were they the same divinity that we see the dictator Camillus, while besieging Veii, address himself to the Juno of the enemy, to induce her to abandon the Etruscan city and pass into his camp. When he is master of the city, he takes the statue, well persuaded that he gains possession of the goddess at the same time, and devoutly transports it to Rome. From that time Rome had two protecting Junos. There is a similar history, a few years later, of a Jupiter that another dictator took from Præneste, though at that time Rome already had three or four of them at home.[14]

The city which possessed a divinity of its own did not wish strangers to be protected by it, or to adore it. More commonly a temple was accessible only to citizens. The Argives alone had the right to enter the temple of Hera at Argos. To enter that of Athene at Athens, one had to be an Athenian.[15] The Romans who adored two Junos at home could not enter the

[13] Homer, *Iliad*, VI. 88.   [14] Livy, V. 21, 22; VI. 29.
[15] Herodotus, VI. 81; V. 72.

temple of a third Juno, who was in the little city of
Lanuvium.[16]

We should not lose sight of the fact that the ancients never
represented God to themselves as a unique being exercising his
action upon the universe. Each of their innumerable gods had
his little domain; to one a family belonged, to another a tribe,
to a third a city. Such was the world which sufficed for the
providence of each of them. As to the god of the human race,
a few philosophers had an idea of him; the mysteries of
Eleusis might have afforded a glimpse of him to the most
intelligent of the initiated; but the vulgar never believed in
such a god. For ages man understood the divine being only as
a force which protected him personally, and every man, or
every group of men, desired to have a god. Even to-day, among
the descendants of those Greeks, we see rude peasants pray to the
saints with fervor, while it is doubtful if they have the idea of
a god. Each one of them wishes to have, among these saints, a
particular protector, a special providence. At Naples, each
quarter of the city has its Madonna; the *lazzaroni* kneel before
that of their own street, while they insult that of the neighboring street: it is not rare to see two *facchini* wrangle, and even
fight with knives, in defence of the merits of their respective
Madonnas. These cases are exceptions to-day and are found
only among certain peoples and in certain classes. They were
the rule among the ancients.

Each city had its corps of priests, who depended upon no
foreign authority. Between the priests of two cities there was
no bond, no communication, no exchange of instruction or of
rites. If one passed from one city to another, he found other
gods, other dogmas, other ceremonies. The ancients had books
of liturgies, but those of one city did not resemble those of
another. Every city had its collection of prayers and practices,
which were kept very secret; it would have thought itself in
danger of compromising its religion and its destiny by opening
this collection to strangers. Thus religion was entirely local,
entirely civic, taking this word in the ancient sense — that is to
say, special to each city.[17]

[16] They acquired this right only by conquest. Livy, VIII. 14.
[17] There existed worships common to several cities only in the
case of confederations. We shall speak of them elsewhere.

Generally a man knew only the gods of his own city, and honored and respected them alone. Each one could say what, in a tragedy of Æschylus, a stranger said to the Argives — "I fear not the gods of your country; I owe them nothing."[18]

Every city looked to its gods for safety. Men invoked them in danger, and thanked them in victory. Often defeat was attributed to them; and they were reproached for having badly fulfilled their duty as defenders of the city. Men even went so far, sometimes, as to overturn their altars and stone their temples.[19]

Ordinarily, these gods took good care of the city whose worship they received; and this was quite natural: these gods were eager for offerings, and they received victims only from their own city. If they wished the continuation of the sacrifices and hecatombes, it was very necessary that they should watch over the city's safety.[20] See, in Virgil, how Juno "strove and labored" that her Carthage might one day obtain the empire of the world. Each of these gods, like the Juno of Virgil, had the grandeur of his city at heart. These gods had the same interests as the citizens themselves, and in times of war marched to battle in the midst of them. In Euripides we see a personage who says, on the eve of battle, "The gods who fight with us are more powerful than those who are on the side of the enemy."[21] The Æginetans never commenced a campaign without carrying with them the statues of their national heroes, the Æacidæ. The Spartans in all their expeditions carried with them the Tyndaridæ.[22] In the combat the gods and the citizens mutually sustained each other, and if they conquered, it was because all had done their duty.

If a city was conquered, the gods were supposed to have been vanquished with it.[23] If a city was taken, its gods themselves were captives.

On this last point, it is true, opinions were uncertain and diverse. Many were persuaded that a city never could be taken

---

18 Æschylus, *Suppl.*, 858.
19 Suetonius, *Calig.*, 5; Seneca, *De Vita Beata*, 36.
20 This idea is often found among the ancients. Theognis, 759.
21 Euripides, *Heracl.*, 347.
22 Herodotus, V. 65; V. 80.
23 Virgil, *Æn.*, I. 68.

so long as its gods remained in it. When Æneas sees the Greeks masters of Troy, he cries that the gods have departed, deserting their temples and their altars. In Æschylus, the chorus of Thebans expresses the same belief when, at the approach of the enemy, it implores the gods not to abandon the city.[24]

According to this opinion, in order to take a city it was necessary to make the gods leave it. For this purpose the Romans employed a certain formula which they had in their rituals, and which Macrobius has preserved: "O thou great one, who hast this city under thy protection, I pray thee, I adore thee, I ask of thee as a favor, to abandon this city and this people, to quit these temples, these sacred places, and having separated thyself from them, to come to Rome, to me and mine. May our city, our temples, and our sacred places be more agreeable and more dear to thee; take us under thy protection. If thou doest this, I will found a temple in thine honor."[25] Now, the ancients were convinced that there were formulas so efficacious and powerful, that, if one pronounced them exactly and without changing a single word, the god could not resist the request of men. The god thus called upon passed over, therefore, to the side of the enemy, and the city was taken.

In Greece we find the same opinions and similar customs. Even in the time of Thucydides, when the Greeks besieged a city, they never failed to address an invocation to its gods, that they might permit it to be taken.[26] Often, instead of employing a formula to attract the god, the Greeks preferred to carry off its statue by stealth. Everybody knows the legend of Ulysses' carrying off the Pallas of the Trojans. At another time the Æginetans, wishing to make war upon Epidaurus, commenced by carrying off two protecting statues of that city, and transported them to their own city.[27]

Herodotus relates that the Athenians wished to make war upon the Æginetans, but the enterprise was hazardous, for Ægina had a protecting hero of great power and of singular fidelity; this was Æacus. The Athenians, after having studied

[24] Æsch., *Sept. Cont. Theb.*, 202
[25] Macrobius, III. 9.
[26] Thucydides, II. 74.
[27] Herodotus, V. 83.

the matter over, put off the execution of their design for thirty years; at the same time they built in their own country a chapel to this same Æacus, and devoted a worship to him. They were persuaded that if this worship was continued without interruption during thirty years, the god would belong no longer to the Æginetans, but to themselves. Indeed, it seemed to them that a god could not accept fat victims for so long a time without placing himself under obligations to those who had offered them. Æacus, therefore, would in the end be forced to abandon the interests of the Æginetans, and to give the victory to the Athenians.[28]

Here is another case from Plutarch. Solon desired that Athens might become mistress of the little Isle of Salamis, which then belonged to the Megarians. He consulted the oracle. The oracle answered, "If you wish to conquer the isle, you must first gain the favor of the heroes who protect it and who inhabit it." Solon obeyed; in the name of Athens he offered sacrifices to the two principal heroes of Salamis. These heroes did not resist the gifts that were offered them, but went over to the Athenian side, and the isle, deprived of protectors, was conquered.[29]

In time of war, if the besiegers sought to gain possession of the divinities of the city, the besieged, on their part, did their best to retain them. Sometimes they bound the god with chains, to prevent him from deserting. At other times they concealed him from all eyes, that the enemy might not find him. Or, still again, they opposed to the formula by which the enemy attempted to bribe the god another formula which had the power to retain him. The Romans had imagined a means which seemed to them to be surer; they kept secret the name of the principal and most powerful of their protecting gods.[30] They thought that, as the enemy could never call this god by his name, he would never abandon their side, and that their city would never be taken.

We see by this what a singular idea the ancients had of the gods. It was a long time before they conceived the Divinity as a supreme power. Every family had its domestic religion,

[28] Herodotus, V. 89.
[29] Plutarch, *Solon,* 9.
[30] Macrobius, III.

every city had its national religion. A city was like a little church, all complete, which had its gods, its dogmas, and its worship. These beliefs appear very crude to us, but they were those of the most intellectual people of ancient times, and have exercised upon this people and upon the Romans so important an influence that the greater part of their laws, of their institutions, and of their history is from this source.

Chapter VII

THE RELIGION OF THE CITY

1. The Public Repasts.

WE have already seen that the principal ceremony of the domestic worship was a repast, which they called a sacrifice. To eat food prepared upon an altar was, to all appearance, the first form which men gave to the religious act. The need of putting themselves in communion with the divinity was satisfied by this repast, to which they invited him, and of which they gave him his part.

The principal ceremony of the city worship was also a repast of this nature; it was partaken of in common by all the citizens, in honor of the protecting divinities. The celebrating of these public repasts was universal in Greece; and men believed that the safety of the city depended upon their accomplishment.[1]

The Odyssey gives us a description of one of these sacred feasts: Nine long tables are spread for the people of Pylos; at each one of them five hundred citizens are seated, and each group has immolated nine bulls in honor of the gods. This repast, which was called the feast of the gods, begins and ends with libations and prayers.[2] The ancient custom of repasts in common is also mentioned in the oldest Athenian traditions. It is related that Orestes, the murderer of his mother, arrived at Athens at the very moment when the city, assembled about its king, was performing the sacred act.[3]

The public meals of Sparta are well known, but the idea

[1] Σωτηρια των πολεων συνδειπνα. Athenæus, V. 2.
[2] Homer, *Odyssey*, III.   [3] Athenæus, X. 49.

which men ordinarily entertain of them is very far from the truth. They imagine the Spartans living and eating always in common, as if private life had not been known among them. We know, on the contrary, from ancient authors, that the Spartans often took their meals in their own houses, in the midst of their families.[4] The public meals took place twice a month, without reckoning holidays. These were religious acts of the same nature as those which were practised at Athens, in Argos, and throughout Greece.[5]

Besides these immense banquets, where all the citizens were assembled, and which could take place only on solemn festivals, religion prescribed that every day there should be a sacred meal. For this purpose, men chosen by the city, were required to eat together, in its name, within the enclosure of the prytaneum, in the presence of the sacred fire and the protecting gods. The Greeks were convinced that, if this repast was interrupted but for a single day, the state was menaced with the loss of the favor of its gods.

At Athens, the men who took part in the common meal were selected by lot, and the law severely punished those who refused to perform this duty. The citizens who sat at the sacred table were clothed, for the time, with a sacerdotal character; they were called *parasites*. This word which, at a later period, became a term of contempt, was in the beginning a sacred title.[6] In the time of Demosthenes the parasites had disappeared; but the prytanes were still required to eat together in the prytaneum. In all the cities there were halls destined for the common meals.[7]

If we observe how matters passed at this meal, we shall easily recognize the religious ceremony. Every guest had a crown upon his head; it was a custom of the ancients to wear a crown

---

[4] Athenæus, IV. 17; IV. 21. Herodotus, VI. 57. Plutarch, *Cleomenes*, 13.

[5] This custom is attested, for Athens, by Xenophon, *Gov. Ath.*, 2; Schol. on Aristophanes, *Clouds*, 393;—for Crete and Thessaly, Athenæus, IV. 22;—for Argos, Boeckh, 1122;—for other cities, Pindar, *Nem.*, XI.; Theognis, 269; Pausanias, V. 15; Athenæus, IV. 32; IV. 61; X. 24 and 25; X. 49; XI. 66.

[6] Plutarch, *Solon*, 24. Athenæus, VI. 26.

[7] Demosthenes, *Pro Corona*, 53. Aristotle, *Politics*, VII. 1, 19. Pollux, VIII. 155.

of leaves or flowers when one performed a solemn religious act. "The more one is adorned with flowers," they said, "the surer one is of pleasing the gods; but if you sacrifice without wearing a crown, they will turn from you."[8] "A crown," they also said, "is a herald of good omen, which prayer sends before it towards the gods."[9] For the same reason the banqueters were clothed in robes of white; white was the sacred color among the ancients, that which pleased the gods.[10]

The meal invariably commenced with a prayer and libations, and hymns were sung. The nature of the dishes and the kind of wine that was to be served were regulated by the rules of each city.

To deviate in the least from the usage followed in primitive times, to present a new dish or alter the rhythm of the sacred hymns, was a grave impiety, for which the whole city was responsible to the gods. Religion even went so far as to fix the nature of the vessels that ought to be employed both for the cooking of the food and for the service of the table. In one city the bread must be served in copper baskets; in another earthen dishes had to be employed. Even the form of the loaves was immutably fixed.[11] These rules of the old religion continued to be observed, and the sacred meals always preserved their primitive simplicity. Creeds, manners, social condition, all changed; but these meals remained unchangeable; for the Greeks were very scrupulous observers of their national religion.

It is but just to add, that when the guests had satisfied the requirements of religion by eating the prescribed food, they might immediately afterwards commence another meal, more expensive and better suited to their taste. This was quite a common practice at Sparta.[12]

The custom of religious meals was common in Italy as well as in Greece. It existed anciently, Aristotle tells us, among the

---

[8] Fragment of Sappho, in Athenæus, XV. 16.

[9] Athenæus, XV. 19.

[10] Plato, *Laws*, XII. 956. Cicero, *De Legib.*, II. 18. Virgil, V. 70, 774; VII. 135; VIII. 274. So, too, among the Hindus, in religious ceremonies, one was required to wear a crown, and to be clothed in white.

[11] Athenæus, I. 58; IV. 32; XI. 66.

[12] Ibid., IV. 19; IV. 20.

peoples known as Œnotrians, Oscans, and Ausonians.[13] Virgil
has mentioned it twice in the Æneid. Old Latinus receives the
envoys of Æneas, not in his home, but in a temple, "consecrated by the religion of his ancestors; there took place the
sacred feasts after the immolation of the victims; there all the
family chiefs sat together at long tables." Farther along, when
Æneas arrives at the home of Evander, he finds him celebrating a sacrifice. The king is in the midst of his people; all are
crowned with flowers; all, seated at the same table, sing a hymn
in praise of the god of the city.

This custom was perpetuated at Rome. There was always a
hall where the representatives of the curies ate together. The
senate, on certain days, held a sacred repast in the Capitol. At
the solemn festivals, tables were spread in the streets, and the
whole people ate at them. Originally the pontiffs presided at
these repasts; later, this care was delegated to special priests,
who were called *epulones*.[14]

These old customs give us an idea of the close tie which
united the members of a city. Human association was a
religion; its symbol was a meal, of which they partook together.
We must picture to ourselves one of these little primitive
societies, all assembled, or the heads of families at least, at the
same table, each clothed in white, with a crown upon his head;
all make the libation together, recite the same prayer, sing the
same hymns, and eat the same food, prepared upon the same
altar; in their midst their ancestors are present, and the protecting gods share the meal. Neither interest, nor agreement,
nor habit creates the social bond; it is this holy communion
piously accomplished in the presence of the gods of the city.

2.   *The Festivals and the Calendar.*

In all ages and in all societies, man has desired to honor his
gods by festivals; he has established that there should be days
during which the religious sentiment should reign in his
soul, without being distracted by terrestrial thoughts and
labors. In the number of days that he has to live he has
devoted a part to the gods.

Every city had been founded with rites which, in the
thoughts of the ancients, had had the effect of establishing the

[13] Aristotle, *Politics*, IV. 9, 3.
[14] Dionysius, II. 23. Aulus Gellius, XII. 8. Livy, XL. 59.

national gods within its walls. It was necessary that the virtue of these rites should be rejuvenated each year by a new religious ceremony. This festival they called the birthday; all the citizens were required to celebrate it.

Whatever was sacred gave occasion for a festival. There was the festival of the city enclosure, *amburbalia*, and that of the territorial limits, *ambarvalia*. On those days the citizens formed a grand procession, clad in white, and crowned with leaves; they made the circuit of the city or territory, chanting prayers; at the head walked priests, leading victims, which they sacrificed at the close of the ceremony.[15]

Afterwards came the festival of the founder. Then each of the heroes of the city, each of those souls that men invoked as protectors, claimed a worship. Romulus had his, and Servius Tullius, and many others, even to the nurse of Romulus, and Evander's mother. In the same way Athens had the festival of Cecrops, that of Erechtheus, that of Theseus; and it celebrated each of the heroes of the country, the guardian of Theseus, and Eurystheus, and Androgeus, and a multitude of others.

There were also the rural festivals, those for ploughing, seedtime, the time for flowering, and that for the vintage. In Greece, as in Italy, every act of the husbandman's life was accompanied with sacrifices, and men performed their work reciting sacred hymns. At Rome the priests fixed, every year, the day on which the vintage was to commence, and the day on which the new wine might be drunk. Everything was regulated by religion. A religious ordinance required the vines to be pruned; for it told man that it would be impious to offer a libation with the wine of an unpruned vine.[16]

Every city had a festival for each of the divinities which it had adopted as a protector, and it often counted many of them. When the worship of a new divinity was introduced into the city, it was necessary to find a new day in the year to consecrate to him. What characterized the religious festivals was the interdiction of labor, the obligation to be joyous, the songs, and the public games. The Athenian religion added, Take care to do each other no wrong on those days.[17]

[15] Tibullus, II. 1. Festus, v. *Amburbiales.*
[16] Varro, VI. 16. Virgil, *Georg.*, I. 340–350. Pliny, XVIII. Festus, v. *Vinalia.* Plutarch, *Rom. Quest.*, 40; *Numa*, 14.
[17] A law of Solon, cited by Demosthenes, *in Timocrat.*

The calendar was nothing more than the order of the religious festivals. It was regulated, therefore, by the priests. At Rome it was long before the calendar was reduced to writing; the first day of the month, the pontiff, after having offered a sacrifice, convoked the people, and named the festivals that would take place in the course of the month. This convocation was called the *calatio,* whence came the name of calends, which was given to this day.

The calendar was regulated neither on the course of the moon nor on the apparent course of the sun. It was governed solely by the laws of religion, mysterious laws, which the priests alone knew. Sometimes religion required that the year should be shortened, and at other times that it should be lengthened. We can form an idea of primitive calendars, if we recollect that among the Albans the month of May had twelve days, and that March had thirty-six.[18]

We can see that the calendar of one city would in no wise resemble that of another, since the religion was not the same in both, and the festivals, as well as the gods, were different. The year had not the same length from one city to another. The months did not bear the same names: at Athens they had quite other names than at Thebes, and at Rome they had not the same names as at Lavinium. This was due to the fact that the name of each month was derived, ordinarily, from the principal festival it contained, and the festivals were not the same. Different cities had no understanding to commence the year at the same time, or to count the series of their years from the same date. In Greece the Olympic festival afforded, in the course of time, a common date; but this did not prevent each city from having its own particular style of reckoning. In Italy every city counted its years from the day of its foundation.

3. *The Census.*

Among the most important ceremonies of the city religion there was one known as the purification. It took place at Athens every year; at Rome it occurred once in five years.[19]

---

[18] Censorinus, 22. Macrobius, I. 14; I. 15. Varro, V. 28; VI. 27.

[19] Diogenes Laertius, *Life of Socrates,* 23. Harpocration, Φαρμακος. They also purified the domestic hearth every year. Æschylus, *Choeph.,* 966.

The rites which were then observed, and the very name which it bore, indicate that the object of this ceremony was to efface the faults committed by the citizens against the worship. Indeed, this religion, with its complicated forms, was a source of terror for the ancients: as faith and purity of intention went for very little, and the religion consisted entirely in the minute practice of innumerable rules, they were always in fear of having been guilty of some negligence, some omission, or some error, and were never sure of being free from the anger or malice of some god. An expiatory sacrifice was necessary, therefore, to reassure the heart of man. The magistrate whose duty it was to offer it (at Rome it was the censor; before the censor, it was the consul, and before the consul, the king) commenced by assuring himself, by the aid of the auspices, that the gods accepted the ceremony. He then convoked the people by means of a herald, who, for this purpose, made use of a certain sacramental formula. All the citizens, on the appointed day, collected outside the walls; there, all being silent, the magistrate walked three times around the assembly, driving before him three victims, a sheep, a hog, a bull (*suovetaurile*) ; these three animals together constituted, among the Greeks, as among the Romans, an expiatory sacrifice. Priests and victims followed the procession. When the third circuit was completed the magistrate pronounced a set form of prayer, and immolated the victims.[20] From this moment every stain was effaced, all negligence in the worship repaired, and the city was at peace with its gods. Two things were necessary for an act of this nature, and of so great importance; one was, that no stranger should be found among the citizens, as this would have destroyed the effect of the ceremony; the other was, that all the citizens should be present, without which the city would have retained some stain. It was necessary, therefore, that this religious ceremony should be preceded by a numbering of the citizens. At Rome and at Athens, they were counted with scrupulous care. It is probable that the number was pro-

[20] Varro, *L. L.*, VI. 86. Valerius Maximus, V. 1, 10. Livy, I. 44; III. 22; VI. 27. Propertius, IV. 1, 20. Servius, *ad Eclog.*, X. 55; *ad Æn.*, VIII. 231. Livy attributes this institution to king Servius; but probably it is older than Rome, and existed in all the cities, as well as at Rome. It is attributed to Servius just because he modified it, as we shall see.

nounced by the magistrate in the formula of prayer, as it was afterwards inserted in the account of the ceremony which the censor drew up.

The loss of citizenship was the punishment of the man who failed to have his name enrolled. This severity is easily explained. The man who had not taken part in the religious act, who had not been purified, for whom the prayer had not been pronounced or the victim sacrificed, could no longer be a member of the city. In the sight of the gods, who had been present at the ceremony, he was no longer a citizen.[21]

We are enabled to judge of the importance of this ceremony by the exorbitant power of the magistrate who presided at it. The censor, before commencing the sacrifice, ranged the people in a certain order; the senators, the knights, and the tribes, each rank in its appropriate place. Absolute master on that day, he fixed the place of each man in the different categories. Then, all having been arranged according to his directions, he performed the sacred act. Now, a result of this was, that from that day to the following lustration, every man preserved in the city the rank which the censor had assigned him in the ceremony. He was a senator if on that day he had been counted among the senators; a knight if he had figured among the knights; if a simple citizen, he formed a part of the tribe in the ranks of which he had been on that day; and if the magistrate had refused to admit him into the ceremony, he was no longer a citizen. Thus the place which one had occupied in the religious act, and where the gods had seen him, was the one he held in the city for five years. Such was the origin of the immense power of the censor.

In this ceremony none but citizens took part; but their wives, their children, their slaves, their property, real and personal, were in a manner purified in the person of the head of the family. It was for this reason that, before the sacrifice, each citizen was required to give to the censor an account of the persons and property belonging to him.

The lustration was accomplished in Augustus's time with the same exactitude and the same rites as in the most ancient times. The pontiffs still regarded it as a religious act, while

[21] Citizens absent from Rome were required to return home for the lustration; nothing could exempt them from this. Volleius II. 15.

statesmen saw in it an excellent measure of administration, at least.

4. Religion in the Assembly, in the Senate, in the Tribunal, in the Army, in the Triumph.

There was not a single act of public life in which the gods were not seen to take a part. As he was under the influence of the idea that they were by turns excellent protectors or cruel enemies, man never dared to act without being sure that they were favorable. The people assembled only on such days as religion permitted. They remembered that the city had suffered a disaster on a certain day; this was, doubtless, because on that day the gods had been either absent or irritated; they would probably be in the same mood at the same season every year, for reasons unknown to mortals. This day, therefore, was forever unlucky; there were no assemblies, no courts; public life was suspended.

At Rome, before an assembly proceeded to business, the augurs were required to declare that the gods were propitious. The assembly commenced with a prayer, which the augur pronounced, and which the consul repeated after him.

There was the same custom among the Athenians. The assembly always commenced by a religious act. Priests offered a sacrifice; a large circle was then traced by pouring lustral water upon the ground and within this sacred circle the citizens assembled.[22] Before any orator began to speak, a prayer was pronounced before the silent people. The auspices were also consulted, and if any unfavorable sign appeared in the heavens, the assembly broke up at once.[23]

The tribune, or speaker's stand, was a sacred place, and the orator never ascended it without a crown upon his head.[24]

The place of assembly of the Roman senate was always a temple. If a session had been held elsewhere than in a sacred place, its acts would have been null and void; for the gods would not have been present. Before every deliberation, the

[22] Aristophanes, *Acharn.*, 44. Æschines, *in Timarch.*, I. 21; *in Ctesiph.*, 176, and Scholiast. Dinarch., *in Aristog.*, 14.
[23] Aristophanes, *Acharn.*, 171.
[24] Aristophanes, *Thesmoph.*, 381, and Scholiast.

president offered a sacrifice and pronounced a prayer. In the hall there was an altar, where every senator, on entering, offered a libation, at the same time invoking the gods.[25]

The Athenian senate was little different. The hall also contained an altar and a sacred fire. A religious ceremony was observed at the opening of each session. Every senator, on entering, approached the altar, and pronounced a prayer. While the session lasted, every senator wore a crown upon his head, as in religious ceremonies.[26]

At Rome, as well as at Athens, courts of justice were open in the city only on such days as religion pronounced favorable. At Athens the session of the court was held near an altar, and commenced with a sacrifice.[27] In Homer's time the judges assembled "in a holy circle."

Festus says, that in the rituals of the Etruscans were directions as to the founding of a city, the consecration of a temple, the arrangement of curies and tribes in a public assembly, and the ranging of an army in order of battle. All these things were marked in the ritual, because all these things were connected with religion.

In war, religion was as influential, at least, as in peace. In the Italian cities[28] there were colleges of priests, called *fetiales*, who presided, like the heralds among the Greeks, at all the sacred ceremonies to which international relations gave rise. A *fetialis*, veiled, and with a crown upon his head, declared war by pronouncing a sacramental formula. At the same time, the consul, in priestly robes, offered a sacrifice, and solemnly opened the temple of the most venerated and most ancient divinity of Italy. Before setting out on an expedition, the army being assembled, the general repeated prayers and offered a sacrifice. The custom was the same at Athens and at Sparta.[29]

During a campaign the army presented the image of the city; its religion followed it. The Greeks took with them the statues

[25] Varro, cited by Aulus Gellius, XIV. 7. Cicero, *ad Famil.*, X. 12. Suetonius, *Aug.*, 35. Dion Cassius, LIV. p. 621. Servius, VII. 153.

[26] Andocides, *De Myst.*, 44, *De Red.*, 15. Antiphon, *Pro Chor.*, 45. Lycurgus, *in Leocr.*, 122. Demosthenes, *in Meidiam*, 114. Diodorus, XIV. 4.

[27] Aristophanes, *Wasps*, 860–865. Homer, *Iliad*, XVIII. 504.

[28] Dionysius, II. 73. Servius, X. 14.

[29] Dionysius, IX. 57. Virgil, VII. 601. Xenophon, *Hellen.*, VI. 5.

of their divinities. Every Greek or Roman army carried with it a hearth, on which the sacred fire was kept up night and day.[30] A Roman army was accompanied by augurs and *pullarii* (feeders of the sacred chickens) : every Greek army had a diviner.

Let us examine a Roman army at the moment when it is preparing for battle. The consul orders a victim to be brought, and strikes it with the axe; it falls: its entrails will indicate the will of the gods. An aruspex examines them, and if the signs are favorable, the consul gives the signal for battle. The most skilful dispositions, the most favorable circumstances, are of no account if the gods do not permit the battle. The fundamental principle of the military art among the Romans was to be able to put off a battle when the gods were opposed to it. It was for this reason that they made a sort of citadel of their camp every day.

Let us now examine a Greek army, and we will take for example the battle of Plataea. The Spartans are drawn up in line; each one has his post for battle. They all have crowns upon their heads, and the flute-players sound the religious hymns. The king, a little in rear of the ranks, slaughters the victims. But the entrails do not give the favorable signs, and the sacrifice must be repeated. Two, three, four victims are successively immolated. During this time the Persian cavalry approach, shoot their arrows, and kill quite a number of Spartans. The Spartans remain immovable, their shields placed at their feet, without even putting themselves on the defensive against the arrows of the enemy. They await the signal of the gods. At last the victims offer the favorable signs; then the Spartans raise their shields, seize their swords, move on to battle, and are victorious.

After every victory they offer a sacrifice; and this is the origin of the triumph, which is so well known among the Romans, and which was not less common among the Greeks. This custom was a consequence of the opinion which attributed the victory to the gods of the city. Before the battle the army had addressed a prayer to them, like the one we read in

[30] Herodotus, VIII. 6. Plutarch, *Agesilaus,* 6; *Publicola,* 17. Xenophon, *Gov. Laced.,* 14. Dionysius, IX. 6. Stobæus, 42. Julius Obsequens, 12, 116.

Æschylus: "To you, O gods, who inhabit and possess our land,
if our arms are fortunate, and if our city is saved, I promise to
sprinkle your altars with the blood of sheep, to sacrifice bulls
to you, and to hang up in your holy temples the trophies conquered by the spear."[31] By virtue of this promise, the victor
owed a sacrifice. The army entered the city to offer it, and
repaired to the temple, forming a long procession, and singing a sacred hymn — θριαμβος.[32]

At Rome the ceremony was very nearly the same. The army
marched in procession to the principal temple of the city. The
priests walked at the head of the cortège, leading victims. On
reaching the temple, the general sacrificed the victims to the
gods. On their way the soldiers all wore crowns, as was becoming in a sacred ceremony, and sung a hymn, as in Greece.
There came a time, indeed, when the soldiers did not scruple
to replace the hymn, which they did not understand, by
barrack songs and raillery at their general; but they still preserved the custom of repeating the refrain Io triumphe.[33]
Indeed, it was this refrain which gave the name to the
ceremony.

Thus, in time of peace, as in war time, religion intervened
in all acts. It was everywhere present, it enveloped man. The
soul, the body, private life, public life, meals, festivals, assemblies, tribunals, battles, all were under the empire of this city
religion. It regulated all the acts of man, disposed of every
instant of his life, fixed all his habits. It governed a human
being with an authority so absolute that there was nothing
beyond its control.

One would have a very false idea of human nature to believe
that this ancient religion was an imposture, and, so to speak, a
comedy. Montesquieu pretends that the Romans adopted a
worship only to restrain the people. A religion never had such
an origin; and every religion that has come to sustain itself
only from motives of public utility, has not stood long. Montesquieu has also said that the Romans subjected religion to
the state. The contrary is true. It is impossible to read many
pages of Livy without being convinced of this. Neither the

[31] Æschylus, Sept. Cont. Theb., 252–260. Eurip., Phœn., 573.
[32] Diodorus, IV. 5. Photius,   .
[33] Varro, L. L., VI. 64. Pliny, N. H., VII. 56. Macrobius, I. 19.

Romans nor the Greeks knew anything of those sad conflicts
between church and state which have been so common in other
societies. But this is due solely to the fact that at Rome as well
as at Sparta and Athens, the state was enslaved by its religion;
or, rather, the state and religion were so completely confounded, that it was impossible even to distinguish the one
from the other, to say nothing of forming an idea of a conflict
between the two.

Chapter VIII

THE RITUALS AND THE ANNALS

THE character and the virtue of the religion of the ancients
was not to elevate human intelligence to the conception of the
absolute; to open to the eager mind a brilliant road, at the
end of which it could gain a glimpse of God. This religion was
a badly connected assemblage of small creeds, of minute practices, of petty observances. It was not necessary to seek the
meaning of them; there was no need of reflecting, or of giving
a reason for them. The word *religion* did not signify what it
signifies for us; by this word we understand a body of dogmas,
a doctrine concerning God, a symbol of faith concerning what
is in and around us. This same word, among the ancients,
signified rites, ceremonies, acts of exterior worship. The doctrine was of small account: the practices were the important
part; these were obligatory, and bound man (*ligare, religio*).
Religion was a material bond, a chain which held man a slave.
Man had originated it, and he was governed by it. He stood in
fear of it, and dared not reason upon it, or discuss it, or
examine it. Gods, heroes, dead men, claimed a material worship from him, and he paid them the debt, to keep them
friendly, and, still more, not to make enemies of them.

Man counted little upon their friendship. They were
envious, irritable gods, without attachment or friendship for
man, and willingly at war with him. Neither did the gods love
man, nor did man love his gods. He believed in their existence,
but would have wished that they did not exist. He feared
even his domestic and national gods, and was continually in

fear of being betrayed by them. His great inquietude was lest he might incur their displeasure. He was occupied all his life in appeasing them. *Paces deorum quærere,* says the poet. But how satisfy them? Above all, how could one be sure that he had satisfied them, and that they were on his side? Men believed that the employment of certain formulas answered this purpose. A certain prayer, composed of certain words, had been followed by the success that was asked for; this was, without doubt, because it had been heard by the god, and had exercised an influence upon him; that it had been potent, more potent than the god, since he had not been able to resist it. They therefore preserved the mysterious and sacred words of this prayer. After the father, the son repeated it. As soon as writing was in use it was committed to writing. Every family, every religious family at least, had a book in which were written the prayers of which the ancestors had made use, and with which the gods had complied.[1] It was an arm which man employed against the inconstancy of the gods. But not a word or syllable must be changed, and least of all the rhythm in which it had been chanted. For then the prayer would have lost its force, and the gods would have remained free. But the formula was not enough; there were exterior acts whose details were minute and unchangeable. The slightest gesture of the one who performed the sacrifice, and the smallest parts of his costume, were governed by strict rules. In addressing one god, it was necessary to have the head veiled; in addressing another, the head was uncovered; for a third, the skirt of the toga was thrown over the shoulder. In certain acts the feet had to be naked. There were certain prayers which were without effect unless the man, after pronouncing them, pirouetted on one foot from left to right. The nature of the victim, the color of the hair, the manner of slaying it, even the shape of the knife, and the kind of wood employed to roast the flesh — all was fixed for every god by the religion of each family, or of each city. In vain the most fervent heart offered to the gods the fattest victims: if one of the innumerable rites of the sacrifice was neglected, the sacrifice was without effect; the least failure made of the sacred act an act of impiety. The slightest altera-

[1] Dionysius, I. 75. Varro, VI. 90. Cicero, *Brutus,* 16. Aulus Gellius, XIII. 19.

tion disturbed and confused the religion of a country, and changed the protecting gods into so many cruel enemies. It was for this reason that Athens was so severe against the priest who made some change in the ancient rites.[2] It was for the same reason that the Roman senate degraded its consuls and its dictators who had committed any error in a sacrifice.

All these formulas and practices had been handed down by ancestors who had proved their efficacy. There was no occasion for innovation. It was a duty to rest upon what the ancestors had done, and the highest piety consisted in imitating them. It mattered little that a belief changed; it might be freely modified from age to age, and take a thousand diverse forms, in accordance with the reflection of sages, or with the popular imagination. But it was of the greatest importance that the formulas should not fall into oblivion, and that the rites should not be modified. Every city, therefore, had a book in which these were preserved.

The use of sacred books was universal among the Greeks, the Romans, and the Etruscans.[3] Sometimes the ritual was written on tablets of wood, sometimes on cloth; Athens engraved its rites upon tablets of copper, that they might be imperishable. Rome had its books of the pontiffs, its books of the augurs, its book of ceremonies, and its collection of Indigitamenta. There was not a city which had not also its collection of ancient hymns in honor of its gods.[4] In vain did language change with manners and beliefs; the words and the rhythm remained unchangeable, and on the festivals men continued to sing these hymns after they no longer understood them. These books and songs, written by the priests, were preserved by them with the greatest care. They were never revealed to strangers. To reveal a rite, or a formula, would have been to betray the religion of the city, and to deliver its gods to the enemy. For greater precaution they were concealed from the citizens themselves, and the priests alone were allowed to know them.

[2] Demosthenes, in Neæram, 116, 117.
[3] Pausanias, IV. 27. Plutarch, Cont. Colot., 17. Pollux, VIII. 128. Pliny, N. H., XIII. 21. Val. Max., I. 1, 3. Varro, L. L., VI. 16. Censorinus, 17. Festus, v. Rituales.
[4] Plutarch, Theseus, 16. Tac., Ann., IV. 43. Ælian, H. V., II. 39.

In the minds of the people, all that was ancient was venerable and sacred. When a Roman wished to say that anything
was dear to him, he said, "That is ancient for me." The
Greeks had the same expression. The cities clung strongly to
their past, because they found in the past all the motives as
well as all the rules of their religion. They had need to look
back, for it was upon recollections and traditions that their
entire worship rested. Thus history had for the ancients a
greater importance than it has for us. It existed a long time
before Herodotus and Thucydides, — written or unwritten; as
simple oral traditions, or in books, it was contemporary with
the birth of cities. There was no city, however small and
obscure it might be, that did not pay the greatest attention to
preserving an account of what had passed within it. This was
not vanity, but religion. A city did not believe it had the right
to allow anything to be forgotten; for everything in its history
was connected with its worship.

History commenced, indeed, with the act of foundation,
and recorded the sacred name of the founder. It was continued
with the legend of the gods of the city, its protecting heroes. It
taught the date, the origin, and the reason of every worship,
and explained its obscure rites. The prodigies which the gods
of the country had performed, and by which they had manifested their power, their goodness, or their anger, were
recorded there; there were described the ceremonies by which
the priests had skilfully turned a bad presage, or had appeased
the anger of the gods; there were recorded the epidemics which
had afflicted the city, on what day a temple had been consecrated, and for what reason a sacrifice had been established;
there were recorded all the events which related to religion,
the victories that proved the assistance of the gods, and in
which these gods had often been seen fighting, the defeats which
indicated their anger, and for which it had been necessary
to institute an expiatory sacrifice. All this was written for the
instruction and the piety of the descendants. All this history
was a material proof of the existence of the national gods; for
the events which it contained were the visible form under
which these gods had revealed themselves from age to age.
Even among these facts there were many that gave rise to
festivals and annual sacrifices. The history of the city told the

citizen what he must believe and what he must adore. Then, too, this history was written by priests. Rome had its annals of the pontiffs; the Sabine priests, the Samnite priests, and the Etruscan priests had similar ones.[5] Among the Greeks there has been preserved to us the recollection of the books or secret annals of Athens, Sparta, Delphi, Naxos, and Tarentum.[6] When Pausanias travelled in Greece, in the time of Hadrian, the priests of every city related to him the old local histories. They did not invent them, but had learned them in their annals. This sort of history was entirely local. It commenced at the foundation, because what had happened before this date was of no interest to the city; and this explains why the ancients have so completely ignored their earliest history. Their records related only to affairs in which the city had been engaged, and gave no heed to the rest of the world. Every city had its special history, as it had its religion and its calendar.

We can easily believe that these city annals were exceedingly dry, and very whimsical, both in substance and in form. They were not a work of art, but a religious work. Later came the writers, the narrators, like Herodotus; the thinkers, like Thucydides. History then left the hands of the priests, and became something quite different. Unfortunately these beautiful and brilliant writings still leave us to regret the early annals of the cities, and all that they would have taught us of the beliefs and the inner life of the ancients. But these books, which appear to have been kept secret, which never left the sanctuaries, which were never copied, and which the priests alone read, have all perished, and only a faded recollection of them has remained.

This trace, it is true, has a great value for us. Without it we should perhaps have a right to reject all that Greece and Rome relate to us of their antiquities; all those accounts, that appear to us so improbable, because they differ so much from our habits and our manner of thinking and acting, might pass for the product of men's imaginations. But this trace of the old

---

[5] Dionysius, II. 49. Livy, X. 33. Cicero, *De Divin.*, II. 41; I. 33; II. 23. Censorinus, 12, 17. Suetonius, *Claudius*, 42. Macrobius, I. 12; V. 19. Solin., II. 9. Servius, VII. 678; VIII. 398. Letters of Marc. Aurel., IV. 4.

[6] Plutarch, *Cont. Colot.*, 17; *Solon*, 11; *Moral.*, 869. Athenæus, XI. 49. Tac., *Ann.*, IV. 43.

annals that has remained shows us the pious respect which the ancients had for their history. Every city had archives, in which the facts were religiously preserved as fast as they took place. In these sacred books every page was contemporary with the event which it recorded. It was materially impossible to alter these documents, for the priests had the care of them; and it was greatly to the interest of religion that they should remain unalterable. It was not even easy for the pontiff, as he wrote the lines, skilfully to insert statements contrary to the truth; for he believed that all events came from the gods; that he re-vealed their will, and that he was giving future generations sub-jects for pious souvenirs, and even for sacred acts. Every event that took place in the city commenced at once to form a part of the religion of the future. With such beliefs we can easily understand that there would be much involuntary error — a result of credulity, of a love for the marvellous, and of faith in the national gods; but voluntary falsehood is not to be thought of; for that would have been impious; it would have violated the sanctity of the annals, and corrupted the religion. We can believe, therefore, that in these books, if all was not true, there was nothing at least that the priests did not believe. Now, for the historian who seeks to pierce the obscurity of those early times, it is a great source of confidence to know that, if he has to deal with errors, he has not to deal with imposture. These errors even, having still the advantage of being contemporary with those ancient ages that he is studying, may reveal to him, if not the details of events, at least the sincere convictions of men.

These annals, it is true, were kept secret; neither Herodotus nor Livy read them. But several passages of ancient authors prove that some parts became public, and that fragments of them came to the knowledge of historians.

There were, moreover, besides the annals, — these written and authentic documents, — oral traditions, which were per-petuated among the people of a city; not vague and indifferent traditions, like ours, but traditions dear to the cities, such as did not vary to please the imagination, such as men were not at liberty to modify; for they formed a part of the worship, and were composed of narrations and songs that were repeated from year to year in the religious festivals. These sacred and

unchangeable hymns fixed the memory of events, and perpetually revived the traditions. Doubtless we should be wrong
in believing that these traditions had the exactitude of the
annals. The desire to praise the gods might be stronger than
the love of truth. Still they must have been at least a reflection
of the annals, and must generally have been in accord with
them. For the priests who drew up and who read the annals
were the same who presided at the festivals where these old
lays were sung.

There came a time, too, when these annals were divulged.
Rome finally published hers; those of other Italian cities were
known; the priests of Greek cities no longer made any scruple
of relating what theirs contained. Men studied and compiled
from these authentic monuments. There was formed a school
of learned men from Varro and Verrius Flaccus to Aulus
Gellius and Macrobius. Light was thrown upon all ancient
history. Some errors were corrected which had found their way
into the traditions, and which the historians of the preceding
period had repeated: men learned, for example, that Porsenna
had taken Rome, and that gold had been paid to the Gauls.
The age of historical criticism had begun. But it is worthy of
remark that this criticism, which went back to the sources, and
studied the annals, found nothing there that authorized it to
reject the historic whole which writers like Herodotus and Livy
had constructed.

Chapter IX

GOVERNMENT OF THE CITY. THE KING

1. Religious Authority of the King.

WE should not picture to ourselves a city, at its foundation,
deliberating on the form of government that it will adopt,
devising and discussing its laws, and preparing its institutions.
It was not thus that laws were made and that governments
were established. The political institutions of the city were
born with the city itself and on the same day with it. Every
member of the city carried them within himself, for the germ
of them was in each man's belief and religion.

Religion prescribed that the hearth should always have a supreme priest. It did not permit the sacerdotal authority to be divided. The domestic hearth had a high priest, who was the father of the family; the hearth of the cury, had its curio, or phratriarch; every tribe, in the same manner, had its religious chief, whom the Athenians called the king of the tribe. It was also necessary that the city religion should have its supreme priest.

This priest of the public hearth bore the name of king. Sometimes they gave him other titles. As he was especially the priest of the prytaneum, the Greeks preferred to call him the prytane; sometimes also they called him the archon. Under these different names of king, prytane, and archon we are to see a personage who is, above all, the chief of the worship. He keeps up the fire, offers the sacrifice, pronounces the prayer, and presides at the religious repasts.

It may be worth while to offer proof that the ancient kings of Greece and Italy were priests. In Aristotle we read, "The care of the public sacrifices of the city belongs, according to religious custom, not to special priests, but to those men who derive their dignity from the hearth, and who in one place are called kings, in another prytanes, and in a third archons."[1] Thus writes Aristotle, the man who best understood the constitution of the Greek cities. This passage, so precise, shows, in the first place, that the three words *king, prytane,* and *archon* were a long time synonymous. So true is this, that an ancient historian, Charon of Lampsacus, writing a book about the kings of Lacedæmon, entitled it *Archons and Prytanes of the Lacedæmonians.*[2] It shows also that the personage to whom was applied indifferently one of these three names — perhaps all of them at the same time — was the priest of the city, and that the worship of the public hearth was the source of his dignity and power.

This sacerdotal character of primitive royalty is clearly indicated by the ancient writers. In Æschylus the daughters of Danaus address the king of Argos in these terms: "Thou art the supreme prytane, and watchest over the hearth of this country."[3] In Euripides, Orestes, the murderer of his mother,

[1] Aristotle, *Polit.,* VII. 5, 11 (VI. 8). Comp. Dionysius, II. 65.
[2] Suidas, v. Χαρων.   [3] Æsch., *Supp.,* 361 (357).

says to Menelaus, "It is just that I, the son of Agamemnon, should reign at Argos." And Menelaus replies, "Art thou, then fit, — thou, a murderer, — to touch the vessels of lustral water for the sacrifices? Art thou fit to slay the victims?"[4] The principal office of a king was, therefore, to perform religious ceremonies. An ancient king of Sicyon was deposed because, having soiled his hands by a murder, he was no longer in a condition to offer the sacrifices.[5] Being no longer fit for a priest, he could no longer be king.

Homer and Virgil represent the kings as continually occupied with sacred ceremonies. We know from Demosthenes that the ancient kings of Attica performed themselves all the sacrifices that were prescribed by the religion of the city; and from Xenophon that the kings of Sparta were the chiefs of the Lacedæmonian religion.[6] The Etruscan Lucumones were, at the same time, magistrates, military chiefs, and pontiffs.[7]

The case was not at all different with the Roman kings. Tradition always represents them as priests. The first was Romulus, who was acquainted with the science of augury, and who founded the city in accordance with religious rites. The second was Numa: he fulfilled, Livy tells us, the greater part of the priestly functions; but he foresaw that his successors, often having wars to maintain, would not always be able to take care of the sacrifices, and instituted the flamens to replace the kings when the latter were absent from Rome. Thus the Roman priesthood was only an emanation from the primitive royalty.

These king-priests were inaugurated with a religious ceremonial. The new king, being conducted to the summit of the Capitoline Hill, was seated upon a stone seat, his face turned towards the south. On his left was seated an augur, his head covered with sacred fillets, and holding in his hand the augur's staff. He marked off certain lines in the heavens, pronounced a prayer, and, placing his hand upon the king's head, supplicated the gods to show, by a visible sign, that this chief was agreeable to them. Then, as soon as a flash of lighting or a

---

[4] Euripides, *Orestes*, 1605.
[5] Nic. Damas., *Frag. Hist. Gr.*, t. III. p. 394.
[6] Demosthenes, *in Neær.* Xenophon, *Gov. Laced.*, 13.
[7] Virgil, X. 175. Livy, V. 1. Censorinus, 4.

flight of birds had manifested the will of the gods, the new king took possession of his charge. Livy describes this ceremony for the installation of Numa; Dionysius assures us that it took place for all the kings, and after the kings, for the consuls; he adds that it was still performed in his time.[8] There was a reason for such a custom; as the king was to be supreme chief of the religion, and the safety of the city was to depend upon his prayers and sacrifices, it was important to make sure, in the first place, that this king was accepted by the gods.

The ancients have left us no account of the manner in which the Spartan kings were elected; but we may be certain that the will of the gods was consulted in the election. We can even see from old customs which survived to the end of the history of Sparta, that the ceremony by which the gods were consulted was renewed every nine years; so fearful were they that the king might lose the favor of the divinity. "Every nine years," says Plutarch, "the Ephors chose a very clear night, but without a moon, and sat in silence, with their eyes fixed upon the heavens. If they saw a star cross from one quarter of the heavens to the other, this indicated that their kings were guilty of some neglect of the gods. The kings were then suspended from their duties till an oracle came from Delphi to relieve them from their forfeiture."[9]

2. *Political Authority of the King.*

Just as in the family the authority was inherent in the priesthood, and the father, as head of the domestic worship, was at the same time judge and master, so the high priest of the city was at the same time its political chief. The altar — to borrow an expression of Aristotle — conferred dignity and power upon him. There is nothing to surprise us in this confusion of the priesthood and the civil power. We find it at the beginning of almost all societies, either because during the infancy of a people nothing but religion will command their obedience, or because our nature feels the need of not submitting to any other power than that of a moral idea.

We have seen how the religion of the city was mixed up with everything. Man felt himself at every moment depend-

8 Livy, I. 18. Dionysius, II. 6; IV. 80.
9 Plutarch, *Agis*, 11.

ent upon his gods, and consequently upon this priest, who was
placed between them and himself. This priest watched over the
sacred fire; it was, as Pindar says, his daily worship that saved
the city every day.[10] He it was who knew the formulas and
prayers which the gods could not resist; at the moment of
combat, he it was who slew the victim, and drew upon the
army the protection of the gods. It was very natural that a man
armed with such a power should be accepted and recognized
as a leader. From the fact that religion had so great a part in
the government, in the courts, and in war, it necessarily followed that the priest was at the same time magistrate, judge,
and military chief. "The kings of Sparta," says Aristotle,[11]
"have three attributes: they perform the sacrifices, they command in war, and they administer justice." Dionysius of
Halicarnassus expresses himself in the same manner regarding
the kings of Rome.

The constitutional rules of this monarchy were very simple;
it was not necessary to seek long for them; they flowed from
the rules of the worship themselves. The founder, who had
established the sacred fire, was naturally the first priest.
Hereditary succession was the constant rule, in the beginning,
for the transmission of this worship. Whether the sacred fire
was that of a family or that of a city, religion prescribed that
the care of supporting it should always pass from father to son.
The priesthood was therefore hereditary, and the power went
with it.[12]

A well-known fact in the history of Greece proves, in a
striking manner that, in the beginning, the kingly office belonged to the man who set up the hearth of the city. We know
that the population of the Ionian colonies was not composed
of Athenians, but that it was a mixture of Pelasgians, Æolians,
Abantes, and Cadmeans. Yet all the hearths of the cities were
placed by the members of the religious family of Codrus.

It followed that these colonists, instead of having for leaders
men of their own race, — the Pelasgi a Pelasgian, the Abantes

---

[10] Pindar, *Nem.*, XI. 5.   [11] Aristotle, *Politics*, III. 9.
[12] We speak here only of the early ages of cities. We shall see,
farther on, that a time came when hereditary succession ceased to be
the rule, and we shall explain why at Rome royalty was not hereditary.

an Albantian, the Æolians an Æolian, — all gave the royalty in their twelve cities to the Codridæ.[13] Assuredly these persons had not acquired their authority by force, for they were almost the only Athenians in this numerous agglomeration. But as they had established the sacred fires, it was their office to maintain them. The royalty was, therefore, bestowed upon them without a contest, and remained hereditary in their families. Battus had founded Cyrene in Africa; and the Battiadæ were a long time in possession of the royal dignity there. Protis founded Marseilles; and the Protiadæ, from father to son, performed the priestly office there, and enjoyed great privileges.

It was not force, then, that created chiefs and kings in those ancient cities. It would not be correct to say that the first man who was king there was a lucky soldier. Authority flowed from the worship of the sacred fire. Religion created the king in the city, as it had made the family chief in the house. A belief, an unquestionable and imperious belief, declared that the hereditary priest of the hearth was the depositary of the holy duties and the guardian of the gods. How could one hesitate to obey such a man? A king was a sacred being; βασιλεῖς ἱεροί, says Pindar. Men saw in him, not a complete God, but at least "the most powerful man to call down the anger of the gods;[14] the man without whose aid no prayer was heard, no sacrifice accepted.

This royalty, semi-religious, semi-political, was established in all cities, from their foundation, without effort on the part of the kings, without resistance on the part of the subjects. We do not see at the origin of the ancient nations those fluctuations and struggles which mark the painful establishment of modern societies. We know how long a time was necessary, after the fall of the Roman empire, to restore the rules of a regular society. Europe saw, during several centuries, opposing principles dispute for the government of the people, and the people at times rejecting all social organization. No such spectacle was seen in ancient Greece, or in ancient Italy; their history does not commence with conflicts: revolutions appeared only at the close.

Among these populations, society formed slowly and by degrees, while passing from the family to the tribe, and from the tribe to the city, but without shock and without a struggle.

[13] Herodotus, I. 142–148. Pausanias, VI. Strabo.
[14] Sophocles, OEdipus Rex, 34.

Royalty was established quite naturally, in the family first, in the city later. It was not devised in the imagination of a few; it grew out of a necessity that was manifest to the eyes of all. During long ages it was peaceable, honored, and obeyed. The kings had no need of material force; they had neither army nor treasury; but, sustained by a faith that had a powerful influence over the mind, their authority was sacred and inviolable.

A revolution, of which we shall speak farther on, overturned the kingly power in every city; but when it fell, it left no rancor in the hearts of men. That contempt, mingled with hatred, which ordinarily attends on fallen grandeur, it never experienced. Fallen as it was, the affection and respect of men remained attached to its memory. In Greece we see something which is not very common in history: in the cities where the royal family did not become extinct, not only was it not expelled, but the same men who had despoiled it of power continued to honor it. At Ephesus, at Marseilles, at Cyrene, the royal family, deprived of power, remained surrounded with the respect of the people, and even retained the title and insignia of royalty.[15]

The people established republican institutions; but the name of king, far from becoming a reproach, remained a venerated title. It is customary to say that this word was odious and despised. This is a singular error; the Romans applied it to the gods in their prayers. If the usurpers dared not assume this title, it was not because it was odious, but rather because it was sacred.[16] In Greece monarchy was many times restored in the cities; but the new monarchs never claimed the right to be called *kings,* and were satisfied to be called *tyrants.* What made the difference in these names was not the more or fewer moral qualities found in the sovereign. It was not the custom to call a good prince *king* and a bad one *tyrant.* Religion was what distinguished one from the other. The primitive kings had performed the duties of priests, and had derived their authority from the sacred fire; the tyrants of a later epoch were merely political chiefs, and owed their elevation to force or election only.

15 Strabo, IV. 171; XIV. 632; XIII. 608. Athenæus, XIII. 576.

16 *Sanctitas regum,* Suetonius, *Julius Cæsar,* 6. Livy, III. 39. Cicero, *Repub.,* I. 33.

Chapter X

THE MAGISTRACY

THE union of the political authority and the priesthood in the same person did not cease with royalty. The revolution which established the republican *régime*, did not separate functions whose connection appeared natural, and was then the fundamental law of human society. The magistrate who replaced the king was, like him, a priest, and at the same time a political chief.

Sometimes this annual magistrate bore the sacred title of king.[1] In other places the title of *prytane*,[2] which he retained, indicated his principal function. In other cities the title of *archon* prevailed. At Thebes, for example, the first magistrate was called by this name; but what Plutarch says of this office shows that it differed little from the priesthood. This archon, during his term of office, was required to wear a crown,[3] as became a priest; religion forbade him to let his hair grow, or to carry any iron object upon his person — a regulation which made him resemble the Roman flamen. The city of Platæa also had an archon, and the religion of this city required that, during his whole term of office, he should be clothed in white[4] — that is to say, in the sacred color.

The Athenian archons, when entering upon their duty, ascended the Acropolis, their heads crowned with myrtle, and offered a sacrifice to the divinity of the city.[5] It was also a custom for them, in the exercise of their duty, to wear a crown of leaves upon their heads.[6] Now, it is certain that the crown, which in the course of time became, and has remained, the symbol of power, was then only a religious emblem, an exterior

---

[1] At Megara, at Samothrace. Livy, XLV. 5. Boeckh, *Corp. Inscr.*, 1052.
[2] Pindar, *Nem.*, XI.
[3] Plutarch, *Rom. Quest.*, 40.
[4] Plutarch, *Aristides*, 21.
[5] Thucydides, VIII. 70. Apollodorus, *Fragment*, 21 (coll. Didot).
[6] Demosthenes, *in Meidiam*, 33. Æschines, *in Timarch.*, 19.

sign, which accompanied prayer and sacrifice.[7] Among the nine archons the one called king was especially a religious chief; but each of his colleagues had some sacerdotal function to fulfil, some sacrifice to offer to the gods.[8]

The Greeks had a general expression to designate magistrates; they said οι εν τελει, — which signified, literally, those who are to accomplish the sacrifice;[9] an old expression, indicating the idea that was entertained of the magistrate in early times. Pindar says of these personages that, by the offerings which they make to the sacred fire, they assure the safety of the city.

At Rome the first act of the consul was to offer a sacrifice in the forum. Victims were brought to the public square; when the pontiff had declared them worthy of being offered, the consul immolated them with his own hand, while a herald enjoined a religious silence upon the multitude, and a flute-player sounded the sacred air.[10] A few days later, the consul repaired to Lavinium, whence the Roman penates had come, and offered another sacrifice.

When we examine the character of the magistrate among the ancients with a little attention, we see how slightly he resembles the chief of state of modern societies. Priesthood, justice, and command are confounded in his person. He represents the city, which is a religious association, as much, at least, as a political one. He has in his hands the auspices, the rites, prayer, the protection of the gods. A consul is something more than a man; he is a mediator between man and the divinity. To his fortune is attached the public fortune; he is, as it were, the tutelary genius of the city. The death of a consul is calamitous to the republic.[11] When the consul Claudius Nero left his army to fly to the succor of his colleague, Livy shows us into how great alarm Rome was thrown for the fate of this army; this was because, deprived of its chief, the army was at the same time deprived of its celestial protection; with the

---

[7] Plutarch, *Nicias*, 3; *Phocion*, 37. Cicero, *in Verr.*, IV. 50.

[8] Pollux, VIII. ch. IX. Lycurgus (coll. Didot), t. II. p. 362.

[9] Thucydides, I. 10; II. 10; III. 36; IV. 65. Comp. Herodotus, I. 133; III. 18; Æschylus, *Pers.*, 204; *Agam.*, 1202; Euripides, *Trach.*, 238.

[10] Cicero, *De Lege Agr.*, II. 34. Livy, XXI. 63. Macrobius, III. 3.

[11] Livy, XXVII. 40.

consul, the auspices have gone — that is to say, religion and the gods.

The other Roman magistracies, which were, in a certain sense, members successively detached from the consulship, like that office, united sacerdotal and political attributes. We have seen the censor, on certain days, with a crown upon his head, offering a sacrifice in the name of the city, and striking down a victim with his own hand. The pretors and the curule ediles presided at religious festivals.[12] There was no magistrate who had not some sacred act to perform; for, in the minds of the ancients, all authority ought to have some connection with religion. The tribunes of the people were the only ones who had no sacrifice to offer; but they were not counted among the real magistrates. We shall see, farther along, that their authority was of an entirely exceptional nature.

The sacerdotal character belonging to the magistrate is shown, above all, in the manner of his election. In the eyes of the ancients the votes of men were not sufficient to establish the ruler of a city. So long as the primitive royalty lasted, it appeared natural that this ruler should be designated by birth, by virtue of the religious law which prescribed that the son should succeed the father in every priestly office; birth seemed sufficiently to reveal the will of the gods. When revolutions had everywhere suppressed this royalty, men appear to have sought, in the place of birth, a mode of election which the gods might not have to disavow. The Athenians, like many Greek peoples, saw no better way than to draw lots; but we must not form a wrong idea of this procedure, which has been made a subject of reproach against the Athenian democracy; and for this reason it is necessary that we attempt to penetrate the view of the ancients on this point. For them the lot was not chance; it was the revelation of the divine will. Just as they had recourse to it in the temples to discover the secrets of the gods, so the city had recourse to it for the choice of its magistrate. It was believed that the gods designated the most worthy by making his name leap out of the urn. This was the opinion of Plato himself, who says, "He on whom the lot falls is the ruler, and is dear to the gods; and this we affirm to be quite just. The

12 Varro, *L. L.*, VI. 54. Athenæus, XIV. 79.

officers of the temple shall be appointed by lot; in this way their election will be committed to God, who will do what is agreeable to him." The city believed that in this manner it received its magistrates from the gods.[13]

Affairs are substantially the same at Rome. The designation of a consul did not belong to men. The will or the caprice of the people could not legitimately create a magistrate. This, therefore, was the manner in which the consul was chosen. A magistrate in charge — that is to say, a man already in possession of the sacred character and of the auspices — indicated among the *dies fasti* the one on which the consul ought to be named. During the night which preceded this day, he watched in the open air, his eyes fixed upon the heavens, observing the signs which the gods sent, whilst he pronounced mentally the name of some candidate for the magistracy.[14] If the presages were favorable, it was because the gods accepted the candidate. The next day the people assembled in the *Campus Martius;* the same one who had consulted the gods presided at the assembly. He pronounced in a loud voice the names of the candidates concerning whom he had taken the auspices. If among those who sought the consulship there was one for

---

13 Plato, *Laws*, III. 690; VI. 759. Comp. Demetrius Phalereus, *Fragm.*, 4. It is surprising that modern historians represent the drawing of lots as an invention of the Athenian democracy. It was, on the contrary, in full rigor under the rule of the aristocracy (Plutarch, *Pericles,* 9), and appears to have been as old as the archonship itself. Nor is it a democratic procedure: we know, indeed, that even in the time of Lysias and of Demosthenes, the names of all the citizens were not put in the urn (Lysias, *Orat., de Invalido, c.* 13; *in Andocidem, c.* 4): for a still stronger reason was this true when the Eupatrids only, or the Pentakosiomedimni could be archons. Passages of Plato show clearly what idea the ancients had of the drawing of lots; the thought which caused it to be employed for magistrate-priests like the archons, or for senators charged with holy duties like the prytanes, was a religious idea, and not a notion of equality. It is worthy of remark, that when the democracy gained the upper hand, it reserved the selection by lot for the choice of archons, to whom it left no real power, and gave it up in the choice of strategi, who then had the true authority. So that there was drawing of lots for magistracies which dated from the aristocratic age, and election for those that dated from the age of the democracy.

14 Valerius Maximus, I. 1, 3. Plutarch, *Marcellus*, 5.

whom the auspices had not been favorable, his name was omitted.[15] The people voted upon those names only which had been pronounced by the president.[16] If the president named but two candidates, the people necessarily voted for them; if he named three, they chose two of them. The assembly never had the right to vote for other men than those whom the president had designated; for the auspices had been for those only, and for those only had the consent of the gods been assured.

This mode of election, which was scrupulously followed in the first ages of the republic, explains some peculiarities of Roman history which at first surprise us. We see, for example, that quite frequently the people are unanimous for two men for the consulship, and still they are not elected. This is because the president has not taken the auspices concerning these two men, or the auspices have not been favorable. On the other hand, we have seen the people elect to the consulship men whom they detested.[17] This was because the president pronounced only these two names. It was absolutely necessary to vote for them, for the vote was not expressed by "yes" or "no;" every vote was required to contain two names, and none could be written except those that had been designated. The people, when candidates were presented who were odious to them, could indeed show their displeasure by retiring without a vote; but there always remained in the enclosure citizens enough to make up a quorum.

Here we see how great was the power of the president of the comitia, and we no longer wonder at the expression, *Creat consules,* which referred not to the people, but to the president of the comitia. It was of him, indeed, rather than of the people, that it might be said, "He creates the consuls;" for he was the one who discovered the will of the gods. If he did not create the consuls, it was at least through him that the gods created them. The power of the people went no farther than to ratify the election, or, at most, to select among three or four names, if the auspices had been equally favorable to three or four candidates.

[15] Livy, XXXIX. 39. Velleius, II. 92. Valerius Maximus, III. 8, 3.
[16] Dionysius, IV. 84; V. 19; V. 72; V. 77; VI. 49.
[17] Livy, II. 42; II. 43.

Doubtless this method of procedure was very advantageous to the Roman aristocracy; but we should deceive ourselves if we saw in all this merely a ruse invented by them. Such a ruse was never thought of in the ages when they believed in this religion. Politically it was useless in the first ages, since at that time the patricians had a majority in voting. It might even have turned against them, by investing a single man with exorbitant power. The only explanation that can be given of this custom, or rather, of these rites of election, is, that every one then sincerely believed that the choice of the magistrates belonged, not to the people, but to the gods. The man in whose hands the religion and the fortune of the city were to be placed, ought to be revealed by the divine voice.

The first rule for the election of a magistrate is the one given by Cicero: "That he be named according to the rites." If, several months afterwards, the senate was told that some rite had been neglected, or badly performed, it ordered the consuls to abdicate, and they obeyed. The examples are very numerous; and if, in case of two or three of them, we may believe that the senate was very glad to be rid of an ill-qualified or ill-intentioned consul, the greater part of the time, on the contrary, we cannot inpute other motives to them than religious scruples.

When the lot or the auspices had designated an archon or a consul, there was, it is true, a sort of proof by which the merits of the newly-elected officer were examined. But even this will show us what the city wished to find in its magistrate; and we shall see that it sought not the most courageous warrior, not the ablest and most upright man in peace, but the one best loved by the gods. Indeed, the Athenian senate inquired of the magistrate elect if he had any bodily defect, if he possessed a domestic god, if his family had always been faithful to his worship, if he himself had always fulfilled his duties towards the dead.[18] Why these questions? Because a bodily defect — a sign of the anger of the gods — rendered a man unfit to fill any priestly office, and consequently to exercise any magistracy; because he who had no family worship ought not to have a national worship, and was not qualified to offer the sacrifices in the name of the city; because, if his family had not always been faithful to his worship, — that is to say, if one of his

18 Plato, *Laws*, VI. Xenophon, *Mem.*, II. Pollux, VIII. 85, 86, 95.

ancestors had committed one of those acts which affect religion, — the hearth was forever contaminated, and the descendants were detested by the gods; finally, because, if he himself had neglected the tomb of his dead, he was exposed to their dangerous anger, and was pursued by invisible enemies. The city would have been very daring to have confided its fortunes to such a man. These are the principal questions that were addressed to one who was about to become a magistrate. It appeared that men did not trouble themselves about his character or his knowledge. They tried especially to assure themselves that he was qualified for the priestly office, and that the religion of the city would not be compromised in his hands.

This sort of examination was also in use at Rome. We have not, it is true, any information as to the questions which the consul was required to answer. But it is enough to know that this examination was made by the pontiffs.[19]

Chapter XI

THE LAW

AMONG the Greeks and Romans, as among the Hindus, law was at first a part of religion. The ancient codes of the cities were a collection of rites, liturgical directions, and prayers, joined with legislative regulations. The laws concerning property and those concerning succession were scattered about in the midst of rules for sacrifices, for burial, and for the worship of the dead.

What remains to us of the oldest laws of Rome, which were called the Royal Laws, relates as often to the worship as to the relations of civil life. One forbade a guilty woman to approach the altars; another forbade certain dishes to be served in the sacred repasts; a third prescribed what religious ceremony a victorious general ought to perform on re-entering the city. The code of the Twelve Tables, although more recent, still contain minute regulations concerning the religious rites of sepulture. The work of Solon was at the same time a code, a constitution, and a ritual; it regulated the order of sacrifices,

[19] Dionysius, II. 73.

and the price of victims, as well as the marriage rites and the worship of the dead.

Cicero, in his Laws, traces a plan of legislation which is not entirely imaginary. In the substance as in the form of his code, he imitates the ancient legislators. Now, these are the first laws that he writes: "Let men approach the gods with purity; let the temples of the ancestors and the dwelling of the Lares be kept up; let the priests employ in the sacred repasts only the prescribed kinds of food; let every one offer to the Manes the worship that is due them." Assuredly the Roman philosopher troubled himself little about the old religion of the Lares and Manes; but he was tracing a code in imitation of the ancient codes, and he believed himself bound to insert rules of worship.

At Rome it was a recognized truth that no one could be a good pontiff who did not know the law, and, conversely, that no one could know the law if he did not understand questions relating to religion. The pontiffs were for a long time the only jurisconsults. As there was hardly an act of life which had not some relation to religion, it followed that almost everything was submitted to the decision of these priests, and that they were the only competent judges in an infinite number of cases. All disputes regarding marriage, divorce, and the civil and religious rights of infants, were carried to their tribunal. They were judges in cases of incest as well as of celibacy. As adoption affected religion, it could not take place without the consent of the pontiff. To make a will was to break the order that religion had established for the transmission of property and of the worship. The will, therefore, in the beginning, required to be authorized by the pontiff. As the limits of every man's land were established by religion, whenever two neighbors had a dispute about boundaries, they had to plead before the priests called *fratres arvales*. This explains why the same men were pontiffs and jurists — law and religion were but one.[1]

At Athens the archon and the king had very nearly the same judicial functions as the Roman pontiff.[2]

[1] Hence this old definition, which the jurisconsults preserved even to Justinian's time—*Jurisprudentia est rerum divinarum atque humanarum notitia.* Cf. Cicero, *De Legib.* II. 9; II. 19; *De Arusp. Resp.*, 7. Dionysius, II. 73. Tacitus *Ann.*, I. 10; *Hist.*, I. 15. Dion Cassius, XLVIII. 44. Pliny, *N. H.*, XVIII. 2. Aulus Gellius, V. 19; XV. 27.

[2] Pollux, VIII. 90.

The origin of ancient laws appears clearly. No man invented them. Solon, Lycurgus, Minos, Numa, might have reduced the laws of their cities to writing, but they could not have made them. If we understand by legislator a man who creates a code by the power of his genius, and who imposes it upon other men, this legislator never existed among the ancients. Nor did ancient law originate with the votes of the people. The idea that a certain number of votes might make a law did not appear in the cities till very late, and only after two revolutions had transformed them. Up to that time laws had appeared to men as something ancient, immutable, and venerable. As old as the city itself, the founder had established them at the same time that he established the hearth — *moresque viris et mœnia ponit.* He instituted them at the same time that he instituted the religion. Still it could not be said that he had prepared them himself. Who, then, was the true author of them? When we spoke above of the organization of the family, and of the Greek and Roman laws which regulated property, succession, wills, and adoption, we observed how exactly these laws corresponded to the beliefs of ancient generations. If we compare these laws with natural equity, we often find them opposed to it, and we can easily see that it was not in the notion of absolute right and in the sentiment of justice, that they were sought for. But place these laws by the side of the worship of the dead and of the sacred fire, compare them with the rules of this primitive religion, and they appear in perfect accord with all this.

Man did not need to study his conscience and say, "This is just; this is unjust." Ancient law was not produced in this way. But man believed that the sacred hearth, in virtue of the religious law, passed from father to son; from this it followed that the house was hereditary property. The man who had buried his father in his field believed that the spirit of the dead one took possession of this field forever, and required a perpetual worship of his posterity. As a result of this, the field, the domain of the dead, and place of sacrifice, became the inalienable property of a family. Religion said, "The son continues the worship — not the daughter;" and the law said, with the religion, "The son inherits — the daughter does not inherit; the nephew by the males inherits, but not the nephew on the female side." This was the manner in which the laws were made; they presented themselves without being sought. They were the direct and necessary consequence of the belief; they were religion itself applied to the relations of men among themselves.

The ancients said their laws came from the gods. The Cretans attributed their laws, not to Minos, but to Jupiter. The Lacedæmonians believed that their legislator was not Lycurgus, but Apollo. The Romans believed that Numa wrote under the dictation of one of the most powerful divinities of ancient Italy — the goddess Egeria. The Etruscans had received their laws from the god Tages. There is truth in all these traditions. The veritable legislator among the ancients was not a man, but the religious belief which men entertained.

The laws long remained sacred. Even at the time when it was admitted that the will of a man or the votes of a people might make a law, it was still necessary that religion should be consulted, and at least that its consent should be obtained. At Rome it was not believed that a unanimous vote was sufficient to make a law binding; the decision of the people required to be ratified by the pontiffs, and the augurs were required to attest that the gods were favorable to the proposed law.[3]

One day, when the tribunes of the people wished to have a law adopted by the assembly of the tribes, a patrician said to them, "What right have you to make a new law, or to touch existing laws? You, who have not the auspices, you, who, in your assemblies, perform no religious acts, what have you in common with religion and sacred things, among which must be reckoned the laws?"[4]

From this we can understand the respect and attachment which the ancients long had for their laws. In them they saw no human work, but one whose origin was holy. It was no vain word when Plato said, "To obey the laws is to obey the gods." He does no more than to express the Greek idea, when, in Crito, he exhibits Socrates giving his life because the laws demanded it of him. Before Socrates, there was written upon the rock of Thermopylæ, "Passer-by, go and tell Sparta that we

[3] Dionysius, IX. 41; IX. 49.
[4] Dionysius, X. 4. Livy, III. 31.

lie here in obedience to its laws." The law among the ancients was always holy, and in the time of royalty it was the queen of the kings. In the time of the republic it was the queen of the people. To disobey it was sacrilege.

In principle the laws were immutable, since they were divine. It is worthy of remark that they were never abrogated. Men could indeed make new ones, but old ones still remained, however they might conflict with the new ones. The code of Draco was not abolished by that of Solon;[5] nor were the Royal Laws by those of the Twelve Tables. The stone on which the laws were engraved was inviolable; or, at most, the least scrupulous only thought themselves permitted to turn it round. This principle was the great cause of the confusion which is observable among ancient laws.

Contradictory laws and those of different epochs were found together, and all claimed respect. In an oration of Isæus we find two men contesting an inheritance; each quotes a law in his favor; the two laws are absolute contraries, and are equally sacred. In the same manner the code of Manu preserves the ancient law which establishes primogeniture, and has another by the side of it which enjoins an equal division among the brothers.

The ancient law never gave any reasons. Why should it? It was not bound to give them; it existed because the gods had made it. It was not discussed — it was imposed; it was a work of authority; men obeyed it because they had faith in it.

During long generations the laws were not written; they were transmitted from father to son, with the creed and the formula of prayer. They were a sacred tradition, which was perpetuated around the family hearth, or the hearth of the city.

The day on which men began to commit them to writing, they consigned them to the sacred books, to the rituals, among prayers and ceremonies. Varro cites an ancient law of the city of Tusculum, and adds that he read it in the sacred books of that city.[6] Dionysius of Halicarnassus, who had consulted the original documents, says that before the time of the Decemvirs all the written laws at Rome were to be found in the books

---

[5] Andocides, I. 82, 83. Demosthenes, in Everg., 71.
[6] Varro, L. L., VI. 16.

of the priests.[7] Later the laws were removed from the rituals, and were written by themselves; but the custom of depositing them in a temple continued, and priests had the care of them.

Written or unwritten, these laws were always formulated into very brief sentences, which may be compared in form to the verses of Leviticus, or the slocas of the book of Manu. It is quite probable, even, that the laws were rhythimical.[8] According to Aristotle, before the laws were written, they were sung.[9] Traces of this custom have remained in language; the Romans called the laws carmina — verses; the Greeks said νομοι — songs.[10]

These ancient verses were invariable texts. To change a letter of them, to displace a word, to alter the rhythm, was to destroy the law itself, by destroying the sacred form under which it was revealed to man. The law was like prayer, which was agreeable to the divinity only on condition that it was recited correctly, and which became impious if a single word in it was changed. In primitive law, the exterior, the letter, is everything; there is no need of seeking the sense or spirit of it. The value of the law is not in the moral principle that it contains, but in the words that make up the formula. Its force is in the sacred words that compose it.

Among the ancients, and especially at Rome, the idea of law was inseparably connected with certain sacramental words. If, for example, it was a question of contract, one was expected to say, Dari spondes? and the other was expected to reply, Spondeo. If these words were not pronounced, there was no contract. In vain the creditor came to demand payment of the debt — the debtor owed nothing; for what placed a man under obligation in this ancient law was not conscience, or the sentiment of justice; it was the sacred formula. When this formula was pronounced between two men, it established between them a legal obligation. Where there was no formula, the obligation did not exist.

The strange forms of ancient Roman legal procedure would

[7] Dionysius, X. 1. [8] Ælian, V. H., II. 39.

[9] Aristotle, Probl., XIX. 28.

[10] Νεμω, to divide; νομος division, measure, rhythm, song. See Plutarch, De Musica, p. 1133; Pindar, Pyth., XII. 41. fragm., 190 (Edit. Heyne). Scholiast on Aristophanes, Knights, 9; Νομοι καλουνται 'οι εις θεους 'υμνοι.

not surprise us if we but recollected that ancient law was a religion, a sacred text, and justice a collection of rites. The plaintiff pursues with the law — *agit lege.* By the text of the law he seizes his adversary: but let him be on his guard; to have the law on his side, he must know its terms, and pronounce them exactly. If he speaks one word for another, the law exists no longer for him, and cannot defend him. Gaius gives an account of a man whose vines had been cut by his neighbor; the fact was settled; he pronounced the law. But the law said trees; he pronounced vines, and lost his case.

Repeating the law was not sufficient. There was also needed an accompaniment of exterior signs, which were, so to say, the rites of this religious ceremony called a contract, or a case in law. For this reason at every sale the little piece of copper and the balance were employed. To buy an article, it was necessary to touch it with the hand — *mancipatio;* and if there was a dispute about a piece of property, there was a feigned combat — *manuum consertio.* Hence were derived the forms of liberation, those of emancipation, those of a legal action, and all the pantomime of legal procedure.

As law was a part of religion, it participated in the mysterious character of all this religion of the cities. The legal formulas, like those of religion, were kept secret. They were concealed from the stranger, and even from the plebeian. This was not because the patricians had calculated that they should possess a great power in the exclusive knowledge of the law, but because the law, by its origin and nature, long appeared to be a mystery, to which one could be initiated only after having first been initiated into the national worship and the domestic worship.

The religious origin of ancient law also explains to us one of the principal characteristics of this law. Religion was purely *civil*, that is to say, peculiar to each city. There could flow from it, therefore, only a *civil* law. But it is necessary to distinguish the sense which this word had among the ancients. When they said that the law was civil, — *jus civile*, νομοι πολιτικοι — they did not understand simply that every city had its code, as in our day every state has a code. They meant that their laws had no force, or power, except between the members of the same city. To live in a city did not make one subject to its laws and place him under their protection; one had to be a citizen. The law did not exist for the slave; no more did it exist for the stranger.

We shall see, further along, that the stranger domiciled in a city could be neither a proprietor there, nor an heir, nor a testator; he could not make a contract of any sort, or appear before the ordinary tribunals of the citizens. At Athens, if he happened to be the creditor of a citizen, he could not sue him in the courts for the payment of the debt, as the law recognized no contract as valid for him.

These provisions of ancient law were perfectly logical. Law was not born of the idea of justice, but of religion, and was not conceived as going beyond it. In order that there should be a legal relation between two men, it was necessary that there should already exist a religious relation; that is to say, that they should worship at the same hearth and have the same sacrifices. When this religious community did not exist, it did not seem that there could be any legal relation. Now, neither the stranger nor the slave had any part in the religion of the city. A foreigner and a citizen might live side by side during long years, without one's thinking of the possibility of a legal relation being established between them. Law was nothing more than one phase of religion. Where there was no common religion, there was no common law.

Chapter XII

THE CITIZEN AND THE STRANGER

THE citizen was recognized by the fact that he had a part in the religion of the city, and it was from this participation that he derived all his civil and political rights. If he renounced the worship, he renounced the rights. We have already spoken of the public meals, which were the principal ceremony of the national worship. Now, at Sparta, one who did not join in these, even if it was not his fault, ceased at once to be counted among the citizens.[1] At Athens, one who did not take part in the festivals of the national gods lost the rights of a citizen.[2]

[1] Aristotle, *Politics*, II. 6, 21 (II. 7).
[2] Boeckh, *Corp. Inscr.*, 3641, *b*.

At Rome, it was necessary to have been present at the sacred ceremony of the lustration, in order to enjoy political rights.[3] The man who had not taken part in this — that is to say, who had not joined in the common prayer and the sacrifice — lost his citizenship until the next lustration.

If we wished to give an exact definition of a citizen, we should say that it was a man who had the religion of the city.[4] The stranger, on the contrary, is one who has not access to the worship, one whom the gods of the city do not protect, and who has not even the right to invoke them. For these national gods do not wish to receive prayers and offering except from citizens; they repulse the stranger; entrance into their temples is forbidden to him, and his presence during the sacrifice is a sacrilege. Evidence of this ancient sentiment of repulsion has remained in one of the principal rites of Roman worship. The pontiff, when he sacrifices in the open air, must have his head veiled: "For before the sacred fires in the religious act which is offered to the national gods, the face of a stranger must not appear to the pontiff; the auspices would be disturbed."[5] A sacred object which fell for a moment into the hands of a stranger at once became profane. It could not recover its religious character except by an expiatory ceremony.[6] If the enemy seized upon a city, and the citizens succeeded in recovering it, above all things it was important that the temples should be purified and all the fires extinguished and rekindled. The presence of the stranger had defiled them.[7]

Thus religion established between the citizen and the stranger a profound and ineffaceable distinction. This same religion, so long as it held its sway over the minds of men,

---

[3] Velleius, II. 15. Soldiers on a campaign were excepted; but the censor was required to have their names taken, so that, having been registered in the ceremony, they were considered as present.

[4] Demosthenes, *in Neæram,* 113, 114. Being a citizen was called, in Greek, συντελειν, that is to say, making the sacrifice together, or μετειναι 'ιερων και 'οσιων.

[5] Virgil, *Æn.,* III. 406. Festus, v. *Exesto: Lictor in quibusdam sacris clamitabat, hostis exesto. Hostis,* as we know, meant stranger (Macrobius I. 17); *hostilis facies,* in Virgil, means the face of a stranger.

[6] *Digest,* XI. tit. 6, 36.

[7] Plutarch, *Aristides,* 20. Livy, V. 50.

forbade the right of citizenship to be granted to a stranger. In the time of Herodotus, Sparta had accorded it to no one except a prophet; and even for this the formal command of the oracle was necessary. Athens granted it sometimes; but with what precautions! First, it was necessary that the united people should vote by secret ballot for the admission of the stranger. Even this was nothing as yet; nine days afterwards a second assembly had to confirm the previous vote, and in this second case six thousand votes were required in favor of the admission — a number which will appear enormous when we recollect that it was very rare for an Athenian assembly to comprise so many citizens. After this a vote of the senate was required to confirm the decision of this double assembly. Finally, any citizen could oppose a sort of veto, and attack the decree as contrary to the ancient laws. Certainly there was no other public act where the legislator was surrounded with so many difficulties and precautions as that which conferred upon a stranger the title of citizen. The formalities to go through were not near so great in declaring war, or in passing a new law. Why should these men oppose so many obstacles to a stranger who wished to become a citizen? Assuredly they did not fear that in the political assemblies his vote would turn the balance. Demosthenes gives us the true motive and the true thought of the Athenians: "It is because the purity of the sacrifices must be preserved." To exclude the stranger was to "watch over the sacred ceremonies." To admit a stranger among the citizens was "to give him a part in the religion and in the sacrifices."[8] Now for such an act the people did not consider themselves entirely free, and were seized with religious scruples; for they knew that the national gods were disposed to repulse the stranger, and that the sacrifices would perhaps be rendered useless by the presence of the new comer. The gift of the rights of a citizen to a stranger was a real violation of the fundamental principles of the national religion; and it is for this reason that, in the beginning, the city was so sparing of it. We must also note that the man admitted to citizenship with so much difficulty could be neither archon nor priest. The city, indeed, permitted him to take part in its worship, but as to presiding at it, that would have been too much.

[8] Demosthenes, *in Neæram*, 89, 91, 92, 113, 114.

No one could become a citizen at Athens if he was a citizen in another city;[9] for it was a religious impossibility to be at the same time a member of two cities, as it also was to be a member of two families. One could not have two religions at the same time.

The participation in the worship carried with it the possession of rights. As the citizen might assist in the sacrifice which preceded the assembly, he could also vote at the assembly. As he could perform the sacrifices in the name of the city, he might be a prytane and an archon. Having the religion of the city, he might claim rights under its laws, and perform all the ceremonies of legal procedure.

The stranger, on the contrary, having no part in the religion, had none in the law. If he entered the sacred enclosure which the priests had traced for the assembly, he was punished with death. The laws of the city did not exist for him. If he had committed a crime, he was treated as a slave, and punished without process of law, the city owing him no legal protection.[10] When men arrived at that stage that they felt the need of having laws for the stranger, it was necessary to establish an exceptional tribunal. At Rome, in order to judge the alien, the pretor had to become an alien himself — prætor peregrinus. At Athens the judge of foreigners was the polemarch — that is to say, the magistrate who was charged with the cares of war, and of all transactions with the enemy.[11]

Neither at Rome nor at Athens could a foreigner be a proprietor.[12] He could not marry; or, if he married, his marriage was not recognized, and his children were reputed illegitimate.[13] He could not make a contract with a citizen; at any rate, the law did not recognize such a contract as valid. At first he could take no part in commerce.[14] The Roman law forbade him to inherit from a citizen, and even forbade a

---

[9] Plutarch, *Solon*, 24. Cicero, *Pro Cæcina*, 34.

[10] Aristotle, *Politics*, III. 1, 3. Plato, *Laws*, VI.

[11] Demosthenes, *in Neæram*, 49. Lysias, *in Pancleonem*.

[12] Gaius, *fr.* 234.

[13] Gaius, I. 67. Ulpian, V. 4–9. Paulus, II. 9. Aristophanes, *Birds*, 1652.

[14] Ulpian, XIX. 4. Demosthenes, *Pro Phorm.; in Eubul.*

citizen to inherit from him.[15] They pushed this principle so far, that if a foreigner obtained the rights of a citizen without his son, born before this event, obtaining the same favor, the son became a foreigner in regard to his father, and could not inherit from him.[16] The distinction between citizen and foreigner was stronger than the natural tie between father and son.

At first blush it would seem as if the aim had been to establish a system that should be vexatious towards foreigners; but there was nothing of this. Athens and Rome, on the contrary, gave him a good reception, both for commercial and political reasons. But neither their good will nor their interest could abolish the ancient laws which religion had established. This religion did not permit the stranger to become a proprietor, because he could not have any part in the religious soil of the city. It permitted neither the foreigner to inherit from the citizen, nor the citizen to inherit from the foreigner; because every transmission of property carried with it the transmission of a worship, and it was as impossible for the citizen to perform the foreigner's worship as for the foreigner to perform the citizen's.

Citizens could welcome the foreigner, watch over him, even esteem him if he was rich and honorable; but they could give him no part in their religion or their laws. The slave in certain respects was better treated than he was, because the slave, being a member of the family whose worship he shared, was connected with the city through his master; the gods protected him. The Roman religion taught, therefore, that the tomb of the slave was sacred, but that the foreigner's was not.[17]

A foreigner, to be of any account in the eyes of the law, to be enabled to engage in trade, to make contracts, to enjoy his property securely, to have the benefit of the laws of the city to protect him, must become the client of a citizen. Rome and Athens required every foreigner to adopt a patron.[18] By choosing a citizen as a patron the foreigner became connected

---

[15] Cicero, *Pro Archia*, 5. Gaius. II. 110.
[16] Pausanias, VIII. 43.
[17] *Digest*, XI. tit. 7, 2; XLVII. tit. 12, 4.
[18] Harpocration, προστατης.

with the city. Thenceforth he participated in some of the benefits of the civil law, and its protection was secured.

Chapter XIII

PATRIOTISM. EXILE

THE word *country,* among the ancients, signified the land of the fathers, *terra patria* — fatherland. The fatherland of every man was that part of the soil which his domestic or national religion had sanctified, the land where the remains of his ancestors were deposited, and which their souls occupied. His little fatherland was the family enclosure with its tomb and its hearth. The great fatherland was the city, with its prytaneum and its heroes, with its sacred enclosure, and its territory marked out by religion. "Sacred fatherland" the Greeks called it. Nor was it a vain word; this soil was, indeed, sacred to man, for his gods dwelt there. State, city, fatherland: these words were no abstraction, as they are among the moderns; they really represented a group of local divinities, with a daily worship and beliefs that had a powerful influence over the soul.

This explains the patriotism of the ancients — an energetic sentiment, which, for them, was the supreme virtue to which all other virtues tended. Whatever man held most dear was associated with the idea of country. In it he found his property, his security, his laws, his faith, his god. Losing it he lost everything. It was almost impossible that private and public interests could conflict. Plato says, "Our country begets us, nourishes us, educates us;" and Sophocles says, "It is our country that preserves us."

Such a country is not simply a dwelling-place for man. Let him leave its sacred walls, let him pass the sacred limits of its territory, and he no longer finds for himself either a religion or a social tie of any kind. Everywhere else, except in his own country, he is outside the regular life and the law; everywhere else he is without a god, and shut out from all moral life. There alone he enjoys his dignity as a man, and his duties. Only there can he be a man.

Country holds man attached to it by a sacred tie. He must love it as he loves his religion, obey it as he obeys a god. He must give himself to it entirely. He must love his country, whether it is glorious or obscure, prosperous or unfortunate. He must love it for its favors, and love it also for its severity. Socrates, unjustly condemned by it, must not love it the less. He must love it as Abraham loved his God, even to sacrificing his son for it. Above all, one must know how to die for it. The Greek or Roman rarely dies on account of his devotion to a man, or for a point of honor; but to his country he owes his life. For, if his country is attacked, his religion is attacked. He fights literally for his altars and his fires, *pro aris et focis;* for if the enemy takes his city, his altars are overturned, his fires are extinguished, his tombs are profaned, his gods are destroyed, his worship is effaced. The piety of the ancients was love of country.

The possession of a country was very precious, for the ancients imagined few chastisements more cruel than to be deprived of it. The ordinary punishment of great crimes was exile.

Exile was really the interdiction of worship. To exile a man was, according to the formula used both by the Greeks and the Romans, to cut him off from both fire and water.[1] By this fire we are to understand the sacred fire of the hearth; by this water the lustral water which served for the sacrifices. Exile, therefore, placed man beyond the reach of religion. "Let him flee," were the words of the sentence, "nor ever approach the temples. Let no citizen speak to or receive him; let no one admit him to the prayers or the sacrifices; let no one offer the lustral water."[2] Every house was defiled by his presence. The man who received him became impure by his touch. "Any one who shall have eaten or drank with him, or who shall have touched him," said the law, "should purify himself." Under the ban of this excommunication the exile could take part in no religious ceremony; he no longer had a worship, sacred repasts, or prayers; he was disinherited of his portion of religion.

1 Herodotus, VII. 231. Cratinus, *in Athenæus,* XI. 3. Cicero, *Pro Domo,* 20. Livy, XXV. 4. Ulpian, X. 3.
2 Sophocles, *OEdipus Rex,* 239. Plato, *Laws,* IX. 881.

We can easily understand that, for the ancients, God was not everywhere. If they had some vague idea of a God of the universe, this was not the one whom they considered as their providence, and whom they invoked. Every man's gods were those who inhabited his house, his canton, his city. The exile, on leaving his country behind him, also left his gods. He no longer found a religion that could console and protect him; he no longer felt that providence was watching over him; the happiness of praying was taken away. All that could satisfy the needs of his soul was far away.

Now, religion was the source whence flowed civil and political rights. The exile, therefore, lost all this in losing his religion and country. Excluded from the city worship, he saw at the same time his domestic worship taken from him, and was forced to extinguish his hearth-fire.[3] He could no longer hold property; his goods, as if he was dead, passed to his children, unless they were confiscated to the profit of the gods or of the state.[4] Having no longer a worship, he had no longer a family; he ceased to be a husband and a father. His sons were no longer in his power;[5] his wife was no longer his wife,[6] and might immediately take another husband. Regulus, when a prisoner of the enemy, the Roman law looked upon as an exile; if the senate asked his opinion, he refused to give it, because an exile was no longer a senator; if his wife and children ran to him, he repulsed their embraces, because for an exile there were no longer wife and children, —

> "Fertur pudicæ conjugis osculum
> Parvosque natos, *ut capitis minor,*
> A se removisse."[7]

"The exile," says Xenophon, "loses home, liberty, country, wife, and children." When he dies, he has not the right to be buried in the tomb of his family, for he is an alien.[8]

[3] Ovid, *Trist.,* I. 3, 43.
[4] Pindar, *Pyth.,* IV. 517. Plato, *Laws,* IX. 877. Diodorus, XIII. 49. Dionysius, XI. 46. Livy, III. 58.
[5] *Institutes of Justinian,* I. 12. Gaius, I. 128.
[6] Dionysius, VIII. 41.
[7] Horace, *Odes,* III.
[8] Thucydides, I. 138.

It is not surprising that the ancient republics almost all permitted a convict to escape death by flight. Exile did not seem to be a milder punishment than death. The Roman jurists called it capital punishment.

Chapter XIV

THE MUNICIPAL SPIRIT

WHAT we have already seen of ancient institutions, and above all of ancient beliefs, has enabled us to obtain an idea of the profound gulf which always separated two cities. However near they might be to each other, they always formed two completely separate societies. Between them there was much more than the distance which separates two cities to-day, much more than the frontier which separates two states; their gods were not the same, or their ceremonies, or their prayers. The worship of one city was forbidden to men of a neighboring city. The belief was, that the gods of one city rejected the homage and prayers of any one who was not their own citizen.

These ancient beliefs, it is true, were modified and softened in the course of time; but they had been in their full vigor at the time when these societies were formed, and these societies always preserved the impression of them.

Two facts we can easily understand: first, that this religion, peculiar to each city, must have established the city in a very strong and almost unchangeable manner; it is, indeed, marvellous how long this social organization lasted, in spite of all its faults and all its chances of ruin; second, that the effect of this religion, during long ages, must have been to render it impossible to establish any other social form than the city.

Every city, even by the requirements of its religion, was independent. It was necessary that each should have its particular code, since each had its own religion, and the law flowed from the religion. Each was required to have its soverign tribunal, and there could be no judicial tribunal superior to that of the city. Each had its religious festivals and its calendar; the months and the year could not be the same in two cities, as the series of religious acts was different. Each had its own money, which at first was marked with its religious emblem. Each had its weights and measures. It was not admitted that there could be anything common between two cities. The line of demarcation was so profound that one hardly imagined marriage possible between the inhabitants of two different cities. Such a union always appeared strange, and was long considered illegal. The legislation of Rome and that of Athens were visibly averse to admitting it. Nearly everywhere children born of such a marriage were confounded with bastards, and deprived of the rights of citizens. To make a marriage legal between inhabitants of two cities, it was necessary that there should be between those cities a particular convention — *jus connubii*, επιγαμια.

Every city had about its territory a line of sacred bounds. This was the horizon of its national religion and of its gods. Beyond these bounds other gods reigned, and another worship was practised.

The most salient characteristic of the history of Greece and of Italy, before the Roman conquest, is the excessive division of property and the spirit of isolation in each city. Greece never succeeded in forming a single state; nor did the Latin or the Etruscan cities, or the Samnite tribes, succeed in forming a compact body. The incurable division of the Greeks has been attributed to the nature of their country, and we are told that the mountains which intersect each other establish natural lines of demarcation among men. But there were no mountains between Thebes and Platæa, between Argos and Sparta, between Sybaris and Crotona. There were none between the cities of Latium, or between the twelve cities of Etruria. Doubtless physical nature has some influence upon the history of a people, but the beliefs of men have a much more powerful one. In ancient times there was something more impassable than mountains between two neighboring cities, there were the series of sacred bounds, the difference of worship, and the hatred of the gods towards the foreigner.

For this reason the ancients were never able to establish, or even to conceive of, any other social organization than the city. Neither the Greeks, nor the Latins, nor even the Romans, for a very long time, ever had a thought that several cities might be united, and live on an equal footing under the same government. There might, indeed, be an alliance, or a temporary association, in view of some advantage to be gained, or some danger to be repelled; but there was never a complete union; for religion made of every city a body which could never be joined to another. Isolation was the law of the city.

With the beliefs and the religious usages which we have seen, how could several cities ever have become united in one state? Men did not understand human association, and it did not appear regular, unless it was founded upon religion. The symbol of this association was a sacred repast partaken of in common. A few thousand citizens might indeed literally unite around the same prytaneum, recite the same prayer, and partake of the same sacred dishes. But how attempt, with these usages, to make a single state of entire Greece? How could men hold the public repasts, and perform all the sacred ceremonies, in which every citizen was bound to take a part? Where would they locate the prytaneum? How would they perform the annual lustration of the citizens? What would become of the inviolable limits which had from the beginning marked out the territory of the city, and which separated it forever from the rest of the earth's surface? What would become of all the local worships, the city divinities, and the heroes who inhabited every canton? Athens had within her limits the hero Œdipus, the enemy of Thebes: how unite Athens and Thebes in the same worship and under the same government?

When these superstitions became weakened (and this did not happen till a late period, in common minds), it was too late to establish a new form of state. The division had become consecrated by custom, by interest, by inveterate hatreds, and by the memory of past struggles. Men could no longer return to the past.

Every city held fast to its *autonomy:* this was the name they gave to an assemblage which comprised their worship, their laws, their government, and their entire religious and political independence.

It was easier for a city to subject another than to annex it.

Victory might make slaves of all the inhabitants of a conquered city, but they could not be made citizens of the victorious city. To join two cities in a single state, to unite the conquered population with the victors, and associate them under the same government, is what was never seen among the ancients, with one exception, of which we shall speak presently. If Sparta conquered Messenia, it was not to make of the Spartans and Messenians a single people. The Spartans expelled the whole race of the vanquished, and took their lands. Athens proceeded in the same manner with Salamis, Ægina, and Melos.

The thought of removing the conquered to the city of the victors could not enter the mind of any one. The city possessed gods, hymns, festivals, and laws, which were its precious patrimony, and it took good care not to share these with the vanquished. It had not even the right to do this. Could Athens admit that a citizen of Ægina might enter the temple of Athene Polias? that he might offer his worship to Theseus? that he might take part in the sacred repasts? that, as a prytane, he might keep up the public fire? Religion forbade it. The conquered population of the isle of Ægina could not, therefore, form a single state with the population of Athens. Not having the same gods, the Æginetans and the Athenians could not have the same laws or the same magistrates.

But might not Athens, at any rate, leaving the conquered city intact, send magistrates within its walls to govern it? It was absolutely contrary to the principles of the ancients to place any man over a city, who was not a citizen of it. Indeed, the magistrate was a religious chief, and his principal function was to sacrifice in the name of the city. The foreigner, who had not the right to offer the sacrifice, could not therefore be a magistrate. Having no religious function, he had not in the eyes of men any regular authority. Sparta attempted to place its harmosts in the cities, but these men were not magistrates; they did not act as judges, or appear in the assemblies. Having no regular relation with the people of the cities, they could not maintain themselves there for any great length of time.

Every conqueror, consequently, had only the alternative of destroying a subdued city and occupying its territory, or of leaving it entirely independent. There was no middle course. Either the city ceased to exist, or it was a sovereign state. So long as it retained its worship, it retained its government; it lost the one only by losing the other; and then it existed no longer. This absolute independence of the ancient city could only cease when the belief on which it was founded had completely disappeared. After these ideas had been transformed and several revolutions had passed over these antique societies, then men might come to have an idea of, and to establish, a larger state, governed by other rules. But for this it was necessary that men should discover other principles and other social bonds than those of the ancient ages.

Chapter XV

RELATIONS BETWEEN THE CITIES. WAR. PEACE. THE ALLIANCE OF THE GODS

This religion, which exercised so powerful an empire over the interior life of the city, intervened with the same authority in all the relations between cities. We may see this by observing how men of those ancient ages carried on war, how they concluded peace, and how they formed alliances.

Two cities were two religious associations which had not the same gods. When they were at war it was not the men alone who fought — the gods also took part in the struggle. Let no one suppose that this was simply a poetical fiction. There was among the ancients a very definite and a very vivid belief, by reason of which each army took its gods along with it. Men believed that these gods took an active part in the battle; the soldiers defended them and they defended the soldiers. While fighting against the enemy, each one believed he was fighting against the gods of another city. These foreign gods he was permitted to detest, to abuse, to strike; he might even make them prisoners. Thus war had a strange aspect. We must picture to ourselves two armies facing each other: in the midst of each are its statues, its altar, and its standards, which are sacred emblems; each has its oracles, which have promised it success; its augurs, and its soothsayers, who assure it the victory. Before the battle each soldier in the two armies thinks and says, like the Greek in Euripides, "The gods who fight for us are more powerful than those of our enemies." Each army pronounces against the other an imprecation like that which Macrobius has preserved — "O gods, spread fear, terror, and misfortune among our enemies. Let these men, and whoever inhabits their lands and cities, be deprived by you of the light of the sun. May their city, and their lands, and their heads, and their persons, be devoted to you." After this imprecation, they rush to battle on both sides, with that savage fury which the notion that they have gods fighting for them and that they are fighting against strange gods inspires in them. There is no mercy for the enemy; war is implacable; religion presides over the struggle, and excites the combatants. There can be no superior rule to moderate the desire for slaughter; they are permitted to kill the prisoners and the wounded.

Even outside the field of battle they have no idea of a duty of any kind towards the enemy. There are never any rights for a foreigner, least of all in time of war. No one was required to distinguish the just from the unjust in respect to him. Mucius Scævola and all the Romans believed it was a glorious deed to assassinate an enemy. The consul Marcius boasted publicly of having deceived the king of Macedonia. Paulus Æmilius sold as slaves a hundred thousand Epirots who had voluntarily surrendered themselves to him.

The Lacedæmonian Phebidas seized upon the citadel of the Thebans in time of peace. Agesilaus was questioned upon the justice of this action. "Inquire only if it is useful," said the king; "for whenever an action is useful to our country, it is right." This was the international law of ancient cities. Another king of Sparta, Cleomenes, said that all the evil one could do to enemies was always just in the eyes of gods and men.

The conqueror could use his victory as he pleased. No human or divine law restrained his vengeance or his cupidity. The day on which the Athenians decreed that all the Mitylenæans, without distinction of age or sex, should be exterminated, they did not dream of transcending their rights; and when, on the next day, they revoked their decree, and contented themselves with putting a thousand citizens to death, and confiscating all the lands, they thought themselves humane and indulgent. After the taking of Platæa, the men were put to death, and the women sold; and yet no one accused the conquerors of having violated any law.

These men made war not only upon soldiers, but upon an entire population, men, women, children, and slaves. They waged it not only against human beings, but against fields and crops. They burned houses and cut down trees; the harvest of the enemy was almost always devoted to the infernal gods, and consequently burned. They exterminated the cattle; they even destroyed the seed which might produce a crop the following year. A war might cause the name and race of an entire people to disappear at a single blow, and change a fertile country into a desert. It was by virtue of this law of war that the Romans extended a solitude around their city; of the territory where the Volscians had twenty-three cities, it made the Pontine marshes; the fifty-three cities of Latium have disappeared; in Samnium, the places where the Roman armies had passed could long be recognized, less by the vestiges of their camps than by the solitude which reigned in the neighborhood.

When the conquerors did not exterminate the vanquished, they had a right to suppress their city — that is to say, to break up their religious and political association. The worship then ceased, and the gods were forgotten. The religion of the city being destroyed, the religion of every family disappeared at the same time. The sacred fires were extinguished. With the worship fell the laws, civil rights, the family, property, everything that depended upon religion.[1] Let us listen to the prisoner whose life is spared; he is made to pronounce the following formula: "I give my person, my city, my land, the water that flows over it, my boundary gods, my temples, my movable property, everything which pertains to the gods, — these I give to the Roman people."[2] From this moment the gods, the temples, the houses, the lands, and the people belonged to the victors. We shall relate, farther on, what the result of this was under the dominion of Rome.

When a war did not end by the extermination or subjection of one of the two parties, a treaty of peace might terminate it.

---

[1] Cicero, *in Verr.*, II. 3, 6. Siculus Flaccus, *passim*. Thucydides, III. 50 and 68.

[2] Livy, I. 38. Plautus, *Amphitr.*, 100–105.

But for this a convention was not sufficient; a religious act was necessary. Every treaty was marked by the immolation of a victim. To sign a treaty is a modern expression; the Latins said, strike a kid, *icere hædus,* or *fœdus;* the name of the victim most generally employed for this purpose has remained in the common language to designate the entire act.[3] The Greeks expressed themselves in a similar manner; they said, offer a libation — σπενδεσθαι. The ceremony of the treaty was always accomplished by priests, who conformed to the ritual.[4] In Italy they were called *feciales,* and *spendophoroi,* or libation-carriers, in Greece.

These religious ceremonies alone gave a sacred and inviolable character to international conventions. The history of the Caudine Forks is well known. An entire army, through its consuls, questors, tribunes, and centurions had made a convention with the Samnites; but no victims had been offered. The senate, therefore, believed itself justified in declaring that the treaty was not valid. In annulling it, no pontiff or patrician believed that he was committing an act of bad faith.

It was the universal opinion among the ancients that a man owed no obligations except to his own gods. We may recall the saying of a certain Greek, whose city adored the hero Alabandos; he was speaking to an inhabitant of another city, that worshipped Hercules. "Alabandos," said he, "is a god, and Hercules is not one."[5] With such ideas it was important, in a treaty of peace, that each city called its own gods to bear witness to its oaths. "We made a treaty, and poured out the libations," said the Platæans to the Spartans; "we called to witness, you the gods of your fathers, we the gods who occupy our country."[6] Both parties tried, indeed, if it was possible, to invoke divinities that were common to both cities. They swore by those gods that were visible everywhere — the sun, which shines upon all, and the nourishing earth. But the gods of each city, and its protecting heroes, touched men much more, and it was necessary to call them to witness, if men wished to have oaths really confirmed by

---

[3] Festus, *Fœdum,* and *Fœdus.*
[4] In Greece they wore a crown. Xenophon, *Hell.,* IV. 7, 3.
[5] Cicero, *De Nat. Deor.,* III. 19.
[6] Thucydides, II.

religion. As the gods mingled in the battles during the war, they had to be included in the treaty. It was stipulated, there- fore, that there should be an alliance between the gods as between the men of the two cities. To indicate this alliance of the gods, it sometimes happened that the two peoples agreed mutually to take part in each other's sacred festivals.[7] Some- times they opened their temples to each other, and made an exchange of religious rites. Rome once stipulated that the city god of Lanuvium should thenceforth protect the Romans, who should have the right to invoke him, and to enter his temple.[8] Afterwards each of the contracting parties engaged to worship the divinities of the other. Thus the Eleans, having concluded a treaty with the Ætolians, thenceforth offered an annual sacrifice to the heroes of their allies.[9]

It often happened, after an alliance, that the divinities of two cities were represented by statues or medals holding one another by the hand. Thus it is that there are medals on which are seen united the Apollo of Miletus and the Genius of Smyrna, the Pallas of the Sideans and the Artemis of Perga, the Apollo of Hierapolis and the Artemis of Ephesus. Virgil, speaking of an alliance between Thrace and the Trojans, represents the Penates of the two nations united and associated.

These strange customs corresponded perfectly with the idea which the ancients had of the gods. As every city had its own, it seemed natural that these gods should figure in battles and treaties. War or peace between two cities was war or peace between two religions.

International law among the ancients was long founded upon this principle. When the gods were enemies, there was war without mercy and without law; as soon as they were friends, the men were united, and entertained ideas of reciprocal duties. If they could imagine that the protecting divinities of two cities had some motive for becoming allies, this was reason enough why the two cities should become so. The first city with which Rome contracted ties of friendship was Cære, in Etruria, and Livy gives the reason for this: in the disaster of the Gallic invasion, the Roman gods had found an asylum in

---

[7] Thucydides, V. 23. Plutarch, *Theseus*, 25, 33.

[8] Livy, VIII. 14.

[9] Pausanias, V. 15.

Cære; they had inhabited that city, and had been adored there; a sacred bond of friendship was thus established between the Roman gods and the Etruscan city.[10] Thenceforth religion would not permit the two cities to be enemies; they were allied forever.[11]

Chapter XVI

THE ROMAN. THE ATHENIAN

THIS same religion which had founded society, and which had governed it for a long time, also gave the human mind its direction, and man his character. By its dogmas and its practices it gave to the Greek and the Roman a certain manner of thinking and acting, and certain habits of which they were a long time in divesting themselves. It showed men gods everywhere, little gods, gods easily irritated and malevolent. It

[10] Livy, V. 50. Aulus Gellius, XVI. 13.

[11] It does not enter into our plan to speak of the numerous confederations or amphictyonies in ancient Greece and Italy. We will only remark here that they were as much religious as political associations. There was not one of them that had not a common worship and a sanctuary. That of the Bœotians worshipped Athene Itonia, that of the Achæans Demeter Panachæa, the god of the Ionians in Asia Minor was Poseidon Helliconius, as that of the Dorian Pentapolis was Apollo Triopicus. The confederation of the Cyclades offered a common sacrifice in the isle of Delos, the cities of Argolis at Calauria. The Amphictyony of Thermopylæ was an association of the same nature. All their meetings took place in temples, and were principally for offering sacrifices. Each of the confederate cities sent citizens clothed for the time with a sacerdotal character, and called *theori*, to take part in these meetings. A victim was slain in honor of the god of the association, and the flesh, cooked upon the altar, was shared among the representatives of the cities. The common meal, with the songs, prayers, and sacred plays that accompanied them, formed the bond of the confederation. The same usage existed in Italy. The cities of Latium had the feriæ Latinæ, in which they shared the flesh of a victim. It was the same with the Etruscan cities. Besides, in all these amphictyonies, the political bond was always weaker than the religious one. The confederate cities preserved perfect independence. They might even make war against each other, provided they observed a truce during the federal festival.

crushed man with the fear of always having gods against him, and left him no liberty in his acts.

We must inquire what place religion occupied in the life of a Roman. His house was for him what a temple is for us. He finds there his worship and his gods. His fire is a god; the walls, the doors, the threshold are gods;[1] the boundary marks which surround his field are also gods. The tomb is an altar, and his ancestors are divine beings.

Each one of his daily actions is a rite; his whole day belongs to his religion. Morning and evening he invokes his fire, his Penates, and his ancestors; in leaving and entering his house he addresses a prayer to them. Every meal is a religious act, which he shares with his domestic divinities. Birth, initiation, the taking of the toga, marriage, and the anniversaries of all these events, are the solemn acts of his worship.

He leaves his house, and can hardly take a step without meeting some sacred object — either a chapel, or a place formerly struck by lightning, or a tomb; sometimes he must step back and pronounce a prayer; sometimes he must turn his eyes and cover his face, to avoid the sight of some ill-boding object.

Every day he sacrifices in his house, every month in his cury, several months a year with his gens or his tribe. Above all these gods, he must offer worship to those of the city. There are in Rome more gods than citizens.

He offers sacrifices to thank the gods; he offers them, and by far the greater number, to appease their wrath. One day he figures in a procession, dancing after a certain ancient rhythm, to the sound of the sacred flute. Another day he conducts chariots, in which lie statues of the divinities. Another time it is a *lectisternium:* a table is set in a street, and loaded with provisions, upon beds lie statues of the gods, and every Roman passes bowing, with a crown upon his head, and a branch of laurel in his hand.[2]

There is a festival for seed-time, one for the harvest, and one for the pruning of the vines. Before corn has reached the ear, the Roman has offered more than ten sacrifices, and in-

[1] St. Augustine, *City of God,* VI. 7. Tertullian, *Ad. Nat.,* II. 15.
[2] Livy, XXXIV. 55; XL. 37.

voked some ten divinities for the success of his harvest. He has, above all, a multitude of festivals for the dead, because he is afraid of them.

He never leaves his own house without looking to see if any bird of bad augury appears. There are words which he dares not pronounce for his life. If he experiences some desire, he inscribes his wish upon a tablet which he places at the feet of the statue of a divinity.

At every moment he consults the gods, and wishes to know their will. He finds all his resolutions in the entrails of victims, in the flight of birds, in the warning of the lightning. The announcement of a shower of blood, or of an ox that has spoken, troubles him and makes him tremble. He will be tranquil only after an expiatory ceremony shall restore him to peace with the gods.

He steps out of his house always with the right foot first. He has his hair cut only during the full moon. He carries amulets upon his person. He covers the walls of his house with magic inscriptions against fire. He knows of formulas for avoiding sickness, and of others for curing it; but he must repeat them twenty-seven times, and spit in a certain fashion at each repetition.[3]

He does not deliberate in the senate if the victims have not given favorable signs. He leaves the assembly of the people if he hears the cry of a mouse. He renounces the best laid plans if he perceives a bad presage, or if an ill-omened word has struck his ear. He is brave in battle, but on condition that the auspices assure him the victory.

This Roman whom we present here is not the man of the people, the feeble-minded man whom misery and ignorance have made superstitious. We are speaking of the patrician, the noble, powerful, and rich man. This patrician is, by turns, warrior, magistrate, consul, farmer, merchant; but everywhere and always he is a priest, and his thoughts are fixed upon the gods. Patriotism, love of glory, and love of gold, whatever power these may have over his soul, the fear of the gods still

[3] Cato, *De Re Rust.*, 160. Varro, *De Re Rust.*, I. 2; I. 37. Pliny, *N. H.*, VIII. 82; XVII. 28; XXVII. 12; XXVIII. 2. Juvenal, X. 55. Aulus Gellius, IV. 5.

governs everything. Horace has written the most striking truth concerning the Romans: —

"Dis te minorem quod geris, imperas."

Men have sometimes called this a political religion; but can we suppose that a senate of three hundred members, a body of three thousand patricians, should have agreed so unanimously to deceive an ignorant people? and that, for ages, during so many rivalries, struggles, and personal hatreds, not a single voice was raised to say, This is a falsehood? If a patrician had betrayed the secrets of his sect, — if, addressing himself to the plebeians, who impatiently supported the yoke of this religion, he had disembarrassed and freed them from these auspices and priesthoods, — this man would immediately have obtained so much credit that he might have become the master of the state. Does any one suppose that if these patricians had not believed in the religion which they practised, such a temptation would not have been strong enough to determine at least one among them to reveal the secret? We greatly deceive ourselves on the nature of man if we suppose a religion can be established by convention and supported by imposture. Let any one count in Livy how many times this religion embarrassed the patricians themselves, how many times it stood in the way of the senate and impeded its action, and then decide if this religion was invented for the convenience of statesmen. It was very late — not till the time of the Scipios — that they began to believe that religion was useful to the government; but then religion was already dead in their minds.

Let us take a Roman of the first days: we will choose one of the greatest commanders, Camillus, who was five times dictator, and who was victorious in more than ten battles. To be just, we must consider him quite as much a priest as a warrior. He belonged to the Furian gens; his surname is a word which designates a priestly function. When a child he was required to wear the *prætexta*, which indicated his caste, and the *bulla*, which kept bad fortune from him. He grew up, taking a daily part in the ceremonies of the worship; he passed his youth in studying religious rites. A war broke out, and the priest became a soldier; he was seen, when wounded in the thigh, in a cavalry combat, to draw the iron from the wound and continue to fight. After several campaigns he was raised to magistracies; as consular tribune he offered the public sacrifices, acted as judge, and commanded the army. A day comes when men think of him for the dictatorship. On that day, the magistrate in office, after having watched during a clear night, consults the gods; his thoughts are fixed upon Camillus, whose name he pronounces in a low voice, and his eyes are fixed upon the heavens, where he seeks the presages. The gods send only good ones, for Camillus is agreeable to them, and he is named dictator.

Now, as chief of the army, he leaves the city, not without having consulted the auspices and slain many victims. He has under his orders many officers and almost as many priests, a pontiff, augurs, aruspices, keepers of the sacred chickens, assistants at sacrifices, and a bearer of the sacred fire. His work is to finish the war against Veii, which for nine years has been besieged without success. Veii is an Etruscan city — that is to say, almost a sacred city; it is against piety, more than courage, that the Romans have to contend. If the Romans have been unsuccessful for nine years, it is because the Etruscans have a better knowledge of the rites that are agreeable to the gods, and the magic formulas that gain their favor. Rome, on her side, has opened the Sibylline books, and has sought the will of the gods there. It appears that the Latin festival has been vitiated by some neglect of form, and the sacrifice is renewed. Still the Etruscans retain their superiority; only one resource is left — to seize an Etruscan priest and learn the secret of the gods from him. A Veientine priest is taken and brought to the senate. "To insure the success of Rome," he says, "the level of the Alban Lake must be lowered, taking good care that the water does not run into the sea." The Romans obey. They dig many canals and ditches, and the water of the lake is lost in the plain.

At this moment Camillus is elected dictator. He repairs to the army at Veii. He is sure of success; for all the oracles have been revealed, all the commands of the gods have been fulfilled. Moreover, before leaving Rome, he has promised the protecting gods festivals and sacrifices. In order to insure success he does not neglect human means; he increases the army, improves its discipline, and constructs a subterranean gallery, to penetrate into the citadel. The day for the attack arrives; Camillus leaves his tent; he takes the auspices and sacrifices victims. The pontiffs and augurs surround him; clothed in the *paludamentum,* he invokes the gods: "Under thy conduct, O Apollo, and by thy will which inspires me, I march to take and destroy the city of Veii: to thee I promise and devote a tenth part of the spoils." But it is not enough to have gods on his side; the enemy also has a powerful divinity that protects him. Camillus invokes this divinity in these words: "Queen Juno, who at present inhabitest Veii, I pray thee come with us conquerors; follow us into our city; let our city become thine." Then, the sacrifices being finished, the prayers pronounced, the formulas recited, when the Romans are sure that the gods are for them, and no god any longer defends the enemy, the assault is made, and the city is taken.

Such was Camillus. A Roman general was a man who understood admirably how to fight, who knew, above all, how to command obedience, but who believed firmly in the augurs, who performed religious acts every day, and who was convinced that what was of most importance was not courage, or even discipline, but the enunciation of certain formulas exactly pronounced, according to the rites. These formulas, addressed to the gods, determined them and constrained them almost always to give him the victory. For such a general the supreme recompense was for the senate to permit him to offer the triumphal sacrifice. Then he ascends the sacred chariot drawn by four white horses; he wears the sacred robe with which the gods are clothed on festal days; his head is crowned, his right hand holds a laurel branch, his left the ivory sceptre; these are exactly the attributes and the costume of Jupiter's statue.[4] With this almost divine majesty he shows himself to the citizens, and goes to render homage to the true majesty of the greatest of the Roman gods. He climbs the slope of the Capitol, arrives before the temple of Jupiter, and immolates victims.

The fear of the gods was not a sentiment peculiar to the Roman; it also reigned in the heart of the Greek. These peoples, originally established by religion, and elevated by it,

[4] Livy, X. 7; XXX. 15. Dionysius, V. 8. Appian, *Punic Wars,* 59. Juvenal, X. 43. Pliny, XXXIII. 7.

long preserved the marks of their first education. We know the scruples of the Spartan, who never commenced an expedition before the full moon, who was continually sacrificing victims to know whether he ought to fight, and who renounced the best planned and most necessary enterprises because a bad presage frightened him. The Athenian was not less scrupulous. An Athenian army never set out on a campaign before the seventh day of the month, and when a fleet set sail on an expedition, great care was taken to regild the statue of Pallas.

Xenophon declares that the Athenians had more religious festivals than any other Greek people.[5] "How many victims offered to the gods!" says Aristophanes,[6] "how many temples! how many statues! how many sacred processions! At every moment of the year we see religious feasts and crowned victims." The city of Athens and its territory are covered with temples and chapels. Some are for the city worship, others for the tribes and demes, and still others for family worship. Every house is itself a temple, and in every field there is a sacred tomb.

The Athenian whom we picture to ourselves as so inconstant, so capricious, such a free-thinker, has, on the contrary, a singular respect for ancient traditions and ancient rites. His principal religion — that which secures his most fervent devotion — is the worship of ancestors and heroes. He worships the dead and fears them. One of his laws obliges him to offer them yearly the first fruits of his harvest; another forbids him to pronounce a single word that can call down their anger. Whatever relates to antiquity is sacred to the Athenian. He has old collections, in which are recorded his rites, from which he never departs. If a priest introduces the slightest innovation into the worship, he is punished with death. The strangest rites are observed from age to age. One day in the year the Athenians offer a sacrifice in honor of Ariadne; and because it was said that the beloved of Theseus died in childbirth, they are compelled to imitate the cries and movements of a woman in travail. They celebrate another festival, called Oschophoria, which is a sort of pantomime, representing the return of Theseus to Attica. They crown the wand of a herald because

[5] Xenophon, *Gov. of the Athenians*, III. 2.
[6] Aristophanes, *Clouds*.

Theseus's herald crowned his staff. They utter a certain cry which they suppose the herald uttered, and a procession is formed, and each wears the costume that was in fashion in Theseus's time. On another day the Athenians did not fail to boil vegetables in a pot of a certain kind. This was a rite the origin of which was lost in dim antiquity, and of which no one knew the significance, but which was piously renewed each year.[7]

The Athenian, like the Roman, had unlucky days: on these days no marriage took place, no enterprise was begun, no assembly was held, and justice was not administered. The eighteenth and nineteenth day of every month was employed in purifications. The day of the Plynteria — a day unlucky above all — they veiled the statue of the great Athene Polias. On the contrary, on the day of the Panathenæa, the veil of the goddess was carried in grand procession, and all the citizens, without distinction of age or rank, made up the *cortège*. The Athenian offered sacrifices for the harvests, for the return of rain, and for the return of fair weather; he offered them to cure sickness, and to drive away famine or pestilence.[8]

Athens has its collection of ancient oracles, as Rome has her Sibylline books, and supports in the Prytaneum men who foretell the future. In her streets we meet at every step soothsayers, priests, and interpreters of dreams. The Athenian believes in portents; sneezing, or a ringing in the ears, arrests him in an enterprise. He never goes on shipboard without taking the auspices. Before marrying he does not fail to consult the flight of birds. The assembly of the people disperses as soon as any one declares that there has appeared in the heavens an ill-boding sign. If a sacrifice has been disturbed by the announcement of bad news, it must be recommenced.[9]

The Athenian hardly commences a sentence without first invoking good fortune. He puts the same words at the head of all his decrees. On the speaker's stand the orator prefers to

---

[7] Plutarch, *Theseus*, 20, 22, 23.
[8] Plato, *Laws*, p. 800. Philochorus, *Fragm.* Euripides, *Suppl.*, 80.
[9] Aristophanes, *Peace*, 1084; *Birds*, 596, 718. *Schol. ad Aves*, 721. Thucyd., II. 8.

commence with an invocation to the gods and heroes who
inhabit the country. The people are led by oracles. The
orators, to give their advice more force, repeat, at every
moment, "The goddess ordains thus."[10]

Nicias belongs to a great and rich family. While still young
he conducts to the sanctuary of Delos a *theoria* — that is to
say, victims, and a chorus to sing the praises of the god during
the sacrifice. Returning to Athens, he offers a part of his
fortune in homage to the gods, dedicating a statue to Athene
and a chapel to Dionysius. By turns he is *hestiator*, and pays
the expense of the sacred repast of his tribe; and *choregus*,
when he supports a chorus for the religious festivals. No day
passes that he does not offer a sacrifice to some god. He has a
soothsayer attached to his house, who never leaves it, and
whom he consults on public affairs, as well as on his own.
Having been appointed a general, he commands an expedition
against Corinth; while he is returning victorious to Athens,
he perceives that two of his dead soldiers have been left, without burial, upon the enemy's territory. He is seized with a
religious scruple; he stops his fleet, and sends a herald to
demand of the Corinthians permission to bury the two bodies.
Some time after, the Athenian people are deliberating upon
the Sicilian expedition. Nicias ascends the speaker's stand, and
declares that his priests and soothsayers announce prestiges
which are opposed to the expedition. Alcibiades, it is true, has
other diviners who interpret the oracles in a contrary sense.
The people are undecided. Men come in who have just arrived
from Egypt; they have consulted the god Ammon, who is
beginning to be quite the fashion, and they report this oracle
from him. The Athenians will capture all the Syracusans. The
people immediately decide for war.[11]

Nicias, much against his will, commands the expedition.
Before setting out, he offers a sacrifice, according to custom.
He takes with him, like other generals, a troop of diviners,
sacrificers, aruspices, and heralds. The fleet carries its sacred
fire; every vessel has an emblem representing some god.

But Nicias has little hope. Is not misfortune announced by
prodigies enough? Crows have injured a statue of Pallas; a

[10] Lycurgus, I. 1. Aristophanes, *Knights*, 903, 999, 1171, 1179.
[11] Plutarch, *Nicias*. Thucydides, VI.

man has mutilated himself upon an altar; and the departure
takes place during the unlucky days of the Plynteria. Nicias
knows only too well that this war will be fatal to him and his
country. During the whole course of his campaign he always
appears timorous and circumspect; he hardly dares to give the
signal for a battle, he whom they know to be so brave a soldier
and so skilful a general. The Athenians cannot take Syracuse,
and, after cruel losses, they are forced to decide upon returning home. Nicias prepares his fleet for the return; the sea is
still free. But an eclipse of the moon happens. He consults his
diviner; the diviner answers that the presage is unfavorable,
and that they must wait three times nine days. Nicias obeys;
he passes all this time inactive, offering many sacrifices to
appease the wrath of the gods. During this delay the enemy
close up the port and destroy his fleet. Nothing is left for him
but to retreat by land, and this is impossible. Neither he nor
any of his soldiers escapes the Syracusans.

What did the Athenians say at the news of this disaster?
They knew the personal courage of Nicias, and his admirable
constancy. Nor did they dream of blaming him for having followed the dictates of religion. They found but one thing to
reproach him for; this was for having taken with him an
ignorant diviner. For this man had been mistaken as to the
meaning of the eclipse of the moon; he ought to have known
that, for an army wishing to retreat, a moon that conceals its
light is a favorable presage.[12]

Chapter XVII

THE OMNIPOTENCE OF THE STATE. THE ANCIENTS
KNEW NOTHING OF INDIVIDUAL LIBERTY

THE city had been founded upon a religion, and constituted
like a church. Hence its strength; hence, also, its omnipotence
and the absolute empire which it exercised over its members.
In a society established on such principles, individual liberty
could not exist. The citizen was subordinate in everything,
and without any reserve, to the city; he belonged to it body

[12] Plutarch, *Nicias*, 23.

and soul. The religion which had produced the state, and the state which supported the religion, sustained each other, and made but one; these two powers, associated and confounded, formed a power almost superhuman, to which the soul and the body were equally enslaved.

There was nothing independent in man; his body belonged to the state, and was devoted to its defence. At Rome military service was due till a man was fifty years old, at Athens till he was sixty, at Sparta always. His fortune was always at the disposal of the state. If the city had need of money, it could order the women to deliver up their jewels, the creditors to give up their claims, and the owners of olive trees to turn over gratuitously the oil which they had made.[1]

Private life did not escape this omnipotence of the state. The Athenian law, in the name of religion, forbade man to remain single.[2] Sparta punished not only those who remained single, but those who married late. At Athens the state could prescribe labor, and at Sparta idleness. It exercised its tyranny even in the smallest things; at Locri the laws forbade men to drink pure wine; at Rome, Miletus, and Marseilles wine was forbidden to women.[3] It was a common thing for the kind of dress to be invariably fixed by each city; the legislation of Sparta regulated the head-dress of women and that of Athens forbade them to take with them on a journey more than three dresses.[4] At Rhodes and Byzantium the law forbade men to shave the beard.[5]

The state was under no obligation to suffer any of its citizens to be deformed. It therefore commanded a father to whom such a son was born, to have him put to death. This law is found in the ancient codes of Sparta and of Rome. We do not know that it existed at Athens; we know only that Aristotle and Plato incorporated it into their ideal codes.

[1] Aristotle, *Econom.*, II.
[2] Pollux, VIII. 40. Plutarch, *Lysander,* 30.
[3] Athenæus, X. 33. Ælian, *V. H.,* II. 37.
[4] *Fragm. Hist. Græc.* Didot, t. II. p. 129, 211. Plutarch, *Solon,* 21.
[5] Athenæus, XIII. Plutarch, *Cleomenes,* 9.
"The Romans thought that no marriage, or rearing of children, nay, no feast or drinking bout, ought to be permitted according to every one's appetite or fancy, without being examined and inquired into." Plutarch, *Cato the Elder,* 23.

There is, in the history of Sparta, one trait which Plutarch and Rousseau greatly admired. Sparta had just suffered a defeat at Leuctra, and many of its citizens had perished. On the receipt of this news, the relatives of the dead had to show themselves in public with gay countenances. The mother who learned that her son had escaped, and that she should see him again, appeared afflicted and wept. Another, who knew that she should never again see her son, appeared joyous, and went round to the temple to thank the gods. What, then, was the power of the state that could thus order the reversal of the natural sentiments, and be obeyed?

The state allowed no man to be indifferent to its interests; the philosopher or the studious man had no right to live apart. He was obliged to vote in the assembly, and be magistrate in his turn. At a time when discords were frequent, the Athenian law permitted no one to remain neutral; he must take sides with one or the other party. Against one who attempted to remain indifferent, and not side with either faction, and to appear calm, the law pronounced the punishment of exile with confiscation of property.

Education was far from being free among the Greeks. On the contrary, there was nothing over which the state had greater control. At Sparta the father could have nothing to do with the education of his son. The law appears to have been less rigorous at Athens; still the state managed to have education in the hands of masters of its own choosing. Aristophanes, in an eloquent passage, shows the Athenian children on their way to school; in order, distributed according to their district, they march in serried ranks, through rain, snow, or scorching heat. These children seem already to understand that they are performing a public duty.[6] The state wished alone to control education, and Plato gives the motive for this:[7] "Parents ought not to be free to send or not to send their children to the masters whom the city has chosen; for the children belong less to their parents than to the city."

The state considered the mind and body of every citizen as belonging to it; and wished, therefore, to fashion this body and mind in a manner that would enable it to draw the

---

[6] Aristophanes, *Clouds*, 960–965.
[7] Plato, *Laws*, VII.

greatest advantage from them. Children were taught gym-
nastics, because the body of a man was an arm for the city,
and it was best that this arm should be as strong and as
skilful as possible. They were also taught religious songs and
hymns, and the sacred dances, because this knowledge was
necessary to the correct performance of the sacrifices and
festivals of the city.[8]

It was admitted that the state had a right to prevent free
instruction by the side of its own. One day Athens made a
law forbidding the instruction of young people without
authority from the magistrates, and another, which specially
forbade the teaching of philosophy.[9]

A man had no chance to choose his belief. He must believe
and submit to the religion of the city. He could hate and
despise the gods of the neighboring city. As to the divinities
of a general and universal character, like Jupiter, or Cybele,
or Juno, he was free to believe or not to believe in them; but
it would not do to entertain doubts about Athene Polias, or
Erechtheus, or Cecrops. That would have been grave impiety,
which would have endangered religion and the state at the
same time, and which the state would have severely punished.
Socrates was put to death for this crime. Liberty of thought
in regard to the state religion was absolutely unknown among
the ancients. Men had to conform to all the rules of worship,
figure in all the processions, and take part in the sacred
repasts. Athenian legislation punished those by a fine who
failed religiously to celebrate a national festival.[10]

The ancients, therefore, knew neither liberty in private life,
liberty in education, nor religious liberty. The human person
counted for very little against that holy and almost divine
authority which was called country or the state. The state had
not only, as we have in our modern societies, a right to
administer justice to the citizens; it could strike when one was
not guilty, and simply for its own interest. Aristides assuredly
had committed no crime, and was not even suspected; but

---

[8] Aristophanes, *Clouds,* 966–968.

[9] Xenophon, *Memor.,* I. 2. Diogenes Laertius, *Theophr.* These two
laws did not continue a long time; but they do not the less prove the
omnipotence that was conceded to the state in matters of instruction.

[10] Pollux, VIII. 46. Ulpian, *Schol. in Demosthenes; in Meidiam.*

the city had the right to drive him from its territory, for the simple reason that he had acquired by his virtues too much influence, and might become dangerous, if he desired to be. This was called *ostracism;* this institution was not peculiar to Athens; it was found at Argos, at Megara, at Syracuse, and we may believe that it existed in all the Greek cities.[11]

Now, *ostracism* was not a chastisement; it was a precaution which the city took against a citizen whom it suspected of having the power to injure it at any time. At Athens a man could be put on trial and condemned for incivism — that is to say, for the want of affection towards the state. A man's life was guaranteed by nothing so soon as the interest of the state was at stake. Rome made a law by which it was permitted to kill any man who might have the intention of becoming king.[12] The dangerous maxim that the safety of the state is the supreme law, was the work of antiquity.[13] It was then thought that law, justice, morals, everything should give way before the interests of the country.

It is a singular error, therefore, among all human errors, to believe that in the ancient cities men enjoyed liberty. They had not even the idea of it. They did not believe that there could exist any right as against the city and its gods. We shall see, farther on, that the government changed form several times, while the nature of the state remained nearly the same, and its omnipotence was little diminished. The government was called by turns monarchy, aristocracy, democracy; but none of these revolutions gave man true liberty, individual liberty. To have political rights, to vote, to name magistrates, to have the privilege of being archon, — this was called liberty; but man was not the less enslaved to the state. The ancients, especially the Greeks, always exaggerated the importance, and above all, the rights of society; this was largely due, doubtless, to the sacred and religious character with which society was clothed in the beginning.

[11] Aristotle, *Pol.,* VIII. 2, 5. Scholiast on Aristoph., *Knights,* 851.
[12] Plutarch, *Publicola,* 12.
[13] Cicero, *De Legib.,* III. 3.

BOOK FOURTH

THE REVOLUTIONS

Chapter I

PATRICIANS AND CLIENTS

CERTAINLY we could imagine nothing more solidly constituted than this family of the ancient ages, which contained within itself its gods, its worship, its priest, and its magistrate. There could be nothing stronger than this city, which also had in itself its religion, its protecting gods, and its independent priesthood, which governed the soul as well as the body of man, and which, infinitely more powerful than the states of our day, united in itself the double authority that we now see shared between the state and the church. If any society was ever established to last, it was certainly that. Still, like everything human, it had its revolutions. We cannot state at what period these revolutions commenced. We can understand that, in reality, this epoch was not the same for the different cities of Greece and Italy. All that is certain is, that from the seventh century before our era, this social organization was almost everywhere discussed and attacked. From that time it was supported only with difficulty, and by a more or less skilful combination of resistance and concessions. It struggled thus for several centuries, in the midst of perpetual contests, and finally disappeared.

The causes of its destruction may be reduced to two. One was the change which took place in the course of time in ideas, resulting from the natural development of the human mind, and which, in effacing ancient beliefs, at the same time caused the social edifice to crumble, which these beliefs had built, and could alone sustain. The other was a class of men who found themselves placed outside this city organization, and who suffered from it. These men had an interest in destroying it, and made war upon it continually.

When, therefore, the beliefs, on which this social *régime* was founded, became weakened, and the interests of the majority of men were at war with it, the system fell. No city escaped this law of transformation; Sparta no more than Athens, Rome no more than Greece. We have seen that the men of Greece and those of Italy had originally the same beliefs, and that the same series of institutions was developed among both; and we shall now see that all these cities passed through similar revolutions.

We must try to understand why and how men became separated from this ancient organization, not to fall, but, on the contrary, to advance towards a social organization larger and better. For under the semblance of disorder, and sometimes of decay, each of their changes brought them nearer an object which they did not comprehend.

Thus far we have not spoken of the lower classes, because we have had no occasion to speak of them. For we have been attempting to describe the primitive organization of the city; and the lower classes counted absolutely for nothing in that organism. The city was constituted as if these classes had not existed. We were able therefore to defer the study of these till we had arrived at the period of the revolutions.

The ancient city, like all human society, had ranks, distinctions, and inequalities. We know the distinction originally made at Athens between the Eupatrids and the Thetes; at Sparta we find the class of Equals and that of the Inferiors; and in Eubœa, that of the Knights and that of the People. The history of Rome is full of the struggles between the Patricians and Plebeians, struggles that we find in all the Sabine, Latin, and Etruscan cities. We can even remark that the higher we ascend in the history of Greece and Italy, the more profound and the more strongly marked the distinction appears — a positive proof that the inequality did not grow up with time, but that it existed from the beginning, and that it was contemporary with the birth of cities.

It is worth while to inquire upon what principles this division of classes rested. We can thus the more easily see by virtue of what ideas or what needs the struggles commenced, what the inferior classes claimed, and on what principles the superior classes defended their empire.

We have seen above that the city grew out of the confederation of families and tribes. Now, before the day on which the
city was founded, the family already contained within itself
this distinction of classes. Indeed, the family was never dismembered; it was indivisible, like the primitive religion of the
hearth. The oldest son alone, succeeding the father, took
possession of the priesthood, the property, and the authority,
and his brothers were to him what they had been to their
father. From generation to generation, from first-born to first-
born, there was never but one family chief. He presided at
the sacrifice, repeated the prayer, pronounced judgment, and
governed. To him alone originally belonged the title of *pater;*
for this word, which signified power, and not paternity, could
be applied only to the chief of the family. His sons, his
brothers, his servants, all called him by this title.

Here, then, in the inner constitution of the family is the
first principle of inequality. The oldest is the privileged one
for the worship, for the succession, and for command. After
several centuries, there were naturally formed, in each of these
great families, younger branches, that were, according to
religion and by custom, inferior to the older branch, and who,
living under its protection, submitted to its authority.

This family, then, had servants, who did not leave it, who
were hereditarily attached to it, and upon whom the *pater,* or
patron, exercised the triple authority of master, magistrate,
and priest. They were called by names that varied with the
locality: the more common names were Clients and Thetes.

Here was another inferior class. The client was inferior not
only to the supreme chief of the family, but to the younger
branches also. Between him and them there was this difference,
that a member of a younger branch, by ascending the series of
his ancestors, always arrived at a *pater,* that is to say, a family
chief, one of those divine ancestors, whom the family invoked
in its prayers. As he was descended from a *pater,* they called
him in Latin *patricius.* The son of a client, on the contrary,
however high he might ascend in his genealogy, never arrived
at anything but a client or a slave. There was no *pater* among
his ancestors. Hence came for him a state of inferiority from
which there was no escape.

The distinction between these two classes of men was mani-

fest in what concerned material interests. The property of the
family belonged entirely to the chief, who, however, shared the
enjoyment of it with the younger branches, and even with the
clients. But while the younger branch had at least an eventual
right to this property, in case of the extinction of the elder
branch, the client could never become a proprietor. The land
that he cultivated he had only in trust; if he died, it returned
to his patron; Roman law of the later ages preserved a vestige
of this ancient rule in what was called *jus applicationis*. The
client's money, even, did not belong to him; the patron was
the true owner of it, and could take it for his own needs. It
was by virtue of this ancient rule that the Roman law required
the client to endow the daughter of the patron, to pay the
patron's fine, and to furnish his ransom, or contribute to the
expenses of his magistracy.

The distinction is still more manifest in religion. The
descendant of the *pater* alone can perform the ceremonies of
the family worship. The client takes a part in it; a sacrifice is
offered for him; he does not offer it for himself. Between him
and the domestic divinity there is always a mediator. He cannot even replace the absent family. If this family becomes
extinct, the clients do not continue the worship; they are
dispersed. For the religion is not their patrimony; it is not of
their blood, it does not come from their own ancestors. It is a
borrowed religion; they have not the enjoyment of the ownership of it.

Let us keep in mind that according to the ideas of ancient
generations, the right to have a god and to pray was hereditary. The sacred tradition, the rites, the sacramental words,
the powerful formulas which determined the gods to act, — all
this was transmitted only with the blood. It was therefore very
natural that in each of these ancient families, the free person
who was really descended from the first ancestor, was alone in
possession of the sacerdotal character. The Patricians or Eupatrids had the privilege of being priests, and of having a religion
that belonged to them alone.

Thus, even before men left the family state, there existed a
distinction of classes; the old domestic religion had established
ranks. Afterwards, when the city was formed, nothing was
changed in the inner constitution of the family. We have

already shown that originally the city was not an association of individuals, but a confederation of tribes, curies, and families, and that in this sort of alliance each of these bodies remained what it had been before. The chiefs of these little groups united with each other, but each remained master in the little society of which he was already chief. This explains why the Roman law so long left to the *pater* the absolute authority over his family, and the control of and the right of judging his clients. The distinction of classes, born in the family, was continued therefore in the city.

The city in its first age was no more than an alliance of the heads of families. There are numerous evidences of a time when they alone were citizens. This rule was kept up at Sparta, where the younger sons had no political rights. We may still see vestiges of it in an ancient law of Athens, which declared that to be a citizen one must have a domestic god.[1] Aristotle remarks that anciently, in many cities, it was the rule that the son was not a citizen during the life of his father, and that, the father being dead, the oldest son alone enjoyed political rights.[2] The law then counted in the city neither the younger branches of the family, nor, for still stronger reason, the clients. Aristotle also adds that the real citizens were at that time very few.

The assembly which deliberated on the general interests of the city was composed, in those ancient times, only of heads of families — *patres*. We may be allowed to doubt Cicero when he tells us that Romulus called the senators *fathers*, to mark their paternal affection for the people. The members of the senate naturally bore this title because they were the chiefs of the *gentes*. At the same time that these men, united, represented the city, each one of them remained absolute master in his *gens*, which was for him a kind of little kingdom. We also see, from the commencement of Rome, another more numerous assembly, that of the curies; but it differs very little from that of the *patres*. These formed the principal element of this assembly; only, every *pater* appeared there surrounded by his family; his relatives, his clients, even, formed his cortege, and marked his power. Each family had, moreover, but one vote

---

[1] Harpocration, Ζευς ερκειος
[2] Aristotle, *Pol.,* VIII. 5, 2–3.

in the comitia.[3] The chief might, indeed, consult his relations, and even his clients, but he alone voted. Besides, the law forbade a client to have a different opinion from his patron. If the clients were connected with the city, it was through their patrician chiefs. They took part in public worship, they appeared before the tribunal, they entered the assembly, but it was in the suite of their patrons.

We must not picture to ourselves the city of these ancient ages as an agglomeration of men living mingled together within the enclosure of the same walls. In the earliest times the city was hardly the place of habitation; it was the sanctuary where the gods of the community were; it was the fortress which defended them, and which their presence sanctified; it was the centre of the association, the residence of the king and the priests, the place where justice was administered; but the people did not live there. For several generations yet men continued to live outside the city, in isolated families, that divided the soil among them. Each of these families occupied its canton, where it had its domestic sanctuary, and where it formed, under the authority of its *pater,* an indivisible group. Then, on certain days, if the interests of the city or the obligations of the common worship called, the chiefs of these families repaired to the city and assembled around the king, either to deliberate or to assist at a sacrifice. If it was a question of war, each of these chiefs arrived, followed by his family and his servants (*sua manus*) : they were grouped by phratries, or curies, and formed the army of the city, under the command of the king.

Chapter II

THE PLEBEIANS

WE must now point out another element of the population, which was below the clients themselves, and which, originally low, insensibly acquired strength enough to break the ancient

[3] Aulus Gellius, XV. 27. We shall see that clientship underwent changes later. We speak here only of the first ages of Rome.

social organization. This class, which became more numerous at Rome than in any other city, was there called the *plebs*. We must understand the origin and character of this class to understand the part it played in the history of the city, and of the family, among the ancients. The plebeians were not the clients; the historians of antiquity do not confound these two classes. Livy, in one place, says, "The plebeians did not wish to take part in the election of the consuls; the consuls were therefore elected by the patricians and their clients." And in another, "The plebeians complained that the patricians had too much influence in the comitia, on account of the votes of their clients."[1] In Dionysius of Halicarnassus we read, "The plebeians left Rome and retired to Mons Sacer; the patricians remained alone in the city with their clients." And farther along, "The plebeians, being dissatisfied, refused to enroll their names. The patricians, with their clients, took arms and carried on the war."[2] These plebeians, completely distinct from the clients, formed no part of what was called the Roman people, at least in the first centuries. In an old prayer, which was still repeated in the time of the Punic wars, the gods were asked to be propitious "to the people and the plebs."[3] The plebs were not, therefore, comprised in the people, at any rate not originally. The people comprised the patricians and the clients: the plebs were excluded.

What constituted the peculiar character of the plebs was, that they were foreign to the religious organization of the city, and even to that of the family. By this we recognize the plebeian, and distinguish him from the client. The client

---

[1] Livy, II. 64; II. 56.

[2] Dionysius, VI. 46; VII. 19; X. 27.

[3] Livy, XXIX. 27: *Ut ea mihi populo plebique Romanæ bene verruncent.* Cicero, *pro Murena,* I. *Ut ea res mihi magistratuique meo, populo plebique Romanæ bene atque feliciter eveniat.* Macrobius (*Saturn.,* I. 17) cites an ancient oracle of the prophet Marcius, which had the words, *Prætor qui jus populo plebique dabit.* That ancient writers have not always paid attention to this essential distinction between *populus* and *plebs* ought not to surprise us, when we recollect that the distinction no longer existed at the time when they wrote. In Cicero's age the *plebs* had for several centuries legally made a part of the *populus.* But the old formulas which Livy, Cicero, and Macrobius cite, remain as memorials of the time when the two classes were not yet confounded.

shared at least in the worship of his patron, and made a part of the family and of the gens. The plebeian, at first, had no worship, and knew nothing of the sacred family.

What we have already seen of the social and religious state of ancient times explains to us how this class took its rise. Religion was not propagated; born in a family, it remained, as it were, shut in there; each family was forced to create its creed, its gods, and its worship. But there must have been, in those times, so distant from us, a great number of families in which the mind had not the power to create gods, to arrange a doctrine, to institute a worship, to invent hymns, and the rhythm of the prayer. These families naturally found themselves in a state of inferiority compared with those who had a religion, and could not make a part of society with them; they entered neither into the curies nor into the city. In the course of time it even happened that families which had a religion lost it either by negligence, forgetting the rites, or by one of those crimes which prevented a man from approaching his hearth and continuing his worship. It must have happened, also, that clients, on account of crime or bad treatment, quitted the family and renounced its religion. The son, too, who was born of a marriage in which the rites had not been performed, was reputed a bastard, like one who had been born of adultery, and the family religion did not exist for him. All these men, excluded from the family and from the worship, fell into the class of men without a sacred fire — that is to say, became plebeians.

We find this class around almost all the ancient cities, but separated by a line of demarcation. Originally a Greek city was double; there was the city, properly so called — πολις, which was built ordinarily on the summit of some hill; it had been built with the religious rites, and enclosed the sanctuary of the national gods. At the foot of the hill was found an agglomeration of houses, which were built without any religious ceremony, and without a sacred enclosure. These were the dwellings of the plebeians, who could not live in the sacred city.

At Rome the difference between the two classes was striking. The city of the patricians and their clients was the one that Romulus founded, according to the rites, on the Palatine. The dwellings of the plebs were in the asylum, a species of en-

closure situated on the slope of the Capitoline Hill, where
Romulus admitted people without hearth or home, whom he
could not admit into his city. Later, when new plebeians came
to Rome, as they were strangers to the religion of the city,
they were established on the Aventine — that is to say, without
the pomœrium, or religious city.

One word characterizes these plebeians — they were without
a hearth; they did not possess, in the beginning, at least, any
domestic altars. Their adversaries were always reproaching
them with having no ancestors, which certainly meant that
they had not the worship of ancestors, and had no family tomb
where they could carry their funeral repast. They had no
father — *pater;* that is to say, they ascended the series of their
ascendants in vain; they never arrived at a religious family
chief. They had no family — *gentem non habent;* that is to
say, they had only the natural family; as to the one which
religion formed and constituted, they had not that.

The sacred marriage did not exist for them; they knew not
its rites. Having no hearth, the union that the hearth established was forbidden to them; therefore the patricians, who
knew no other regular union than that which united husband
and wife in presence of the domestic divinity, could say, in
speaking of the plebeians, "*Connubia promiscua habent more
ferarum.*" There was no family for them, no paternal authority. They had the power over their children which strength
gave them; but that sacred authority with which religion
clothed the father, they had not.

For them there was no right of property; for all property
was established and consecrated by a hearth, a tomb, and
termini — that is to say, by all the elements of the domestic
worship. If the plebeian possessed land, that land had no
sacred character; it was profane, and had no boundaries. But
could he hold land in the earliest times? We know that at
Rome no one could exercise the right of property if he was
not a citizen; and the plebeian, in the first ages of Rome, was
not a citizen. According to the jurisconsult, one could not be
a proprietor except by quiritary right; but the plebeians were
not counted at first among the Quirites. At the foundation of
Rome the *ager Romanus* was divided up among the tribes, the
curies, and the gentes. Now, the plebeians, who belonged to

none of these groups, certainly did not share in the division. These plebeians, who had no religion, had not the qualification which enabled a man to make a portion of the soil his own. We know that they long inhabited the Aventine, and built houses there; but it was only after three centuries, and many struggles, that they finally obtained the ownership of this territory.

For the plebeians there was no law, no justice, since the law was the decision of religion, and the procedure was a body of rites. The client had the benefit of the Roman franchise through his patron; but for the plebeian this right did not exist. An ancient historian says formally that the sixth king of Rome was the first to make laws for the plebs, whilst the patricians had had theirs for a long time.[4] It appears even that these laws were afterwards withdrawn from the plebs, or that, not being founded upon religion, the patricians refused to pay any attention to them. For we see in the historian that, when tribunes were created, a special law was required to protect their lives and liberty, and that this law was worded thus: "Let no one undertake to strike or kill a tribune as he would one of the plebs."[5] It seems, therefore, that any one had a right to strike or to kill a plebeian; or, at least, that this misdeed committed against a man who was beyond the pale of the law was not punished.

The plebeians had no political rights. They were not at first citizens, and no one among them could be a magistrate. For two centuries there was no other assembly at Rome than that of the curies; and the curies did not include the plebeians. The plebs did not even enter into the composition of the army so long as that was distributed by curies.

But what manifestly separated the plebeian from the patrician was, that the plebeian had no part in the religion of the city. It was impossible for him to fill the priestly office. We may even suppose that in the earliest ages prayer was forbidden him, and that the rites could not be revealed to him. It was as in India where "the Sudra should always be ignorant of the sacred formulas." He was a foreigner, and consequently his presence alone defiled the sacrifice. He was repulsed by the

[4] Dionysius, IV. 43.
[5] Dionysius, VI. 89.

gods. Between him and the patrician there was all the distance that religion could place between two men. The plebs were a despised and abject class, beyond the pale of religion, law, society, and the family. The patrician could compare such an existence only with that of the brutes — *more ferarum.* The touch of the plebeian was impure. The decemvirs, in their first ten tables, had forgotten to interdict marriage between the two orders; for these first decemvirs were all patricians, and it never entered the mind of one of them that such a marriage was possible.

We see how many classes in the primitive age of the cities were superposed one above another. At the head was the aristocracy of family chiefs, those whom the official language of Rome called *patres,* whom the clients called *reges,* whom the Odyssey names βασιλεις or ανακτες. Below were the younger branches of the families; still lower were the clients; and lowest were the plebs.

This distinction of classes came from religion. For at the time when the ancestors of the Greeks, the Italians, and the Hindus still lived together in Central Asia, religion had said, "The oldest shall offer prayer." From this came the pre-eminence of the oldest in everything; the oldest branch in every family had been the sacerdotal and dominant branch. Still religion made great account of the younger branches, who were a species of reserve, to replace the older branch some day, if it should become extinct, and to save the worship. It also made some account of the client, and even of the slave, because they assisted in the religious acts. But the plebeian, who had no part in the worship, it reckoned as absolutely of no account. The ranks had been thus fixed.

But none of the social arrangements which man studies out and establishes is unchangeable. This carried in itself the germ of disease and death, which was too great an inequality. Many men had an interest in destroying a social organization that had no benefits for them.

Chapter III

FIRST REVOLUTION

1. Political Authority taken from the kings.

WE have said that, originally, the king was the religious chief of the city, the high-priest of the public hearth, and that he had added political authority to the priestly, because it appeared natural that the man who represented the religion of the city should at the same time be the president of the assembly, the judge, and the head of the army. By virtue of this principle, it happened that all the powers of the state became united in the hands of the king.

But the heads of families, the *patres,* and above them the chiefs of the phratries and tribes, formed, by the side of this king, a very powerful aristocracy. The king was not the only king; every *pater* was king in his own gens: even at Rome it was an ancient custom to call each one of these powerful patrons by the name of king. At Athens every phratry and every tribe had its chief, and by the side of the king of the city there were the kings of the tribes, φυλοβασιλεις. It was a hierarchy of chiefs, all having, in a more or less extended domain, the same attributes and the same inviolability. The king of the city did not exercise his authority over the entire population; the interior of families and all the clients escaped his action. Like the feudal king who had as subjects only a few powerful vassals, this king of the ancient city commanded only the chiefs of the tribes and the gentes, each one of whom might be individually as powerful as he, and who, united, were much more powerful. We can easily believe that he had some difficulty in commanding obedience. Men would have great respect for him, because he was the head of the worship, and guardian of the sacred hearth; but they might not be very submissive, since he had little power. The governors and the governed were not long in perceiving that they were not of the same opinion on the measure of obedience that was due. The kings wished to be powerful, and the *patres* preferred

that they should not be. A struggle then commenced in all
the cities, between the aristocracy and the kings.

Everywhere the issue of the struggle was the same. Royalty
was vanquished. But we must not forget that this primitive
royalty was sacred. The king was the man who pronounced
the prayers, who offered the sacrifice, who had, in fine, by
hereditary right, the power to call down upon the city the
protection of the gods. Men could not think, therefore, of
doing away with the king; one was necessary to their religion;
one was necessary to the safety of the city. So we see in all the
cities whose history is known to us, that they did not at first
touch the religious authority of the king, and contented themselves with taking away his political power. This was only a
sort of appendix, which the kings had added to their priesthood, and was not, like that, sacred and inviolable. It might
be taken from the kings without imperilling religion.

Royalty was, therefore, preserved; but, shorn of its power,
it was no longer anything but a priesthood. "In very ancient
times," says Aristotle, "kings had absolute power in peace and
war; but in the course of time some renounced this power
voluntarily, from others it was taken by force, and nothing was
left to these kings but the care of the sacrifices." Plutarch gives
a similar account: "As the kings displayed pride and rigor in
their commands, the greater part of the Greeks took away their
power, and left them only the care of religion."[1] Herodotus,
speaking of the city of Cyrene, says, "They left to Battus, a
descendant of the kings, the care of the worship and the
possession of the sacred lands, but they took away all the
power which his fathers had enjoyed."

This royalty, thus reduced to a priesthood, continued, in
most cases, to be hereditary in the sacred family that had long
before established the hearth and commenced the national
worship. In the time of the Roman empire — that is to say,
seven or eight centuries after this revolution — there were yet at
Ephesus, at Marseilles, and at Thespiæ, families who preserved
the title and insignia of ancient royalty, and who still presided
over religious ceremonies.[2] In the other cities the sacred

[1] Aristotle, *Politics,* III. 9, 8. Plutarch, *Rom. Quest.,* 63.
[2] Strabo, IV.; IX. Diodorus, IV. 29.

families were extinct, and the kingly office had become elective, and generally annual.

2. History of this Revolution at Sparta.

Sparta always had kings, and still the revolution of which we speak was accomplished here as well as in the other cities.

It appears that the first Dorian kings reigned as absolute masters. But in the third generation the struggle commenced between the kings and the aristocracy. During two centuries there was a series of struggles, which made Sparta one of the most unquiet cities in Greece. We know that one of these kings, the father of Lycurgus, was killed by the blow of a stone in a civil war.[3]

Nothing is more obscure than the history of Lycurgus. His ancient biographer commences with these words: "We can say nothing of him that is not subject to controversy." It seems certain, at least, that Lycurgus appeared in a time of dissensions, "at a time when the government floated in the midst of perpetual agitation." What appears the most clearly from all the information that has come down to us concerning him, is, that his reform dealt royalty a blow from which it never recovered. "Under Charilaus," says Aristotle, "the monarchy gave place to an aristocracy."[4] Now, this Charilaus was king when Lycurgus made his reform. We know, moreover, from Plutarch, that Lycurgus was intrusted with the duty of making laws only when a civil disturbance arose, during which king Charilaus sought safety in a temple. Lycurgus had for a moment the power to suppress royalty: he took good care not to do this, judging that royalty was necessary, and the royal family inviolable. But he arranged so that the kings were thenceforth subordinate to the senate in whatever concerned the government, and that they were no longer anything more than presidents of this assembly, and the executors of its decrees. A century later, royalty was still farther weakened; the executive power was taken away and was intrusted to annual magistrates, who were called *ephors*.

[3] Strabo, VIII. 5. Plutarch, *Lycurgus*, 2.

[4] Aristotle, *Politics*, VIII. 10, 3 (V. 10). Heracleides of Pontus, in *Fragm. Hist. Græc.*, coll. Didot, t. II. p. 11. Plutarch, *Lycurgus*, 4.

It is easy to judge by the duties of the ephors what those were that were left to the king. The ephors pronounced judgment in civil cases, while the senate tried criminal cases. The ephors, with the advice of the senate, declared war, or settled the articles of treaties of peace. In time of war two ephors accompanied the king and watched over him; they decided on the plan of the campaign, and superintended all the operations.[5] What remained, then, for the kings, if the law, the foreign relations, and military operations were taken from them? They had the priesthood left. Herodotus describes their prerogatives: "If the city offers a sacrifice, they have the first place at the sacred repast; they are served first, and have a double portion. They are the first also to make a libation, and the skins of the victims belong to them. Each one receives, twice a month, a victim, which he sacrifices to Apollo."[6] "The kings," says Xenophon, "offer the public sacrifices, and they have the best parts of the victims." If they did not act as judges either in civil or in criminal affairs, they still had reserved to them the right of deciding in all affairs which concerned religion. In case of war, one of the kings always proceeded at the head of the troops, offering sacrifices and consulting the presages. In presence of the enemy he slew victims, and when the signs were favorable, he gave the signal for battle. During the combat he was surrounded by diviners, who indicated to him the will of the gods, and flute-players, who sounded the sacred hymns. The Spartans said the king commanded, because he was in possession of both religion and the auspices; but the ephors and the polemarchs directed all the movements of the army.[7]

We can therefore justly say that the royalty of Sparta was

[5] Thucydides, V. 63. Hellanicus, II. 4. Xenophon, *Gov. of Laced.*, 14 (13); *Hell.*, VI. 4. Plutarch, *Agesilaus*, 10, 17, 23, 28; *Lysander*, 23. The king had so little, of his own right, the direction of military affairs, that a special act of the senate was necessary to confirm the command of the army to Agesilaus, who thus united exceptionally the functions of king and general. Plutarch, *Agesilaus*, 6; *Lysander*, 23. It had been the same previously, in the case of king Pausanias. Thucydides, I. 128.

[6] Herodotus, VI. 56, 57.

[7] Xenophon, *Gov. of Laced.*

merely an hereditary priesthood. The same revolution which suppressed the political power of the kings in other cities suppressed it also in Sparta. The power belonged really to the senate, which directed, and to the ephors, who executed. The kings, in all that did not concern religion, obeyed the ephors. Herodotus could therefore say that Sparta did not know the monarchial *régime;* and Aristotle, that the government of Sparta was an aristocracy.[8]

3. *The same Revolution at Athens.*

We have seen above what the primitive population of Attica was. A certain number of families, independent and without any bond of union among them, occupied the country; each one of them formed a society, governed by an hereditary chief. Later these families were united in groups, and from their association grew the Athenian city. The great work of completing the unity of Attica is attributed to Theseus. But the traditions add — and we can easily believe — that Theseus must have met with strong resistance. The class of men who opposed him were not the clients, or the poor, who were scattered about in the villages and the γενη. These men rejoiced, rather, at a change which gave a chief to their chiefs, and assured to themselves a refuge and a protection. The ones who suffered by the change were the chiefs of families, and the chiefs of villages and tribes, the βασιλεις, φυλοβασιλεις, those Eupatrids who, by hereditary right, held the supreme authority in their γενος, or in their tribe. These stoutly defended their independence, and when it was lost they lamented its loss.

At any rate they retained all they could of their ancient independence. Each remained the absolute chief of his tribe, or of his γενος. Theseus could not destroy an authority which religion had established, and which it rendered inviolable. Still further, if we examine the traditions which relate to this epoch, we shall see that these powerful Eupatrids agreed to associate for the purpose of forming a city only after stipulating that the government should be really federative, and that each one of themselves should have a part in it. There was, indeed, a supreme king; but as soon as the common interest

[8] Herodotus, V. 92. Aristotle, *Politics,* VIII. 10 (V. 10).

was at stake, the assembly of the chiefs was convoked, and nothing of importance could be done without the consent of this species of a senate.

These traditions, in the language of succeeding generations, were expressed somewhat after this manner: "Theseus changed the government of Athens from a monarchy to a republic." This is the account of Aristotle, Isocrates, Demosthenes, and Plutarch. In this somewhat deceptive statement there is a foundation of truth. Theseus did, indeed, as tradition says, "restore the sovereign authority to the hands of the people." Only the word people, δημος, which the tradition has preserved, had not, in the time of Theseus, so extended an application as it had in the time of Demosthenes. This people, or political body, was then no other than an aristocracy — that is to say, the entire body of the chiefs of the γενη.

Theseus, in establishing this assembly, was not necessarily an innovator. But in spite of him the formation of the great Athenian unity changed the conditions of the government. As soon as these Eupatrids, whose authority remained intact in the families, were united in the same city, they formed a powerful body, which had its rights, and might make its claims. The king of the little rock of Cecrops became the king of all Attica; but instead of being, as in his little village, an absolute king, he was now only the chief of a federative state — that is to say, the first among equals. A conflict between this aristocracy and royalty could not be long delayed. "The Eupatrids regretted the really royal power which each one of them had previously exercised in his village. It appears that these warrior priests placed religion in the front rank, and pretended that the authority of the local worships had been diminished. If it is true, as Thucydides says, that Theseus attempted to destroy the prytanea of the villages, it is not surprising that the religious sentiment was aroused against him. It is impossible to say how many contests he had to sustain, how many risings he had to repress, by address or by force. What is certain is, that he was finally vanquished; that he was driven from Athens, and died in exile.

The Eupatrids then had full sway; they did not suppress royalty, but they set up a king of their choice, Menestheus. After him, the family of Theseus recovered the power, and held it during three generations. It was then replaced by another family — that of the Melanthidæ. This whole period must have been very unquiet; but no definite account of the civil wars has been preserved.

The death of Codrus coincides with the final victory of the Eupatrids. They did not yet suppress royalty, for their religious notions forbade this; but they took away its political power. The traveller Pausanias, who lived long after these events, but who carefully consulted the traditions, says that royalty then lost a great part of its attributes, and "became dependent," which signifies, doubtless, that it was thenceforth subordinate to the senate of the Eupatrids. Modern historians call this period of Athenian history that of the archonships, and rarely fail to say that royalty was then abolished. But this is not strictly true. The descendants of Codrus succeeded each other from father to son during thirteen generations. They had the title of archon, but there are ancient documents which give them also that of king,[9] and we have already said that these two titles were exactly synonymous. Athens, therefore, during this long period, still had hereditary kings; but it had taken away their power, and had left them only the religious functions. This is what had been done at Sparta.

At the end of three centuries, the Eupatrids found that this religious royalty was still more powerful than they desired, and they weakened it still more. They decided that the same man should not be clothed with this high sacerdotal dignity for more than ten years. But they continued to believe that the ancient royal family was alone qualified to fill the office of archon.[10]

About forty years passed thus. But one day the royal family was stained with a crime, and men thought it could no longer fill the priestly office:[11] that thenceforth the archons should be chosen outside this family, and that this dignity should be accessible to all the Eupatrids. Forty years later, in order to enfeeble this royalty, or to distribute it into more hands, they made it annual, and divided it into two distinct magistracies.

---

9 See *Parian Marbles,* and Comp. Pausanias, I. 3, 2; VII. 2, 1; Plato, *Menexenes,* p. 238, c.; Ælian, *V. H.,* V. 13.

10 Pausanias, IV. 3.

11 Heracleides of Pontus, I. 3. Nicholas of Damascus, *Fragm.* 51.

Up to that time the archon was at the same time king; but thenceforth these two titles were separated. A magistrate called an archon, and another magistrate called a king, shared the attributes of the ancient religious royalty. The duty of watching over the perpetuation of families, of authorizing or forbidding adoption, of receiving wills, of deciding questions relating to real property — everything in which religion was interested — devolved upon the archon. The duty of offering the solemn sacrifices, and that of judging cases of impiety, were reserved to the kings. Thus the title of king — a sacred title, which was necessary to religion — was perpetuated in the city with the sacrifices and the national worship. The king and the archon, together with the polemarch and the six thesmothetæ, who had perhaps existed for a long time, completed the number of nine annual magistrates, whom it was the custom to call the nine archons, from the name of the first among them.

The revolution that took from royalty its political power, was carried through under different forms in all the cities. At Argos, from the second generation of Dorian kings, royalty was so weakened "that there was left to the descendants of Temenus only the name of king, without any power;" still this royalty remained hereditary during several centuries.[12] At Cyrene the descendants of Battus at first united in their hands the priesthood and the political power; but after the fourth generation nothing was left them but the priesthood.[13] At Corinth royalty was at first transmitted hereditarily in the family of the Bacchidæ. The effect of the revolution was to render the office annual, but without taking it from this family, whose members held it by turns for a century.

4. The same Revolution at Rome.

At first, royalty was at Rome what it had been in Greece. The king was the high priest of the city; he was at the same time the supreme judge; he also commanded the armed citizens. Next to him were the patres, who formed a senate. There was but one king, because religion enjoined unity in the priesthood and unity in the government. But it was

12 Pausanias, II. 19.
13 Herodotus, IV. 161. Diodorus, VIII.

understood that on all important affairs the king must consult the heads of the confederated families.[14] From this time historians mention an assembly of the people. But we must inquire what was then the meaning of the word people (*populus*), that is to say, what was the body politic in the time of the first kings. All the witnesses agree that the people always assembled by curies; now the curies were the collection of the gentes; every gens repaired there in a body, and had but one vote. The clients were there, ranged round the pater, consulted perhaps, perhaps giving their advice, contributing towards the single vote which the gens cast, but with no power to give an opinion contrary to that of the pater. This assembly of the curies was, then, nothing but the patrician city united in presence of the kings.

By this we see that Rome was in the same state as the other cities. The king was in the presence of an aristocratic body very strongly organized, and which derived its power from religion. The same conflicts which we have seen in Greece, therefore, took place in Rome. The history of the seven kings is the history of this long quarrel. The first wished to increase his power and free himself from the authority of the senate. He sought the favor of the inferior classes, but the Fathers were hostile to him; and he perished, assassinated in an assembly of the senate.

The aristocracy immediately dream of abolishing royalty, and the Fathers fill by turns the place of the king. The lower classes are agitated, it is true; they do not wish to be governed by the chiefs of the gentes, and demand the restoration of royalty.[15] But the patricians satisfy themselves by deciding that henceforth it shall be elective, and they fix the forms of election with marvellous skill. The senate must choose the candidate; the patrician assembly of the curies must confirm this choice; and, finally, the patrician augurs must declare whether this newly-elected king is pleasing to the gods.

Numa was elected according to these rules. He was very religious — rather a priest than a warrior, a very scrupulous observer of all the rites of worship, and consequently very strongly attached to the religious constitution of the families

14 Cicero, *De Repub.*, II. 8.
15 Livy, I. Cicero, *De Repub.*, II.

and the city. He was a king after the hearts of the patricians, and died peaceably in his bed.

It should seem that, under Numa, royalty had been reduced to its priestly functions, as it had been in the Greek cities. It is at least certain that the religious authority of the king was entirely distinct from his political, and that one did not necessarily accompany the other. What proves this is, that there was a double election. By virtue of the first, the king was merely a religious chief; if to this dignity he wished to join the political power, *imperium,* it was necessary that the city should confer it upon him by a special decree. This conclusion follows clearly from what Cicero has told us of the ancient constitution. Thus the priesthood and the political power were distinct; they might be placed in the same hands, but for that two comitia and a double election were necessary.

The third king certainly united them in his own hands. He held both the priestly office and the command; he was even more warrior than priest; he neglected, and wished to diminish, the religious element, the strength of the aristocracy. We see him welcome a multitude of strangers to Rome, in spite of the religious principle which excluded them; he even dared to live in the midst of them on the Cælian Hill. We also see him distribute to plebeians lands, the revenue of which, up to that time, had been appropriated to defraying the expenses of the sacrifices. The patricians accused him of having neglected the rites, and, what was even worse, of having modified and altered them. And so he died like Romulus; the gods of the patricians destroyed him and his sons with a thunderbolt. This event restored the supremacy to the senate, which set up a king of its own choice. Ancus scrupulously observed all the religious rites, made war as seldom as possible, and passed his life in the temples. Dear to the patricians, he died in his bed.

The fifth king was Tarquin, who obtained the throne in spite of the senate, and by the help of the lower classes. He was troubled little with religious scruples; indeed, he was very incredulous; nothing less than a miracle could convince him of the science of the augurs. He was an enemy of the ancient families; he created patricians, and changed the old religious constitution of the city as much as possible. Tarquin was assassinated.

The sixth king gained possession of the throne by stratagem: it should seem, indeed, that the senate never recognized him as a legitimate king. He flattered the lower classes, distributed lands among them without regard to the rights of property, and even conferred political rights upon them. Servius was murdered on the steps of the senate house.

The quarrel between the kings and the aristocracy assumed the character of a social struggle. The kings sided with the people, and depended for support upon the clients and the plebs. To the patrician order, so powerfully organized, they opposed the lower classes, so numerous at Rome. The aristocracy then found itself threatened by a double peril, the worst of which was not the necessity of giving way before royalty. It saw rising in its rear the classes that it despised. It saw the plebs organizing, a class without religion and without a sacred fire. It saw itself in danger of being attacked by its clients, within the family itself, whose constitution, rights, and religion were discussed and jeopardized. In the eyes of the aristocracy, therefore, the kings were odious enemies, who, to augment their own power, were planning to overthrow the sacred organization of the family and of the city.

The second Tarquin succeeded Servius; he disappointed the hopes of the senators who had elected him, and wished to be master — *de rege dominus exstitit.* He weakened the patricians to the extent of his power; he struck off the highest heads; reigned without consulting the Fathers, and made war and peace without asking their approval. The patricians seemed completely subdued.

Finally, an occasion presented itself. Tarquin was far from Rome; his army — that is to say, his support — was also away. The city was, for a time, in the hands of the patricians. The prefect of the city — that is to say, the one who held the civil power during the absence of the king — was a patrician, Lucretius. The commander of the cavalry — that is to say, the one whose military authority was next to that of the king — was a patrician, Junius.[16] These two men prepared the insurrection. They had, as associates, other patricians, Valerius and Tarquinius Collatinus. The place of meeting was not at Rome, but at the little city of Collatia, which was the property of

[16] The Junian family was patrician. Dionysius, IV. 68.

one of the conspirators. There they showed the people the body of a woman; they said this woman had taken her own life as a punishment for the crime of a son of the king. The people of Collatia revolt and move on to Rome; there the same scene is renewed. Men are taken by surprise; the king's partisans are disconcerted, and besides, at this very moment, the legal power in Rome belongs to Junius and Lucretius.

The conspirators take good care not to assemble the people, but to repair to the senate house. The senate declares Tarquin dethroned and royalty abolished. But the decree of the senate must be confirmed by the city. Lucretius, as prefect of the city, has the right to convoke the assembly. The curies are assembled, and they agree with the conspirators; they declare for the deposition of Tarquin, and the creation of two consuls.

This principal point being decided, they leave the nomination of the consuls to the assembly by centuries. But will not this assembly, in which some plebeians vote, protest against what the patricians have done in the senate and the curies? It cannot. For every Roman assembly is presided over by a magistrate, who states the object of the vote, and no other question can come up for deliberation. More than this, none but the president at this period has the right to speak. If a law is to be voted upon, the centuries can vote only yes or no. If it is an election, the president presents the candidates, and no candidate except those presented can be voted for. In the present case, the president appointed by the senate is Lucretius, one of the conspirators. He states that the only object of the meeting is the election of two consuls. He presents two names, those of Junius and Tarquinius Collatinus, as candidates for the office. These two men are necessarily elected. The senate now ratify the election, and lastily the augurs confirm it in the name of the gods.

This revolution did not please every body at Rome. Many plebeians joined the king, and followed his fortunes. On the other hand, a rich Sabine patrician, the powerful chief of a numerous gens, the haughty Attus Clausus, found the new government so much to his taste that he came to Rome to live.

Still it was political royalty only that was suppressed: religious royalty was sacred, and must endure. Therefore men hastened to name a king, but one who was king only for the sacrifices — *rex sacrorum*. All imaginable precautions were taken that this king-priest should never take advantage of the great prestige which his office gave him, and seize upon the civil power.

Chapter IV

THE ARISTOCRACY GOVERNS THE CITIES

THE same revolution, under forms slightly varied, took place at Athens, at Sparta, at Rome, in all the cities, in fine, whose history is known to us. Everywhere it was the work of the aristocracy; everywhere it resulted in suppressing political royalty and continuing religious royalty. From this epoch, during a period whose duration was very unequal in different cities, the government of the city was in the hands of the aristocracy.

This aristocracy rested at the same time on birth and religion. It had its foundation in the religious constitution of the family. It originated in the same rules that we have noticed above, in the domestic worship and in private law — that is to say, the law of the hereditary descent of the sacred fire, the right of primogeniture, and the right of pronouncing the prayers, which was the prerogative of birth. An hereditary religion was the title of this aristocracy to absolute dominion, and gave it rights that appeared sacred. According to ancient ideas, he alone could be an owner of land who had a domestic worship; he alone was a member of the city who embodied the religious character which constituted the citizen; he alone could be a priest who was a descendant of a family having a worship; he alone could be a magistrate who had the right to offer the sacrifices. A man who had no hereditary worship might be the client of another man; or, if he preferred it, he could remain without the pale of all society. For many generations it did not enter the minds of men that this inequality was unjust. No one had thought of establishing human society upon any other principles.

At Athens, from the death of Codrus to the time of Solon, all authority was in the hands of the Eupatrids. They alone were priests and archons. They alone acted as judges, and knew the laws, which were not written, and whose sacred formulas were transmitted from father to son.

These families preserved as much as possible the ancient forms of the patriarchal *régime*. They did not live united in the city, but continued to live in the various cantons of Attica, each on its vast domain, surrounded by its numerous servants, governed by its Eupatrid chief, and practising its hereditary worship in absolute independence.[1] During four centuries the Athenian city was merely a confederation of these powerful heads of families, who assembled on certain days for the celebration of the central worship, or for the pursuit of common interests.

Men have often remarked how mute history is regarding this long period in the life of Athens, and in general in the life of Greek cities. They are surprised that, when it has preserved the memory of so many events from the times of the ancient kings, it has recorded so few of the time of the aristocratic governments. The reason is doubtless because at that time very few acts of general interest took place. The return of the patriarchal *régime* had almost suspended the national life. Men lived apart, and had few common interests. The horizon of each one was the small group and the small hamlet where he lived, as Eupatrid or as servant.

At Rome, too, each patrician family lived upon its estate, surrounded by its clients. Men came to the city to celebrate the festivals of the public worship, and for the public assemblies. During the years that followed the expulsion of the kings, the power of the aristocracy was absolute. None but a patrician could fill the priestly office in the city; the vestals, the pontiffs, the salii, the flamens, and the augurs, were chosen exclusively from the sacred caste. Patricians alone could be consuls; they alone composed the senate. Though they did not suppress the assembly by centuries, to which the plebeians had access, they at any rate regarded the assembly by curies as the only one that was legitimate and sacred. The centuries had, in appearance, the election of the consuls; but we have seen

[1] Thucydides, II. 15, 16.

that they could vote only on the names that the patricians presented, and, besides, their decisions were submitted to the triple ratification of the senate, the curies, and the augurs. Patricians alone administered justice, and knew the forms of the law.

This political system lasted at Rome only a few years. In Greece, on the contrary, there was a long period during which the aristocracy was master. The Odyssey presents us with a faithful picture of this social state in the western portion of Greece. We see there a patriarchal *régime* strongly resembling what we have remarked in Attica. A few great and rich families own the whole country. Numerous slaves cultivate the soil, or tend the flocks; the manner of living is simple — a single table suffices for the chief and the servants. These chiefs are called by a name which becomes, under other circumstances, a pompous title — ανακτες, βασιλεις. Thus it happened that the Athenians of primitive times gave the chief of the γενος the title of βασιλευς, and that at Rome the clients preserved the custom of calling the chief of the gens *rex*. These heads of families have a sacred character; the poet calls them divine kings. Ithaca is very small, yet it contains a great number of these kings. Among them there is indeed a supreme king; but he is of little importance, and appears to have no other prerogative than that of presiding at the council of the chiefs. It appears, even, from certain indications, that this office is elective, and it is clear the Telemachus will not be the supreme chief of the isle, unless the other chiefs, his equals, wish to elect him. Ulysses, returning to his country, appears to have no other subjects than the servants who belong to him personally. When he has slain some of the chiefs, their servants take up arms and sustain a contest which the poet does not think blameworthy. Among the Phæacians, Alcinous has supreme authority; but we see him repair to an assembly of the chiefs; and we may remark that he does not convoke the council, but that the council summons the king. The poet describes an assembly of the Phæacian city. It is far from being an assembly of the multitude; the chiefs alone, individually convoked by a herald, as at Rome for the *comitia calata*, assemble; they occupy seats of stone; the king makes an address, and calls his auditors sceptre-bearing kings.

In Hesiod's city, the rocky Ascra, we find a class of men whom the poet calls the chiefs, or kings. They are those who administer justice to the people. Pindar also shows us a class of chiefs among the Cadmæans; at Thebes he extols the sacred race of the Sparti, from which, at a later date, Epaminondas derives his descent. We can hardly read Pindar without being struck with the aristocratic spirit which still reigned in Greek society in the time of the Persian wars. From this we may imagine how powerful the aristocracy was a century or two earlier. For what the poet boasts of the most in his heroes, is their family; and we must suppose that this sort of praise was at that time highly valued, and that birth still seemed the supreme good. Pindar shows us the great families which were then conspicuous in each city; in the single city of Ægina he names the Midylidæ, the Theandridæ, the Euxenidæ, the Blepsiadæ, the Chariadæ, the Balychidæ. At Syracuse he extols a priestly family of the Iamidæ; at Agrigentum, that of the Emmenidæ, and so on for all the cities of which he has occasion to speak.

At Epidaurus, the entire body of the citizens — that is to say, of those who had political rights — was for a long time composed of no more than one hundred and eighty members. All the rest "were outside the city."[2] The real citizens were still fewer at Heraclea, where the younger members of the great families had no political rights.[3] The case was a long time the same at Cnidus, at Istros, and at Marseilles. At Thera all the power was in the hands of a few families which were reputed sacred. It was the same at Apollonia.[4]

At Erythræ there was an aristocratic class called the Basilidæ. In the cities of Eubœa the ruling class were called the knights.[5] We may remark here that among the ancients, as in the middle ages, it was a privilege to fight on horseback.

The monarchy had already ceased to exist at Corinth when a colony set out from there to found Syracuse. The new city, therefore, knew nothing of royalty, and was ruled from the first by an aristocracy. This class was called Geomori, that is

[2] Plutarch, Gr. Quest., I.
[3] Aristotle, Politics, VIII. 5, 2.
[4] Aristotle, Politics, III. 9, 8; VI. 3, 8.
[5] Aristotle, Politics, VIII. 5, 10.

to say, proprietors. It was composed of families which, on the day of the foundation, had distributed among themselves, with all the ordinary rites, the sacred parts of the territory. This aristocracy remained for several generations absolute master of the government, and it preserved its title of *proprietors*, which seems to indicate that the lower classes had not the right of property in the soil. An aristocracy of the same kind ruled for a long time at Miletus and at Samos.[6]

Chapter V

SECOND REVOLUTION. CHANGE IN THE CONSTITUTION OF THE FAMILY. THE RIGHT OF PRIMOGENITURE DISAPPEARS. THE GENS IS DISMEMBERED

THE revolution which had overturned royalty had modified the exterior form of the government rather than changed the constitution of society. It had not been the work of the lower classes, who had an interest in destroying the old institutions, but of the aristocracy, who wished to maintain them. It had not been undertaken in order to overturn the ancient constitution of the family, but rather to preserve it. The kings had often been tempted to elevate the inferior classes and to weaken the gentes, and for this the kings themselves had been dethroned. The aristocracy had brought about a political revolution only to prevent a social one. They had taken the power in hand, less from the pleasure of ruling than to protect their old institutions, their ancient principles, their domestic worship, their paternal authority, the *régime* of the gens — in fine, the private law which the primitive religion had established.

This great and general effort of the aristocracy was to meet a danger. Now, it appears that, in spite of these efforts, and of the victory itself, the danger continued. The old institutions begin to totter, and grave changes were about to be introduced into the inner constitution of the family. The old rule of the gens, founded by the domestic religion, had not been destroyed

6 Diodorus, VIII. 5. Thucydides, VIII. 21. Herodotus, VII. 155.

at the time when men passed to the government of the city. They had not wished, they had not been able; immediately to renounce it, as the chiefs clung to their authority, and the lower classes had not at first the desire to free themselves. The rule of the gens was therefore reconciled with that of the city. But these were in reality two antagonistic forms of government, which men could not hope to ally forever, and which must sooner or later be at war with each other. The family, indivisible and numerous, was too strong and too independent for the social power not to feel the temptation, and even the need, of weakening it. Either the city could not last, or it must in the course of time break up the family.

The ancient gens, with its single hearth, its sovereign chief, and its indivisible domain, was a convenient arrangement so long as the state of isolation continued, and no other form of society than itself existed. But as soon as men were united in cities, the authority of the ancient chief was necessarily diminished; for though he was sovereign in his own gens, he was a member of a community; as such, the general interests obliged him to make sacrifices, and general laws commanded obedience. In his own eyes, and, above all, in the eyes of his inferiors, his dignity was impaired. Then, in this community, aristocratically as it was constituted, the lower classes counted for something, if only on account of their numbers. The family which comprised several branches, and which attended the comitia, surrounded by a multitude of clients, naturally had greater authority in the general deliberations than a small family that counted few hands and few soldiers. Now, these inferiors were not slow to see their importance and strength. A certain sentiment of pride, and the desire for a better fate, grew up among them. Added to this was the rivalry of the heads of families striving for influence and seeking mutually to weaken each other. Then, too, they were ambitious of the magistracies of the city. To obtain these they sought popularity, and, to hold them, they neglected or forgot their little sovereignties. These causes produced by degrees a sort of relaxation in the constitution of the gens; those for whose interest it was to maintain this constitution held to it less, while those who had an interest in modifying it became bolder and stronger.

The force of individuality, at first strong in the family, insensibly became weaker. The right of primogenture, which was the condition of its unity, disappeared. We ought not to expect that any writer of antiquity should furnish us the exact date of this great change. It is probable that there was no date, because the change did not take place in a year. It was effected by degrees — at first in one family, then in another, and little by little in all. It happened, so to speak, without any one's perceiving it.

We can easily perceive, also, that men did not pass at once from the indivisibility of the patrimony to the equal division among the brothers. There was apparently a transition period between these two conditions of property. Affairs probably took the same course in Greece and Italy as in ancient Hindu society, where the religious law after having prescribed the indivisibility of the patrimony, left the father free to give some portion of it to his younger sons; then, after having required that the oldest should have at least a double portion, permitted the apportionment to be equal, and finished by recommending this arrangement.

But we have no precise information upon these points. A single fact is certain — that the right of primogeniture existed at an ancient epoch, and that afterwards it disappeared.

This change was not accomplished at the same time, nor in the same manner, in all the cities. In some legislation maintained it for a long time. At Thebes and at Corinth it was still in vigor in the eighth century. At Athens legislation still showed some preference for the oldest. At Sparta the right of primogeniture continued until the triumph of democracy. There were cities where it disappeared only after an insurrection. At Heraclea, Cnidus, Istros, and Marseilles the younger branches took up arms to destroy at the same time the right of primogeniture and the paternal authority.[1] From that time Greek cities that had not before counted more than a hundred men enjoyed political rights, could count five or six hundred. All the members of aristocratic families were citizens, and magistracies and the senate were open to them.

It is impossible to tell at what time the privilege of birth disappeared at Rome. It is probable that the kings, in the

[1] Aristotle, *Politics*, VIII. 5, 2, ed. B. Saint Hilaire.

midst of their struggle against the aristocracy, did all that lay in their power thus to suppress and disorganize the gentes. At the beginning of the republic, we see a hundred new members enter the senate. Livy believed that they came from the plebs;[2] but it is not possible that the hard rule of the patricians could have commenced with a concession of this nature. These new senators must have been taken from patrician families; they had not the same title as the old members of the senate; these latter were called *patres* (chiefs of families); the new ones were called *conscripti* (chosen).[3] Does not this difference of name make it probable that the hundred new senators, who were not family chiefs, belonged to younger branches of patrician gentes? We may suppose that this class of the younger branches, being numerous and energetic, lent its support to the enterprise of Brutus and the *fathers,* only on the condition of receiving civil and political rights. These branches thus acquired, through the need which the patres had of them, what the same class conquered by its arms at Heraclea, Cnidus, and Marseilles.

The right of primogeniture, then, disappeared everywhere — an important revolution which began to transform society. The Italian gens and the Hellenic γενos lost their primitive unity. The different branches separated; thenceforth each had its share of the property, its domicile, its own interests, and its independence. *Singuli singulas familias incipiunt habere,* says the jurisconsult. There is in the Latin language an old expression which appears to date from this epoch; *familiam ducere,* they said of one who separated from the gens, and established a new stock, just as they said *ducere coloniam* of one who quitted the metropolis, and went to found a colony. The brother who thus separated from the oldest brother had thenceforth his own sacred fire, which, doubtless, he had lighted at the common fire of the gens, as the colony lighted its fire at the prytaneum of the metropolis. The gens no longer preserved anything more than a sort of religious authority over

[2] He contradicts himself elsewhere. *Ex primoribus ordinis equestris,* he says. Now, the *primores* of the equestrian order—that is to say, the knights of the first six centuries—were patricians. See Belot, *Hist. des chevaliers romains,* liv. I. ch. 2.

[3] Festus, v. *Conscripti, Allecti.* Plutarch, *Rom. Quest.,* 58. For several centuries the *patres* were distinguished from the *conscripti.*

the different families that had left it. Its worship had the supremacy over theirs. They were not allowed to forget that they had sprung from this gens; they continued to bear its name; on fixed days they assembled around the common fire, to venerate the ancient ancestor or the protecting divinity. They continued even to have a religious chief, and it is probable that the oldest preserved his privilege of the priesthood, which long remained hereditary. With this exception, they were independent.

This dismemberment of the gens led to important consequences. The antique priestly family, which had formed a group so firmly united, so strongly constituted, so powerful, was forever weakened. This revolution paved the way for other changes, and rendered them easier.

Chapter VI

THE CLIENTS BECOME FREE

1. What Clientship was at first, and how it was transformed.

HERE is another revolution, the date of which we cannot indicate, but which certainly modified the constitution of the family and of society itself. The ancient family comprised, under the authority of a single chief, two classes of unequal rank; on the one side were the younger branches — that is to say, individuals naturally free; on the other, the servants or clients, inferior by birth, but connected with the chief by their participation in the domestic worship. We have just seen one of these classes emerge from its inferior condition; the second also aspired at an early date to become free. It succeeded in the course of time; clientship became modified, and finally disappeared.

This was an immense change, which the ancient writers have given us no account of. In the same way, in the middle ages, the chroniclers do not tell us how the rural population were transformed by degrees. There has been in the existence of human societies a great number of revolutions no trace of which has been handed down to us in any document.

Writers have not noticed them, because they were accomplished slowly, in an insensible manner, without any apparent struggle; profound and silent revolutions, which moved the foundations of human society, without anything appearing on the surface, and which remained concealed even from the generations that took part in them. History can seize them only a long time after they have taken place, when, in comparing two epochs in the life of a people, it sees differences between them, which show that a great revolution has been accomplished.

If we credit the picture which writers have traced of the primitive clientship of Rome, that must have been truly a golden age. Who could be more humane than this patron, who defended his client before the courts, who sustained him with his money if he was poor, and who provided for the education of his children? What could be more touching than to see this client sustain the patron when he had fallen into debt, paying his debts, giving all he had to procure his ransom? But there was not so much sentiment among the ancients. Disinterested affection and devotion were never institutions. We must have another idea of client and patron.

What we know with the greatest certainty concerning the client is, that he could not leave one patron and choose another, and that he was bound, from father to son, to the same family. If we knew only this, it would be sufficient to convince us that his condition could not be a very desirable one. Let us add that the client was not a proprietor of the soil; the land belonged to the patron, who, as chief of a domestic worship, and also as a member of a city, was the only one qualified to be a proprietor. If the client cultivated the soil, it was in the name and for the profit of the master. He was not even the owner of personal property, of his money, of his *peculium*. As a proof of this, the patron could take from him all these things to pay his own debts or his ransom. Thus nothing belonged to the client. True, the patron owed him and his children a living; but, in turn, his labor was due to the patron. We cannot say that he was precisely a slave; but he had a master, to whom he belonged, and to whose will he was in all things subject. During his whole life he was a client, and his sons after him were clients.

There is some analogy between the client of ancient times and the serf of the middle ages. The principle which condemned them to obedience was not the same, it is true. For the serf, this principle was the right of property, which was exercised at the same time over the soil and over man; for the client, this principle was the domestic religion, to which he was bound under the authority of the patron, who was its priest. Otherwise the subordination of the client and of the serf was the same; the one was bound to his patron as the other was bound to his lord; the client could no more quit the gens than the serf could quit the glebe. The client, like the serf, remained subject to a master, from father to son. A passage in Livy leads us to suppose that he was forbidden to marry outside the gens, as the serf was forbidden to marry outside the village. It is certain that he could not contract marriage without the permission of his patron. The patron could take possession of the soil which the client cultivated, and the money which he possessed, as the lord could do in the case of the serf. If the client died, all that he had been in possession of returned of right to the patron, just as the succession of the serf belonged to the lord.

The patron was not only a master; he was a judge; he could condemn a client to death. He was, moreover, a religious chief. The client bent under this authority, at the same time material and moral, which held both body and soul. His religion, it is true, imposed duties upon the patron, but they were duties of which he alone was the judge, and for whch there was no sanction. The client saw nothing that protected him: he was not of himself a citizen; if he wished to appear before the tribunal of the city, his patron might conduct him there, and speak for him. Did he ask the protection of the laws? He did not know the sacred formulas; and if he knew them, the first law for him was never to testify or to speak against his patron. Without the patron there was no justice; against the patron there was no recourse.

The client did not exist at Rome only; he was found among the Sabines and the Etruscans, making a part of the *manus* of every chief. He existed in the ancient Hellenic gens as well as in that of Italy. We must not look for him in the Dorian cities, it is true, where the rule of the gens disappeared at an early date, and where the conquered peoples were bound, not to a master, but to a lot of land. We find a similar class at Athens, and in the Ionian and Æolian cities, under the name of *Thetes*, or *Pelatæ*.

So long as the aristocratic government lasted, these Thetes did not make a part of the city. Shut up in families, which they could not leave, they were in the power of the Eupatrids, who had the same character and the same authority as the Roman patrons.

We can easily believe that at an early date there was hatred between the patron and the client. It is not difficult to picture to one's self the kind of life that was passed in that family where one had the authority and the other had no rights; where obedience, without reserve and without hope, was placed by the side of unrestrained power; where the best master had his angry moods and his caprices; where the most resigned servant had his rancor, his complaints, and his hatred. Ulysses was a good master; see what a paternal affection he has for Eumæus and Philætius. But he orders to be put to death a servant who has insulted him without knowing him, and others who have fallen into the bad ways to which his absence has exposed them. He is responsible to the city for the death of his dependants; but for the death of his servants no one asks any reason.

In the state of isolation in which the family had long lived, clientship sprang up and maintained itself. The domestic religion was then all-powerful over the soul. The man who was its priest by hereditary right appeared to the inferior classes as a sacred being. More than man, he was an intercessor between man and God. From his mouth went forth the powerful prayer, the irresistible formula, which brought down the favor or the anger of the divinity. Before such a power he felt compelled to bow; obedience was commanded both by faith and by religion; and, besides, what temptation could the client have to free himself? He saw no horizon beyond this family, to which everything belonged. In it alone he found life calm and subsistence assured; in it alone, although he had a master, he had also a protector; in it alone, in fine, he found an altar which he could approach, and gods whom he was

permitted to invoke. To quit this family was to place himself
outside all social organization and all law; it was to lose his
gods and to renounce the right of prayer.

But when the city had been founded, the clients of the
different families could see each other, could confer together,
could make an interchange of their desires and griefs, compare
their masters, and obtain a glimpse of a better fate. Then their
view began to extend beyond the limits of the family. They
saw that beyond their circle there existed society, rules, laws,
altars, temples, and gods. To quit the family was no longer,
therefore, for them, an evil without a remedy. The temptation
became every day stronger; clientship seemed to them a bur-
den every day heavier, and they ceased to believe that the
master's authority was legitimate and sacred. Then sprang up
in the hearts of these men an ardent desire to be free. True,
we do not find in the history of any city mention made of a
general insurrection among this class. If there were armed
struggles, they were shut up and concealed within the circle
of each family. For more than one generation there were on
one side energetic efforts for independence, and implacable
repression on the other. There took place in each house a long
and dramatic series of events which it is impossible to-day to
retrace. All that we can say is, that the efforts of the lower
classes were not without results. An invincible necessity obliged
the masters, little by little, to relinquish some of their omnipotence. When authority ceases to appear just to the subjects,
time must still elapse before it will cease to appear so to the
masters. But this happens after a while, and then the master,
who no longer believes in the justice of his authority, defends
it badly, or ends by renouncing it. Besides, this inferior class
was useful; by cultivating the earth, it accumulated the riches
of the master, and by carrying arms, it constituted his strength
in the midst of family rivalries. It was therefore wise to satisfy
these men, and interest united with humanity to recommend
concessions.

It appears certain that the condition of clients improved by
degrees. At first they lived in the master's house, cultivating
the common domain together. Later a separate lot of land
was assigned to each. The client must already have found

himself happier. He still worked for his master's profit, it is true; the field was not his; he rather belonged to that. Still he cultivated it for a long succession of years, and he loved it. There grew up between it and him, not that bond which the religion of property had created between it and the master, but another bond — that which labor and suffering even can form between the man who gives his care, and the earth which gives its fruits.

Later came new progress. He no longer worked for the master, but for himself. On condition of an annual rent, which at first was perhaps variable, but which afterwards became fixed, he had the benefit of the harvest. He thus found some recompense for his labor, and his life was at the same time freer and more independent. "The chiefs of families," says one of the ancients, "assigned portions of land to their inferiors, as if they had been their own children."[1] So, too, we read in the Odyssey, "A kind master gives his servant a house and a field;" and Eumæus adds, a "desired wife," because the client could not yet marry without the consent of the master, and it was his master who chose his companion for him.

But this field, where, thenceforward, his life was passed, where he found all his labor and all his enjoyment, was not yet his property. For this client did not possess that sacred character which enabled him to hold property. The lot that he occupied continued to be bounded by the sacred landmarks — the god Terminus, whom the family of the master had formerly placed there. These inviolable bounds attested that the field, attached to the family of the master by a sacred tie, could never become the absolute property of a freed client. In Italy the field, and the house which the *villicus* — the client of the patron — occupied, contained a sacred fire, a *Lar familiaris;* but this fire did not belong to the cultivator; it was the master's fire.[2] This established at the same time the right of property in the patron, and the religious subordination of the client, who, so long as he belonged to the patron, still followed the patron's worship.

The client, as soon as he came into possession of property,

1 Festus, v. *Patres.*
2 Cato, *De Re Rust.,* 143. Columella, XI. 1, 19.

suffered from not being the proprietor, and aspired to become such. It became his ambition to remove from this field — which seemed to be his by the right of labor — those sacred bounds which made it forever the property of the former master.

We see clearly that in Greece the clients attained their object; but we do not know by what means. How much time and how many efforts were required for this we can only guess. Possibly the same series of social changes took place in antiquity which Europe saw in the middle ages, when the slaves in the country became serfs of the glebe, when the latter, from serfs, taxable at will, were changed to serfs with a fixed rent, and when finally they were transformed, in the course of time, into peasant proprietors.

2. *Clientship disappears at Athens. The Work of Solon.*

This sort of a revolution is clearly marked in the history of Athens. The effect of the overthrow of royalty had been to revive the *régime* of the γενος, families had returned to their isolated condition, and each had begun to form a little state, with a Eupatrid for a chief, and a multitude of clients for subjects. This government appears to have weighed heavily upon the Athenian population, for they retained an unfavorable recollection of it. The people thought themselves so unhappy that the preceding period appeared to have been a sort of golden age. They regretted their kings, and began to imagine that under the monarchy they had been happy and free; that they had then enjoyed equality, and that it was only since the fall of the kings that inequality and suffering had commenced. This was such an illusion as men often entertain. Popular tradition placed the commencement of the inequality at the time when the people began to find it odious. This clientship, this sort of slavery, which was as old as the constitution of the family, they dated from the time when men had first felt its weight and understood its injustice. It is very certain, however, that it was not in the seventh century that the Eupatrids established the hard laws of clientship. They did no more than to preserve them. In this alone was their injustice; they maintained these laws beyond the time when men accepted them without complaint, and maintained them against the will of the people. The Eupatrids of this epoch were perhaps easier masters than their ancestors had been; and yet they were more heartily detested.

It appears that even under the rule of this aristocracy the condition of the lower class was improved; for certainly at that time it obtained possession of lots of land on the single condition of paying a rent, which was fixed at one sixth of the harvest. These men were thus almost emancipated; having a home and living no longer under the master's eye, they breathed more freely and labored for their own profit.

But such is human nature that these men, as their condition improved, felt more keenly the inequality that remained. Not to be a citizen, and to have no part in the administration of the city, doubtless touched them somewhat; but not to be capable of owning the soil upon which they were born and died, affected them much more. What rendered their condition supportable, let us add, lacked stability. For though they were really in possession of the soil, no formal law assured them either this possession or the independence that flowed from it. We see in Plutarch that the former patron could renew his claim upon his former servant. If the annual rent was not paid, or for any other cause, these men relapsed into a sort of slavery.

Grave questions were agitated in Attica, therefore, during a series of four or five generations. It was hardly possible that men of the lower class could remain in this unstable and anomalous position towards which an insensible progress had conducted them. One of two things was sure to follow: either, losing this position, they must relapse into the bonds of an onerous clientship, or, completely freed by a still farther progress, they must rise to the rank of landed proprietors and free men.

We can imagine all the efforts on the part of the laborer, the former client, and all the resistance on the part of the proprietor, the former patron. It was not a civil war. The Athenian annals have not preserved the record of a single combat. It was a domestic war in each hamlet, in each house, from father to son.

These struggles appear to have had various fortunes, according to the nature of the soil in different cantons in Attica. In the plain where the Eupatrid had his principal domain, and where he was always present, his authority over the little group of servants who were always under his eye remained almost intact; the Pedieis — or men of the plain — therefore, generally showed themselves faithful to the old *régime*. But the Diacrii, — those who cultivated the sides of the mountain with severe toil, — being farther from the master, more habituated to an independent life, more hardy and more courageous, laid up in their hearts a violent hatred for the Eupatrid, and a firm resolve to be free. These especially were the men who were indignant to see about the fields the "sacred bounds" of the master, and to feel that "their soil was enslaved."[3] As to the inhabitants of the cantons near the sea, — the Paralii, — the ownership of the soil tempted them less; they had the sea before them, and commerce, and trade. Several had become rich, and with riches they were nearly free. They therefore did not share the ardent desire of the Diacrii, and did not feel any vigorous hatred of the Eupatrids. They had not, however, the base resignation of the Pedieis; they demanded more stability in their condition, and better assured rights.

Solon satisfied these wishes so far as was possible. There is a part of the work of this legislator which the ancients have very imperfectly explained to us, but which appears to have been the principal part of it. Before his time, the greater part of the inhabitants of Attica still held but a precarious possession of the soil, and might be reduced to personal servitude. After him this class was no longer found; the right of property was accessible to all; there was no longer any slavery for the Athenian; the families of the lower classes were forever freed from the authority of the Eupatrid families. Here was a great change, whose author could be no other than Solon.

According to Plutarch's account, it is true, Solon did no more than to soften the rigor of the law of debt by abolishing the right of the creditor to enslave the debtor. But we should carefully examine what a writer so long after this period says of those debts that troubled the Athenian city, as well as all the cities of Greece and Italy. It is difficult to believe that before Solon there was so great a circulation of money that there were many borrowers and lenders. We are not to judge

[3] Solon, Ed. Bach, pp. 104, 105.

those times by the period that followed. There was at that time very little commerce; bills of exchange were unknown, and credits must have been very rare. On what security could a man borrow who owned nothing? Men are not much accustomed, in any society, to lend to the poor. The assertion is made, it is true, on the faith of the translator of Plutarch rather than on Plutarch himself, that the borrower mortgaged his land; but, supposing this land was his property, he could not have mortgaged it, for mortgages were not then known, and were contrary to the nature of proprietary right. In those debtors of whom Plutarch speaks we must see the former clients; in their debts, the annual rent which they were to pay to their former masters; and in the slavery into which they fell if they failed to pay, the former clientship, to which they were again reduced.

Perhaps Solon suppressed the rent; or, more probably, reduced the amount of it, so that the payment became easy. He added the provision, that in future the failure to pay should not reduce the laborer to servitude.

He did more. Before him these former clients, when they came into possession of the soil, could not become the owners of it; for upon their fields the sacred and inviolable bounds of the former patron still stood. For the enfranchisement of the soil and of the cultivator, it was necessary that these bounds should disappear. Solon abolished them. We find the evidence of this great reform in some verses of Solon himself: "It was an unhoped-for work," said he; "I have accomplished it with the aid of the gods. I call to witness the goddess Mother, the black earth, whose landmarks I have in many places torn up, the earth, which was enslaved, and is now free." In doing this, Solon had accomplished a considerable revolution. He had put aside the ancient religion of property, which, in the name of the immovable god Terminus, retained the land in a small number of hands. He had wrested the earth from religion to give it to labor. He had suppressed, with the Eupatrid's authority over the soil, his authority over man, and he could say in his verses, "Those who in this land suffered cruel servitude and trembled before a master, I have made free." It is probable that this enfranchisement is what the contemporaries of Solon called σεισαχθεια (shaking off the burdens).

Later generations, who, once habituated to liberty, would not, or could not, believe that their forefathers had been serfs, explained this word as if it merely marked an abolition of debts. But there is an energy in it which reveals a greater revolution. Let us add here this sentence of Aristotle, which, without entering into an account of Solon's labors, simply says, "He put an end to the slavery of the people."[4]

3. Transformation of Clientship at Rome.

This war between clients and patrons also filled a long period of Rome's history. Livy, indeed, says nothing of it, because he is not accustomed closely to observe the changes in institutions; besides, the annals of the pontiffs, and similar documents, from which the ancient historians whom Livy consulted had drawn, could have contained no account of these domestic struggles.

One thing, at least, is certain. There were clients in the very beginning of Rome; there has even come down to us very precise evidence of the dependence in which their patrons held them. If, several centuries afterwards, we look for these clients, we no longer find them. The name still exists, but not clientship. For there is nothing more distinct from the clients of the primitive period than these plebeians of Cicero's time, who called themselves the clients of some rich man in order to have the right to the *sportula*.

There were those who more nearly resembled the ancient clients; these were the freedmen.[5] No more did one freed from servitude at once become a free man and a citizen at the end of the republic, than in the first ages of Rome. He remained subject to a master. Formerly they called him a client, now they call him a freedman; the name only is changed. As to the master, his name does not even change; formerly they called him patron, and they still call him by the same name. The freedman, like the client of earlier days, remains attached to the family; he takes its name, like the ancient client. He depends upon the patron; he owes him not only gratitude, but a veritable service, whose measure the master himself fixes.

[4] Aristotle, *Gov. of Ath., Fragm.*, coll. Didot, t. II. p. 107.
[5] The freedman became a client. The identity of these two terms is marked in a passage of Dionysius, IV. 23.

The patron has the right to judge the freedman, as he had to judge the client; he can remit to slavery for the crime of ingratitude.[6] The freedman, therefore, recalls the ancient client. Between them there is but one difference: clientship formerly passed from father to son; now the condition of freedman ceases in the second, or, at farthest, in the third generation. Clientship, then, has not disappeared; it still seizes a man at the moment when servitude gives him up; only it is no longer hereditary. This alone is a considerable change; but we are unable to state when it took place.

We can easily discover the successive improvements that were made in the condition of the client, and by what degrees he arrived at the right to hold property. At first the chief of the gens assigned him a lot of land to cultivate;[7] he soon became the temporary possessor of this lot, on condition that he contributed to all the expenses of his former master. The severe conditions of the old law, which obliged him to pay his patron's ransom, the dowry of his daughter, or his legal fines, clearly prove that when this law was written he was already the temporary possessor of the soil. The client made one farther step of progress; he obtained the right of transmitting, at his death, this lot to his son; in default of a son, the land returned, it is true, to the patron. But now comes new progress: the client who leaves no son obtains the right of making a will. Here custom hesitates and varies; sometimes the patron takes half the property, sometimes the will of the testator is fully respected; in any case his will is never invalid.[8] Thus the client, if he cannot yet call himself a proprietor, has, at least, as extended an enjoyment of property as is possible.

True, this was not complete enfranchisement. But no document enables us to fix the epoch when the clients were definitively detached from the patrician families. There is a passage of Livy (II. 16) which, if we take it literally, shows that from the first years of the republic the clients were citizens. There is a strong probability that they were already

[6] *Digest,* XXV. tit. 2, 5; L. tit. 16, 195. Valerius Maximus, V. 1, 4. Suetonius, *Claudius,* 25. Dion Cassius, LV. The legislation was the same at Athens; see Lysias and Hyperides in Harpocration, v. Ἀποστασιου. Demosthenes *in Aristogitonem,* and Suidas, v. Ἀναγκαιον.

[7] Festus, v. *Patres.*

[8] *Institutes* of Justinian, III. 7.

citizens in the time of king Servius; perhaps they even voted in the *comitia curiata* from the foundation of Rome. But we cannot conclude from this that they were then entirely enfranchised, since it is possible that the patricians found it for their interest to give their clients political rights without consenting on that account to give them civil rights.

It does not appear that the revolution which freed the clients at Rome was accomplished at once, as at Athens. It took place very slowly and imperceptibly, without ever having been consecrated by any formal laws. The bonds of clientship were relaxed little by little, and the client was removed insensibly from the patron.

King Servius introduced a great reform to the advantage of the clients; he changed the organization of the army. Before his reign the army was divided into tribes, curies, and gentes; this was the patrician division; every chief of the gens was at the head of his clients.

Servius divided the army into centuries; each had his rank according to his wealth. By this arrangement the client no longer marched by the side of his patron; he no longer recognized him as a chief in battle; and he became accustomed to independence.

This change produced another in the constitution of the comitia. Formerly the assembly was divided into curies and gentes, and the client, if he voted at all, voted under the eye of the master. But the division by centuries being established for the comitia as well as for the army, the client no longer found himself in the same division as the patron. The old law, it is true, commanded him to vote the same as his patron voted, but how could his vote be known?

It was a great step to separate the client from the patron in the most solemn moments of life, at the moment of combat, and at the moment of voting. The authority of the patron was greatly diminished, and what remained to him was more hotly contested daily. As soon as the client had tasted of independence, he wished for the complete enjoyment of it. He aspired to separate from the gens and to join the plebs, where he might be free. How many occasions presented themselves! Under the kings, he was sure of being aided by them, for they asked nothing better than to enfeeble the gentes. Under the republic, he found the protection of the plebs themselves, and of the tribunes. Many clients were thus freed, and the gens could not recover them. In 472 B. C., the number of clients was still considerable, since the plebs complained that by their votes in the *comitia centuriata,* they caused the balance to incline in favor the patricians.[9] About the same time, the plebs having refused to enroll, the patricians were able to form an army with their clients.[10] It appears, however, that these clients were no longer numerous enough alone to cultivate the lands of the patricians, and that the latter were obliged to borrow the labor of the plebs.[11] It is probable that the creation of the tribuneship, by protecting the escaped clients against their former patrons, and by rendering the condition of the plebs more enviable and more secure, hastened this gradual movement towards enfranchisement. In the year 372 there were no longer any clients, and Manlius could say to the plebs, "As many clients as you have been about a single patron, so many now shall you be against a single enemy."[12] Thenceforth we no longer see in the history of Rome these ancient clients, these men hereditarily attached to the gens. Primitive clientship gave place to a clientship of a new kind, a voluntary, almost fictitious bond, which no longer imposed the same obligations. We no longer see in Rome the three classes, patricians, clients, and plebeians. Only two remain; the clients are confounded with the plebs.

The Marcelli appear to be a branch thus detached from the Claudian gens. They were Claudii; but as they were not patricians, they belonged to the gens only as clients. Free at an early period, and enriched, by what means we know not, they were first raised to plebeian dignities, and later to those of the city. For several centuries the Claudian gens seems to have forgotten its rights over them. One day, however, in Cicero's time,[13] it recalled them to mind very unexpectedly. A freedman or client of the Marcelli died, leaving property,

9 Livy, II. 56.
10 Dionysius, VII. 19; X. 27.
11 *Inculti per secessionem plebis agri.* Livy, II. 34.
12 Livy, VI. 18.
13 Cicero, *De Oratore,* I. 39.

which, according to law, would revert to the patron. The patrician Claudii claimed that the Marcelli, being clients, could not themselves have clients, and that their freedmen and their property should belong to the chief of the patrician gens, who alone was capable of exercising the rights of a patron. This suit very much astonished the public, and embarrassed the lawyers: Cicero himself thought the question very obscure. But it would not have been so four centuries earlier, and the Claudii would have gained their cause. But in Cicero's time the laws upon which they founded their claim were so old that they had been forgotten, and the court easily decided the case in favor of the Marcelli. The ancient clientship no longer existed.

Chapter VII

THIRD REVOLUTION. THE PLEBS ENTER THE CITY

1. General History of this Revolution.

THE changes which, in the course of time, had taken place in the constitution of the family, brought with them others in the constitution of the city. The old aristocratic and sacerdotal family became weakened. The right of primogeniture having disappeared, this family lost its unity and vigor; the clients having been for the most part freed, it lost the greater part of its subjects.

The people of the lower orders were no longer distributed among the gentes, but lived apart, and formed a body by themselves. Thus the city assumed quite another aspect. Instead of being, as at an earlier date, a fully united assemblage of as many little states as there were families, a union was formed on the one side among the patrician members of the gentes, and on the other side between men of the lower orders. There were thus two great bodies, two hostile societies, placed face to face. It was no longer, as in a preceding period, an obscure struggle in each family; there was open war in each city. One of these classes wished to maintain the religious constitution of the city, and to continue the government and the priesthood in the hands of the sacred families. The other wished to break down the barriers that placed it beyond the pale of the law, of religion, and of politics.

In the beginning of the struggle, the advantage was with the aristocracy of birth. It had not, indeed, its former subjects, and its material strength had disappeared; but there remained its religious prestige, its regular organization, its habit of command, its traditions, and its hereditary pride. It never doubted the justice of its cause, and believed that in defending itself it was defending religion. The people, on the other hand, had nothing but numbers on their side. They were held back by a habit of respect, of which they could not easily free themselves. Then, too, they had no leaders, and every principle of organization was wanting. There were, in the beginning, a multitude without any bond of union, rather than a vigorous and well-constituted body. If we bear in mind that men had not yet discovered any other principle of association than the hereditary religion of the family, and that they had no idea of any authority that was not derived from a worship, we shall easily understand that the plebs, who had been excluded from all the rites of religion, could not at first form a regular society, and that much time was required for them to discover the elements of discipline and the rules of a regular government. This inferior class, in its weakness, saw at first no other means of combating the aristocracy than by meeting it with monarchy.

In the cities where the popular class had been already consolidated in the time of the ancient kings, it sustained them with all its strength, and encouraged them to increase their power. At Rome it demanded the restoration of monarchy after Romulus, and caused Hostilius to be nominated; it made Tarquinius Priscus king; it loved Servius, and regretted Tarquinius Superbus. When the kings had been everywhere overthrown, and the aristocracy had become supreme, the people did not content themselves with regretting the monarchy; they aspired to restore it under a new form. In Greece, during the sixth century, they succeeded generally in procuring leaders; not wishing to call them kings, because this title implied the idea of religious functions, and could only be borne by the sacerdotal families, they called them tyrants.[1]

Whatever might have been the original sense of this word, it certainly was not borrowed from the language of religion. Men could not apply it to the gods, as they applied the word king; they did not pronounce it in their prayers. It designated, in fact, something quite new among men — an authority that was not derived from the worship, a power that religion had not established. The appearance of this word in the Greek language marks a principle which the preceding generations had not known — the obedience of man to man. Up to that time there had been no other chiefs of the state than those who had been chiefs of religion; those only governed the city who offered the sacrifices and invoked the gods for it. In obeying them, men obeyed only the religious law, and made no act of submission except to the divinity. Obedience to a man, authority given to this man by other men, a power human in its origin and nature — this had been unknown to the ancient Eupatrids, and was never thought of till the day when the inferior orders threw off the yoke of the aristocracy and attempted a new government.

Let us cite a few examples. At Corinth, "the people supported the government of the Bacchiadæ very unwillingly; Cypselus, understanding this hatred, and seeing that the people sought a chief to conduct them to freedom," offered himself to become their chief. The people accepted him, set him up as their tyrant, drove out the Bacchiadæ, and obeyed Cypselus. Miletus had as a tyrant a certain Thrasybulus; Mitylene obeyed Pittacus, and Samos Polycrates. We find tyrants at Argos, at Epidaurus, and at Megara in the sixth century; Sicyon had tyrants during a hundred and thirty years, without interruption. Among the Greeks of Italy we see tyrants at Cumæ, at Crotona, at Sybaris — indeed everywhere. At Syracuse, in 485, the lower orders made themselves masters of the city, and banished the aristocratic class; but they could

[1] The name of king was sometimes given to these popular chiefs when they were descended from religious families. Herodotus, V. 92.

neither maintain nor govern themselves, and at the end of a year they had to set up a tyrant.[2]

Everywhere these tyrants, with more or less violence, had the same policy. A tyrant of Corinth one day asked advice concerning government of a tyrant of Miletus. The latter, in reply, struck off the heads of grain that were higher than the others. Thus their rule of conduct was to cut down the high heads, and to strike at the aristocracy, while depending upon the people.

The Roman plebs at first formed conspiracies to restore Tarquin. They afterwards tried to set up tyrants, and cast their eyes by turns upon Publicola, Spurius Cassius, and Manlius. The accusation which the patricians so often addressed to those of their own order who became popular, cannot have been pure calumny. The fear of the great attests the desire of the plebs.

But we ought to remark that, if the people in Greece and Rome sought to restore monarchy, it was not from real attachment to this sort of government. They loved tyrants less than they detested aristocracy. For them the monarchy was a means of conquering and avenging themselves; but this government, which was the result of force alone, and never rested upon any sacred tradition, took no root in the hearts of the people. They set up a tyrant for the needs of the struggle; they left him the power afterwards from gratitude or from necessity. But when a few years had elapsed, and the recollection of the hard oligarchy had been effaced, they let the tyrant fall. This government never had the affection of the Greeks; they accepted it only as a temporary resource, while the popular party should find a better one and should feel strong enough to govern itself.

The inferior class increased by degrees. Progress sometimes works obscurely, yet decides the future of a class, and transforms society. About the sixth century before our era, Greece and Italy saw a new source of riches appear. The earth no longer sufficed for all the wants of man; tastes turned towards beauty and luxury; the arts sprang up, and then industry and commerce became necessary. Personal property was created by

[2] Nicholas of Damascus, *Fragm.* Aristotle, *Pol.*, V. 9. Thucydides, I. 126. Diodorus, IV. 5.

degrees; coins were struck, and money appeared. Now, the appearance of money was a great revolution. Money was not subject to the same conditions as landed property. It was, according to the expression of the lawyers, *res nec mancipi,* and could pass from hand to hand without any religious formality, and without difficulty could reach the plebeians. Religion, which had given its stamp to the soil, had no power over money.

Men of the lower orders now learned other occupations besides that of cultivating the earth; there were artisans, sailors, manufacturers, and merchants; and soon there were rich men among them. Here was a singular novelty. Previously, the chiefs of the gentes alone could be proprietors, and here were former clients and plebeians who were rich and who displayed their wealth. Then, too, the luxury which enriched the plebeian impoverished the noble. In many cities, especially at Athens, were a part of the aristocratic body seen to become miserably poor. Now, in a society where wealth is changing hands, rank is in danger of being overthrown. Another consequence of this change was, that among the people themselves, distinctions of rank arose, as must happen in every human society. Some families were prominent; some names increased in importance. A sort of aristocracy was formed among the people. This was not an evil; the people ceased to be a confused mass, and began to resemble a well-constituted body. Having rank among themselves, they could select leaders without any longer having to take from the patricians the first ambitious man who wished to reign. This plebeian aristocracy soon had the qualities which ordinarily accompany wealth acquired by labor — that is to say, the feeling of personal worth, the love of tranquil liberty, and that spirit of wisdom which, though desiring improvements, fears risking too much. The plebs followed the lead of this new aristocracy, which they were proud of possessing. They renounced tyrants as soon as they felt that they possessed among themselves the elements of a better government. Indeed, riches became, for some time, as we shall see by and by, a principle of social organization.

There is one other change of which we must speak, for it greatly aided the lower class to rise — the change that took

place in the military art. In the first ages of the history of
cities, the strength of armies was in their cavalry. The real
warrior was the one who fought from a horse or from a
chariot. The foot-soldier, of little service in combat, was
slightly esteemed. The ancient aristocracy, therefore everywhere reserved to themselves the right to fight on horseback.[3]
In some cities the nobles even gave themselves the title of
knights. The *celeres* of Romulus, the Roman knights of the
earlier ages, were all patricians. Among the ancients the
cavalry was always the noble arm. But by degrees infantry
became more important. Improvement in the manufacture of
arms, and in discipline, enabled it to resist cavalry. When this
point was reached, infantry took the first rank in battle, for it
was more manageable, and its manœuvres easier. The legionaries and the hoplites thenceforth formed the main strength of
armies. Now the legionaries and the hoplites were plebeians.
Add to this that maritime operations became more extended,
especially in Greece, that there were naval battles, and that
the destiny of a city was often in the hands of the rowers —
that is to say, of the plebeians. Now, a class that is strong
enough to defend a people is strong enough to defend its
rights, and to exercise a legitimate influence. The social and
political state of a nation always bears a certain relation to
the nature and composition of its armies.

Finally, the inferior class succeeded in having a religion of
its own. These men had in their hearts, we may suppose, that
religious sentiment which is inseparable from our nature, and
which renders adoration and prayer necessary to us. They
suffered, therefore, to find themselves shut out from all religion
by the ancient principle which prescribed that every god
belonged to a family, and that the right of prayer was transmitted with the blood. They strove, therefore, to have a
worship of their own.

It is impossible to enter here into the details of the efforts
that they made, of the means which they invented, of the
difficulties or the resources that occurred to them. This work,
for a long time a separate study for each individual, was long
the secret of each mind; we can see only the results. Sometimes
a plebeian family set up a hearth of its own, whether it dared

[3] Aristotle, *Politics,* VI. 3, 2.

to light the fire itself or procured the sacred fire elsewhere. Then it had its worship, its sanctuary, its protecting divinity, and its priesthood, in imitation of the patrician family. Sometimes the plebeian, without having any domestic worship, had recourse to the temples of the city. At Rome those who had no sacred fire, and consequently no domestic festival, offered their annual sacrifices to the god Quirinus.[4] When the upper class persisted in driving the lower orders from the temples, the latter built temples of their own. At Rome they had one on the Aventine, which was sacred to Diana; they also had the temple of Plebeian Modesty. The Oriental worships, which began in the sixth century to overrun Greece and Italy, were eagerly received by the plebs; these were forms of worship which, like Buddhism, excluded no caste, or people. Often, too, the plebeians would make themselves gods, like those of the patrician curies and tribes. Thus king Servius erected an altar in every quarter of the city, so that the multitude might have places to sacrifice; just as Peisistratus set up Hermæ in the streets and squares of Athens.[5] Those were the gods of the democracy. The plebeians, previously a multitude without worship, thenceforth had religious ceremonies and festivals. They could pray; this in a society where religion made the dignity of man was a great deal.

When once the lower orders had gained these points; when they had among themselves rich men, soldiers, and priests; when they had gained all that gave man a sense of his own worth and strength; when, in fine, they had compelled the aristocracy to consider them of some account, — it was impossible to keep them out of social and political life, and the city could be closed to them no longer.

The entry of this inferior class into the city was a revolution, which, from the seventh to the fifth century, filled the history of Greece and Italy.

The efforts of the people were everywhere successful, but not everywhere in the same manner, or by the same means. In some cases the people, as soon as they felt themselves to be strong, rose, sword in hand, and forced the gates of the city where they had been forbidden to live. Once masters, they

4 Varro, *L. L.*, VI. 13.
5 Dionysius, IV. 5. Plato, *Hipparchus.*

either drove out the nobles and occupied their houses, or contented themselves with proclaiming an equality of rights. This is what happened at Syracuse, at Erythræ, and at Miletus.

In other cases, on the contrary, the people employed means less violent. Without an armed struggle, and merely by the moral force which their last step had given them, they constrained the great to make concessions. They then appointed a legislator, and the constitution was changed. This was the course of events at Athens.

Sometimes the inferior class arrived by degrees, and without any shock, at its object. Thus, at Cumæ, the number of members of the city, very few in the beginning, was increased at first by the admission of those of the people who were rich enough to keep a horse. Later the number of citizens was raised to one thousand, and by degrees the city reached a democratic form of government.[6]

In a few cities, the admission of the plebs among the citizens was the work of the kings; this was the case at Rome. In others it was the work of popular tyrants, as at Corinth, at Sicyon, and at Argos. When the aristocracy regained the supremacy, they generally had the good sense to leave to the lower orders the rights of citizens which the kings or tyrants had given them. At Samos the aristocracy did not succeed in its struggle with the tyrants until it had freed the lower classes. It would occupy us too long to enumerate all the different forms under which this great revolution appeared. The result was everywhere the same; the inferior class entered the city, and became a part of the body politic.

The poet Theognis has given us a very clear idea of this revolution, and of its consequences. He tells us that in Megara, his country, there were two sorts of men. He calls one the class of the *good, αγαθοι;* this, indeed, is the name which they took in most of the Greek cities. The other he calls the class of the *bad, κακοι;* this, too, is the name by which it was customary to designate the inferior class. The poet describes the ancient condition of this class: "Formerly it knew neither tribunals nor laws;" this is as much as to say that it had not the right of the citizenship. These men were not even

---

6 Heracleides of Pontus. *Fragm.,* coll. Didot, t. 11, p. 217.

permitted to approach the city; "they lived without, like wild beasts." They took no part in the religious repasts; they had not the right to marry into the families of the *good*.

But how changed is all this! Rank has been overthrown; "the bad have been placed above the good." Justice is disturbed; the ancient laws are no more, and laws of strange novelty have replaced them. Riches have become the only object of men's desires, because wealth gives power. The man of noble race marries the daughter of the rich plebeian, and "marriage confounds the races."

Theognis, who belonged to an aristocratic family, vainly strove to resist the course of events. Condemned to exile, and despoiled of his property, he could no longer protest and fight except in his verses. But if he no longer hoped for success, at least he never doubted the justice of his cause. He accepted defeat, but he still preserved a sense of his rights. In his eyes, the revolution which had taken place was a moral evil, a crime. A son of the aristocracy, it seemed to him that this revolution had on its side neither justice nor the gods, and that it was an attempt against religion. "The gods," he says, "have quitted the earth; no one fears them. The race of pious men has disappeared; no one now cares for the Immortals."

But these regrets are useless, and he knows it well. If he complains thus, it is as a sort of pious duty; it is because he has received from the ancients "the holy tradition," and his duty is to perpetuate it. But he labors in vain; the tradition itself will perish; the sons of the nobles will forget their nobility; soon all will be seen united by marriage to plebeian families; "they will drink at their festivals and eat at their tables;" they will soon adopt their sentiments. In Theognis' time, regret was all that was left for the Greek aristocracy, and even this regret was soon to disappear.

In fact, after Theognis the nobility were nothing but a recollection. The great families continued piously to preserve the domestic worship and the memory of their ancestors, but this was all. There were still men who amused themselves by counting their ancestors; but such men were ridiculed. They preserved the custom of inscribing upon some tombs that the deceased was of noble race, but no attempt was made to restore a system forever fallen. Isocrates said, with truth, that in his time the great families of Athens no longer existed except in their tombs.

Thus the ancient city was transformed by degrees. In the beginning it was an association of some hundred chiefs of families. Later the number of citizens increased, because the younger branches obtained a position of equality. Later still, the freed clients, the plebs, all that multitude which, during centuries, had remained outside the political and religious association, sometimes even outside the sacred enclosure of the city, broke down the barriers which were opposed to them, and penetrated into the city, where they immediately became the masters.

2. History of this Revolution at Athens.

The Eupatrids, after the overthrow of royalty, governed Athens during four centuries. Upon this long dominion history is silent; we know only one fact — that it was odious to the lower orders, and that the people tried to change the government.

In the year 598, the discontent, which appeared general, and certain signs which showed a revolution to be at hand, aroused the ambition of a Eupatrid, Cylon, who undertook to overthrow the government of his caste, and to establish himself as a popular tyrant. The energy of the archons frustrated the enterprise, but the agitation continued after him. In vain the Eupatrids employed all the resources of their religion. In vain did they announce that the gods were irritated, and that spectres had appeared. In vain did they purify the city from the crimes of the people, and raise two altars to Violence and Insolence to appease these two divinities, whose malign influence had agitated all minds.[7] All this was to no purpose. The feeling of hatred was not appeased. They brought from Crete the pious Epimenides, a mysterious personage, who was said to be the son of a goddess, and he performed a series of expiatory ceremonies; they hoped, by thus striking the imaginations of the people, to revive religion, and consequently to fortify

[7] Diogenes Laertius, I. 110. Cicero, De Leg., II. 11. Athenæus, p. 602.

the aristocracy. But the people were not moved; the religion of the Eupatrids no longer had any influence upon their minds; they persisted in demanding reform.

For sixteen years longer the fierce opposition of the peasants of the mountain and the patient opposition of the rich men of the shore waged war against the Eupatrids. Finally, those who were wisest among the three parties agreed to intrust to Solon the care of terminating the discords, and of preventing still greater misfortunes. Solon had the rare fortune to belong at the same time to the Eupatrids by birth, and to the merchants by the occupation of his earlier years. His poetry exhibits him to us as a man entirely free from the prejudice of caste. By his conciliatory spirit, by his taste for wealth and luxury, by his love of pleasure, he was far removed from the old Eupatrids. He belonged to new Athens.

We have said above that Solon began by freeing the land from the old domination which the religion of the Eupatrid families had exercised over it. He broke the chains of clientship. So great a change in the social state brought with it another in the political order.

The lower orders needed thenceforth, according to the expression of Solon himself, a shield to defend their newly-found liberty. This shield was political rights.

Solon's constitution is far from being well known to us; it appears, however, that all the Athenians made from that time a part of the assembly of the people, and that the senate was no longer composed of Eupatrids alone; it appears even that the archons could be elected outside the ancient priestly caste. These grave innovations destroyed all the ancient rules of the city. The right of suffrage, magistracies, priesthood, the direction of society, all these had to be shared by the Eupatrid with the inferior caste. In the new constitution no account was taken of the rights of primogeniture. There were still classes, but men were no longer distinguished except by wealth. The rule of the Eupatrids disappeared. The Eupatrid was no longer of any account, unless he was rich; he had influence through his wealth, and not through birth. Thenceforth the poet could say, "In poverty the noble is of no account," and the people applauded in the theatre this line of the poet:

"Of what rank is this man? — Rich, for those are now the
noble."[8]

The system which was thus founded had two sorts of
enemies — the Eupatrids, who regretted their lost privileges,
and the poor, who still suffered from the inequality of their
rank.

Hardly had Solon finished his work when agitation recommenced. "The poor," says Plutarch, "showed themselves the
fierce enemies of the rich." The new government displeased
them, perhaps, quite as much as that of the Eupatrids. Besides,
seeing that the Eupatrids could still be archons and senators,
many imagined that the revolution had not been complete.
Solon had maintained the republican forms; now the people
still entertained a blind hatred against these forms of government under which they had seen, for four centuries, nothing
but the reign of the aristocracy. After the example of many
Greek cities, they wished for a tyrant.

Peisistratus, a Eupatrid, but following his own personal
ambition, promised the poor a division of the lands, and
attached them to himself. One day he appeared in the assembly, and, pretending that he had been wounded, asked for a
guard. The men of the higher classes were about to reply and
unveil his falsehood, but "the people were ready to resort to
violence to sustain Peisistratus; the rich, seeing this, fled in
disorder." Thus one of the first acts of the popular assembly
recently established was to enable a man to become master of
his country.

But it does not appear that the reign of Peisistratus offered
any check to the development of the destinies of Athens. Its
principal effect, on the contrary, was to guarantee this great
social and political reform, which had just taken place, against
a reaction. The Eupatrids never regained their lost power.

The people showed themselves little desirous of recovering
their liberty. Twice a coalition of the great and the rich overthrew Peisistratus; twice he returned to power, and his sons
governed Athens after him. The intervention of the Lacedæmonian army was required in Attica to put an end to this
family's rule.

[8] Euripides, *Phœniss.* Alexis, in Athenæus, IV. 49.

The ancient aristocracy had for a moment the hope of profiting by the fall of Peisistratus, and regaining its privileges. They not only failed of this, but received a still ruder blow. Cleisthenes, who belonged to this class, but who was of a family which it had covered with opprobrium, and had seemed to reject for three generations, found the surest means of taking away the little of its power that still remained. Solon, in changing the constitution, had retained the old religious organization of Athenian society. The population remained divided into two or three hundred gentes, into twelve phratries, and four tribes. In each one of these groups there were, as in the preceding period, an hereditary worship, a priest, who was a Eupatrid, and a chief, who was the same as the priest. All this was a relic of the past, which disappeared slowly. Through this the traditions, the usages, the rules, the distinctions that existed in the old social state, were perpetuated. All these had been established by religion, and in their turn they maintained religion — that is to say, the power of the great families. There were in each of these organizations two classes of men. On the one side were the Eupatrids, who had, by right of birth, the priesthood and the authority; on the other, men of an inferior condition, who were no longer either slaves or clients, but who were still retained by religion under the authority of the Eupatrids. In vain did the laws of Solon declare that all Athenians were free. The old religion seized a man as he went out of the assembly where he had voted freely, and said to him, "Thou art bound to the Eupatrid through worship; thou owest him respect, deference, submission; as a member of the city, Solon has freed thee; but as a member of a tribe, thou obeyest the Eupatrid; as a member of a phratry, thou also hast a Eupatrid for a chief; in the family itself, in the gens where thou wert born, and which thou canst not leave, thou still findest the authority of the Eupatrid." Of what avail was it that the political law had made a citizen of this man, if religion and manners persisted in making him a client? For several generations, it is true, many men lived outside these organizations, whether they had come from foreign countries, or had escaped from the gens and the tribe, to be free. But these men suffered in another way; they found themselves in a state of moral inferiority compared with other men, and a sort of ignominy was attached to their independence. There was, therefore, after the political reform of Solon, another reform to be made in the domain of religion. Cleisthenes accomplished it by suppressing the four old religious tribes, and replacing them with ten tribes, which were divided into demes.

These tribes and demes resembled in appearance the ancient tribes and gentes. In each one of these organizations there were a worship, a priest, a judge, assemblies for religious ceremonies, and assemblies to deliberate upon the common interests.[9] But the new groups differed from the old in two essential points. First, all the free men of Athens, even those who had not belonged to the old tribes and gentes, were included in the divisions of Cleisthenes.[10] This was a great reform; it gave a worship to those who before had none, and included in a religious association those who had previously been excluded from every association. In the second place, men were distributed in the tribes and demes, not according to birth, as formerly, but according to their locality. Birth was of no account; men were equal, and privileges were no longer known. The worship for which the new tribe and deme were established was no longer the hereditary worship of an ancient family; men no longer assembled around the hearth of a Eupatrid. The tribe or deme no longer venerated an ancient Eupatrid as a divine ancestor; the tribes had new eponymous heroes chosen from among the ancient personages of whom the people had preserved a grateful recollection, and as for the demes, they uniformly adopted as their protecting gods, *Zeus, the guardian of the walls,* and *the paternal Apollo.* Henceforth there was no reason why the priesthood should be hereditary in the deme, as it had been in the gens, or why the priest should always be a Eupatrid. In the new groups the priestly office, as well as that of the chief, was annual, and every member might enjoy it in his turn.

This reform completed the overthrow of the aristocracy of

---

9 Æschines, *in Ctesiph.,* 30. Demosthenes, *in Eubul.* Pollux, VIII. 19, 95, 107.

10 Aristotle, *Politics,* III. 1, 10; VII. 2. Scholiast on Æschines, edit. Didot, p. 511.

the Eupatrids. From this time there was no longer a religious caste, no longer any privileges of birth, either in religion or in politics. Athenian society was completely transformed.[11]

Now, the suppression of the old tribes, replaced by new ones, to which all men had access, and in which they were equal, was not a fact peculiar to the history of Athens. The same change took place at Cyrene, Sicyon, Elis, and Sparta, and probably in many other Greek cities.[12] Of all the means calculated to weaken the ancient aristocracy, Aristotle saw none more efficacious than this: "If one wished to found a democracy," he says, "he would proceed as Cleisthenes did at Athens; he would establish new tribes and new phratries; for the hereditary family sacrifices he would substitute sacrifices where all men might be admitted, and he would associate and blend the people together as much as possible, being careful to break up all anterior associations."[13]

When this reform has been accomplished in all the cities, it may be said that the ancient mould of society has been broken, and that a new social body has been formed. This change in the organizations which the ancient hereditary religion had established, and which it had declared immutable, marks the end of the religious government of the city.

3. History of this Revolution at Rome.

At Rome the plebs had a great influence at an early date. The situation of the city, between the Latins, the Sabines, and the Etruscans, condemned it to perpetual war, and war required that there should be a numerous population. The kings, therefore, had welcomed and invited all foreigners, without regard to their origin. Wars succeeded each other without intermission, and as there was a need of men, the most common result of every victory was to take away the inhabitants of the conquered city and transfer them to Rome. What became of these men, brought with the booty? If there

---

[11] The ancient phratries and the γενη were not suppressed; they continued, on the contrary, down to the close of Greek history; but they were thenceforth only religious bodies, and of no account politically.

[12] Herodotus, V. 67, 68. Aristotle, *Politics,* VII. 2, 11. Pausanias, V. 9.

[13] Aristotle, *Politics,* VII. 3, 11 (VI. 3).

were found among them patrician and priestly families, the patricians hastened to associate them with themselves. As to the multitude, some of them became the clients of the great, or of the king, and a part were left with the plebs.

Still other elements entered into the composition of this class. Many foreigners flocked to Rome, as a place whose situation rendered it convenient for commerce. The discontented among the Sabines, the Etruscans, and the Latins, found a refuge there. All this class joined the plebs. The client who succeeded in escaping from the gens became a plebeian. The patrician, who formed a misalliance, or was guilty of any crime that lost him his rank, fell into the inferior class. Every bastard was cast out by religion from pure families, and counted among the plebs.

For all these reasons the plebs increased in numbers. The struggle which had begun between the patricians and the king increased their importance. The kings and the plebs early felt that they had the same enemies. The ambition of the kings was to cut loose from the old principles of government, which limited the exercise of their power. The ambition of the plebeians was to break the ancient barriers which excluded them from the religious and political associations. A tacit alliance was established — the kings protected the plebs, and the plebs sustained the kings.

The traditions and testimony of antiquity place the great progress of the plebeians under the reign of Servius. The hatred which the patricians preserved for this king sufficiently shows what his policy was. His first reform was to give lands to the plebeians, not, it is true, in the *ager Romanus*, but in the territory taken from the enemy; still, this conferring the right to own land upon families that had previously cultivated only the fields of others was none the less an innovation.[14]

What was graver still, was that he published laws for the plebs, which had never been done before. These laws, for the most part, related to obligations which the plebeian might contract with the patrician. It was the commencement of a

[14] Livy, I. 47. Dionysius, IV. 13. The preceding kings had already distributed the lands taken from the enemy; but it is not certain that they admitted the plebs to share in the division.

common law between the two orders, and for the plebs it was the commencement of equality.[15]

Later this same king established a new division in the city. Without destroying the three ancient tribes, where the patrician families and clients were classed according to rank, he formed four new tribes, in which the entire population was distributed according to residence. We have seen this reform at Athens, and we know what were its effects; they were the same at Rome. The plebeians, who did not enter the ancient tribes, were admitted into the new ones.[16] This multitude, up to that time a floating mass, a species of nomadic population that had no connection with the city had thenceforth its fixed divisions and its regular organization. The formation of these tribes, in which the two orders were mingled, really marked the entrance of the plebs into the city. Every tribe had a hearth and sacrifices. Servius established Lares in every public place in the city, in every district of the country. They served as divinities for those who had no rank. The plebeian celebrated the religious festivals of his quarter, and of his burgh (*compitalia, paganalia*), as the patrician celebrated the sacrifice of his gens and of his cury. The plebeian had a religion.

At the same time a great change took place in the sacred ceremony of the lustration. The people were no longer ranged by curies, to the exclusion of those whom the curies did not admit. All the free inhabitants of Rome, all those who formed a part of the new tribes, figured in the sacred act. For the first time all men, without distinction of patrician, or client, or plebeian, were united. The king walked around this mixed assembly, driving victims before him, and singing solemn hymns. The ceremony finished, all alike found themselves citizens.

Before Servius, only two classes of men were distinguished at Rome — the sacerdotal caste of patricians with their clients, and the plebeian class. No other distinction was known than that which religion had established. Servius marked a new division, which had wealth for its foundation. He divided the inhabitants of Rome into two great categories; in the one were those who owned property, in the other those who had

15 Dionysius, IV. 13; IV. 43.
16 Dionysius, I. 26.

nothing. The first was divided into five classes, in which men were divided off according to the amount of their fortune.[17] By this means Servius introduced an entirely new principle into Roman society; wealth began to indicate rank, as religion had done before.

Servius applied this division of the Roman population to the military service. Before him, if the plebeians fought, it was not in the ranks of the legion. But as Servius had made proprietors and citizens of them, he could also make them legionaries. From this time the army was no longer composed of men exclusively from the curies; all free men, all those at least who had property, made a part of it, and the poor alone continued to be excluded. The rank of patrician or client no longer determined the armor of each soldier and his post in battle; the army was divided by classes, exactly like the population, according to wealth. The first class, which had complete armor, and the two following, which had at least the shield, the helmet, and the sword, formed the three first lines of the legion. The fourth and the fifth, being light-armed, made up the body of skirmishers and slingers. Each class was divided into companies, called *centuries*. The first of these consisted, we are told, of eighty men; the four others twenty or thirty each. The cavalry was a separate body, and in this arm also Servius made a great innovation. Whilst up to that time the young patricians alone made up the centuries of the knights, Servius admitted a certain number of plebeians, chosen from the wealthiest, to fight on horseback, and formed of these twelve new centuries.

Now, the army could not be touched without at the same time modifying the political constitution. The plebeians felt that their importance in the state had increased: they had arms, discipline, and chiefs; every century had its centurion and its sacred ensign. This military organization was perma-

17 Modern historians generally reckon six classes. In reality there were but five: Cicero, *De Repub.*, II. 22; Aulus Gellius, X. 28. The knights on the one hand, and the *proletarii*, poor inhabitants, on the other, were not counted in the classes. We must note, moreover, that the word *classis* had not, in the ancient language, a sense similar to our word class; it was applied to a military body; and this shows that the division established by Servius was rather military than political.

nent; peace did not dissolve it. The soldiers, it is true, on their return from a campaign, quitted their ranks, as the law forbade them to enter the city in military order. But afterwards, at the first signal, the citizens resumed their arms in the *Campus Martius,* where each returned to his century, his centurion, and his banner. Now, it happened, twenty-five years after Servius Tullius, the army was called together without any intention of making a military expedition. The army being assembled, and the man having taken their ranks, every century having its centurion at its head, and its ensign in the centre, the magistrate spoke, proposed laws, and took a vote. The six patrician centuries and the twelve of the plebeian knights voted first; after them the centuries of infantry of the first class, and the others in turn. Thus was established in a short time the *comitia centuriata,* where every soldier had the right of suffrage, and where the plebeian and the patrician were hardly distinguished.[18]

All these reforms made a singular change in the appearance of the Roman city. The patricians remained, with their hereditary worship, their curies, their senate. But the plebeians became accustomed to independence, wealth, arms, and reli-

[18] It appears to us incontestable that the comitia by centuries were identical with the Roman army. What proves this is, first, that this assembly is often called the *army* by Latin writers: *urbanus exercitus* (Varro, VI. 93); *quum comitiorum causa exercitus eductus esset* (Livy, XXXIX. 15); *miles ad suffragia vocatur et comitia centuriata dicuntur* (Ampelius, 48): second, that these comitia were convoked exactly as the army was when it entered on a campaign — that is to say, at the sound of a trumpet (Varro, V. 91); two standards floated from the citadel, one red, to call the infantry, the other dark-green for the cavalry: third, that these comitia were always held in the Campus Martius, because the army could not assemble within the city (Aulus Gellius, XV. 27): fourth, that every voter went with his arms (Dion Cassius, XXXVII.): fifth, that the voters were distributed by centuries, the infantry on one side, and the cavalry on the other: sixth, that every century had at its head its centurion and its ensign, 'ὥσπερ εν πολεμω (Dionysius, VII. 59) : seventh, that men more than sixty years of age, not being a part of the army, had not the right to vote in these comitia (Macrobius, I. 5; Festus, v. *Depontani*). Then, in the ancient language, the word *classis* signified a military body, and the word *centuria* designated a military company. The *proletarii* did not appear in this assembly at first; still, as it was a custom in the army to form a century of laborers, they might form a century in the comitia.

gion. The plebs were not confounded with the patricians, but became strong by the side of them.

The patricians, it is true, took their revenge. They commenced by killing Servius; later, they banished Tarquin. The defeat of royalty was the defeat of the plebs.

The patricians attempted to take away from them all the conquests which they had made under the kings. One of the first acts was to take from them the lands that Servius had given them; and we must remark, the only reason given for despoiling them thus, was that they were plebeians.[19] The patricians, therefore, restored the old principle, which required that hereditary religion alone should establish the right of property, and which did not permit a man without religion and without ancestors to exercise any right over the soil.

The laws that Servius had made for the plebs were also withdrawn. If the system of classes and the comitia centuriata were not abolished by the patricians, it was because the state of war did not allow them to disorganize the army, and also because they understood how to surround the comitia with formalities such that they could always control the elections. They dared not take from the plebs the title of citizens, and allowed them to figure in the census. But it is clear that, while allowing the plebs to form a part of the city, they shared with them neither political rights nor religion, nor the laws. In name, the plebs remained in the city; in fact, they were excluded.

Let us not unreasonably accuse the patricians, or suppose that they coldly conceived the design of oppressing and crushing the plebs. The patrician who was descended from a sacred family, and felt himself the heir to a worship, understood no other social system than that whose rules had been traced by the ancient religion. In his eyes the constituent element of every society was the gens, with its worship, its hereditary chief, and its clientship. For him the city could not be anything except an assembly of the chiefs of the gentes. It did not enter his mind that there could be any other political system than that which rested upon worship, or other magistrates than those who performed the public sacrifices, or other laws

[19] Cassius Hemina, in Nonius, Book II. v. *Plevitas.*

than those whose sacred formulas religion had dictated. It was useless to say to him that the plebeians also had within a short time adopted a religion, and that they offered sacrifices to the Lares of the public squares. He would reply that this religion had not the essential character of a real religion, that it was not hereditary, that the fires were not ancient fires, and that these Lares were not real ancestors. He would have added, that the plebeians, in adopting a worship, had done what they had no right to do, and to obtain one, had violated all principle; that they had taken only the external forms of worship, and had neglected the essential principle; it was not hereditary; that, in fine, this image of religion was absolutely the opposite of religion.

Since the patrician persisted in thinking that hereditary religion alone should govern men, it followed that he saw no religion possible for the plebs. He could not understand how the social power could be regularly exercised upon this class of men. The sacred law could not be applied to them; justice was sacred ground, which was forbidden to them. So long as there had been kings, they had taken upon themselves to govern the plebs, and they had done this according to certain rules, which had nothing in common with the ancient religion, and which necessity or the public interest had produced. But by the revolution, which had abolished royalty, religion had assumed its empire; it necessarily followed that the whole plebeian class were placed beyond the reach of social laws.

The patricians then established a government conformable to their own principles; but they had not dreamed of establishing one for the plebs. The patricians had not the courage to drive the plebeians from Rome, but they no longer found the means of organizing them into a regular society. We thus see, in the midst of Rome, thousands of families for which there existed no fixed laws, no social order, no magistrates. The city, the *populus*, — that is to say, the patrician society, with the client that had remained to it, — arose powerful, organized, majestic. About it lived a plebeian multitude, which was not a people, and did not form a body. The consuls, the chiefs of the patrician city, maintained order in this confused population; the plebeians obeyed: feeble, generally poor, they bent under the power of the patrician body.

The problem that was to decide the future of Rome was this: How can the plebs become a regular society?

Now, the patricians, governed by the rigorous principles of their religion, saw only one means of resolving this problem; this was to adopt the plebs, as clients, into the sacred organization of the gentes. It appears that one attempt was made in this direction. The question of debts, which agitated Rome at this period, can only be explained, if we see in it the more grave question of clientship and slavery. The Roman plebs, robbed of their lands, were no longer able to support themselves. The patricians calculated that, by the sacrifice of a little money, they could bring this poor class into their hands. The plebeian began to borrow. In borrowing, he gave himself up to the creditor — sold himself. It was so much a sale that it was a transaction *per æs et libram* — that is to say, with the solemn formality which was commonly employed to confer upon a man the right of property in any object.[20] The plebeian, it is true, took security against slavery. By a sort of fiduciary contract, he stipulated that he should retain his rank of freeman until the day of the payment, and that on that day he should recover full possession of himself on paying the debt. But on that day, if the debt was not paid, he lost the benefit of his contract. He was in the power of his creditor, who took him to his house and made him his client and servant. In all this the creditor did not think he was committing any act of inhumanity; the ideal of society being, in his eyes, the government of the gens, he saw nothing more legitimate or more commendable than to bring men into it by any means possible. If this plan had succeeded, the plebs would have disappeared in little time, and the Roman city would have been nothing but an association of patrician gentes, sharing among them a multitude of clients.

But this clientship was a chain which the plebeian held in horror. He fought against the patrician who, armed with his debt, wished to make a client of him. Clientship was for him equivalent to slavery; the patrician's house was, in his eyes, a prison (*ergastulum*). Many a time the plebeian, seized by the patrician, called upon his associates, and stirred up the ple-

[20] Varro, *L. L.*, VII. 105. Livy, VIII. 28. Aulus Gellius XX. 1. Festus, v. *Nexum*.

beians, crying that he was a free man, and displaying the wounds which he had received in the defence of Rome. The calculation of the patricians only served to irritate the plebs. They saw the danger, and strove with all their energy to free themselves from this precarious state, in which the fall of the royal government had placed them. They wished to have laws and rights.

But it does not appear that these men aspired at first to share the laws and rights of the patricians. Perhaps they thought, with the patricians themselves, that there could be nothing in common between the two orders. No one thought of civil and political equality. That the plebeians could raise themselves to the level of the patricians, never entered the minds of the plebeian of the first centuries any more than it occurred to the patrician.

Far, therefore, from claiming equality of rights and laws, these men seem to have preferred, at first, complete separation. In Rome they found no remedy for their sufferings; they saw but one means of escaping from their inferiority — this was to depart from Rome.

The historian has well expressed their thoughts when he attributes this language to them: ˙ Since the patricians wish to possess the city alone, let them enjoy it at their ease. For us Rome is nothing. We have neither hearths, nor sacrifices, nor country. We only leave a foreign city; no hereditary religion attaches us to this place. Every land is good for us; where we find liberty, there shall be our country."[21] And they went to take up their abode on the Sacred Mount, beyond the limits of the *ager Romanus.*

In view of such an act the senate was divided in opinion. The more ardent of the patricians showed clearly that the departure of the plebs was far from afflicting them. Thenceforth the patricians alone would remain at Rome with the clients that were still faithful to them. Rome would renounce its future grandeur, but the patricians would be masters there. They would no longer have these plebeians to trouble them, to whom the rules of ordinary government could not be applied, and who were an embarrassment to the city. They ought, perhaps, to have been driven out at the same time with

[21] Dionysius, VI. 45, 79.

the kings; but since they had of themselves taken the resolution to depart, the patricians ought to let them go, and rejoice at their departure.

But others, less faithful to old principles, or solicitous for the grandeur of Rome, were afflicted at the departure of the plebs. Rome would lose half its soldiers. What would become of it in the midst of the Latins, Sabines, and Etruscans — all enemies? The plebs had good qualities; why could not these be made use of for the interests of the city? These senators desired, therefore, at a cost of a few concessions, of which they did not perhaps see all the consequences, to bring back to the city those thousands of arms that made the strength of the legions.

On the other side, the plebs perceived, at the end of a few months, that they could not live upon the Sacred Mount. They procured, indeed, what was materially necessary for existence, but all that went to make up an organized society was wanting. They could not found a city there, because they could not find a priest who knew how to perform the religious ceremony of the foundation. They could not elect magistrates, for they had no prytaneum with its perpetual fire, where the magistrate might sacrifice. They could find no foundation for social laws, since the only laws of which men then had any idea were derived from the patrician religion. In a word, they had not among them the elements of a city. The plebs saw clearly that by being more independent they were not happier; that they did not form a more regular society than at Rome; and that the problem, whose solution was so important to them, was not solved. They had gained nothing by leaving Rome; it was not in the isolation of the Sacred Mount that they could find the laws and the rights to which they aspired.

It was found, therefore, that the plebs and patricians, though they had almost nothing in common, could not live without each other. They came together and concluded a treaty of alliance. This treaty appears to have been made on the same terms as those which terminate a war between two different peoples. Plebeians and patricians were indeed neither the same people nor the same city. By this treaty the patrician did not agree that the plebeian should make a part of the religious and political city; it does not appear that the plebs demanded it. They agreed merely that in the future the plebs, having been organized into something like a regular society, should have chiefs taken from their own number. This is the origin of the tribuneship of the plebs — an entirely new institution, which resembled nothing that the city had known before.

The power of the tribunes was not of the same nature as the authority of the magistrates; it was not derived from the city worship. The tribune performed no religious ceremony. He was elected without the auspices, and the consent of the gods was not necessary to create him.[22] He had neither curule chair, nor purple robe, nor crown of leaves, nor any of those insignia which, in all the ancient cities, designated magistrates and priests, for the veneration of men. He was never counted among the Roman magistrates. What, then, was the nature, and what was the principle, of his power? Here we must banish from our minds all modern ideas and habits, and transport ourselves as much as possible into the midst of the ideas of the ancients. Up to that time men had understood political authority only as an appendage to the priesthood. Thus, when they wished to establish a power that was not connected with worship, and chiefs who were not priests, they were forced to resort to a singular device. For this, the day on which they created the first tribune, they performed a religious ceremony of a peculiar character.[23] Historians do not describe the rites; they merely say that the effect was to render these first tribunes *sacrosancti*. Now, these words signified that the body of the tribune should be reckoned thenceforth among the objects which religion forbade to be touched, and whose simple touch made a man unclean.[24] Thus it happened, if some devout Roman, some patrician, met a tribune in the public street, he made it a duty to purify himself on returning home, "as if his body had been defiled simply by the meeting."[25] This *sacrosanct* character remained attached to the

---

[22] Dionysius, X. Plutarch, *Rom. Quest.*, 84.

[23] Livy, III. 55.

[24] This is the proper sense of the word *sacer*. Plautus Bacch., IV. 6, 13. Catullus, XIV. 12. Festus, v. *Sacer*. Macrobius, III. 7. According to Livy, the epithet *sacrosanctus* was not at first applied to the tribune, but to the man who injured the person of the tribune.

[25] Plutarch, *Rom. Quest.*, 81.

tribune during the whole term of his office; then in *creating* his successor, he transmitted the same character to him, just as the consul, in *creating* other consuls, passed to them the auspices, and the power to perform the sacred rites. Later, the tribuneship having been interrupted during two years, it was necessary, in order to establish the new tribunes, to renew the religious ceremony which had been performed on the Sacred Mount.

We do not sufficiently understand the ideas of the ancients, to say whether this *sacrosanct* character rendered the person of the tribune honorable in the eyes of the patricians, or marked him, on the contrary, as an object of malediction and horror. The second conjecture is more in accordance with probability. What is certain is, that in every way the tribune was inviolable; the hand of a patrician could not touch him without grave impiety.

A law conferred and guaranteed this inviolability; it declared that "no person should use violence towards a tribune, or strike him, or kill him." It added that "whoever committed one of these acts against a tribune should be impure, that his property should be confiscated to the profit of the temple of Ceres, and that one might kill him with impunity." The law concluded in these words, whose vagueness powerfully aided the future progress of the tribuneship: "No magistrate, or private person, shall have the right to do anything against a tribune." All the citizens took an oath by which they agreed always to observe this strange law, calling down upon their heads the wrath of the gods if they violated it, and added that whoever rendered himself guilty of an attempt against a tribune "should be tainted with the deepest impurity."[26]

This privilege of inviolability extended as far as the body of the tribune could extend its direct action. If a plebeian was maltreated by a consul who condemned him to imprisonment, or by a creditor who laid hands on him, the tribune appeared, placed himself between them (*intercessio*), and stayed the patrician hand. Who would have dared "to do anything against a tribune," or expose himself to be touched by him.

But the tribune exercised this singular power only where he was present. Out of his presence plebeians might be mal-

26 Dionysius, VI. 89; X. 32, 42.

treated. He had no power over what took place beyond the reach of his hands, of his sight, of his word.[27]

The patricians had not given the plebeians rights; they had only agreed that certain ones among them should be inviolable. Still this was enough to afford some security to all. The tribune was a sort of living altar, to which the right of refuge was attached.

The tribunes naturally became the chiefs of the plebs, and assumed the power of deciding causes for them. They had not, it is true, the right of citing before them even a plebeian, but they could seize upon a person.[28] Once in their hands, the man obeyed. It was sufficient even to be found within the circle where their voice could be heard; this word was irresistible, and a man had to submit, even if he were a patrician or a consul.

The tribune had no political authority. Not being a magistrate, he could not convoke the curies or the centuries. He could make no proposition in the senate; it was not supposed, in the beginning, that he could appear there. He had nothing in common with the real city — that is to say, with the patrician city, where men did not recognize any authority of his. He was not the tribune of the people; he was the tribune of the plebs.

There were then, as previously, two societies in Rome — the city and the plebs; the one strongly organized, having laws, magistrates, and a senate; the other a multitude, which remained without rights and laws, but which found in its inviolable tribunes protectors and judges.

In succeeding years we can see how the tribunes took courage, and what unexpected powers they assumed. They had no authority to convoke the people, but they convoked them. Nothing called them to the senate; they sat at first at the door of the chamber; later they sat within. They had no power to judge the patricians; they judged them and condemned them. This was the result of the inviolability attached to them as *sacrosancti*. Every other power gave way before

[27] *Tribuni antiquitus creati, non juri dicundo nec causis querelisque de absentibus noscendis, sed intercessionibus faciendis quibus præsentes fuissent, ut injuria quæ coram fieret arceretur.* Aulus Gellius, XIII. 12.

[28] Aulus Gellius, XV. 27. Dionysius, VIII. 87; VI. 90.

them. The patricians were disarmed the day they had pronounced, with solemn rites, that whoever touched a tribune should be impure. The law said, "Nothing shall be done against a tribune." If, then, this tribune convoked the plebs, the plebs assembled, and no one could dissolve this assembly, which the presence of the tribune placed beyond the power of the patricians and the laws. If the tribune entered the senate, no one could compel him to retire. If he seized a consul, no one could take the consul from his hand. Nothing could resist the boldness of a tribune. Against a tribune no one had any power, except another tribune.

As soon as the plebs thus had their chiefs, they did not wait long before they had deliberative assemblies. These did not in any manner resemble those of the patricians. The plebs, in their comitia, were distributed into tribes; the domicile, not religion or wealth, regulated the place of each one. The assembly did not commence with a sacrifice; religion did not appear there. They knew nothing of presages, and the voice of an augur, or a pontiff, could not compel men to separate. It was really the comitia of the plebs, and they had nothing of the old rules, or of the religion of the patricians.

True, these assemblies did not at first occupy themselves with the general interests of the city; they named no magistrates, and passed no laws. They deliberated only on the interests of their own order, named the plebeian chiefs, and carried *plebiscita*. There was at Rome, for a long time, a double series of decrees — *senatusconsulta* for the patricians, *plebiscita* for the plebs. The plebs did not obey the senatusconsulta, nor the patricians the plebiscita. There were two peoples at Rome.

These two peoples, always in presence of each other, and living within the same walls, still had almost nothing in common. A plebeian could not be consul of the city, nor a patrician tribune of the plebs. The plebeian did not enter the assembly by curies, nor the patrician the assembly of the tribes.[29]

[29] Livy, II. 60. Dionysius, VII. 16. Festus, v. *Scita plebis*. We speak only of the earliest times. The patricians were enrolled in the tribes, but certainly took no part in assemblies which met without auspices and without a religious ceremony, and in which for a long time they recognized no legal authority.

They were two peoples that did not even understand each other, not having — so to speak — common ideas. If the patrician spoke in the name of religion and the laws, the plebeian replied that he did not know this hereditary religion, or the laws that flowed from it. If the patrician alleged a sacred custom, the plebeian replied in the name of the law of nature. They reproached each other with injustice; each was just according to his own principles, and unjust according to the principles and beliefs of the other. The assembly of the curies and the reunion of the patres seemed to the plebeian odious privileges. In the assembly of the tribes the patrician saw a meeting condemned by religion. The consulship was for the plebs an arbitrary and tyrannical authority; the tribuneship, in the eyes of the patrician, was something impious, abnormal, contrary to all principles; he could not understand this sort of chief, who was not a priest, and who was elected without auspices. The tribuneship deranged the sacred order of the city; it was what a heresy is in religion — the public worship was destroyed. "The gods will be against us," said a patrician, "so long as we have among us this ulcer, which is eating us up, and which extends its corruption to the whole social body." The history of Rome, during a century, was filled with similar discords between these two peoples, who did not seem to speak the same language. The patricians persisted in keeping the plebs without the body politic, and the plebs established institutions of their own. The duality of the Roman population became from day to day more manifest.

And yet there was something which formed a tie between these two peoples: this was war. The patricians were careful not to deprive themselves of soldiers. They had left to the plebeians the title of citizens, if only to incorporate them into the legions. They had taken care, too, that the inviolability of the tribunes should not extend outside of Rome, and for this purpose had decided that a tribune should never go out of the city. In the army, therefore, the plebs were under control; there was no longer a double power; in presence of the enemy Rome became one.

Then, thanks to the custom, begun after the expulsion of the kings, of assembling the army to consult on public interests and on the choice of magistrates, there were mixed assemblies, where the plebeians appeared by the side of the patricians. Now we see clearly in history that the comitia by centuries became more and more important, and became insensibly what were called the great comitia. Indeed, in the conflict which sprang up between the assembly by curies and the assembly by tribes, it seemed natural that the comitia centuriata should become a sort of neutral ground, where general interest would be debated.

The plebeian was not always poor. Often he belonged to a family which was originally from another city, which was there rich and influential, and whom the fate of war had transported to Rome without taking away his wealth, or the sentiment of dignity that ordinarily accompanies it. Sometimes, too, the plebeian had become rich by his labor, especially in the time of the kings. When Servius had divided the population into classes according to their fortunes, some plebeians belonged to the first class. The patricians had not dared, or had not been able, to abolish this division into classes. There was no want of plebeians, therefore, who fought by the side of the patricians in the foremost ranks of the legion, and who voted with them in the first centuries.

This class, rich, haughty, and prudent as well, who could not have been pleased with disturbances, and must have feared them, who had much to lose if Rome fell, and much to gain if it prospered, was a natural mediator between the two hostile orders.

It does not appear that the plebs felt any repugnance at seeing distinctions of wealth established among them. Thirty-six years after the establishment of the tribuneship, the number of tribunes was increased to ten, that there might be two for each of the five classes. The plebs, then, accepted and clung to the division which Servius had established. And even the poorer portion, which was not comprised in the classes, made no complaint; it left the privileges to the wealthier, and did not demand its share of the tribunes.

As to the patricians, they had little fear of the importance which wealth assumed, for they also were rich. Wiser or more fortunate than the Eupatrids of Athens, who were annihilated on the day that the direction of affairs fell to the rich, the patricians never neglected agriculture, or commerce, or even manufactures. To increase their fortunes was always their great care. Labor, frugality, and good speculations were always their virtues. Besides, every victory over an enemy, every conquest, increased their possessions; and so they saw no great evil in uniting power and wealth. The habits and character of the nobles were such that they could not feel contempt for a rich man even though he was a plebeian. The rich plebeian approached them, lived with them, and many relations of interest and friendship were established. This perpetual contact brought about a change of ideas. The plebeian made the patrician understand, little by little, the wishes and the rights of his class. The patrician ended by being convinced. Insensibly he came to have a less firm and haughty opinion of his superiority; he was no longer so sure about his rights. Now, an aristocracy, when it comes to doubt that its empire is legitimate, either no longer has the courage to defend it, or defends it badly. As soon as the prerogatives of the patricians were no longer an article of faith for them, this order might be said to be half vanquished.

The rich men appear to have exercised an influence of another kind on the plebs, from whom they sprang, and from whom they did not yet separate. As they desired the greatness of Rome, they wished for the union of the two orders. Besides, they were ambitious; they calculated that the absolute separation of the two orders forever limited their own career, by chaining them forever to the inferior class, whilst a union would open a way to them, the end of which they could not see. They tried, therefore, to give the ideas and wishes of the plebeians another direction. Instead of persisting in forming a separate order, instead of making laws for themselves which the other order would never recognize, instead of working slowly by plebiscita to make a species of laws for their own use, and to prepare a code which would have no official value, they inspired the plebs with the idea of penetrating into the patrician city, and sharing its laws, institutions, and dignities. From that time the desires of the plebs turned to a union of the two orders on the condition of equality.

The plebs, once started in this direction, began to demand a code. There were laws at Rome, as in all cities, unchangeable and holy laws, which were written, and the text of which was

preserved by priests.[30] But these laws, which were a part of
the religion, applied only to the members of the religious city.
The plebeians had no right to know them; and we may
believe that they had no right to claim their protection. These
laws existed for the curies, for the gentes, for the patricians
and their clients, but not for others. They did not recognize
the right to hold property in one who had no *sacra;* they
granted justice to no one who had not a patron. It was the
exclusively religious character of the law that the plebs wished
to abolish. They demanded not only that the laws should be
reduced to writing and made public, but that there should be
laws that should be equally applicable to the patricians and
themselves.

The tribunes wished at first, it appears, that the laws should
be drawn up by the plebeians. The patricians replied, that
apparently the tribunes were ignorant of what a law was, for
otherwise they would not have made such a claim. "It is a
complete impossibility," said they, "for the plebeians to
make laws. You who have no auspices, you who do not perform
religious acts, what have you in common with sacred things,
among which the laws must be counted?"[31] This notion of
the plebeians appeared monstrous to the patricians; and the
old annals, which Livy and Dionysius of Halicarnassus consulted in this part of their histories, mention frightful prodigies
— the heavens on fire, spectres leaping in the air, and showers
of blood.[32] The real prodigy was that the plebeians thought
of making laws. Between the two orders, each of which was
astonished at the persistence of the other, the republic remained eight years in suspense. Then the tribunes made a
compromise. "Since you are unwilling that the laws should
be written by the plebeians," they said, "choose the legislators
in the two orders." By this they thought they were conceding
a great deal; but it was little according to the rigorous
principles of the patrician religion. The senate replied that it
was in no way averse to the preparation of a code, but that
this code could be drawn up only by patricians. Finally, they
found a means of conciliating the interests of the plebs with

[30] Dionysius, X. 1.
[31] Livy, III. 31. Dionysius, X. 4.
[32] Julius Obsequens, 16.

the religious requirements on which the patricians depended. They decided that the legislators should all be patricians, but that their code, before being promulgated and put in force, should be exhibited to the eyes of the public, and submitted to the approbation of all classes.

This is not the moment to analyze the code of the decemvirs. It is only necessary at present to remark, that the work of the legislators, primarily exposed in the forum, and freely discussed by all the citizens, was afterwards accepted by the comitia centuriata — the assembly in which the two orders were confounded. In this there was a grave innovation. Adopted by all the classes, the law thenceforth was applied to all. We do not find, in what remains to us of the code, a single word that implies any inequality between the plebeian and the patrician, either in the rights of property, or in contracts and obligations, or in legal proceedings. From that moment the plebeian appeared before the same tribunal as the patrician, proceeded in the same manner, and was judged according to the same law. Now, there could not have been a more radical revolution; the daily usages, the manners, the sentiments of man towards man, the idea of personal dignity, the principles of law, all were changed in Rome.

As there remained laws to make, new decemvirs were appointed, and among them were three plebeians. Thus, after it had been proclaimed with so much energy that the making of laws belonged to the patrician class, so rapid was the progress of ideas that at the end of a year plebeians were admitted among the legislators.

The manners tended towards equality. Men were upon an incline where they could no longer hold back. It had become necessary to make a law forbidding marriage between the two orders — a certain proof that religion and manners no longer sufficed to prevent this. But hardly had they had time to make the law, when it fell before an almost universal reprobation. A few patricians persisted, indeed, in calling upon their religion. "Our blood will be attainted, and the hereditary worship of every family will be destroyed by it; no one will any longer know of what race he is born, to what sacrifices he belongs; it will be the overthrow of all institutions, human and divine." The plebeians did not heed these arguments, which appeared to them mere quibbles without weight. To discuss articles of faith before men who had no religion was time lost. Besides, the tribunes replied very justly, "If it is true that your religion speaks so loud, what need have you of this law? It is of no account; withdraw it, you remain as free as before not to ally yourselves with plebeian families." The law was withdrawn.

At once marriages became frequent between the two orders. The rich plebeians were so sought after, that, to speak only of the Licinii, they allied themselves with three of the patrician gentes, the Fabii, the Cornelii, and the Manlii.[33] It could then be seen that the law had been for a moment the only barrier which separated the two orders. Thenceforth the patrician blood and plebeian blood were mingled.

As soon as equality was conquered in private life, the great difficulty was overcome, and it seemed natural that equality should also exist in politics. The plebs then asked why the consulship was closed to them, and they saw no reason why they should be withheld from it.

There was, however, a very potent reason. The consulship was not simply a command; it was a priesthood. To be a consul it was not sufficient to offer guarantees of intelligence, of courage, of probity; the consul must also be able to perform the ceremonies of the public worship. It was necessary that the rites should be duly observed, and that the gods should be satisfied. Now, the patricians alone possessed the sacred character which permitted them to pronounce the prayers, and to call down the divine protection upon the city. The plebeian possessed nothing in common with the worship; religion, therefore, forbade him to be consul — *nefas plebeium consulem fieri.*

We may imagine the surprise and indignation of the patricians, when plebeians claimed for the first time the right to be consuls. Religion itself appeared to be menaced. The nobles took a great deal of pains to make the plebs understand this; they told them how important religion was to the city, that religion had founded the city, and that it presided over all public acts, directed the deliberative assemblies, and gave the republic its magistrates. They added, that this religion was, according to ancient customs (*more majorum*), the patrimony

[33] Livy, V. 12; VI. 34, 39.

of the patricians, that its rites could be known and practised only by them, and, in fine, that the gods would not accept the sacrifice of a plebeian. To propose to have plebeian consuls was to wish to suppress the religion of the city. Thenceforth the worship would be impure, and the city would no longer be at peace with its gods.[34]

The patricians used all their influence and all their address to keep the plebeians from the magistracies. They were defending at the same time their religion and their power. As soon as they saw that the consulship was in danger of falling into the hands of plebeians, they separated from it the religious function which was the most important of all, — that which consisted in making the lustration of the citizens, — and thus the censorship was established. At the moment when it seemed impossible to resist the claims of the plebeians, the consulship was replaced by the military tribuneship. But the plebs showed great patience; they waited seventy-five years before their hopes were realized. It is clear that they displayed less ardor in obtaining the high magistracies than they had shown in conquering the tribuneship and a code.

But if the plebs were somewhat indifferent, there was a plebeian aristocracy that was ambitious. Here is a legend of this period: "Fabius Ambustus, one of the most distinguished of the patricians, had married his two daughters, one to a patrician, who became a military tribune, the other to Licinius Stolo, a prominent plebeian. This plebeian's wife was one day at the house of her sister, when the lictors, conducting the military tribune to his house, struck the door with their fasces. As she was ignorant, of this usage, she showed signs of fear. The laughter and the ironical questions of her sister showed her how much a plebeian marriage had degraded her by placing her in a house where dignities and honors could never enter. Her father guessed her cause of trouble, and consoled her by promising that she should see at her own house what she had seen at her sister's. He planned with his son-in-law, and both worked with the same object in view." This legend teaches us two things — one, that the plebeian aristocracy, by living with the patricians, shared their ambitions, and aspired

[34] Livy, VI. 41.

to their dignities; the other, that there were patricians who encouraged and excited the ambition of this new aristocracy, which was united with them by the closest ties.

It appears that Licinius and Sextius, who was joined with him, did not calculate that the plebs would make great efforts to gain the right of being consuls; for they thought it necessary to propose three laws at the same time. The one, the object of which was to make it imperative that one of the consuls should be chosen from the plebs, was preceded by two others, one of which diminished the debts, and the other granted lands to the people. The two first, it is evident, were intended to warm up the zeal of the plebs in favor of the third. For a moment the plebs were too clear-sighted; they fell in with the laws that were for them, — the reduction of debts, and the distribution of lands, — and gave little heed to the consulship. But Licinius replied that the three laws were inseparable, and that they must be accepted or rejected together. The Roman constitution authorized this course. Very naturally, the plebs preferred to accept all, rather than to lose all. But it was not enough that the plebs wished to make these laws. It was also necessary at that time that the senate should convoke the great comitia, and should afterwards confirm the decree.[35] It refused for ten years to do this. Finally an event took place which Livy has left too much in the shade.[36] It appears that the plebs took arms, and that civil war raged in the streets of Rome. The patricians, when conquered, approved and confirmed in advance, by a senatusconsultum, all the decrees which the people should pass during that year. Now, nothing prevented the tribunes from passing their three laws. From that time the plebs had every year one of the two consuls, and they were not long in succeeding to other magistracies. The plebeian wore the purple dress, and was preceded by the fasces; he administered justice; he was a senator; he governed the city, and commanded the legions.

The priesthoods remained, and it did not seem as if these could be wrested from the patricians; for, in the old religion, it was an unchangeable dogma that the right of reciting the prayers, and of touching sacred objects, was transmitted with

[35] Livy, IV. 49.
[36] Livy, IV. 42.

the blood. The knowledge of the rites, like the possession of the gods, was hereditary. In the same manner as the domestic worship was a patrimony, in which no foreigner could take part, the worship of the city, also, belonged exclusively to the families that had formed the primitive city. Assuredly, in the first centuries of Rome, it would not have entered the mind of any one that a plebeian could be a pontiff; but ideas had changed. The plebeians, by taking from religion its hereditary character, had made a religion for their own use. They had made for themselves domestic Lares, altars in public squares, and a hearth for the tribes. At first the patricians had nothing but contempt for this parody upon their religion. But, with the lapse of time, it became a serious thing, and the plebeian came to believe that, even as to worship and the gods, he was equal to the patrician.

Here were two opposing principles in action. The patrician persisted in declaring that the sacerdotal character and the right of adoring the divinity were hereditary. The plebs freed religion and the priesthood from the old hereditary character, and maintained that every man was qualified to pronounce prayers, and that, provided one was a citizen, he had the right to perform the ceremonies of the city worship. He thus arrived at the conclusion that a plebeian might be a priest.

If the priestly offices had been distinct from the military commands, and from politics, it is possible that the plebeians would not have coveted them so ardently. But all these things were confounded. The priest was a magistrate; the pontiff was a judge; the augur could dissolve the public assemblies. The plebeians did not fail to perceive that, without the priesthoods, they had not really civil or political equality. They therefore claimed that the pontificate should be shared by the two orders, as the consulship had been.

It became difficult to allege their religious incapacity as an objection, since, for sixty years, plebeians had been seen, as consuls, performing the sacrifices; as censors, making the lustrations; as conquerors of the enemy, fulfilling the sacred formalities of the triumph. Through the magistracies the plebs had already gained possession of a part of the priestly offices; it was not easy to save the rest. Faith in the hereditary principle of religion had been destroyed among the patricians themselves. In vain a few among them invoked the ancient rules, declaring, "The worship will be changed and sullied by unworthy hands; you are attacking the gods themselves; take care that their anger is not felt against our city." It does not seem that these arguments had much influence with the plebs, or even that the majority of the patricians were moved by them. The new manners gave the advantage to the plebeian principle. It was decided, therefore, that half of the pontiffs and augurs should, from that time, be chosen among the plebs.[87]

This was the last conquest of the lower orders; they had nothing more to wish for. The patricians had lost even their religious superiority. Nothing distinguished them now from the plebs; the name patrician was now only a souvenir. The old principle upon which the Roman city, like all ancient cities, had been founded, had disappeared. Of this ancient, hereditary religion, which had so long governed men, and which had established ranks among them, there now remained only the exterior forms. The plebeian had struggled against it for four centuries, — under the republic and under the kings, — and had conquered.

Chapter VIII

CHANGES IN PRIVATE LAW. THE CODE OF THE TWELVE TABLES. THE CODE OF SOLON

It is not in the nature of law to be absolute and unchangeable; it is modified and transformed, like every human work. Every society has its laws, which are formulated and developed with it, which change with it, and which, in fine, always follow the movements of its institutions, its manners, and its religious beliefs.

Men of the early ages had been governed by a religion which influenced their minds in proportion to its rudeness. This

---

[87] The dignities of king of the sacrifices, of flamens, salii, and vestals, to which no political importance was attached, were left without danger in the hands of the patricians, who always remained a sacred caste, but who were no longer a dominant caste.

religion had made their law, and had given them their political institutions. But finally society was transformed. The patriarchal rule which this hereditary religion had produced was
dissolved, with the lapse of time, in the rule of the city. Insensibly the gens was dismembered. The younger members
separated from the older, the servant from the chief. The
inferior class increased; it took arms, and finished by vanquish-
ing the aristocracy, and conquering equal rights. This change
in the social state necessarily brought another in law; for as
strongly as the Eupatrids and patricians were attached to the
old family religion, and consequently to ancient law, just so
strongly were the lower classes opposed to this religion, which
had long caused their inferiority, and to this ancient law,
which had oppressed them. Not only did they detest it, but
they did not even understand it. As they had not the belief on
which it was founded, this law appeared to them to be without
foundation. They found it unjust, and from that time it
became impossible for the law to maintain its ground.

If we place ourselves back to the time when the plebs had
increased and entered the body politic, and compare the law
of this epoch with primitive law, grave changes appear at the
first glance. The first and most salient is, that the law has been
rendered public, and is known to all. It is no longer that
sacred and mysterious chant which men repeated, with pious
respect, from age to age; which priests alone wrote, and which
men of the religious families alone could know. The law has
left the rituals and the books of the priests; it has lost its
religious mystery; it is a language which each one can read
and speak.

Something still more important is manifest in these codes.
The nature of the law and its foundation are no longer the
same as in the preceding period. Formerly the law was a
religious decision; it passed for a revelation made by the gods
to the ancestors, to the divine founder, to the sacred kings, to
the magistrate-priests. In the new code, on the contrary, the
legislator no longer speaks in the name of the gods. The
decemvirs of Rome receive their powers from the people. The
people also invested Solon with the right to make laws.
The legislator, therefore, no longer represents religious tradition, but the popular will. The principle of the law, hence-

forth, is the interest of men, and its foundation, the consent of the greatest number.

Two consequences flow from this fact. The first is, that the law is no longer presented as an immutable and undisputable formula. As it becomes a human work, it is acknowledged to be subject to change. The Twelve Tables say, "What the votes of the people have ordained in the last instance is the law."[1] Of all the passages of this code that remain to us, there is not one more important than this, or one which better marks the character of the revolution that had then taken place in the law. The law was no longer a sacred tradition — *mos;* it was simply a text — *lex;* and as the will of men had made it, the same will could change it.

The other consequence is this: The law, which before had been a part of religion, and was consequently the patrimony of the sacred families, was now the common property of all the citizens. The plebeian could plead in the courts. At most, the Roman patrician, more tenacious or more cunning than the Eupatrid of Athens, attempted to conceal the legal procedure from the multitude; but even these forms were not long in being revealed.

Thus the law was changed in its nature. From that time it could no longer contain the same provisions as in the preceding period. So long as religion had controlled it, it had regulated the relations of men to each other according to the principles of this religion. But the inferior class, who brought other principles into the city, understood nothing either of the old rules of the right of property, or of the ancient right of succession, or of the absolute authority of the father, or of the relationship of agnation, and wished to do away with all that.

This transformation of the law, it is true, could not be accomplished at once. If it is sometimes possible for man quickly to change his political institutions, he cannot change his legislation and his private law except slowly and by degrees. The history of Roman law, as well as that of Athenian law, proves this.

The Twelve Tables, as we have seen above, were written in

[1] Livy, VII. 17; IX. 33, 34.

the midst of social changes; patricians made them, but they were made upon the demand of the plebs, and for their use. This legislation, therefore, is no longer the primitive law of Rome; neither is it pretorian law; it is a transition between the two.

Here, then, are the points in which it does not yet deviate from the antique law: it maintains the power of the father; it allows him to pass judgment upon his son, to condemn him to death, or to sell him. While the father lives, the son never reaches his majority. As to the law of succession, this also follows the ancient rules: the inheritance passes to the agnates, and in default of agnates, to the *gentiles*. As to the cognates, that is to say, those related through females, the law does not yet recognize them. They do not inherit from each other; the mother does not succeed to the son, nor the son to the mother.[2]

Emancipation and adoption preserve the character and effects which these acts had in antique law. The emancipated son no longer takes part in the worship of his family, and, as a consequence, he loses the right of succession.

The following points are those on which this legislation deviates from primitive law: —

It formally admits that the patrimony may be divided among the brothers, since it grants the *actio familiæ erciscundæ*.[3]

It declares that the father cannot sell his son more than three times, and that after the third sale, the son shall be free.[4] This is the first blow struck by Roman law at the paternal authority.

Another change still more important was that which gave a man the right to transmit his property by will. Before this period the son was a *self-successor and a necessary:* in default of sons, the nearest agnate inherited; in default of agnates, the property returned to the gens, a trace of the time when the gens, still undivided, was sole proprietor of the domain, which afterwards had been divided. The Twelve Tables threw aside those old principles; they treated property as belonging,

---

[2] Gaius, III. 17, 24. Ulpian, XVI. 4. Cicero, *De Invent.,* II. 50.
[3] Gaius, III. 19.
[4] *Digest,* X. tit. 2, 1.

not to the gens, but to the individual; they therefore recognized in man the right of disposing of his property by will.

Still the will was not entirely unknown in primitive law. Even then a man might choose a legatee outside the gens, but on the condition that his choice should be ratified by the assembly of the curies; so that nothing less than the entire city could change the order which religion had formerly established. The new legislation freed the will from this vexatious rule, and gave it a more convenient form — that of a pretended sale. The man feigned to sell his property to the one whom he had chosen as heir; in reality, he made a will; in this case he had no need of appearing before the assembly of the people.

This form of will had the great advantage of being permitted to the plebeians. He who had nothing in common with the curies, had, up to that time, found no means of making a will.[5] But now he could employ the process of a pretended sale, and dispose of his property. The most remarkable fact in this period of the history of Roman legislation is, that by the introduction of certain new forms, the law extended its action and its benefits to the inferior orders. Ancient rules and formalities had only been applicable and were still applied only to religious families; but new rules and new methods of procedure were prepared which were applicable to the plebeians.

For the same reason, and in consequence of the same needs, innovations were introduced into that part of the law which related to marriage. It is clear that the plebeian families did not contract the sacred marriage, and that for them the conjugal union rested only upon the mutual agreement of the parties (*mutuus consensus*), and on the affection which they had promised each other (*affectio maritalis*). No formality, religious or civil, took place. This plebeian marriage finally prevailed in custom and in law; but in the beginning the laws of the patrician city did not recognize it as at all binding. This fact had important consequences; as the marital and paternal authority in the eyes of the patricians flowed only from the

---

[5] There was, indeed, the testament *in procinctu*, but we are not well informed as to this sort of will; perhaps it was to the testament *calatis comitiis* what the assembly by centuries was to the assembly by curies.

religious ceremony which had initiated the wife into the worship of the husband, it followed that the plebeian had not this power. The law recognized no family as his, and for him private law did not exist. This was a situation that could not last. A formality was therefore devised for the use of the plebeians, which, in civil affairs, had the same effect as the sacred marriage. They had recourse, as in case of the will, to a fictitious sale. The wife was bought by the husband — *coemptio;* from that time she was recognized in law as a part of his property — *familia.* She was in his hands, and ranked as his daughter, absolutely as if the religious ceremony had been performed.[6]

We cannot affirm that this proceeding was not older than the Twelve Tables. It is at least certain that the new legislation recognized it as legitimate. It thus gave the plebeian a private law, which was analogous in its effects to the law of the patricians, though it differed widely in principle. *Usus* corresponds to *coemptio;* these are two forms of the same act. Every object may be acquired in either of two ways — by purchase or by use; the same is the case with the fictitious property in the wife. Use here was one year's cohabitation; it established between husband and wife the same legal ties as purchase or the religious ceremony. It is hardly necessary to add that the cohabitation was to be preceded by marriage, at least by the plebeian marriage, which was contracted by the consent and affection of the parties. Neither the *coemptio* nor the *usus* created a moral union between husband and wife. They came after marriage — merely established a legal right. These were not, as has been too often repeated, modes of marriage; they were only means of acquiring the marital and paternal power.[7]

But the marital authority of ancient times had consequences, which, at the epoch of history to which we have arrived, began to appear excessive. We have seen that the wife was subjected without reserve to the husband, and that the power of the latter went so far that he could alienate or sell

[6] Gaius, I. 114.

[7] Gaius, I. 111; *quæ anno continuo* NUPTA *perseverabat.* So little was the *coemptio* a mode of marriage that a wife might contract it with another besides her husband — with a guardian, for example.

her.[8] In another point of view the power of the husband also produced effects which the good sense of the plebeian could hardly comprehend. Thus the woman placed in the hands of her husband was separated absolutely from her paternal family. She inherited none of its property, and had no tie of relationship with it in the eyes of the law. This was very well in primitive law, when religion forbade the same person to belong to two gentes, or to sacrifice at two hearths, or inherit from two houses. But the power of the hubsand was no longer conceived to be so great, and there were several excellent motives for wishing to escape these hard consequences. The code of the Twelve Tables, while providing that a year's cohabitation should put the wife in the husband's power, was compelled to leave him the liberty of contracting a union less binding. If each year the wife interrupted the cohabitation by an absence of no more than three nights, it was sufficient to prevent the husband's power from being established. Thus the wife preserved a legal connection with her own family, and could inherit from it.

Without entering into further details, we see that the code of the Twelve Tables already departed considerably from primitive law. Roman legislation was transformed with the government and the social state. Little by little, and in almost every generation, some new change took place. As the lower classes progressed in political order, new modifications were introduced into the rules of law. First, marriage was permitted between patrician and plebeian. Next, it was the Papirian law which forbade the debtor to pledge his person to the creditor. The procedure became simplified, greatly to the advantage of the plebeian, by the abolition of the *actions of the law.* Finally, the pretor, continuing to advance in the road which the Twelve Tables had opened, traced out, by the side of the ancient law, an entirely new system, which religion did not dictate, and which approached continually nearer to the law of nature.

An analogous revolution appears in Athenian law. We know

[8] Gaius, I. 117, 118. That this mancipation was merely fictitious in Gaius's time, is beyond doubt; but it was, perhaps, real in the beginning. The case was not the same, moreover, with the marriage by simple *consensus* as with the sacred marriage, which established between husband and wife an indissoluble bond.

that two codes were prepared at Athens, with an interval of thirty years between them; the first by Draco, the second by Solon.

The code of Draco was written when the struggle of the two classes was at its height, and before the Eupatrids were vanquished. Solon prepared his at the moment when the inferior class gained the upper hand. The difference between these codes, therefore, is great.

Draco was a Eupatrid; he had all the sentiments of his caste, and was "learned in the religious law." He appears to have done no more than to reduce the old customs to writing without in any way changing them. His first law is this: "Men should honor the gods and heroes of the country, and offer them annual sacrifices, without deviating from the rites followed by our ancestors." Memorials of his laws concerning murder have been preserved. They prescribe that the guilty one shall be kept out of the temple, and forbid him to touch the lustral water, or the vessels used in the ceremonies.[9]

His laws appeared cruel to succeeding generations. They were, indeed, dictated by an implacable religion, which saw in every fault an offence against the divinity, and in every offence against the divinity an unpardonable crime. Theft was punished with death, because theft was an attempt against the religion of property.

A curious article of this legislation which has been preserved shows in what spirit it was made.[10] It grants the right of prosecution for a murder only to the relatives of the dead and the members of his gens. We see by this how powerful the gens still was at that period, since it did not permit the city to interfere in its affairs, even to avenge it. A man still belonged to the family more than to the city.

In all that has come down to us of this legislation we see that it does no more than reproduce the ancient law. It had the severity and inflexible character of the old unwritten law. We can easily believe that it established a very broad distinction between the classes; for the inferior class always detested it, and at the end of thirty years demanded a new code.

[9] Aulus Gellius, XI. 18. Demosthenes, *in Lept.*, 158. Porphyry, *De Abstinentia*, IX.
[10] Demosthenes, *in Everg.*, 71; *in Macart.*, 57.

The code of Solon is entirely different; we can see that it corresponded to a great social revolution. The first peculiarity that we remark in it is, that the laws are the same for all. They establish no distinction between the Eupatrids, the simple free men, and the Thetes. These names are not even found in any of the articles that have been preserved. Solon boasts in his verses of having written the same laws for the great and the small.

Like the Twelve Tables, the code of Solon departed in many points from the ancient law; on other points he remained faithful to it. This is not to say that the Roman decemvirs copied the laws of Athens, but the two codes, works of the same period and consequences of the same social revolution, could not but resemble each other. Still, this resemblance is little more than in the spirit of the two codes; a comparison of their articles presents numerous differences. There are points on which the code of Solon remains nearer to primitive law than the Twelve Tables, as there are others on which he departs more widely from it.

The very early laws had prescribed that the eldest son alone should inherit. The code of Solon changed this, and prescribed in formal terms that the brothers should share the patrimony. But the legislator did not depart from primitive law enough to give the sister a part in the inheritance. "The division," he says, "shall be *among the sons.*"[11]

Further, if a father left only a daughter, this daughter could not inherit; the property fell to the nearest agnate. In this Solon conformed to the old law; but he succeeded in giving the daughter the enjoyment of the patrimony by compelling the heir to marry her.[12] Relationship through women was unknown in the primitive law. Solon admitted it in the new code, but placed it below the relationship through males. Here is his law:[13] "If a father leaves only a daughter, the nearest agnate inherits by marrying the daughter. If he leaves no children, his brother inherits, and not his sister, — his brother by the same father, and not his uterine brother. In default of brothers and the sons of brothers, the succession

11 Isæus, VI. 25.
12 Isæus, III. 42.
13 Isæus, VII. 19; XI. 1, 11.

falls to the sister. If there are neither brothers, nor sisters, nor nephews, the cousins and the children of cousins inherit. If no cousins are found in the paternal branch (that is to say, among the agnates), the succession is conferred on the collaterals of the maternal branch (the cognates)." Thus women began to enjoy rights of inheritance, but rights inferior to those of men. The law formally declared this principle: "Males and the descendants through males exclude women and the descendants of women." But this sort of relationship was recognized and took its place in the laws — a certain proof that natural right began to speak almost as loud as the ancient religion.

Solon also introduced into Athenian legislation something entirely new — the will. Before him property passed necessarily to the nearest agnate, or, in default of agnates, to the *gennetes* (*gentiles*) ; this was because goods were considered as belonging, not to the individual, but to the family. But in Solon's time men began to take another view of the right of property. The dissolution of the old γενος had made every domain the property of an individual. The legislator therefore permitted them to dispose of their fortunes, and to choose their legatees. Still, while suppressing the rights which the γενος had over each of its members, he did not suppress the rights of the natural family, — the son remained the necessary heir. If the deceased left only a daughter, he could choose his heir only on condition that this heir should marry the daughter. A man without children was free to will his property according to his fancy.[14]

This last rule was absolutely new in Athenian legislation, and we can see by this how many new ideas concerning the family sprang up at that time.

The primitive religion had given the father sovereign authority in his own house. The ancient law of Athens went so far as to permit a father to sell his son, or to put him to death.[15] Solon, conforming to new manners, limited this power.[16] It is certainly known that he forbade a father to sell his daughter, and it is probable that the same injunction pro-

---

[14] Isæus, III. 41, 68, 73; VI. 9; X. 9, 13. Plutarch, *Solon*, 21.
[15] Plutarch, *Solon*, 13.
[16] Plutarch, *Solon*, 23.

tected the son. The paternal authority went on diminishing as the ancient religion lost its power, — an event which happened earlier at Athens than at Rome. The Athenian law, therefore, was not satisfied to say, like the Twelve Tables, "After a triple sale, the son shall be free." It permitted the son, on reaching a certain age, to escape from the paternal power. Custom, if not the laws, insensibly came to establish the majority of the son during the lifetime of his father. There was an Athenian law which enjoined the son to support his father when old or infirm. Such a law necessarily indicates that the son might own property, and consequently that he was freed from parental authority. This law did not exist at Rome, because the son never possessed anything, and always remained a minor.

As for females, the law of Solon still conformed to the earlier law, when it forbade her to make a will because a woman was never a real proprietor, and could have only the usufruct. But it deviated from the ancient code when it permitted women to claim their dower.[17]

There were still other innovations in this code. In opposition to Draco, who permitted only the family of the victim to prosecute one for a crime, Solon granted this right to every citizen.[18] Here was one more old patriarchal right abolished.

Thus at Athens, as at Rome, law began to undergo a change. For the new social state a new code sprang up. Beliefs, manners, and institutions having been modified, laws which had before appeared just and wise ceased to appear so, and by slow degrees were abolished.

[17] Isæus, VII. 24, 25. Dion Chrysostomus, Περι απιστιας. Harpocration, Περα μεδιμνου. Demosthenes, in Evergum; in Bœotum de dote; in Neœram, 51, 52.
[18] Plutarch, Solon, 18.

Chapter IX

THE NEW PRINCIPLE OF GOVERNMENT. THE PUBLIC INTEREST AND THE SUFFRAGE

THE revolution which overthrew the rule of the sacerdotal class, and raised the lower class to a level with the ancient chiefs of gentes, marked a new period in the history of cities. A sort of social reconstruction was accomplished. It was not simply replacing one class of men in power by another. Old principles had been thrust aside, and new rules adopted that were to govern human societies. The new city, it is true, preserved the exterior forms of the preceding period. The republican system remained; almost everywhere the magistrates preserved their ancient names. Athens still had its archons, and Rome its consuls. Nor was anything changed in the ceremonies of the public religion; the repasts of the prytaneum, the sacrifices at the opening of the public assembly, the auspices and the prayers, — all were preserved. It is quite common with man, when he rejects old institutions, to wish to preserve their exterior forms.

In reality all was changed. Neither institutions, nor laws, nor beliefs, nor manners were in this new period what they had been in the preceding. The old system disappeared, carrying with it the rigorous rules which it had established in all things; a new order of things was established, and human life changed its aspect.

During long ages religion had been the sole principle of government. Another principle had to be found capable of replacing it, and which, like it, might govern human institutions, and keep them as much as possible clear of fluctuations and conflicts. The principle upon which the governments of cities were founded thenceforth was public interest.

We must observe this new dogma which then made its appearance in the minds of men and in history. Heretofore the superior rule whence social order was derived was not interest, but religion. The duty of performing the rites of

worship had been the social bond. From this religious necessity
were derived, for some the right to command, for others the
obligation to obey. From this had come the rules of justice
and of legal procedure, those of public deliberations and
those of war. Cities did not ask if the institutions which they
adopted were useful; these institutions were adopted because
religion had wished it thus. Neither interest nor convenience
had contributed to establish them. And if the sacerdotal class
had tried to defend them, it was not in the name of the public
interest; it was in the name of religious tradition. But in the
period which we now enter, tradition no longer holds empire,
and religion no longer governs. The regulating principle from
which all institutions now derive their authority — the only
one which is above individual wills, and which obliges them
all to submit — is public interest. What the Latins call *res
publica*, the Greeks το κοινον, replaces the old religion. This is
what, from this time, establishes institutions and laws, and by
this all the important acts of cities are judged. In the deliberations of senates, or of popular assemblies, when a law is dis-
cused, or a form of government, or a question of private right,
or a political institution, no one any longer asks what religion
prescribes, but what the general interest demands.

A saying is attributed to Solon which well characterizes this
new *régime*. Some one asked him if he had given his country
the best constitution. "No," he replied, "but the one which is
the best suited to it." Now it was something quite new to
expect in forms of government, and in laws, only a relative
merit. The ancient constitutions, founded upon the rules of a
worship, were proclaimed infallible and immutable. They possessed the rigor and inflexibility of the religion. Solon indicated by this answer that, in future, political constitutions
should conform to the wants, the manners, and the interests
of the men of each age. There was no longer a question of
absolute truth; the rules of government were for the future
to be flexible and variable. It is said that Solon wished at the
most that his laws might be observed for a hundred years.

The precepts of public interest are not so absolute, so clear,
so manifest, as are those of religion. We may always discuss
them; they are not perceived at once. The way that appeared

the simplest and surest to know what the public interest demanded was to assemble the citizens, and consult them. This
course was thought to be necessary, and was almost daily
employed. In the preceding period the aupices had borne the
chief weight of the deliberations; the opinion of the priest, of
the king, of the sacred magistrate was all-powerful. Men voted
little, and then rather as a formality than to express an
opinion. After that time they voted on every question; the
opinion of all was needed in order to know what was for
the interest of all. The suffrage became the great means of
government. It was the source of institutions and the rule of
right; it decided what was useful and even what was just. It
was above the magistrates and above the laws; it was sovereign
in the city.

The nature of government was also changed. Its essential
function was no longer the regular performance of religious
ceremonies. It was especially constituted to maintain order and
peace within and dignity and power without. What had
before been of secondary importance was now of the first.
Politics took precedence of religion, and the government
of men became a human affair. It consequently happened
either that new offices were created, or, at any rate, that old
ones assumed a new character. We can see this by the example
of Athens, and by that of Rome. At Athens, during the
domination of the aristocracy, the archons had been especially
priests. The care of deciding causes, of administering the law,
and of making war was of minor importance, and might,
without inconvenience, be joined to the priesthood. When the
Athenians rejected the old religious form of government, they
did not suppress the archonship, for they had an extreme
repugnance to abolishing what was ancient. But by the side
of the archons they elected other magistrates, who, by the
nature of their duties, corresponded better with the wants of
the age. These were the *strategi*. The word signifies chief of
the army, but the authority of these officers was not purely
military; they had the care of the relations with other cities,
of the finances, and of whatever concerned the police of the
city. We may say that the archons had in their hands the
state religion and all that related to it, and that the strategi

had the political power. The archons preserved the authority such as the ancient ages had conceived it; the strategi had what new wants had caused to be established. Finally a time came when the archons had only the semblance of power, and the strategi had all the reality. These new magistrates were no longer priests; they hardly performed the ceremonies that were indispensable in time of war. The government tended more and more to free itself from religion. The strategi might be chosen outside the Eupatrids. In the examination which they had to undergo before they were appointed ($\delta o\kappa\iota\mu\alpha\sigma\iota\alpha$), they were not asked, as the archons were, if they had a domestic worship, and if they were of a pure family; it was sufficient if they had always performed their duties as citizens, and held real property in Attica.[1] The archons were designated by lot,— that is to say, by the voice of the gods; it was otherwise with the strategi. As the government became more difficult and more complicated, as piety was no longer the principal quality, and as skill, prudence, courage, and the art of commanding became necessary, men no longer believed the choice by lot was sufficient to make a good magistrate. The city no longer desired to be bound by the pretended will of the gods, and claimed to have a free choice of its chiefs. That the archon, who was a priest, should be designated by the gods, was natural; but the strategus, who held in his hands the material interests of the city, was better elected by the citizens.

If we closely observe the institutions of Rome, we see that changes of the same kind were going on there. On the one hand, the tribunes of the people so augmented their importance that the direction of the republic — at least, whatever related to internal affairs — finally belonged to them. Now, those tribunes who had no priestly character bore a great resemblance to the strategi. On the other hand, the consulship itself could subsist only by changing its character. Whatever was sacerdotal in it was by degrees effaced. The respect of the Romans for the traditions and forms of the past required, it is true, that the consul should continue to perform the ceremonies instituted by their ancestors; but we can easily understand that, the day when plebeians became consuls, these

[1] Deinarchus, I. 171 (coll. Didot).

ceremonies were no longer anything more than vain formalities. The consulship was less and less a priesthood, and more and more a command. This transformation was slow, insensible, unperceived, but it was not the less complete. The consulship was certainly not, in the time of the Scipios, what it had been in Publicola's day. The military tribuneship, which the senate instituted in 443, and about which the ancients give us very little information, was perhaps the transition between the consulship of the first period and that of the second.

We may also remark that there was a change in the manner of nominating the consuls. Indeed, in the first ages, the vote of the centuries in the election of the magistrates was, as we have seen, a mere formality. It reality, the consul of each year was *created* by the consul of the preceding year, who transmitted the auspices to him after having obtained the assent of the gods. The centuries voted on the two or three candidates presented by the consul in office; there was no debate. The people might detest a candidate; but they were none the less compelled to vote for him. In the period at which we have now arrived, the election is quite different, although the forms are still the same. There is still, as formerly, a religious ceremony and a vote; but the religious ceremony is the formality, and the vote is the reality. The candidate is still presented by the consul who presides; but the consul is obliged, if not by law, at least by custom, to accept all candidates, and to declare that the auspices are equally favorable to all. Thus the centuries name those whom they honor. The election no longer belongs to the gods; it is in the hands of the people. The gods and the auspices are no longer consulted, except on the condition that they will be impartial towards all the candidates. Men make the choice.

Chapter X

AN ARISTOCRACY OF WEALTH ATTEMPTS TO ESTABLISH ITSELF. ESTABLISHMENT OF DEMOCRACY. FOURTH REVOLUTION

THE government which succeeded to the rule of the religious aristocracy was not at first a democracy. We have seen, from the example of Athens and Rome, that the revolution which took place was not the work of the lowest classes. There were, indeed, some cities where these classes rose first; but they could found nothing durable. The protracted disorders into which Syracuse, Miletus, and Samos fell are a proof of this. The new governments were not established with any solidity, except where a class was at once found to take in hand, for a time, the power and moral authority which the Eupatrids and the patricians had lost. What could this new aristocracy be? The hereditary religion being thrown aside, there was no longer any other social distinction than wealth. Men demanded, therefore, that wealth should establish rank; for they could not admit at once that equality should be absolute.

Thus Solon did not think best to do away with the ancient distinction founded on hereditary religion, except by establishing a new division, which should be founded on riches. He divided the citizens into four ranks, and gave them unequal rights; none but the rich could hold the highest offices; none below the two intermediate classes could belong to the senate, or sit in the tribunals.[1]

The case was the same at Rome. We have seen that Servius destroyed the power of the patricians only by founding a rival aristocracy. He created twelve centuries of knights, chosen from the richest plebeians. This was the origin of the equestrian order, which was from that time the rich order at Rome. The plebeians who did not possess the sum required for a

---

[1] Plutarch, *Solon*, 18; *Aristides*, 13. Aristotle, cited by Harpocration, at the words Ἱππεῖς, θῆτες. Pollux, VIII. 129.

knight were divided into five classes, according to the amount of their fortunes. The poorest people were left out of all the classes. They had no political rights; if they figured in the comitia by centuries, it is certain that they did not vote.[2] The republican constitution preserved these distinctions, established by a king, and the plebeians did not at first appear very desirous of establishing equality among themselves.

What is seen so clearly at Athens and at Rome appears in almost all the other cities. At Cumæ, for example, political rights were given at first only to those who, owning horses, formed a sort of equestrian order; later, those who ranked next below them in wealth obtained the same rights, and this last measure raised the number of citizens only to one thousand. At Rhegium the government was for a long time in the hands of a thousand of the wealthiest men of the city. At Thurii, a large fortune was necessary to enable one to make a part of the body politic. We see clearly in the poetry of Theognis that at Megara, after the fall of the nobles, the wealthy took their places. At Thebes, in order to enjoy the rights of a citizen, one could be neither an artisan nor a merchant.[3]

Thus the political rights which, in the preceding epoch, belonged to birth, were, during some time, enjoyed by fortune alone. This aristocracy of wealth was established in all the cities, not by any calculation, but by the very nature of the human mind, which, escaping from a *régime* of great inequality, could not arrive at once at complete equality.

We have to remark that these new nobles did not found their superiority simply upon wealth. Everywhere their ambition was to become the military class. They undertook to defend the city at the same time that they governed it. They reserved for themselves the best arms and the greater part of the perils in battle, desiring to imitate in this the nobility which they had replaced. In all the cities the wealthiest men formed the cavalry, the well-to-do class composed the body of hoplites, or legionaries. The poor were excluded from the army, or at most they were employed as skirmishers or light-

[2] Livy, I. 43.
[3] Aristotle, *Politics,* III. 3, 4; VI. 4, 5 (edit. Didot).

armed soldiers, or among the rowers of the fleet.[4] Thus the organization of the army corresponded with perfect exactitude to the political organization of the city. The dangers were proportioned to the privileges, and the material strength was found in the same hands as the wealth.[5]

There was thus, in almost all the cities whose history is known to us, a period during which the rich class, or at any rate the well-to-do class, was in possession of the government. This political system had its merits, as every system may have, when it conforms to the manners of the epoch, and the religious ideas are not opposed to it. The sacerdotal nobility of the preceding period had assuredly rendered great services. They were the first to establish laws and found regular governments. They had enabled human societies to live, during several centuries, with calmness and dignity. The aristocracy of wealth had another merit; it impressed upon society and the minds of men a new impulse. Having sprung from labor in all its forms, it honored and stimulated the laborer. This new government gave the most political importance to the most laborious, the most active, or the most skilful man; it was, therefore, favorable to industry and commerce. It was also favorable to intellectual progress; for the acquisition of this wealth, which was gained or lost, ordinarily, according to each one's merit, made instruction the first need, and intelligence the most powerful spring of human affairs. We are not, therefore, surprised that under this government Greece and Rome

[4] Lycias, *in Alcib.*, I. 8; II. 7. Isæus, VII. 39. Xenophon, *Hellen.*, VII. 4. Harpocration, θητες.

[5] The relation between military service and political rights is manifest: at Rome the centuriate assembly was no other than the army. So true is this, that men who had passed the age for military service no longer had the right to vote in these comitia. Historians do not tell us that there was a similar law at Athens; but there are figures that are significant. Thucydides says (II. 31, 13) that at the beginning of the war, Athens had thirteen thousand hoplites; if to these we add the knights, numbered by Aristophanes (in the *Wasps*) at about a thousand, we arrive at the number of fourteen thousand soldiers. Now, Plutarch tells us, that at the same date there were fourteen thousand citizens. The proletariat, therefore, who could not serve among the hoplites, were not counted among the citizens. The Athenian constitution, then, in 430 was not yet completely democratic.

enlarged the limits of their intellectual culture, and advanced their civilization.

The rich class did not hold the empire so long as the ancient hereditary nobility had held it. Their title to dominion was not of the same value. They had not the sacred character with which the ancient Eupatrid was clothed. They did not rule by virtue of a belief and by the will of the gods. They had no quality that had power over consciences, that compelled men to submit. Man is little inclined to bow, except before what he believes to be right, or before what his notions teach him is far above him. He had long been made to bend before the religious superiority of the Eupatrid, who repeated the prayers and possessed the gods. But wealth did not overawe him. In presence of wealth, the most ordinary sentiment is not respect; it is envy. The political inequality that resulted from the difference of fortunes soon appeared to be an iniquity, and men strove to abolish it.

Besides, the series of revolutions, once commenced, could not be arrested. The old principles were overturned, and there were no longer either traditions or fixed rules. There was a general sense of the instability of affairs, which prevented any constitution from enduring for any great length of time. The new aristocracy was attacked, as the old had been; the poor wished to be citizens, and in their turn began to make efforts to enter the body politic.

It is impossible to enter into the details of this new struggle. The history of cities, as it gets farther from their origin, becomes more and more diversified. They follow the same series of revolutions; but these revolutions appear under a great variety of forms. We can, at any rate, make this remark—that in the cities where the principal element of wealth was the possession of the soil, the rich class was longer respected, and held its dominion longer; and that, on the contrary, in cities like Athens, where there were few landed estates, and where men became rich especially by industry, manufactures, and commerce, the instability of fortunes sooner awakened the cupidity or hopes of the lower orders, and the aristocracy was sooner attacked.

The rich class of Rome offered a much stronger resistance than that of Greece; this was due to causes which we shall state

presently. But when we read Grecian history, we are somewhat suprised that the new nobles defended themselves so
feebly. True, they could not, like the Eupatrids, oppose to
their adversaries the great and powerful argument of tradition and piety. They could not call to their aid their ancestors
and the gods. They had no point of support in their own
religious notions; nor had they any faith in the justice of their
privileges.

They had, indeed, superiority in arms; but this superiority
finally failed them. The constitutions which the states adopted
would have lasted longer, no doubt, if each state could have
remained isolated, or, at least, if it could have lived in peace.
But war deranges the machinery of constitutions, and hastens
changes. Now, between these cities of Greece and Italy war was
almost perpetual. Military service weighed most heavily upon
the rich class, as this class occupied the front rank in battle.
Often, at the close of a campaign, they returned to the city
decimated and weakened, and consequently not prepared to
make head against the popular party. At Tarentum, for
example, the higher class having lost the greater part of its
members in a war against the Iapygians, a democratic government was at once established in the city. The course of events
was the same at Argos, some thirty years before; at the close
of an unsuccessful war against the Spartans, the number of
real citizens had become so small that it was found necessary
to grant the rights of citizens to a multitude of *Periœci*.[6] It was to
avoid falling into this extremity that Sparta was so sparing of
the blood of the real Spartans. As to Rome, its revolutions are
explained, in a great measure, by its continual wars. First, war
destroyed its patricians; of the three hundred families which
this caste comprised under the kings, there remained hardly
a third part, after the conquest of Samnium. War afterwards
harvested the primitive plebeians, those rich and courageous
plebeians who filled the five classes and formed the legions.

One of the effects of war was that the cities were almost
always brought to the strait of putting arms into the hands of
the lower orders. It was in this way that at Athens, and in all
the maritime cities, the need of a navy and the battles upon

6 Aristotle, *Politics*, VIII. 2, 8 (V. 2).

the water gave the poor class that importance which the constitution refused them. The Thetes, raised to the rank of rowers, of sailors, and even of soldiers, and holding in their hands the safety of their country, felt their importance, and took courage. Such was the origin of the Athenian democracy. Sparta was afraid of war. We can see in Thucydides how slow she was, and how unwilling, to commence a campaign. She allowed herself to be dragged, in spite of herself, into the Peloponnesian war; but how many efforts she made to withdraw! This was because she was forced to arm her υπομειονες, her Neodamodes, her Mothaces, her Laconians, and even her Helots; she well knew that every war, by giving arms to the classes that she was oppressing, threatened her with revolution, and that she would be compelled, on disbanding the army, either to submit to the law of her Helots or to find means to have them massacred without disturbance. The plebeians calumniated the Roman senate when they reproached it with always seeking new wars. The senate was too wise for that. It knew how many concessions and checks in the forum its wars cost. But it could not avoid them.

It is therefore beyond a doubt that war slowly lessened the distance which the aristocracy of wealth had placed between itself and the lower orders. Thus it soon happened that constitutions were found to be at disaccord with the social state, and required modification. Besides, it must have been seen that all privileges were necessarily in contradiction to the principle which then governed men. The public interest was not a principle that could long authorize an inequality among them. It inevitably conducted societies to a democracy.

So true is this, that a little sooner, or a little later, it was necessary to give all free men political rights. As soon as the Roman plebeians wished to hold comitia of their own, they were constrained to admit the lowest class, and could not hold to the division into classes. Most of the cities thus saw real popular assemblies formed and universal suffrage established.

Now, the right of suffrage had at that time a value incomparably greater than it can have in modern states. By means of it the last of the citizens had a hand in all affairs, elected magistrates, made laws, decided cases, declared for war or peace, and prepared treaties of alliance. This extension of the right of suffrage, therefore, made the government really democratic.

We must make a last remark. The ruling class would perhaps have avoided the advent of democracy if they had been able to found what Thucydides calls ολιγαρχια ισονομος, — that is to say, the government for a few, and liberty for all. But the Greeks had not a clear idea of liberty; individual liberty never had any guarantee among them. We learn from Thucydides, who certainly is not suspected of too much zeal for democratic government, that under the rule of the oligarchy the people were subjected to many vexatious, arbitrary condemnations, and violent executions. We read in this historian "that democratic government was needed to give the poor a refuge and the rich a check." The Greeks never knew how to reconcile civil with political equality. That the poor might be protected in their personal interests, it seemed necessary to them that they should have the right of suffrage, that they should be judges in the tribunal, and that they might be elected as magistrates. If we also call to mind that among the Greeks the state was an absolute power, and that no individual right was of any value against it, we can understand what an immense interest every man had, even the most humble, in possessing political rights, — that is to say, in making a part of the government; the collective sovereign being so omnipotent that a man could be nothing unless he was a part of this sovereign. His security and his dignity depended upon this. He wished to possess political rights, not in order to enjoy true liberty, but to have at least what might take its place.

Chapter XI

RULES OF DEMOCRATIC GOVERNMENT. EXAMPLES OF ATHENIAN DEMOCRACY

As the revolutions followed their course, and men departed from the ancient system, to govern them became more difficult. More minute rules, more machinery, and that more delicate, became necessary. This we can see from the example of the Athenian government.

Athens had a great number of magistrates. In the first place she had preserved all those of the preceding epoch — the archon, who gave his name to the year and watched over the perpetuation of the domestic worship; the king, who performed the sacrifices; the polemarch, who figured as chief of the army, and decided the causes of foreigners; the six thesmothetæ, who appeared to pass judgment, but who, in reality, merely presided over juries: there were also the ten ʽιεροποιοι, who consulted the oracles and offered certain sacrifices; the παρασιτοι, who accompanied the archon and the king in the ceremonies; the ten athlothetæ, who remained four years in office to prepare the festival of Bacchus; and, finally, the prytanes, who, to the number of fifty, were continually occupied to attend to keeping up the public fire and the sacred repasts. We see from this that Athens remained faithful to the traditions of ancient times. So many revolutions had not yet completely destroyed this superstitious respect. No one dared to break with the old forms of the national religion; the democracy continued the worship instituted by the Eupatrids.

Afterwards came the magistrates specially created for the democracy, who were not priests, and who watched over the material interests of the city. First were the strategi, who attended to affairs of war and politics; then followed the ten astynomi, who had charge of the police; the ten agoranomi, who watched over the markets of the city and of the Piræeus; the fifteen sitophylaces, who superintended the sales of grain; the fifteen metronomi, who controlled weights and measures; ten guards of the treasury; the ten receivers of the accounts; the *eleven* who were charged with the execution of sentences. In addition to this, the greater part of these magistracies were repeated in each tribe and in each deme. The smallest group of people in Attica had its archon, its priest, its secretary, its receiver, its military chief. One could hardly take a step in the city or in the country without meeting an official.

These offices were annual; so that there was hardly a man who might not hope to fill some one of them in his turn. The magistrate-priests were chosen by lot. The magistrates who attended only to public order were elected by the people. Still there was a precaution against the caprices of the lot, as well as against that of universal suffrage. Every newly elected official was subjected to an examination, either before the senate, or before the magistrates going out of office, or, lastly, before the Areopagus — not that they demanded proofs of capacity or talent, but an inquiry was made concerning the probity of the man, and concerning his family; every magistrate was also required to have a property in real estate.

It would seem that these magistrates, elected by the suffrages of their equals, named for only a single year, responsible and even removable, could have had little prestige and authority. We need only read Thucydides and Xenophon, however, to assure ourselves that they were respected and obeyed. There was always in the character of the ancients, even in that of the Athenians, a great facility in submitting to discipline. It was perhaps a consequence of the habits of obedience with which the religious government had inspired them. They were accustomed to respect the state, and all those who, in any degree, represented it. They never thought of despising a magistrate because they had elected him; suffrage was reputed one of the most sacred sources of authority.

Above the magistrates, who had no other duty than that of seeing to the execution of the laws, there was the senate. It was merely a deliberative body, a sort of council of state; it passed no acts, made no laws, exercised no sovereignty. Men saw no inconvenience in renewing it every year, for neither superior intelligence nor great experience was required of its members. It was composed of fifty prytanes from each tribe, who performed the sacred duties in turn, and deliberated all the year upon the religious and political interests of the city. It was probably because the senate was only the assembly of the prytanes, — that is to say, of the annual priests of the sacred fire, — that it was filled by lot. It is but just to say, that after the lot had decided, each name was examined, and any one was thrown out who did not appear sufficiently honorable.[1]

Above even the senate there was the assembly of the people. This was the real sovereign. But, just as in a well-constituted

[1] Æschines, III. 2; Andocides, II. 19; I. 45–55.

monarchy, the monarch is surrounded with safeguards against his own caprices and errors, this democracy also had invariable rules, to which it submitted.

The assembly was convoked by the prytanes or the strategi. It was holden in an enclosure consecrated by religion; since morning the priests had walked around the Pnyx, immolating victims and calling down the protection of the gods. The people were seated on stone benches. Upon a sort of platform were the prytanes, and in front of them the prœdri, who presided over the assembly. An altar stood near the speaker's stand, and the stand itself was reckoned a sort of altar. When all were seated, a priest (κηρυξ) proclaimed, "Keep silence, religious silence (ευφημια); pray the gods and goddesses [here he named the principal divinities of the country] that all may pass most prosperously in the assembly for the greatest advantage of Athens and the happiness of its citizens." Then the people, or some one in their name, replied, "We invoke the gods that they may protect the city. May the advice of the wisest prevail. Cursed be he who shall give us bad counsel, who shall attempt to change the decrees and the law, or who shall reveal our secrets to the enemy."[2]

Then the herald, by order of the presidents, declared the subjects with which the assembly was to occupy itself. A question, before being presented to the people, was discussed and studied by the senate. The people had not what is called, in modern language, the initiative. The senate offered a draught of a decree (the bill); the people could reject or adopt it, but could not deliberate on any other question.

When the herald had read the proposed law, the discussion was opened. The herald said, "Who wishes to speak?" The orators ascended the speaker's stand according to age. Any man could speak, without distinction of fortune or profession, but on the condition that he had proved that he enjoyed political rights, that he was not a debtor to the state, that his habits of life were correct, that he was lawfully married, that he was a land-owner in Attica, that he had fulfilled all his duties

[2] Æschines, I. 23; III. 4. Deinarchus, II. 14. Demosthenes, *in Aristocr.*, 97. Aristophanes, *Acharn.*, 43, 44, and Scholiast, *Thesmoph.*, 295–310.

towards his parents, that he had taken part in all the military expeditions to which he had been assigned, and that he had never thrown his shield away in any battle.[3]

These precautions against eloquence once taken, the people gave themselves entirely up to it. The Athenians, as Thucydides says, did not believe that words could damage actions. On the contrary, they felt the need of being enlightened. Politics were no longer, as under the preceding government, an affair of tradition and faith. Men reflected and weighed reasons. Discussion was necessary, for every question was more or less obscure, and discussion alone could bring the truth to light. The Athenian people desired to have every question presented in all its different phases, and to have both sides clearly shown. They made great account of their orators, and, it is said, paid them in money for every discourse delivered to the people.[4] They did even better; they listened to them. For we are not to picture to ourselves a noisy and turbulent multitude; the attitude of the people was quite the contrary. The comic poet represents them motionless upon their stone seats, listening open-mouthed.[5] Historians and orators frequently describe these popular assemblies. We rarely see an orator interrupted; whether it was Pericles or Cleon, Æschines or Demosthenes, the people were attentive; whether the orators flattered them or upbraided them, they listened. They allowed the most opposite opinions to be expressed, with a patience that was sometimes admirable. There were never cries or shouts. The orator, whatever he might say, could always reach the end of his discourse.

At Sparta eloquence was little known. The principles of government were not the same. The aristocracy still governed and had fixed traditions, which saved the trouble of a long discussion upon every question. At Athens the people desired to be informed. They could decide only after a contradictory debate; they acted only after they had been convinced, or thought they had been. To put universal suffrage in operation, discussion is necessary; eloquence is the spring of demo-

---

[3] Æschines, I. 27–33. Deinarchus, I. 71.

[4] At least this is what Aristophanes gives us to understand. *Wasps*, 711 (689). See the Scholiast.

[5] Aristophanes, *Knights*, 1119.

cratic government. The orators, therefore, soon received the title of demagogues, — that is to say, of conductors of the city; and indeed they did direct its action, and determined all its resolutions.

The case where an orator should make a proposition contrary to existing laws had been anticipated. Athens had special magistrates called guardians of the laws. Seven in number, they watched over the assembly, occupying high seats, and seemed to represent the law, which was above even the people. If they saw that the law was attacked, they stopped the orator in the midst of his discourse, and ordered the immediate dissolution of the assembly. The people separated without having a right to reach a vote.[6]

There was a law, little applicable indeed, that punished every orator convicted of having given the people bad advice. There was another that forbade access to the speaker's stand to any orator who had three times advised resolutions contrary to the existing laws.[7]

Athens knew very well that democracy could be sustained only by respect for the laws. The care of preparing the changes that it might be useful to propose belonged especially to the thesmothetæ. Their propositions were presented to the senate, which had the right to reject, but not to convert them into laws. In case of approval the senate convoked the assembly, and presented the bill of the thesmothetæ. But the people could decide nothing at once; they put off the discussion to another day. Meanwhile they designated five orators, whose special mission should be to defend the existing laws, and to point out the inconveniences of the innovation proposed. On the day fixed the people again assembled and heard, first, the orators charged with the defence of the old laws, and afterwards those who supported the new. When speeches had been heard, the people did not decide yet. They contented themselves with naming a commission, very numerous, but composed exclusively of men who had held the office of judge. This commission returned to the examination of the affair, heard the orators anew, discussed, and deliberated. If the com-

---

[6] Pollux, VIII. 94. Philochorus, *Fragm.*, coll. Didot, p. 407.

[7] Athenæus, X. 73. Pollux, VIII. 52. See G. Perrot, *Hist. du droit public d'Athènes,* chap. II.

missioners rejected the proposed law, their decision was without appeal. If they approved it, the people were again assembled; and this third time they voted, and by their votes the bill became a law.[8]

Notwithstanding so much prudence, an unjust or unwise proposition might still be adopted; but the new law forever carried the name of its author, who might afterwards be prosecuted and punished. The people, as the real sovereign, were reputed infallible, but every orator always remained answerable for the advice he had given.[9]

Such were the rules which the democracy obeyed. But we are not to conclude from this that they never made mistakes. Whatever the form of government, — monarchy, aristocracy, or democracy, — there are days when reason governs, and others when passion rules. No constitution ever suppressed the weaknesses and vices of human nature. The more minute the rules, the more difficult and full of peril they show the direction of society to be. Democracy could last only by force of prudence.

We are astonished, too, at the amount of labor which this democracy required of men. It was a very laborious government. See how the life of an Athenian is passed. One day he is called to the assembly of his deme, and has to deliberate on the religious and political interests of this little association. Another day he must go to the assembly of his tribe; a religious festival is to be arranged, or expenses are to be examined, or decrees passed, or chiefs and judges named. Three times a month, regularly, he takes part in the general assembly of the people; and he is not permitted to be absent. The session is long. He does not go simply to vote; having arrived in the morning, he must remain till a late hour, and listen to the orators. He cannot vote unless he has been present from the opening of the session, and has heard all the speeches. For him this vote is one of the most serious affairs. At one time political or military chiefs are to be elected, — that is to say, those to whom his interests and his life are to be confided for a year; at another a tax is to be imposed, or a

[8] Æschines, *in Ctesiph.*, 38. Demosthenes, *in Timocr.; in Leptin.* Andocides, I. 83.

[9] Thucydides, III. 43. Demosthenes, *in Timocratem.*

law to be changed. Again, he has to vote on the question of war, knowing well that, in case of war, he must give his own blood or that of a son. Individual interests are inseparably united with those of the state. A man cannot be indifferent or inconsiderate. If he is mistaken, he knows that he shall soon suffer for it, and that in each vote he pledges his fortune and his life. The day when the disastrous Sicilian expedition was decided upon, there was no citizen who did not know that one of his own family must make a part of it, and who was not required to give his whole attention to weighing the advantages of such an expedition against the dangers it presented. It was of the greatest importance that one should see the subject in a clear light; for a check received by his country was for every citizen a diminution of his personal dignity, of his security, and of his wealth.

The duty of a citizen was not limited to voting. When his turn came, he was required to act as a magistrate in his deme or in his tribe. Every third year[10] he was a heliast, and passed all that year in the courts of justice, occupied in hearing cases and applying the law. There was hardly a citizen who was not called upon twice in his life to be a senator. Then for a year he sat every day from morning till evening, receiving the depositions of magistrates, demanding their accounts, replying to foreign ambassadors, drawing up instructions for Athenian ambassadors, examining into all affairs that were to be submitted to the people, and preparing all the laws. Finally, he might be a magistrate of the city, an archon, a strategus, or an astynome, if the lot or suffrage designated him. It was, we see, a heavy charge to be a citizen of a democratic state. There was enough to occupy almost one's whole existence, and there remained very little time for personal affairs and domestic life. Therefore Aristotle says, very justly, that the man who had to labor in order to live could not be a citizen. Such were the requirements of a democracy. The citizens, like the public functionary of our day, was required to devote himself entirely to the state. He gave it his blood in war and his time during peace. He was not free to lay aside public affairs in order to

10 There were 5,000 heliasts out of 14,000 citizens; but we may deduct from this second number 3,000 or 4,000, who might have been thrown out by the δοκιμασια.

give more attention to his own; it was rather his own that he was required to neglect in order to labor for the profit of the city. Men passed their lives in governing themselves. Democracy could not last except through the incessant labor of all citizens. Let their zeal diminish ever so little, and it perished or became corrupt.

Chapter XII

RICH AND POOR. DEMOCRACY PERISHES. THE POPULAR TYRANTS

WHEN a series of revolutions had produced an equality among men, and there was no longer occasion to fight for principles and rights, men began to make war for interests. This new period in the history of cities did not commence for all at the same time. In some it closely followed the establishment of democracy; in others it appeared only after several generations that had know how to govern themselves with moderation. But all the cities sooner or later passed through these deplorable struggles.

As men departed from the ancient system, a poor class began to grow up. Before, when every man belonged to a gens, and had his master, extreme poverty was almost unknown. A man was supported by his chief; the one to whom he owed obedience was bound in turn to provide for his wants. But the revolutions which had dissolved the γενος had also changed the conditions of human life. The day when man was freed from the bonds of clientship, he saw the necessities and the difficulties of existence stand out before him. Life had become more independent, but it was also more laborious and subject to more accidents. Thenceforth each one had the care of his own well-being, his enjoyments, and his task. One became rich by his activity or his good fortune, while another remained poor. Inequality of wealth is inevitable in every society which does not wish to remain in the patriarchal state or in that of the tribe.

The democracy did not suppress poverty, but, on the contrary, rendered it more perceptible. Equality of political rights made the inequality of conditions appear still more plainly.

As there was no authority that was above rich and poor at the same time, and could constrain them to keep the peace, it could have been wished that economic principles and the conditions of labor had been such as to compel the two classes to live on good terms. If, for example, the one had stood in need of the other, — if the wealthy could not have enriched themselves except by calling upon the poor for their labor, and the poor could have found the means of living by selling their labor to the rich, — then the inequality of fortunes would have stimulated the activity and the intelligence of man, and would not have begotten corruption and civil war.

But many cities were absolutely without manufactures and commerce; they had, therefore, no means of augmenting the amount of public wealth in order to give a part of it to the poor without despoiling any one. Where there was commerce, nearly all its benefits were for the rich in consequence of the high rate of interest. If there were manufactures, the workmen were slaves. We know that the rich men of Athens, and of Rome, had in their houses weavers, carvers, and armorers, all slaves. Even the liberal professions were almost closed to the citizen. The physician was often a slave, who cured diseases for the benefit of his master; bank-clerks, many architects, ship-builders, and the lower state officials were slaves. Slavery was a scourge from which free society itself suffered. The citizen found few employments, little to do; the want of occupation soon rendered him indolent. As he saw only slaves at work, he despised labor. Thus economic habits, moral dispositions, prejudices, all combined to prevent the poor man escaping from his misery and living honestly. Wealth and poverty were not constituted in a way to live together in peace.

The poor man had equality of rights; but assuredly his daily sufferings led him to think equality of fortunes far preferable. Nor was he long in perceiving that the equality which he had might serve him to acquire that which he had not, and that, master of the votes, he might become master of the wealth of his city.

He began by undertaking to live upon his right of voting. He asked to be paid for attending the assembly, or for deciding causes in the courts. If the city was not rich enough to afford such an expense, the poor man had other resources. He sold his vote, and, as the occasions for voting were frequent, he could live. At Rome this traffic was regular, and was carried on in broad day; at Athens it was better concealed. At Rome, where the poor man did not act as a judge, he sold himself as a witness; at Athens, as a judge. All this did not relieve the poor man from his misery, and reduced him to a state of degradation.

These expedients did not suffice, and the poor man used more energetic means. He organized regular warfare against wealth. At first this war was disguised under legal forms; the rich were charged with all the public expenses, loaded with taxes, made to build triremes, and to entertain the people with shows. Then fines were multiplied, and property confiscated for the slightest fault. No one can tell how many men were condemned to exile for the simple reason that they were rich. The fortune of the exile went into the public treasury, whence it afterwards flowed, under the form of the triobolon, to be distributed among the poor. But even all this did not suffice; for the number of poor continued to increase. The poor then began to use their right of suffrage either to decree an abolition of debts, or a grand confiscation, and a general subversion.

In earlier times they had respected the right of property, because it was founded in a religious belief. So long as each patrimony was attached to a worship, and was reputed inseparable from the domestic gods of a family, no one had thought of claiming the right to despoil a man of his field; but at the time to which the revolutions have conducted us, these old beliefs are abandoned, and the religion of property has disappeared. Wealth is no longer a sacred and inviolable domain. It no longer appears as a gift of the gods, but as a gift of chance. A desire springs up to lay hold of it by despoiling the possessor, and this desire, which formerly would have seemed an impiety, begins to appear right. Men no longer saw the superior principle that consecrates the right of property. Each felt only his own wants, and measured his rights by them.

We have already seen that the city, especially among the Greeks, had unlimited power, that liberty was unknown, and that individual rights were nothing when opposed to the will of the state. It followed that a majority of votes might decree the confiscation of the property of the rich, and that the Greeks saw neither illegality nor injustice in this. What the state had declared was right. This absence of individual liberty was for Greece a cause of misfortunes and disorders. Rome, which had a little more respect for the rights of man, suffered less.

At Megara, as Plutarch relates, after an insurrection, it was decreed that debts should be abolished, and that the creditors, besides the loss of their capital, should be held to reimburse the interest already paid.[1]

"At Megara, as in other cities," says Aristotle,[2] "the popular party, having got the power into their hands, began by confiscating the property of a few rich families. But, once on this road, it was impossible to stop. A new victim was necessary every day; and, finally, the number of the rich who were despoiled or exiled became so great that they formed an army."

In 412, "the people of Samos put to death two hundred of their adversaries, exiled four hundred more, and divided up the lands and houses."[3]

At Syracuse, hardly were the people freed from the tyranny of Dionysius, when they decreed the partition of the lands.[4]

In this period of Greek history, whenever we see a civil war, the rich are on one side, and the poor are on the other. The poor are trying to gain possession of the wealth, and the rich are trying to retain or to recover it. "In every civil war," says a Greek historian, "the great object is to change fortunes."[5] Every demagogue acted like that Molpagoras of Cios,[6] who delivered to the multitude those who possessed money, massacred some, exiled others, and distributed their property among the poor. At Messene, as soon as the popular party gained the upper hand, they exiled the rich, and distributed their lands.

1 Plutarch, *Greek Quest.*, 18.
2 Aristotle, *Politics*, VIII. 4 (V. 4).
3 Thucydides, VII. 21.
4 Plutarch, *Dion.*, 37, 48.
5 Polybius, XV. 21.
6 Polybius, VII. 10.

The upper classes among the ancients never had intelligence or ability enough to direct the poor towards labor, and thus help them to escape honorably from their misery and corruption. A few benevolent men attempted it, but they did not succeed. The result was, that the cities always floated between two revolutions, one to despoil the rich, the other to enable them to recover their fortunes. This lasted from the Peloponnesian war to the conquest of Greece by the Romans.

In every city the rich and the poor were two enemies living by the side of each other, the one coveting wealth, and the other seeing their wealth coveted. No relation, no service, no labor united them. The poor could acquire wealth only by despoiling the rich. The rich could defend their property only by extreme skill or by force. They regarded each other with the eyes of hate. There was a double conspiracy in every city; the poor conspired from cupidity, the rich from fear. Aristotle says the rich took the following oath among themselves: "I swear always to remain the enemy of the people, and to do them all the injury in my power."[7]

It is impossible to say which of the two parties committed the most cruelties and crimes. Hatred effaced in their hearts every sentiment of humanity. "There was at Miletus a war between the rich and the poor. At first the latter were successful, and drove the rich from the city; but afterwards, regretting that they had not been able to slaughter them, they took their children, collected them into some threshing-floors, and had them trodden to death under the feet of oxen. The rich afterwards returned to the city, and became masters of it. They took, in their turn, the children of the poor, covered them with pitch, and burnt them alive."[8]

---

[7] Aristotle, *Politics*, VIII. 7, 19 (V. 7). Plutarch, *Lysander*, 19.

[8] Heracleides of Pontus, in Athenæus, XII. 26. It is quite the fashion to accuse the Athenian democracy of having set Greece the example in these excesses and disorders. Athens was, on the contrary, the only Greek city, known to us, that did not see this atrocious war between rich and poor within its walls. This intelligent and wise people saw, from the day when this series of revolutions commenced, that they were moving towards a goal where labor alone could save society. They therefore encouraged it and rendered it honorable. Solon directed that all men who had not an occupation should be deprived of political rights. Pericles desired that no slave should

What, then, became of the democracy? They were not precisely responsible for these excesses and crimes; still they were the first to be affected by them. There were no longer any governing rules; now, the democracy could live only under the strictest and best observed rules. We no longer see any government, but merely factions in power. The magistrate no longer exercised his authority for the benefit of peace and law, but for the interests and greed of a party. A command no longer had a legitimate title or a sacred character; there was no longer anything voluntary in obedience; always forced, it was always wanting for an opportunity to take its revenge. The city was now, as Plato said, only an assemblage of men, where one party was master and the other enslaved. The government was called aristocratic when the rich were in power, democratic when the poor ruled. In reality, true democracy no longer existed.

From the day when it was mastered by material interests, it was changed and corrupted. Democracy, with the rich in power, had become a violent oligarchy; the democracy of the poor had become a tyranny. From the fifth to the second century before our era, we see in all the cities of Greece and of Italy, Rome still excepted, that the republican forms are imperilled, and that they have become odious to one party. Now, we can clearly see who wish to destroy it, and who desire its preservation. The rich, more enlightened and more haughty, remain faithful to republican government, while the poor, for whom political rights have less value, are ready to adopt a tyrant as their chief. When this poor class, after several civil wars, saw that victories gained them nothing, that the opposite party always returned to power, and that, after many interchanges of confiscations and restitutions, the struggle always recommenced, they dreamed of establishing a monarchical government which should conform to their interests, and

labor in the construction of the great monuments which he raised, and reserved all this labor for free men. Moreover, property was so divided up, that a census, taken at the end of the fifth century, shows little Attica to have contained more than ten thousand proprietors. Besides, Athens, living under a somewhat better economical *régime* than the other cities enjoyed, was less violently agitated than the rest of Greece; the quarrels between rich and poor were calmer, and did not end in the same disorders.

which, by forever suppressing the opposite party, should assure them, for the future, the fruits of their victory. And so they set up tyrants. From that moment the parties changed names; they were no longer aristocracy or democracy; they fought for liberty or for tyranny. Under those two names wealth and poverty were still at war. Liberty signified the government where the rich had the rule, and defended their fortunes; tyranny indicated exactly the contrary.

It is a general fact, and almost without exception in the history of Greece and of Italy, that the tyrants sprang from the popular party, and had the aristocracy as enemies. "The mission of the tyrant," says Aristotle, "is to protect the people against the rich; he has always commenced by being a demagogue, and it is the essence of tyranny to oppose the aristocracy." "The means of arriving at a tyranny," he also says, "is to gain the confidence of the multitude; and one does this by declaring himself the enemy of the rich. This was the course of Peisistratus at Athens, of Theagenes at Megara, and of Dionysius at Syracuse."[9]

The tyrant always made war upon the rich. At Megara, Theagenes surprises the herds of the rich in the country and slaughters them. At Cumæ, Aristodemus abolishes debts, and takes the lands of the rich to give them to the poor. This was the course of Nicocles at Sicyon, and of Aristomachus at Argos. All these tyrants writers represent as very cruel. It is not probable that they were all so by nature; but they were urged by the pressing necessity, in which they found themselves, of giving lands or money to the poor. They could maintain their power only while they satisfied the cravings of the multitude, and administered to their passions.

The tyrant of the Greek cities was a personage of whom nothing in our day can give us an idea. He was a man who lived in the midst of his subjects, without intermediate officers and without ministers, and who dealt with them directly. He was not in that lofty and independent position which the sovereign of a great state occupies. He had all the little passions of the private man; he was not insensible to the profits of a confiscation; he was accessible to anger and to the desire of personal revenge; he was disturbed by fear; he knew that he

[9] Aristotle, *Politics*, V. 8; VIII. 4, 5; V. 4.

had enemies all about him, and that public opinion approved assassination, when it was a tyrant that was struck down. We can imagine what the government of such a man must have been. With two or three honorable exceptions, the tyrants who were set up in all the Greek cities in the fourth and third centuries reigned only by flattering all that was worst in the multitude, and by destroying all that was superior in birth, wealth, or merit. Their power was unlimited. The Greeks could see how easily a republican government, when it did not profess a great respect for individual rights, was changed into a despotism. The ancients had conferred such powers upon the state that, the day when a tyrant took this omnipotence in hand, men no longer had any security against him, and he was legally the master of their lives and their fortunes.

Chapter XIII

REVOLUTIONS OF SPARTA

WE are not to believe that Sparta remained ten centuries without seeing a revolution. Thucydides tells us, on the contrary, "that it was torn by dissensions more than any other Greek city."[1] The history of these internal dissensions, it is true, is little known to us; but this is due to the fact that the government of Sparta made a rule and a custom of surrounding itself with the most profound mystery.[2] The greater part of the struggles that took place there have been concealed and forgotten; but we know enough of them, at least, to say, that if the history of Sparta differs materially from that of other cities, it has none the less passed through the same series of revolutions.

The Dorians were already united into a people when they overran Peloponnesus. What had caused them to leave their country? Was it the invasion of a foreign nation? or was it an internal revolution? We do not know. But it appears certain that, at this stage in the life of the Dorians, the old rule of

[1] Thucydides, I. 18.
[2] Thucydides, V. 68.

the gens had already disappeared. We no longer distinguish among them this ancient organization of the family; we no longer find traces of the patriarchal government, or vestiges of the religious nobility, or of hereditary clientship; we see only warriors, all equal, under a king. It is probable, therefore, that a first social revolution had already taken place, either in Doris or on the road which conducted this people to Sparta. If we compare Dorian society of the ninth century with Ionian society of the same epoch, we perceive that the former was much farther advanced than the other in the series of changes. The Ionian race entered later upon the revolutionary road, but passed over it quicker.

Though the Dorians, on their arrival at Sparta, no longer had the government of the gens, they had not been able so completely to free themselves from it as not to retain some of its institutions, — as, for example, the right of primogeniture and the inalienability of the patrimony. These institutions could not fail to establish an aristocracy in Spartan society.

All the traditions show us that, at the time when Lycurgus appeared, there were two classes among the Spartans, and that they were hostile to each other. Royalty had a natural tendency to take part with the lower class. Lycurgus, who was not king, became the chief of the aristocracy, and at the same blow weakened royalty, and brought the people under the yoke.

The declamations of a few of the ancients, and of many of the moderns, on the wisdom of Spartan institutions, on the unchangeable good fortune which the Spartans enjoyed, on their equality, and on their living in common, ought not to blind us. Of all the cities that ever were upon the earth, Sparta is perhaps the one where the aristocracy reigned the most oppressively, and where equality was the least known. It is useless to talk of the division of the land. If that division ever took place, it is at least quite certain that it was not kept up; for, in Aristotle's time, "some possessed immense domains; others had nothing, or almost nothing. One could reckon hardly a thousand proprietors in all Laconia."[3]

If we leave out the Helots and the Laconians, and examine only Spartan society, we shall find a hierarchy of classes superposed one above the other. First, there are the Neodamodes,

[3] Aristotle, *Politics*, II. 6, 10 and 11.

who appear to be former slaves freed;[4] then come the Epeunactæ, who had been admitted to fill up the gaps made by war among the Spartans;[5] in a rank a little above figured the Mothaces, who, very similar to domestic clients, lived with their masters, composed their *cortège*, shared their occupations, their labors, and their festivals, and fought by their side;[6] then came the class of bastards, who, though descended from true Spartans, were separated from them by religion and law.[7] There was still another class, called the inferiors, 'ὑπομείονες,[8] who were probably the younger, disinherited sons of families. Finally, above all these was raised the aristocratic class, composed of the men called the Equals — 'ὅμοιοι. These men were indeed equal among themselves, but were much superior to all the rest. The number of this class is not known; we know only that it was very small. One day one of their enemies counted them in the public square, and found some sixty of them in the midst of a multitude of four thousand people.[9] These Equals alone had a part in the government of the city. "To be outside this class," says Xenophon, "is to be outside the body politic."[10] Demosthenes says that a man who entered the class of Equals became by that alone "one of the masters of the government."[11] "They were called Equals," he further says, "because equality ought to reign between the members of an oligarchy."

On the composition of this body we have no precise information. It was recruited, as it should seem, by election; but the right of electing belonged to the body itself, and not to the people. To be admitted to it was what they called, in the official language of Sparta, *the reward of virtue*. We do not know how much wealth, rank, merit, and age were required to compose this *virtue*. It is evident that birth was not sufficient, since there was an election. We may suppose that it was rather wealth which determined the choice in a city

4 Myron of Priene, in Athenæus, VI.
5 Theopompus, in Athenæus, VI.
6 Athenæus, VI. 102. Plutarch, *Cleomenes*, 8. Ælian, XII. 43.
7 Aristotle, *Politics*, VIII. 6 (V. 6). Xenophon, *Hellenica*, V. 3, 9.
8 Xenophon, *Hellenica*, III. 3, 6.
9 Xenophon, *Hellenica*, III. 3, 5.
10 Xenophon, Gov. of Laced., 10.
11 Demosthenes, *in Leptin.*, 107.

"which had the love of money in the highest degree, and where everything was permitted to wealth."[12]

However this may be, these Equals alone had the rights of citizens; they alone composed the assembly; they alone formed what was called at Sparta *the people*. From this class came, by election, the senators, to whom the constitution gave very great authority; for Demosthenes says that the day a man entered the senate he became a despot toward the multitude.[13] This senate, of which the kings were simple members, governed the state according to the habitual custom of aristocratic bodies; annual magistrates, whose election belonged indirectly to it, exercised in its name an absolute authority. Thus Sparta had a republican government; it even had all the externals of a democracy — king-priests, annual magistrates, a deliberative senate, and an assembly of the people. But this people was an association of some two or three hundred men.

Such was, after Lycurgus, and especially after the establishment of the ephors, the government of Sparta. An aristocracy, composed of a few rich men, placed an iron yoke upon the Helots, upon the Laconians, and even upon the greater number of the Spartans. By its energy, ability, unscrupulousness, and disregard of all moral laws, it succeeded in holding its power during five centuries; but it stirred up cruel hatreds, and had to suppress a great number of insurrections.

We have not spoken of the plots of the Helots. All those of the Spartans are not known. The government was too wise not to seek to suppress even the recollection of them. Still there are a few which history has not been able to overlook. We know that the colonists who founded Tarentum were Spartans who had attempted to overthow the government. An indiscretion of the poet Tyrtæus revealed to all Greece that, during the Messenian wars, a party had conspired to obtain a division of the lands.

What saved Sparta was the extreme division which existed in the lower orders. The Helots did not agree with the

---

[12] Ἀ φιλοχρηματια Σπαρταν ἑλοι; it was already a proverb in Greece in Aristotle's time. Zenobius, II. 24. Aristotle, *Pol.*, VIII. 6, 7 (V. 6).

[13] Demosthenes, *in Leptin.*, 107. Xenophon, *Gov. of Laced.*, 10.

Laconians; and the Methaces despised the Neodamodes. No coalition was possible; and the aristocracy — thanks to its military education and the close union of its members! — was always strong enough to make head against any one class of its enemies.

The kings attempted what no class could realize. All those among them who aspired to escape from the state of inferiority in which the aristocracy held them sought support among the lower classes. During the Persian war Pausanias formed the project of elevating royalty and the lower orders at the same time by overthrowing the oligarchy. The Spartans put him to death, accusing him of having conspired with the king of Persia; his real crime was, rather, entertaining the thought of freeing the Helots.[14] We can see in history how numerous were the kings who were exiled by the ephors. The cause of these condemnations is easily guessed; and Aristotle says, "The kings of Sparta, in order to make head against the ephors and the senate, became demagogues."[15]

In 397 B. C. a conspiracy came near overthrowing this oligarchic government. A certain Cinadon, who did not belong to the class of Equals, was the chief of the conspirators. He would bring one whom he wished to join in this plot to the public square, and make him count the citizens; by including the ephors and the senators, they would reach the number of about seventy. Cinadon would then say to him, "Those men are our enemies; all the others, on the contrary, who fill the square to the number of more than four thousand, are our allies." He would add, "When you meet a Spartan in the country, see in him an enemy and a master; all other men are friends." Helots, Laconians, Neodamodes, υπομειονες, all were united this time, and were the accomplices of Cinadon. "For all," says the historian, "had such a hatred for their masters that there was not a single one among them who did not declare that it would be agreeable to him to eat them raw." But the government of Sparta was admirably served; no secret could be kept from it. The ephors pretended that the entrails

14 Aristotle, *Politics*, VIII. 1 (V. 1). Thucydides, I. 13, 2.
15 Aristotle, *Politics*, II. 6, 14.

of the victims had revealed the plot to them. No time was left for the conspirators to act; they were seized and secretly put to death. The oligarchy was once more saved.[16]

Favored by this government, the inequality continued to increase. The Peloponnesian war and the expedition into Asia had caused money to flow to Sparta; but it had been distributed in a very unequal manner, and had enriched those only who were already rich. At the same time small properties disappeared. The number of proprietors, who in Aristotle's time amounted to a thousand, was reduced to a hundred a century after him.[17] The entire soil was in a few hands at a time when there was neither manufacture nor commerce to furnish occupation for the poor, and when the rich employed slaves in cultivating their immense domains.

On the one hand were a few men who had everything, on the other a very great number who had absolutely nothing. In the life of Agis, and in that of Cleomenes, Plutarch presents us with a picture of Spartan society. We there see an unbridled love of wealth; everything is made secondary to this. Among a few there are luxury, effeminacy, and the desire endlessly to augment their fortunes. Beyond these there is a miserable crowd, indigent, without political rights, of no weight in the city, envious, full of hatred, and condemned by their condition to desire a revolution.

When the oligarchy had thus pushed affairs to the last possible limits, revolution was inevitable, and the democracy, so long arrested and repressed, finally broke down the barriers. We can also easily believe that, after ages of compression, the democracy would not stop with political changes, but would arrive with the first bound at social reforms.

The small number of Spartans by birth (there were, including all the different classes, no more than seven hundred) and the debasement of character, a result of long oppression, explain why the signal for changes did not come from the lower classes. It came from a king. Agis undertook to accomplish this inevitable revolution by legal means, which increased for him the difficulties of the enterprise. He presented to the senate — that is to say, to the rich men themselves — two bills

[16] Xenophon, *Hellenica*, III. 3.
[17] Plutarch, *Agis*, 5.

for the abolition of debts and the partition of the lands. We cannot be too much surprised that the senate did not reject these propositions. Agis had perhaps taken his measures to have them accepted. But the laws, once voted, remained to be put in execution; and these reforms are always so difficult to carry through that the boldest fail. Agis, stopped short by the opposition of the ephors, was constrained to go outside the law; he deposed those magistrates, and named others by his sole authority. He then armed his partisans, and established, for a year, a reign of terror. During that time he was enabled to apply the law concerning debts, and to burn in the public square all evidences of debt; but he had not time to divide up the land. We do not know whether Agis hesitated at this point, frightened at his own work, or whether the oligarchy circulated well-devised accusations against him. At any rate the people left him, and allowed him to fall. The ephors put him to death, and the aristocratic government was re-established.

Cleomenes took up the projects of Agis, but with more skill and fewer scruples. He began by massacring the ephors; he boldly suppressed this magistracy, which was odious to the kings and to the popular party, and proscribed the rich. After these measures he carried through the revolution; he distributed the lands, and gave the rights of citizens to four thousand Laconians. It is worthy of remark that neither Agis nor Cleomenes avowed that he was carrying through a revolution, and that both, claiming to act in the name of the old legislator, Lycurgus, pretended that they were bringing Sparta back to her ancient usages. Assuredly the constitution of Cleomenes was very far from them. The king was really an absolute master; there was no other authority as a counterpoise. He reigned after the manner of the tyrants who then held sway in most of the Greek cities, and the Spartan people, satisfied to have obtained lands, appeared to care very little for political liberty. This situation did not continue long. Cleomenes wished to extend the democratic rule to all Peloponnesus, where Aratus, at the very same time, was laboring to establish liberty and a well-regulated aristocracy. In all the cities, the popular party agitated in the name of Cleomenes, hoping, like Sparta, to obtain an abolition of debts and a distribution of lands. It was this unexpected insurrection of

the lower classes that obliged Aratus to change all his plans.
He thought he could count upon Macedonia, whose king,
Antigonus Doson, was then acting on the plan of attacking
the tyrants and the popular party everywhere, and therefore
introduced him into Peloponnesus. Antigonus and the Achæans
conquered Cleomenes at Sellasia. The Spartan democracy
were again overthrown, and the Macedonians re-established the
ancient government (B. C. 222).

But the oligarchy could no longer support itself. Disturbances continued a long time; one year, three ephors, who were
favorable to the popular party, massacred their two colleagues;
the following year the five ephors belonged to the oligarchs.
The people took arms and killed them all. The oligarchy
wanted no kings; the people were in favor of kings; one was
nominated and elected outside the royal family — a thing that
had never been known before at Sparta. This king, named
Lycurgus, was twice dethroned, once by the people, because
he refused to divide the lands, and a second time by the aristocracy, because they suspected him of wishing to make the
partition. It is not known how he closed his reign; but after
him there was a tyrant, Machanidas, at Sparta — a certain
proof that the popular party had gained the ascendency.

Philopœmen, who, at the head of the Achæan league, made
war everywhere upon democratic tyrants, conquered and killed
Machanidas. The Spartan democracy immediately set up
another tyrant, Nabis. This man gave the rights of citizens to
all freemen, raising the Laconians themselves to the rank of
Spartans. He even freed the Helots. Following the custom of
the tyrants of the Greek cities, he became the leader of the
poor against the rich, and proscribed or put to death those
whose riches raised them above others.

This new democratic Sparta was not wanting in grandeur.
Nabis established such order in Laconia as had not been
known there for a long time. He brought Messenia, Elisis, and
a part of Arcadia under Spartan rule, and seized Argos. He
formed a navy, which was very far from the ancient traditions
of the Spartan aristocracy. With his fleet he commanded all the
islands that surround Peloponnesus, and extended his influence even over Crete. He everywhere raised the democracy:
master of Argos, his first care was to confiscate the property

of the rich, abolish debts, and distribute the lands. We can see in Polybius what a hatred the Achæan league had for this democratic tyrant. The league determined Flaminius to make war upon him in the name of Rome. Ten thousand Laconians, without counting mercenaries, took arms to defend Nabis. After a check, he desired to make peace; but the people refused: so much was the tyrant's cause that of the democracy. Flaminius, as victor, took away a part of his forces, but allowed him to reign in Laconia; either because the impossibility of re-establishing the old government was too evident, or because it was for the interest of Rome that there should be a few tyrants, as a counterpoise to the Achæan league. Nabis was afterwards assassinated by an Æolian; but his death did not restore the oligarchy. The changes which he had made in the social state were maintained after him, and Rome herself refused to restore Sparta to her ancient condition.

BOOK FIFTH

THE MUNICIPAL REGIME DISAPPEARS

Chapter I

NEW BELIEFS. PHILOSOPHY CHANGES THE PRINCIPLES AND THE RULES OF POLITICS

In what precedes we have seen how the municipal governments were constituted among the ancients. A very ancient
religion had at first founded the family, and afterwards the
city. At first it had established domestic law and the government of the gens; afterwards it had established civil laws and
municipal government. The state was closely allied with
religion; it came from religion, and was confounded with it.
For this reason, in the primitive city all political institutions
had been religious institutions, the festivals had been ceremonies of the worship, the laws had been sacred formulas, and
the kings and magistrates had been priests. For this reason,
too, individual liberty had been unknown, and man had not
been able to withdraw even his conscience from the omnipotence of the city. For this reason, also, the state remained
bounded by the limits of a city, and had never been able to
pass the boundaries which its national gods had originally
traced for it. Every city had not only its political independence, but also its worship and its code. Religion, law, government, all were municipal. The city was the single living force;
there was nothing above and nothing below it; neither
national unity nor individual liberty.

It remains for us to relate how this system disappeared, —
that is to say, how, the principle of human association being
changed, government, religion, and law threw off this municipal character which they had borne in antiquity.

The ruin of the governments which Greece and Italy had
created was due to two principal causes. One belonged to the
order of moral and intellectual facts, the other to the order of

material facts; the first is the transformation of beliefs, the
second is the Roman conquest. These two great facts belong
to the same period; they were developed and accomplished
together during the series of six centuries which preceded
our era.

The primitive religion, whose symbols were the immovable
stone of the hearth, and the ancestral tomb, — a religion which
had established the ancient family, and had afterwards
organized the city, — changed with time, and grew old. The
human mind increased in strength, and adopted new beliefs.
Men began to have an idea of immaterial nature; the notion
of the human soul became more definite, and almost at the
same time that of a divine intelligence sprang up in their
minds.

Could they still believe in the divinities of the primitive
ages, of those dead men who lived in the tomb, of those Lares
who had been men, of those holy ancestors whom it was necessary to continue to nourish with food? Such a faith became
impossible. Such beliefs were no longer on a level with the
human mind. It is quite true that these prejudices, though
rude, were not easily eradicated from the vulgar mind. They
still reigned there for a long time; but from the fifth century
before our era, reflecting men freed themselves from these
errors. They had other ideas of death. Some believed in an-
nihilation, others in a second and entirely spiritual existence
in a world of spirits. In these cases they no longer admitted
that the dead lived in the tomb, supporting themselves upon
offerings. They also began to have too high an idea of the
divine to persist in believing that the dead were gods. On
the contrary, they imagined the soul going to seek its recompense in the Elysian Fields, or going to pay the penalty of its
crimes; and by a notable progress, they no longer deified any
among men, except those whom gratitude or flattery placed
above humanity.

The idea of the divinity was slowly transformed by the
natural effect of the greater power of the mind. This idea,
which man had at first applied to the invisible force which
he felt within himself, he transported to the incomparably
grander powers which he saw in nature, whilst he was elevating himself to the conception of a being who was without and

above nature. Then the Lares and Heroes lost the adoration of all who thought. As to the sacred fire, which appears to have had no significance, except so far as it was connected with the worship of the dead, that also lost its prestige. Men continued to have a domestic fire in the house, to salute it, to adore it, and to offer it libations; but this was now only a customary worship, which faith no longer vivified.

The public hearth of the city, or prytaneum, was insensibly drawn into the discredit into which the domestic fire had fallen. Men no longer knew what it signified; they had forgotten that the ever-living fire of the prytaneum represented the invisible life of the national ancestors, founders, and heroes. They continued to keep up this fire, to have public meals, and to sing the old hymns — vain ceremonies, of which they dared not free themselves, but the sense of which no one understood.

Even the divinities of nature, which they had associated with the sacred fire, changed their character. After having commenced by being domestic divinities, after having become city divinities, they were transformed again. Men finally perceived that the different beings whom they called by the name of Jupiter, might be only one and the same being; and thus of other gods. The mind was oppressed with the multitude of divinities, and felt the need of reducing their number. Men understood that the gods no longer belonged each to a family or to a city, but that they all belonged to the human race, and watched over the universe. Poets went from city to city, and taught men, instead of the old hymns of the city, new songs, wherein neither Lares nor city-protecting divinities appeared, and where the legends of the great gods of heaven and earth were related; and the Greek people forgot their old domestic and national hymns for this new poetry, which was not the daughter of religion, but of art and of a free imagination. At the same time a few great sanctuaries, like those of Delphi and Delos, attracted men, and made them forget their local worship. The mysteries and the doctrines which these taught accustomed them to disdain the empty and meaningless religion of the city.

Thus an intellectual revolution took place slowly and obscurely. Even the priests made no opposition, for as long as the sacrifices continued to be offered on designated days, it seemed to them that the ancient religion was preserved. Ideas might change, and faith perish provided the rites received no attack. It happened, therefore, without the practices being modified, that the beliefs were transformed and that the domestic and municipal religion lost all influence over the minds of men.

Then philosophy appeared, and overthrew all the rules of the ancient polity. It was impossible to touch the opinions of men without also touching the fundamental principles of their government. Pythagoras, having a vague conception of the Supreme Being, disdained the local worships; and this was sufficient to cause him to reject the old modes of government, and to attempt to found a new order of society.

Anaxagoras comprehended the God-Intelligence which reigns over all men and all beings. In rejecting ancient religious notions, he also rejected ancient polity. As he did not believe in the gods of the prytaneum, he no longer fulfilled all the duties of a citizen; he avoided the assemblies, and would not be a magistrate. His doctrine was an attack upon the city; and the Athenians condemned him to death.

The Sophists came afterwards, and exercised more influence than these two great minds. They were men eager to combat old errors. In the struggle which they entered against whatever belonged to the past, they did not spare the institutions of the city more than they spared religious prejudices. They boldly examined and discussed the laws which still reigned in the state and in the family. They went from city to city, proclaiming new principles, teaching, not precisely indifference to the just and the unjust, but a new justice, less narrow, less exclusive than the old, more humane, more rational, and freed from the formulas of preceding ages. This was a hardy enterprise, which stirred up a tempest of hatred and rancor. They were accused of having neither religion, nor morals, nor patriotism. The truth is, that they had not a very well settled doctrine, and thought they had done enough when they had attacked old prejudices. They moved, as Plato says, what before had been immovable. They placed the rule of religious sentiment, and that of politics, in the human conscience, and not in the customs of ancestors, in immutable tradition. They taught the Greeks that to govern a state it was not enough to appeal to old customs and sacred laws, but that men should be persuaded and their wills should be influenced. For the knowledge of ancient customs they substituted the art of reasoning and speaking — dialectics and rhetoric. Their adversaries quoted tradition to them, while they, on the other hand, employed eloquence and intellect.

When reflection had thus been once awakened, man no longer wished to believe without giving a reason for his belief, or to be governed without discussing his institutions. He doubted the justice of his old social laws, and other principles dawned upon his mind. Plato puts these remarkable words in the mouth of a Sophist: "All you who are here, I regard as related to each other. Nature, in default of law, has made you citizens. But the law, that tyrant of man, does violence to nature on many occasions." Thus to oppose nature to law and custom was to attack the ancient political system at its foundation. In vain did the Athenians banish Protagoras and burn his writings: the blow had been struck: the result of the teachings of the Sophists had been immense. The authority of the old institutions perished with the authority of the national gods, and the habit of free examination became established in men's homes and in the public squares.

Socrates, while reproving the abuse which the Sophists made of the right to doubt, was still of their school. Like them he rejected the empire of tradition, and believed that the rules of conduct were graven in the human conscience. He differed from them only in this; he studied conscience religiously, and with a firm desire to find there an obligation to be just and to do good. He ranked truth above custom, and justice above the law. He separated morals from religion: before him, men never thought of a duty except as a command of the ancient gods. He showed that the principle of duty is in the human mind. In all this, whether he wished it or not, he made war upon the city worship. In vain he took pains to be present at all the festivals and took part in the sacrifices; his belief and his words contradicted his conduct. He founded a new religion, which was the opposite of the city religion. He was justly accused of not adoring the gods whom the state adored. Men put him to death for having attacked the customs and the beliefs of their ancestors, or, as they expressed it, for having corrupted the present generation. The unpopularity of Socrates and the violent rage of the citizens are explained if we think of the religious habits of that Athenian society where there were so many priests, and where they were so powerful. But the revolution which the Sophists had commenced, and which Socrates had taken up with more moderation, was not stopped by the death of the old man. Greek society was enfranchised more and more, daily, from the empire of old beliefs and old institutions.

After him philosophers freely discussed the principles and rules of human association. Plato, Crito, Antisthenes, Speusippus, Aristotle, Theophrastus, and many others wrote treatises on politics. They studied and examined; the great problems of the organization of a state, of authority and obedience, of obligations and rights, were presented to all minds.

Doubtless thought could not easily free itself from the bonds which habit had made for it. Plato still yielded, in certain points, to the empire of old ideas. The state which he imagines is still the ancient city: it is small; it must not contain more than five thousand members. Its government is still regulated on ancient principles: liberty is unknown in it; the object which the legislator proposes to himself is less the perfection of man than the security and grandeur of the association. The family, even, is almost suppressed, that it may not come into competition with the city: the state is the only proprietor; it alone is free: the state alone has a will; only the state has a religion and a belief, and whoever does not believe with it must perish. And yet in the midst of all this the new ideas appear. Plato proclaims, with Socrates and the Sophists, that the moral and political guide is in ourselves; that tradition is nothing, that reason must be consulted, and that laws are just only when they conform to human nature.

These ideas are still more precise in Aristotle. "The law," he says, "is reason." He teaches that we are to seek, not what conforms to the customs of ancestors, but what is good in itself. He adds that, as time progresses, institutions should be modified. He puts aside respect for ancestors. "Our first ancestors, whether they came from the bosom of the earth, or survived some deluge, resembled, in all probability, those who to-day are the most degraded and the most ignorant among men. It would be an evident absurdity to cling to the opinions of those men." Aristotle, like all the philosophers, absolutely disregards the religious origin of human society: he does not speak of the prytaneum; he does not admit that these local worships were the foundation of the state. "The state," he says, "is nothing else but an association of equal beings seeking in common a happy and comfortable existence." Thus philosophy rejects the old principles of society, and seeks a new foundation on which it may support social laws and the idea of country.[1]

The Cynic school goes farther. It denies the ties of country itself. Diogenes boasted that he had the rights of a citizen nowhere, and Crates said that his country was a contempt for the opinions of others. The Cynics added this truth, then quite new — that man is a citizen of the universe, and that his country is not the narrow territory of a city. They considered municipal patriotism as a prejudice, and excluded love of the city from the moral sentiments.

From disgust or disdain, philosophers avoided public affairs more and more. Socrates had fulfilled the duties of a citizen; and Plato had attempted to work for the state by reforming it. Aristotle, still more indifferent, confined himself to the part of an observer, and made the state an object of scientific study. The Epicureans paid no attention to public affairs. "Do not meddle with them," said Epicurus, "unless some higher power compels you to." The Cynics did not wish even to be citizens.

The Stoics returned to politics. Zeno, Cleanthes, and Chrysippus wrote numerous treatises on the government of states. But their principles were far removed from the old municipal politics. These are the terms in which one of the ancients speaks of the doctrines which their writings contained: "Zeno, in his treatise on government, has undertaken to show us that we are not the inhabitants of such a deme, or such a city, separated from each other by a particular code, or exclusive laws, but that we should see citizens in all men, as if we all belonged to the same deme and the same city."[2] We see from

[1] Aristotle, *Politics*, II. 5, 12; IV. 5; 7, 2, VII. 4 (VI. 4).
[2] Pseudo Plutarch, *Fortune of Alexander*, 1.

this how far ideas had advanced since the age of Socrates, who thought himself bound to adore, as far as he was able, the gods of the state. Even Plato did not plan any other government than that of a city. Zeno passed beyond these narrow limits of human associations. He disdained the divisions which the religion of ancient ages had established. As he believed in a God of the universe, so he had also the idea of a State into which the whole human race should enter.[3]

But here is a still newer principle. Stoicism, by enlarging human association, emancipates the individual. As it rejects the religion of the city, it rejects also the servitude of the citizen. It no longer desires that the individual man shall be sacrificed to the state. It distinguishes and separates clearly what ought to remain free in man, and frees at least the conscience. It tells man that he ought to shut himself up within himself, to find in himself duty, virtue, and reward. It does not forbid him to meddle with public affairs; it even invites him to affairs of state, still warning him, however, that his principal labor ought to have for its object his individual improvement, and that whatever the government may be, his conscience ought to remain free, — a great principle which the ancient city had always disregarded, but which was destined to become one of the most sacred rules of politics.

Men now begin to understand that there are other duties besides those towards the state, other virtues besides civic virtue. The mind is attached to other objects besides country. The ancient city had been so powerful and so tyrannical that man had made it the object of all his labor and of all his virtues. It had been his standard of the beautiful and the good, and except for that there was no heroism. But now Zeno teaches man that he has a dignity, not as a citizen, but as a man; that besides his obligations to the law, he has others to himself; and that the supreme merit is not to live or to die for the state, but to be virtuous and to please the Deity. These were somewhat selfish virtues, which left national independ-

[3] The idea of the universal city is expressed by Seneca, *ad Marciam,* 4, *De Tranquillitate,* 14; by Plutarch, *De Exsilio;* by Marcus Aurelius: "As Antoninus, I have Rome for my country; as a man, the world."

ence and liberty to fall; but they gave the individual more importance. The public virtues went on declining, while the personal virtues were evolved and came forth into the world. They had at first to struggle both against the general corruption and against despotism. But they became rooted in the minds of men by degrees, and, as time went on, became a power which every government had to take into account; and it was of the first importance that the rules of politics should be modified, so that a free place might be made for them.

Thus were these religious notions transformed, little by little; the municipal religion, the basis of the city, disappeared, and the municipal governments, such as the ancients had conceived them, were forced to fall with it. Insensibly men departed from those rigorous rules, and from those narrow forms of government. Higher ideas prompted men to form more extensive societies. They were attracted towards unity; this was the general aspiration for two centuries preceding our era. The fruits which these revolutions of knowledge bore were, it is true, very slow to mature; but we shall see, in studying the Roman conquest, that events moved in the same direction with these ideas, that, like them, they tended to the ruin of the old municipal system, and that they prepared new modes of government.

Chapter II

THE ROMAN CONQUEST

At first it appears very surprising that among the thousand cities of Greece and Italy one was found capable of subduing all the others. Yet this great event is due to the ordinary causes that determine the course of human affairs. The wisdom of Rome consisted, like all wisdom, in profiting by the favorable circumstance that fell in its way.

We can distinguish two periods in the work of the Roman conquest. One corresponds to the time when the old municipal spirit was still strong; it was then that Rome had the greatest number of obstacles to surmount. The second belonged to the time when the municipal spirit was much weakened; conquest then became easy, and was accomplished rapidly.

1. The Origin and Population of Rome.

The origin of Rome and the composition of its people are worthy of remark. They explain the particular character of its policy, and the exceptional part that fell to it from the beginning in the midst of other cities.

The Roman race was strangely mixed. The principal element was Latin, and originally from Alba; but these Albans themselves, according to traditions which no criticism authorizes us to reject, were composed of two associated, but not confounded, populations. One was the aboriginal race, real Latins. The other was of foreign origin, and was said to have come from Troy with Æneas, the priest-founder; it was, to all appearance, not numerous, but was influential from the worship and the institutions which it had brought with it.[1]

These Albans, a mixture of two races, founded Rome on a spot where another city had already been built — Pallantium, founded by the Greeks. Now, the population of Pallantium remained in the new city, and the rites of the Greek worship were preserved there.[2] There was also, where the Capitol afterwards stood, a city which was said to have been founded by Hercules, the families of which remained distinct from the rest of the Roman population during the entire continuance of the republic.[3]

Thus at Rome all races were associated and mingled; there were Latins, Trojans, and Greeks; there were, a little later, Sabines, and Etruscans. Of the several hills, the Palatine was the Latin city, after having been the city of Evander. The Capitoline, after having been the dwelling-place of the companions of Hercules, became the home of the Sabines of Tatius. The Quirinal received its name from the Sabine Quirites, or from the Sabine god Quirinus. The Cœlian hill

[1] The Trojan origin of Rome was a received opinion even before Rome was in regular communication with the East. A soothsayer, in a prediction which related to the second Punic war, applied to the Romans the epithet *Trojugena*. Livy, XXV. 12.

[2] Livy, I. 5. Virgil, VIII. Ovid, *Fasti*, I. 579. Plutarch, *Rom. Quest.*, 56. Strabo, V. p. 230.

[3] Dionysius, I. 85. Varro, *L. L.*, V. 42. Virgil, VIII. 358.

appears to have been inhabited from the beginning by Etruscans.[4] Rome did not seem to be a single city; it appeared like a confederation of several cities, each one of which was attached by its origin to another confederation. It was the centre where the Latins, Etruscans, Sabellians, and Greeks met.

Its first king was a Latin; the second, a Sabine; the fifth was, we are told, the son of a Greek; the sixth was an Etruscan.

Its language was composed of the most diverse elements. The Latin predominated, but Sabellian roots were numerous, and more Greek radicals were found in it than in any other of the dialects of Central Italy. As to its name, no one knew to what language that belonged. According to some, Rome was a Trojan word; according to others, a Greek word. There are reasons for believing it to be Latin, but some of the ancients thought it to be Etruscan.

The names of Roman families also attest a great diversity of origin. In the time of Augustus there were still some fifty families who, by ascending the series of their ancestors, arrived at the companions of Æneas.[5] Others claimed to be descendants of the Arcadian Evander, and from time immemorial the men of these families wore upon their shoes, as a distinctive sign, a small silver crescent.[6] The Potitian and Pinarian families were descended from those who were called the companions of Hercules, and their descent was proved by the hereditary worship of that god. The Tullii, Quinctii, and Servilii came from Alba after the conquest of that city. Many families joined to their name a surname which recalled their foreign origin. There were thus the Sulpicii Camerini, the Cominii Arunci, the Sicinii Sabini, the Claudii Regillenses, and the Aquillii Tusci. The Nautian family was Trojan, the Aurellii were Sabines; the Cæcilii came from Præneste, and the Octavii were originally from Velitræ.

The effect of this mixing of the most diverse nations was, that from the beginning Rome was related to all the peoples that it knew. It could call itself Latin with the Latins, Sabine

[4] Of the three names of the primitive tribes, the ancients always believed that one was Latin, another Sabine, and the third Etruscan.

[5] Dionysius, I. 85.

[6] Plutarch, *Rom. Quest.*, 76.

with the Sabines, Etruscan with the Etruscans, and Greek with the Greeks.

Its national worship was also an assemblage of several quite different worships, each one of which attached it to one of these nations. It had the Greek worship of Evander and Hercules, and boasted of possessing the Trojan Palladium. Its Penates were in the Latin city of Lavinium, and it adopted from the beginning the Sabine worship of the god Consus. Another Sabine god, Quirinus, was so firmly established at Rome that he was associated with Romulus, its founder. It had also the gods of the Etruscans, and their festivals, and their augurs, and even their sacerdotal insignia.

At a time when no one had the right to take part in the religious festivals of a nation unless he belonged by birth to that nation, the Roman had this incomparable advantage of being able to take part in the Latin holidays, the Sabine festivals, the Etruscan festivals, and the Olympic games.[7] Now, religion was a powerful bond. When two cities had a single worship, they called themselves relations; they were required to regard themselves as allies, and to aid each other. In ancient times men knew of no other union than that which religion established. Rome therefore preserved with great care whatever could serve as an evidence of this precious relationship with other nations. To the Latins it presented its traditions of Romulus; to the Sabines its legend of Tarpeia and Tatius; to the Greeks it quoted the old hymns which it had preserved in honor of Evander's mother, hymns which Romans no longer understood, but which they persisted in singing. They also preserved the recollection of Æneas with the greatest care; for if they could claim relationship with the Peloponnesians through Evander,[8] they were related through Æneas to more than thirty cities,[9] scattered through Italy, Sicily, Greece, Thrace, and Asia Minor, all having had Æneas for a founder, or being colonies of cities founded by him, — all having, consequently, a common worship with Rome. We can see in the wars which they waged in Sicily against Carthage, and in

[7] Pausanias, V. 23, 24. Comp. Livy, XXIX. 12; XXXVII. 37.
[8] Pausanias, VIII. 43. Strabo, V. p. 232.
[9] Servius, ad Æn., III. 12.

Greece against Philip, what advantage they derived from this
ancient relationship.

The Roman population was, then, a mixture of several
races, its worship was an assemblage of several worships, and
its national hearth an association of several hearths. It was
almost the only city whose municipal religion was not isolated
from all others. It was related to all Italy and all Greece.
There was hardly a people that it could not admit to its
hearth.

2.   *First Aggrandizement of Rome* (B. C. 753–350).

During the period when the municipal religion was everywhere powerful, it governed the policy of Rome.

We are told that the first act of the new city was to seize
some Sabine women — a legend which appears very improbable when we reflect on the sanctity of marriage among the
ancients; but we have seen above that the municipal religion
forbade marriage between persons of different cities unless
these two cities had a common origin or a common worship.
The first Romans had the right of intermarriage with Alba,
from which they originally came, but not with their other
neighbors, the Sabines. What Romulus wished to obtain first
of all was not a few women; it was the right of intermarriage,
— that is to say, the right of contracting regular relations with
the Sabine population. For this purpose a religious bond must
be established between them; he therefore adopted the worship
of the Sabine god Consus, and celebrated his festival.[10] Tradition adds that during this festival he carried off the women.
If he had done this, the marriages could not have been celebrated according to the rites, since the first and most necessary
act of the marriage was the *traditio in manum*, — that is to say,
the giving away of the daughter by the father; Romulus would
have failed of his object. But the presence of the Sabines and
their families at the religious ceremony, and their participation
in the sacrifice, established between the two nations a bond
such that the *connubium* could no longer be refused. There
was no need of a seizure; the right of intermarriage was a
natural consequence of the festival. And the historian Diony-

[10] Dionysius, II. 30.

sius, who consulted ancient documents and hymns, assures us that the Sabines were married according to the most solemn rites, which is confirmed by Plutarch and Cicero. It is worthy of remark that the result of the first effort of the Romans was to throw down the barriers which the municipal religion had placed between two neighboring nations. No similar legend relative to Etruria has come down to us, but it appears quite certain that Rome had the same relations with that country as with Latium and the Sabines. The Romans therefore had the address to unite themselves, by worship and by blood, with all the nations around them. They took care to have the *connubium* with all the cities; and what proves that they well understood the importance of this bond is, that they would not permit other cities, their subjects, to have it among themselves.[11]

Rome then entered upon the long series of its wars. The first was against the Sabines of Tatius; it was terminated by a religious and political alliance between these two little nations. It next made war upon Alba. The historians say that the Romans dared to attack this city, though they were a colony from it. It was precisely because they were a colony from Alba that they judged it necessary to destroy that city. Indeed, every metropolis exercised a religious supremacy over its colonies, and religion then had so great an influence that while Alba remained standing, Rome could be only a dependent city, and her progress would be forever arrested.

After the destruction of Alba, Rome was no longer content to remain a colony, but claimed to take the rank of a metropolis, by inheriting the rights and the religious supremacy which up to that time Alba had exercised over the thirty colonies of Latium. The Romans sustained long wars to obtain the presidency of the sacrifice at the *feriæ Latinæ*. This was a means of acquiring the single kind of superiority and dominion which was understood at that time.

They built at home a temple to Diana; they obliged the Latins to come and offer sacrifices there, and even attracted the Sabines to it.[12] By this means they habituated these two

---

[11] Livy, IX. 43; XXIII. 4.
[12] Livy, I. 45. Dionysius, IV. 48, 49.

nations to share with them, under their presidency, the festivals, the prayers, and the sacred flesh of the victims. Rome thus united them under her religious supremacy.

Rome was the only city that understood how to augment her population by war. The Romans pursued a policy unknown to the rest of the Græco-Italian world; they annexed all that they conquered. They brought home the inhabitants of captured cities, and gradually made Romans of them. At the same time they sent colonists into the conquered countries, and in this manner spread Rome everywhere; for their colonists, while forming distinct cities, in a political point of view, preserved a religious community with the metropolis; and this was enough to compel the colonies to subordinate their policy to that of Rome, to obey her, and to aid her in all her wars.

One of the remarkable peculiarities of the policy of Rome was, that she attracted to her all the worships of the neighboring cities. She obtained possession of a Juno from Veii, a Jupiter from Præneste, a Minerva from Falerii, a Juno from Lanuvium, a Venus from the Samnites, and many others that we do not know.[13] "For it was the custom of the Romans," says one of the ancients,[14] "to take home the religions of the conquered cities; sometimes they distributed them among the gentes, and sometimes they gave them a place in their national religion." Montesquieu praises the Romans for a refinement of skillful policy in not having imposed their gods upon the conquered nations. But that would have been contrary to their ideas, and to those of all the ancients. Rome conquered the gods of the vanquished, and did not give them hers. She kept her protectors for herself, and even labored to increase the number. She tried to possess more worships and more tutelary gods than any other city.

As, moreover, these worships and gods were, for the most part, taken from the conquered, Rome was placed by them in religious communion with all the surrounding nations. The ties of a common origin, the possession of the *connubium*, that of the presidency of the *feriæ Latinæ*, that of the vanquished

---

[13] Livy, V. 21, 22; VI. 29. Ovid, Fasti, III. 837, 843. Plutarch, *Parallel of Greek and Roman Hist.*, 75.

[14] Cincius, cited by Arnobius, *Adv. Gentes*, III. 38.

gods, the right, which they pretended to have, of sacrificing at Olympia and at Delphi, were so many means by which the Romans prepared their dominion. Like all the cities, Rome had her municipal religion, the source of her patriotism; but she was the only city which made this religion serve for her aggrandizement. Whilst other cities were isolated by their religion, Rome had the address or the good fortune to employ hers to draw everything to herself, and to dominate over all.

3. How Rome acquired Empire (B. C. 350–140).

Whilst Rome grew thus slowly by the means which religion and the ideas of that age placed at her disposal, a series of social and political changes was taking place in all the cities and in Rome itself, transforming at the same time the govern-ments of men and their ways of thinking. We have already traced this revolution. What is important to remark here is, that it coincides with the great development of the Roman power.

These two results, which took place at the same time, were not without influence upon each other. The conquests of Rome would not have been so easy if the old municipal spirit had not been everywhere extinct; and we may also believe that the municipal system would not have fallen so soon if the Roman conquest had not dealt it the final blow.

In the midst of the changes which took place in institutions, in manners, in religious ideas, and in laws, patriotism itself had changed its nature; and this is one of the events which contributed most to the great progress of Rome. We have described this sentiment as it was in the first ages of the city. It was a part of religion; men loved their country because they loved its protecting gods, because they there found a pry-taneum, a holy fire, festivals, prayers, and hymns, and because beyond its borders they no longer found either gods or a wor-ship. This patriotism was faith and piety. But when the domination had been withdrawn from the sacerdotal caste, this sort of patriotism disappeared with other old religious notions. Love of the city still survived, but it took a new form.

Men no longer loved their country for its religion and its gods; they loved it only for its laws, for its institutions, and for the rights and security which it afforded its members. We see in the funeral oration which Thucydides puts into the mouth of Pericles what the reasons are that Athens was loved; they are because this city "wishes all to be equal before the law;" "because she gives men liberty, and opens the ways of honor to all; because she maintains public order, assures authority to the magistrates, protects the weak, and gives to all spectacles and festivals, which are the education of the mind." And the orator closes by saying, "This is why our warriors have died heroically rather than allow their country to be torn from them; this is why those who survive are all ready to suffer, and to devote themselves for it." Man, therefore, still owes duties to the city; but these duties do not flow from the same principle as before. He still gives his blood and his life, but it is no longer to defend his national divinity and the hearth of his fathers; it is to defend the institutions which he enjoys, and the advantages which the city procures him.

Now, this new patriotism had not exactly the same effects as that of the ancient ages. As the heart was no longer attached to the prytaneum, to the protecting gods, and to the sacred soil, but simply to the institutions and the laws, — and as, moreover, the latter, in the state of instability in which all the cities then found themselves, changed frequently, — patriotism became a variable and inconsistent sentiment, which depended upon circumstances, and which was subject to the same fluctuations as the government itself. One loved his country only as much as he loved the form of government that prevailed there for the moment; and he who found its laws bad had no longer anything to attach him to it.

Municipal patriotism thus became weakened and died out in men's minds. Every man's opinion was more precious to him than his country, and the triumph of his faction became much dearer to him than the grandeur or glory of his city. Each one, if he did not find in his own city the institutions that he loved, began to prefer some other city, where he saw these institutions established. Men then began to emigrate more freely, and feared exile less. What did it matter if they were excluded from the prytaneum and the lustral water? They thought little now of the protecting gods, and were easily accustomed to live away from their country.

From this to taking up arms against it was not a great step.

Men joined a hostile city to make their party victorious in their own. Of two Argives, one preferred an aristocratic government; he preferred Sparta to Argos: the other preferred democracy; he preferred Athens. Neither cared a great deal for the independence of his own city, and was not much averse to becoming the subject of another city, provided that city sustained his faction in Argos. It is clear, from Thucydides and Xenophon, that it was this disposition of men's minds that brought on and sustained the Peloponnesian war. At Platæa the rich were of the Theban and Lacedemonian party, the democrats were in favor of Athens. At Corcyra the popular faction were for Athens, and the aristocracy for Sparta.[15] Athens had allies in all the cities of Peloponnesus, and Sparta had them in all the Ionian cities. Thucydides and Xenophon agree in saying that there was not a single city where the people were not favorable to the Athenians, and the aristocracy to the Spartans.[16] This war represents a general effort which the Greeks made to establish everywhere a single constitution with the hegemony of a city; but a part desired an aristocracy under the protection of Sparta, while others favored a democracy with the support of Athens. It was the same in Philip's time. The aristocratic party, in all the cities, desired the domination of Macedon. In Philopœmen's time the cases were reversed, but the sentiments remained the same; the popular party accepted the empire of Macedon, and all who were in favor of the aristocracy joined the Achæan league. Thus the wishes and the affections of men no longer had the city as the object. There were few Greeks who were not ready to sacrifice municipal independence in order to obtain the constitution which they preferred.

As to honest and scrupulous men, the perpetual dissensions which they saw disgusted them with the municipal system. They could not love a form of society, where it was necessary to fight every day, where the rich and the poor were always at war, and where they saw popular violence and aristocratic vengeance alternate without end. They wished to escape from a *régime* which, after having produced real grandeur, no longer produced anything but suffering and hatred. They

15 Thucydides, II. 2; III. 65, 70; V. 29, 76.
16 Thucydides, III. 47. Xenophon, *Hell.*, VI. 3.

began to feel the necessity of abandoning the municipal system, and of arriving at some other form of government than the city. Many men dreamed at last of establishing above the cities a sort of sovereign power, which should look to the maintenance of order, and compel those turbulent little societies to live in peace. It was thus that Phocion, a good citizen, advised his compatriots to accept the authority of Philip, and promised them, at this price, concord and security.

In Italy affairs were in much the same condition as in Greece. The cities of Latium, of the Sabines, and of Etruria were distracted by the same revolutions and the same struggles, and love of the city disappeared. As in Greece, every man was ready to join a foreign city, in order to make his opinions and interests prevail in his own.

These dispositions of mind made the fortune of the Romans. They everywhere supported the aristocracy; everywhere, too, the aristocracy were their allies. Let us take a few examples. The Claudian gens left the Sabines because Roman institutions pleased them better than those of their own country. At the same epoch many Latin families emigrated to Rome, because they did not like the democratic government of Latium, and the Romans had just established the reign of the patricians.[17] At Ardea, the aristocracy and the plebs being at enmity, the plebs called the Volscians to their aid, and the aristocracy delivered the city to the Romans.[18] Etruria was full of dissensions; Veii had overthrown her aristocratic government; the Romans attacked this city, and the other Etruscan cities, where the sacerdotal aristocracy still held sway, refused to aid the Veientines. The legend adds that in this war the Romans carried away a Veientine aruspex, and made him deliver them an oracle that assured them the victory. Does not this legend signify that the Etruscan priests delivered the city to the Romans?

Later, when Capua revolted against Rome, it was remarked that the knights — that is to say, the aristocratic body — took no part in that insurrection.[19] In 313, the cities of Ausona, Sora, Minturnæ, and Vescia were delivered to the Romans by

17 Dionysius, VI. 2.
18 Livy, IV. 9, 10.
19 Livy, VIII. 11.

the aristocratic party.[20] When the Etruscans were seen to form a coalition against Rome, it was because popular governments had been established among them. A single city — that of Arretium — refused to enter this coalition; and this was because the aristocracy still prevailed in Arretium. When Hannibal was in Italy, all the cities were agitated; but it was not a question of independence. In every city the aristocracy were for Rome, and the plebs for the Carthaginians.[21]

The manner in which Rome was governed will explain this constant preference which the aristocracy entertained for it. The series of revolutions continued as in other cities, but more slowly. In 509, when the Latin cities already had tyrants, a patrician reaction had succeeded at Rome. The democracy rose afterwards, but gradually, and with much moderation and self-restraint. The Roman government was, therefore, for a longer time aristocratic than any other, and was long the hope of the aristocratic party.

The democracy, it is true, finally carried the day in Rome; but even then the proceedings, and what one might call the artifices, of the government remained aristocratic. In the comitia centuriata the votes were distributed according to property. It was not altogether different with the comitia tributa: legally, no distinction of wealth was admitted there; in fact, the poor class, being included in the four city tribes, had but four votes to oppose to the thirty-one of the class of proprietors. Besides, nothing was more quiet, ordinarily, than these assemblies; no one spoke there, except the president, or some one whom he called upon. Orators were little heard there, and there was little discussion. More generally there was simply a vote of yes or no, and a count of the votes. This last operation, being very complicated, demanded much time and patience. Add to this that the senate was not renewed annually, as in the democratic cities of Greece; it sat for life, and very nearly recruited itself. It was really an oligarchic body.

The manners of the Romans were still more aristocratic than their institutions. The senators had seats reserved at the theatre. The rich alone served in the cavalry; the grades of the army were in great part reserved for the young men of the

[20] Livy, IX. 24, 25; X. 1.
[21] Livy, XXIII. 13, 14, 39; XXIV. 2, 3.

great families. Scipio was not sixteen years old when he already commanded a squadron.

The rule of the rich class was kept up longer at Rome than in any other city. This was due to two causes. One was, that Rome made great conquests, and the profits of these went to the class that was already rich; all lands taken from the conquered were possessed by them; they seized upon the commerce of the conquered countries, and joined with it the benefits derived from the collection of duties and the administration of the provinces. These families, thus increasing their wealth with every generation, became immeasurably opulent, and each one of them was a power, compared with the people. The other cause was, that the Roman, even the poorest, had an innate respect for wealth. Long after real clientship had disappeared, it was, in a certain sense, resuscitated under the form of a homage paid to great fortunes; and it became a custom for the poor to go every morning to salute the rich.

It does not follow from this that the struggle between rich and poor was not seen at Rome, as well as in other cities; but it commenced only in the time of the Gracchi, — that is to say, after the conquest was almost achieved. Besides, this struggle never had at Rome that character of violence which it assumed everywhere else. The lower orders of Rome never ardently coveted riches. They aided the Gracchi in a lukewarm manner; they refused to believe that these reformers were working for them, and abandoned them at the decisive moment. The agrarian laws, so often presented to the rich as a menace, always left the people quite indifferent, and agitated them only on the surface. It is clear that they were not very eager to possess lands; for, if they were offered a share in the public lands, — that is to say, in the domain of the state, — they at least never had a thought of despoiling the rich of their property. Partly from inveterate respect, and partly from a habit of doing nothing, they loved to live by the side of the rich, and as it were in their shadow.

The rich class had the wisdom to admit to its circle the most considerable families of the subject and allied cities. All who were rich in Italy came gradually to form the rich class of Rome. This body continued to increase in importance, and became the master of the state. The rich alone filled the magistracies, because these cost a great sum to purchase. They alone composed the senate, because it required a very large property to be a senator. Thus we see this strange fact, that, in spite of democratic laws, a nobility was formed, and that the people, who were all-powerful, suffered this nobility to take rank above them, and never made any real opposition to it.

Rome, therefore, from the third to the second century before our era, was the most aristocratically governed city that existed in Italy or Greece. Finally, let us remark that, if the senate was obliged to manage the multitude on home questions, it was absolute master so far as concerned foreign affairs. It was the senate that received ambassadors, that concluded alliances, that distributed the provinces and the legions, that ratified the acts of the generals, that determined the conditions allowed to the conquered — all acts which everywhere else belonged to the popular assembly. Foreigners, in their relations with Rome, had, therefore, nothing to do with the people. The senate alone spoke, and the idea was held out that the people had no power. This was the opinion which a Greek expressed to Flaminius. "In your country," said he, "riches alone govern, and all else is submissive to it."[22]

As a result of this, in all the cities the aristocracy turned their eyes towards Rome, counted upon it, looked to it for protection, and followed its fortunes. This seemed so much the more natural, as Rome was a foreign city to nobody; Sabines, Latins, and Etruscans saw in it a Sabine, Latin, or Etruscan city, and the Greeks recognized Greeks in it.

As soon as the Romans appeared in Greece, the aristocracy surrendered to them. Hardly anybody thought then that they were choosing between independence and subjection; for most men the question was only between aristocracy and the popular party. In all the cities the latter was for Philip, Antiochus, or Perseus, and the former for Rome. We may see in Polybius and Livy that when Argos opened her gates, in B. C. 198, to the Macedonians, the people had the sway there; that the next year, it was the party of the rich that gave up Opuntii to the Romans; that, among the Acarnanians, the aristocracy made a treaty of alliance with Rome, and that in the following year

22 Livy, XXXIV. 31.

this treaty was broken, because, in the interval, the people had recovered the ascendency; that Thebes was allied with Philip so long as the popular party had the power, and sided with Rome the moment the aristocracy became the masters; that at Athens, at Demetrias, and at Phocæa the populace were hostile to the Romans; that Nabis, the democratic tyrant, made war upon them; that the Achæan league, as long as it was governed by the aristocracy, was favorable to them; that men like Philopœmen and Polybius desired national independence, but preferred Roman rule to democracy; that in the Achæan league itself there came a moment when the popular party rose in its turn, and from that moment the league was the enemy of Rome; that Diæus and Critolaus were at the same time the chiefs of the popular faction and the generals of the league against the Romans, and that they fought bravely at Scarphea and at Leucopetra, less perhaps for the independence of Greece than for the triumph of democracy.

Such facts show clearly enough how Rome, without any very great efforts, obtained the empire. The municipal spirit gradually disappeared. The love of independence became a very rare sentiment, and all hearts were entirely enlisted in the interests and passions of parties. Insensibly men forgot the city. The barriers which had previously separated cities, and had made of them so many distinct little worlds, whose horizons bounded the wishes and thoughts of every one, fell one after another. In all Italy and in all Greece, only two groups of men were distinguished: on one hand was an aristocratic class, on the other a popular party. One party labored for the supremacy of Rome, the other opposed it. The aristocracy were victorious, and Rome acquired the empire.

4.   Rome everywhere destroys the Municipal System.

The institutions of the ancient city had been weakened, and almost exhausted, by a series of revolutions. One of the first results of the Roman dominion was to complete their destruction, and to efface what still remained of them. This we can see by observing the condition into which the nations fell as they became subject to Rome.

We must first banish from our minds all the customs of modern politics, and not picture to ourselves the nations entering the Roman state, one after another, as in our day provinces are annexed to a kingdom, which, on receiving these new members, extends its boundaries. The Roman state (*civitas Romana*) was not enlarged by conquests; it never included any families except those that figured in the religious cere• mony of the census. The Roman territory (*ager Romanus*) never increased. It remained enclosed within the immutable limits which the kings had traced for it, and which the ceremony of the *Ambarvalia* sanctified every year. What in• creased with every conquest was the dominion of Rome (*imperium Romanum*).

So long as the republic lasted, it never entered the mind of any one that the Romans and the other peoples could form a single nation. Rome might, indeed, receive a few of the con• quered, allow them to live within her walls, and transform them, in the course of time, into Romans; but she could not assimilate a whole foreign people to her people, an entire territory to her territory. Still this was not peculiar to the policy of Rome, but a principle that held through all an• tiquity; it was a principle from which Rome would sooner have departed than any other city, but from which she could not entirely free herself. Whenever, therefore, a people was conquered, it did not enter the Roman state; it entered only the Roman dominion. It was not united to Rome, as provinces are to-day united to a capital; between other nations and itself Rome knew only two kinds of connection — subjection or alliance.

From this it would seem that municipal institutions must have subsisted among the conquered, and that the world must have been an assemblage of cities distinct from each other, and having at their head a ruling city. But it was nothing of the kind. The effect of the Roman conquest was to work in every city a complete transformation.

On one side were the subjects *dedititii*, or those who, having pronounced the formula of the *deditio*, had delivered to the Roman people "their persons, their walls, their lands, their waters, their houses, their temples, and their gods."

They had therefore renounced, not only their municipal government, but all that appertained to it among the ancients, — that is to say, their religion and their private law. From that moment these men no longer formed a political body among themselves; nothing that goes to make up a regular society remained to them. Their city (*urbs*) might remain standing, but the state (*civitas*) had perished. If they continued to live together, they lived without institutions, laws, or magistrates. The arbitrary authority of a *præfectus* sent by Rome maintained material order among them.[23] On the other hand were the allies — *fœderati*, or *socii*. They were less cruelly treated. The day on which they entered the Roman dominion, it had been stipulated that they should preserve their municipal government, and should remain organized into cities. They therefore continued to have in every city a constitution, magistracies, a senate, a prytaneum, laws, and judges. The city was supposed to be independent, and seemed to have no other relations with Rome than those of an ally with its ally. Still, in the terms of the treaty which had been drawn up at the time of the conquest, Rome had been careful to insert these words: *Majestatem populi Romani comiter conservato.*[24] These terms established the dependence of the allied city upon the metropolitan city, and as they were very vague, it happened that the measure of this dependence was always in accordance with the will of the stronger. These cities, which were called free, received orders from Rome, obeyed proconsuls, and paid taxes to the collectors of the revenue. Their magistrates rendered their accounts to the governor of the province, who also heard the appeals from the judges.[25] Now, such was the nature of the municipal system among the ancients that it needed complete independence, or it ceased to exist. Between the maintenance of the institutions of the city and their subordination to a foreign power, there was a contradiction which perhaps does not clearly appear to the eyes of the moderns, but which must have struck every man of that period. Municipal liberty and the government of Rome were irreconcilable; the first could be only an appearance, a falsehood, an amusement calculated to divert the minds of men.

[23] Livy, I. 38; VII. 31; IX. 20; XXVI. 16; XXVIII. 34. Cicero, *De Lege Agr.*, I. 6; II. 32. Festus, v. *Præfecturæ.*

[24] Cicero, *Pro Balbo,* 16.

[25] Livy, XLV. 18. Cicero, *ad Attic.*, VI. 1, 2. Appian, *Civil Wars,* I. 102. Tacitus, XV. 45.

Each of those cities sent, almost every year, a deputation to Rome, and its most minute and most private affairs were regulated by the senate. They still had their municipal magistrates, their archons, and their strategi, freely elected by themselves; but the archon no longer had any other duty than to inscribe his name on the registers for the purpose of marking the year, and the strategus, in earlier times the chief of the army and of the state, now had no other care than to keep the streets in order, and inspect the markets.[26]

Municipal institutions, therefore, perished among the nations that were called allies as well as among those that bore the name of subjects; there was only this difference, that the first preserved the exterior forms. Indeed, the city, as antiquity had understood it, was no longer seen anywhere, except within the walls of Rome.

Then, too, the Romans, while everywhere destroying the municipal system, substituted nothing in its place. To the people whose institutions they took away, they did not give their own instead. The Romans never thought of creating new institutions for their use; they never made a constitution for the people of their empire, and did not understand how to establish fixed rules for their government. Even the authority which Rome exercised over the cities had no regularity. As they made no part of her state, or of her city, she had no legal power over them. Her subjects were strangers to her — a reason why she exercised this irregular and unlimited power which ancient municipal law allowed citizens to exercise towards foreigners and enemies. It was on this principle that the Roman administration was a long time regulated, and this is the manner in which it was carried on.

Rome sent one of her citizens into a country. She made that country the *province* of this man, — that is to say, his charge, his own care, his personal affair; this was the sense of the word *provincia*. At the same time she conferred upon this citizen the *imperium;* this signified that she gave up in his favor, for a determined time, the sovereignty which she held over the country. From that time this citizen represented in his person all the rights of the republic, and by this means he was an

[26] Philostratus, *Lives of the Sophists*, I. 23. Boeckh., *Corp. Inscr.*, passim.

absolute master. He fixed the amount of taxes; he exercised the military power, and administered justice. His relations with the subjects, or the allies, were limited by no constitution. When he sat in his judgment-seat, he pronounced decisions according to his own will; no law controlled him, neither the provincial laws, as he was a Roman, nor the Roman laws, as he passed judgment upon provincials. If there were laws between him and those that he governed, he had to make them himself, for he alone could bind himself. Therefore the *imperium* with which he was clothed included the legislative power; and thus it happened that the governors had the right, and established the custom, on entering the provinces, of publishing a code of laws, which they called their Edict, and to which they morally promised to conform. But as the governors were changed annually, these codes changed every year, for the reason that the law had its source only in the will of the man who was for the time invested with the *imperium*. This principle was so rigorously applied that, when a judgment had been pronounced by a governor, but had not been entirely executed at the time of his departure from the province, the arrival of his successor completely annulled this judgment, and the proceedings were recommenced.[27]

Such was the omnipotence of the governor. He was the living law. As to invoking the justice of Rome against his acts of violence or his crimes, the provincials could not do this unless they could find a Roman citizen who would act as their patron,[28] for, as to themselves, they had no right to demand the protection of the laws of the city, or to appeal to its courts. They were foreigners; the judicial and official language called them *peregrini;* all that the law said of the *hostis* continued to be applied to them.

The legal situation of the inhabitants of the empire appears clearly in the writings of the Roman jurisconsults. We there see that the people are considered as no longer having their own laws, and as not yet having those of Rome. For them, therefore, the law did not exist in any manner. In the eyes of the Roman jurisconsult, a provincial was neither husband nor father, — that is to say, the law recognized neither his

[27] Gaius, IV. 103, 105.
[28] Cicero, *De Orat.*, I. 9.

marital nor his paternal authority. For him property did not exist. It was a double impossibility for him to become a proprietor; it was impossible by reason of his personal condition, because he was not a Roman citizen, and impossible by reason of the condition of the land, because it was not Roman territory, and the law admitted the complete right of ownership only within the limits of the *ager Romanus.* For the lawyers taught that the land in the provinces was never private property, and that men could have only the possession and usufruct thereof.[29] Now, what they said in the second century of our era of the provincial territory had been equally true of the Italian soil before Italy obtained the Roman franchise, as we shall presently see.

It is certain, then, that the people, as fast as they entered the Roman empire, lost their municipal religion, their government, and their private law. We can easily believe that Rome softened in practice whatever was destructive in this subjection. We see, indeed, that, though the Roman laws did not recognize the paternal authority in the subject, they allowed this authority still to subsist in practice. If they did not permit a certain man to call himself a proprietor of the soil, they still allowed him the possession of it; he cultivated his land, sold it, and devised it by will. It was not said that this land was his, but they said it was as good as his, *pro suo.* It was not his property, *dominium,* but it was among his goods, *in bonis.*[30] Rome thus invented for the benefit of the subject a multitude of turns and artifices of language. Indeed, the Roman genius, if its municipal traditions prevented it from making laws for the conquered, could not suffer society to fall into dissolution. In principle the provincials were placed outside the laws, while in fact they lived as if they had them; but with the exception of this, and the tolerance of the conquerors, all the institutions of the vanquished and all their laws were allowed to disappear. The Roman empire presented, for several generations, this singular spectacle: A single city remained intact, preserving its institutions and its laws, while all the rest — that is to say, more than a hundred millions of souls — either had no kind of laws, or had such as were not recognized by the

[29] Gaius, II. 7. Cicero, *Pro Flacco,* 32.
[30] Gaius, I. 52; II. 5, 6, 7.

ruling city. The world then was not precisely in a state of chaos, but force, arbitrary rule, and convention, in default of laws and principles, alone sustained society.

Such was the effect of the Roman conquest on the nations that successively became its prey. Of the city everything went to ruin; religion first, then the government, and finally private law. All the municipal institutions, already for a long time shaken, were finally overthrown and destroyed; but no regular society, no system of government, replaced at once what had disappeared. There was a period of stagnation between the moment when men saw the municipal governments dissolve and that in which another form of society appeared. The nation did not at once succeed the city, for the Roman empire in no wise resembled a nation. It was a confused multitude, where there was real order only in one central point, and where all the rest enjoyed only a factitious and transitory order, and obtained this only at the price of obedience. The conquered nations succeeded in establishing themselves as an organized body only by conquering in their turn the rights and institutions which Rome was inclined to keep for itself. In order to do this they had to enter the Roman city, make a place for themselves there, press forward, and transform that city also, in order to make of themselves and Rome one body. This was a long and difficult task.

5.   *The Conquered Nations successively enter the Roman City.*

We have seen how deplorable was the condition of the Roman subject, and how the condition of the citizen was to be envied. Not vanity alone, but the most real and dearest interests had to suffer. Whoever was not a Roman citizen was not reputed to be either a husband or a father; legally he could be neither proprietor nor heir. Such was the value of the title of Roman citizen, that without it one was outside the law, and with it he entered regular society. It happened, therefore, that this title became the object of the most lively desires of men. The Latin, the Italian, the Greek, and, later, the Spaniard and the Gaul, aspired to be Roman citizens — the single means of having rights and of counting for something. All, one after another, nearly in the order in which they entered the Roman empire, labored to enter the Roman city, and, after long efforts, succeeded. This slow introduction into the Roman state is the last act in the long history of the social transformations of the ancients. To observe this great event in all its successive phases, we must examine its commencement, in the fourth century before our era.

Latium had been conquered; of the forty small peoples who inhabited it, Rome had exterminated half. She had despoiled some of their lands, and had left to others the title of allies. In B. C. 340 the latter perceived that the alliance was entirely to their detriment, that they were expected to obey in everything, and that they were required every year to lavish their blood and money for the sole benefit of Rome. They formed a coalition; their chief, Annius, thus stated their demands in the Roman senate: "Give us equality. Let us have the same laws; let us form but a single state — *una civitas;* let us have but a single name; let us all alike be called Romans." Annius thus announced, in the year 340, the desire which all the nations of the empire, one after another expressed, and which was to be completely realized only after five centuries and a half. Then such a thought was new and very unexpected; the Romans declared it monstrous and criminal. It was, indeed, contrary to the old religion and the old law of the cities. The consul, Manlius, replied, that if such a proposition should be accepted, he would slay with his own hand the first Latin who should come to take his seat in the senate; then, turning towards the altar, he called upon the god to witness, saying, "Thou hast heard, O Jupiter, the impious words that have come from this man's mouth. Canst thou tolerate, O Jupiter, that a foreigner should come to sit in thy sacred temple as a senator, as a consul?" Thus Manlius expressed the old sentiment of repulsion that separated the citizen from the foreigner. He was the organ of the ancient religious law, which prescribed that the foreigner should be detested by the men because he was cursed by the gods of the city. It appeared to him impossible that a Latin should be a senator because the place of meeting for the senate was a temple, and the Roman gods could not suffer the presence of a foreigner in their sanctuary.

War followed: the Latins, being conquered, surrendered, — that is to say, they gave up to the Romans their cities, their worships, their laws, and their lands. Their position was cruel.

A consul said in the senate that, if they did not wish Rome to be surrounded by a vast desert, the fate of the Latins should be settled with some regard to clemency. Livy does not clearly explain what was done. If we are to trust him, the Latins obtained the right of Roman citizenship without including in the political privileges the right of suffrage, or in the civil the right of marriage. We may also note, that these new citizens were not counted in the census. It is clear that the senate deceived the Latins in giving them the name of Roman citizens. This title disguised a real subjection, since the men who bore it had the obligations of citizens without the rights. So true is this, that several Latin cities revolted, in order that this pretended citizenship might be withdrawn.

A century passed, and, without Livy's notice of the fact, we might easily discover that Rome had changed her policy. The condition of the Latins having the rights of citizens, without suffrage and without *connubium,* no longer existed. Rome had withdrawn from them the title of citizens, or, rather, had done away with this falsehood, and had decided to restore to the different cities their municipal governments, their laws, and their magistracies.

But by a skilful device Rome opened a door which, narrow as it was, permitted subjects to enter the Roman city. It granted to every Latin who had been a magistrate in his native city the right to become a Roman citizen at the expiration of his term of office.[31] This time the gift of this right was complete and without reserve; suffrage, magistracies, census, marriage, private law, all were included. Rome resigned itself to share with the foreigner its religion, its government, and its laws; only its favors were individual, and were addressed not to entire cities, but to a few men in each of them. Rome admitted to her bosom only what was best, wealthiest, and most estimable in Latium.

This right of citizenship then became precious, first, because it was complete, and secondly, because it was a privilege. Through it a man figured in the comitia of the most powerful city of Italy; he might be consul and commander of the legions. There was also the means of satisfying more modest ambitions; thanks to this right, one might ally himself, by

[31] Appian, *Civil Wars,* II. 26.

marriage, to a Roman family; or he might take up his abode
at Rome, and become a proprietor there; or he might carry
on trade in Rome, which had already become one of the
first commercial towns in the world. One might enter the
company of farmers of the revenue, — that is to say, take a
part in the enormous profits which accrued from the collection
of the revenue, or from speculations in the lands of the *ager
publicus.* Wherever one lived he was effectually protected; he
escaped the authority of the municipal magistrate, and was
sheltered from the caprices of the Roman magistrates themselves. By being a citizen of Rome, a man gained honor,
wealth, and security.

The Latins, therefore, became eager to obtain this title, and
used all sorts of means to acquire it. One day, when Rome
wished to appear a little severe, she found that twelve thousand of them had obtained it through fraud.

Ordinarily, Rome shut her eyes, knowing that by this means
her population increased, and that the losses of war were
thus repaired. But the Latin cities suffered; their richest inhabitants became Roman citizens, and Latium was impoverished. The taxes, from which the richest were exempt as
Roman citizens, became more and more burdensome, and the
contingent of soldiers that had to be furnished to Rome was
every year more difficult to fill up. The larger the number of
those who obtained the Roman franchise, the harder was the
lot of those who had not that right. There came a time when
the Latin cities demanded that this franchise should cease to
be a privilege. The Italian cities, which, having been conquered two centuries before, were in nearly the same condition
as those of Latium, and also saw their richest inhabitants
abandon them to become Romans, demanded for themselves
the Roman franchise. The fate of subjects and allies had
become all the less supportable at this period, from the fact
that the Roman democracy was then agitating the great question of the agrarian laws. Now, the principle of all these laws
was, that neither subject nor ally could be an owner of the
soil, except by a formal act of the city, and that the greater
part of the Italian lands belonged to the republic. One party
demanded, therefore, that these lands, which were nearly all
occupied by Italians, should be taken back by the state, and

distributed among the poor of Rome. Thus the Italians were menaced with general ruin. They felt keenly the need of civil rights, and they could only come into possession of these by becoming Roman citizens.

The war that followed was called the *social war;* the allies of Rome took up arms that they might no longer be allies, but might become Romans. Rome, though victorious, was still constrained to grant what was demanded, and the Italians received the rights of citizenship. Thenceforth assimilated to the Romans, they could vote in the forum; in private life they were governed by Roman laws; their right to the soil was recognized, and the Italian lands, as well as Roman soil, could be owned by them in fee simple. Then was established the *jus Italicum:* this was the law, not of the Italian person, since the Italian had become a Roman, but of the Italian soil, which was susceptible of ownership, just as if it had been the *ager Romanus.*[32]

From that time all Italy formed a single state. There still remained the provinces to enter into the Roman unity.

We must make a distinction between Greece and the provinces of the west. In the west were Gaul and Spain, which, before the conquest, knew nothing of the real municipal system. The Romans attempted to create this form of government among them, either thinking it impossible to govern them otherwise, or judging that, in order gradually to assimilate them to the Italian nations, it would be necessary to make them pass over the same route which the Italians had followed. Hence it happened that the emperors who suppressed all political life at Rome, kept up the forms of municipal liberty in the provinces. Thus cities were formed in Gaul; each had its senate, its aristocratic body, its elective magistrates; each had even its local worship, its *Genius,* and its city-protecting divinity, after the manner of those in ancient Greece and ancient Italy. Now, this municipal system, thus established, did not prevent men from arriving at the Roman citizenship; on the contrary, it prepared them for it. A gradation, skilfully arranged among these cities, marked the steps by which they were insensibly to approach Rome, and finally to become

[32] Thenceforth also called *res mancipi.* See Ulpian

assimilated with it. There were distinguished, first, the allies, who had a government and laws of their own, and no legal bond with Roman citizens; second, the colonies, which enjoyed the civil rights of the Romans, without having political rights; third, the cities of the Italian right, — that is to say, those to whom, by the favor of Rome, the complete right of property over their lands had been granted, as if these lands had been in Italy; fourth, the cities of the Latin right, — that is to say, those whose inhabitants could, following the custom formerly established in Latium, become Roman citizens after having held a municipal office. These distinctions were so deep, that between persons of two different classes no marriage or other legal relation was possible. But the emperors took care that the cities should rise in the course of time, and one after another, from the condition of subjects or allies, to the Italian right, from the Italian right to the Latin right. When a city had arrived at this point, its principal families became Romans one after another.

Greece entered just as little into the Roman state. At first every city preserved the forms and machinery of the municipal government. At the moment of the conquest, Greece showed a desire to preserve its autonomy; and this was left to it longer, perhaps, than it would have wished. At the end of a few generations it aspired to become Roman; vanity, ambition, and interest worked for this.

The Greeks had not for Rome that hatred which is usually borne towards a foreign master. They admired it; they had a veneration for it; of their own accord they devoted a worship to it, and built temples to it as to a god. Every city forgot its protecting divinity, and worshipped in its place the goddess Rome and the god Cæsar; the greatest festivals were for them, and the first magistrates had no higher duty than celebrating with great pomp the Augustan games. Men thus became accustomed to lift their eyes above their cities; they saw in Rome the model city, the true country, the prytaneum of all nations. The city where one was born seemed small. Its interests no longer occupied their minds; the honors which it conferred no longer satisfied their ambition. Men thought themselves nothing if they were not Roman citizens. Under the emperors, it is true, this title no longer conferred political rights; but it offered more solid advantages, since the man who was clothed with it acquired at the same time the full right to hold property, the right to inherit, the right to marry, the paternal authority, and all the private rights of Rome. The laws which were found in each city were variable and without foundation; they were merely tolerated. The Romans despised them, and the Greeks had little respect for them. In order to have fixed laws, recognized by all as truly sacred, it was necessary to have those of Rome.

We do not see that all Greece, or even a Greek city, formally asked for this right of citizenship, so much desired; but men worked individually to acquire it, and Rome bestowed it with a good grace. Some obtained it through the favor of the emperor; others bought it. It was granted to those who had three children, or who served in certain divisions of the army. Sometimes to construct a merchant vessel of a certain tonnage, or to carry grain to Rome, was sufficient to obtain it. An easy and prompt means of acquiring it was to sell one's self as a slave to a Roman citizen, for the act of freeing him according to legal forms conferred the right of citizenship.[33] One who had the title of Roman citizen no longer formed a part of his native city, either civilly or politically. He could continue to live there, but he was considered an alien; he was no longer subject to the laws of the city, he no longer obeyed its magistrates, no longer supported its pecuniary burdens.[34] This was a consequence of the old principle, which did not permit a man to belong to two cities at the same time.[35] It naturally happened that, after several generations, there were in every Greek city quite a large number of men, and these ordinarily the wealthiest, who recognized neither its government nor its laws. Thus slowly, and as if by a natural death, perished the municipal system. There came a time when the city was a mere framework that contained nothing, where the local laws

[33] Suetonius, Nero, 24. Petronius, 57. Ulpian, III. Gaius, I. 16, 17.

[34] He became an alien even in respect to his own family, if it had not, like him, the right of citizenship. He did not inherit its property. Pliny, Panegyric, 37.

[35] Cicero, Pro Balbo, 28; Pro Archia, 5; Pro Cæcina, 36. Cornelius Nepos, Atticus, 3. Greece long before had abandoned this principle, but Rome held faithfully to it.

applied to hardly a person, where the municipal judges no
longer had anything to adjudicate upon.

Finally, when eight or ten generations had sighed for the
Roman franchise, and all those who were of any account had
obtained it, there appeared an imperial decree which granted
it to all free men without distinction.

What is remarkable here is, that no one can tell the date of
this decree or the name of the prince who issued it. The honor
is given, with some probability of truth, to Caracalla, — that is
to say, to a prince who never had very elevated views; and this
is attributed to him as simply a fiscal measure. We meet in
history with few more important decrees than this. It abolished
the distinction which had existed since the Roman conquest
between the dominant nation and the subject peoples; it even
caused to disappear a much older distinction, which religion
and law had made between cities. Still the historians of that
time took no note of it, and all we know of it we glean from
two vague passages of the jurisconsults and a short notice in
Dion Cassius.[36] If this decree did not strike contemporaries,
and was not remarked by those who then wrote history, it is
because the change of which it was the legal expression had
been accomplished long before. The inequality between
citizens and subjects had been lessened every generation, and

---

[36] *"Antoninus Pius jus Romanæ civitatis omnibus subjectis dona-
vit."* Justinian, *Novels,* 78, ch. 5. *"In orbe Romano qui sunt, ex con-
stitutione imperatoris Antonini, cives Romani effecti sunt."* Ulpian,
in *Digest,* I. tit. 5, 17. It is known, moreover, from Spartianus, that
Caracalla was called Antoninus in official acts. Dion Cassius says that
Caracalla gave all the inhabitants of the empire the Roman franchise
in order to make general the impost of tithes on enfranchisements
and successions. The distinction between *peregrini,* Latins, and
citizens did not entirely disappear; it is found in Ulpian and in the
Code. Indeed, it appeared natural that enfranchised slaves should
not immediately become Roman citizens, but should pass through
all the old grades that separated servitude from citizenship. We also
judge from certain indications that the distinction between the
Italian lands and the provincial lands still continued for a long time.
(*Code,* VII. 25; VII. 31; X. 39. *Digest,* L. tit. 1.) Thus the city of Tyre,
in Phœnicia, even later than Caracalla, enjoyed as a privilege the
jus Italicum. (*Digest,* IV. 15.) The continuance of this distinction is
explained by the interest of the emperors, who did not wish to be
deprived of the tribute which the provincial lands paid into the
treasury.

had been gradually effaced. The decree might pass unperceived under the veil of a fiscal measure; it proclaimed and caused to pass into the domain of law what was already an accomplished fact.

The title of citizen then began to fall into desuetude; or, if it was still employed, it was to designate the condition of a free man as opposed to that of a slave. From that time all that made a part of the Roman empire, from Spain to the Euphrates, formed really one people and a single state. The distinction between cities had disappeared; that between nations still appeared, but was hardly noticed. All the inhabitants of this immense empire were equally Romans. The Gaul abandoned his name of Gaul, and eagerly assumed that of Roman; the Spaniard, the inhabitant of Thrace, or of Syria, did the same. There was now but a single name, a single country, a single government, a single code of laws.

We see how the Roman city developed from age to age. At first it contained only patricians and clients; afterwards the plebeian class obtained a place there; then came the Latins, then the Italians, and finally the provincials. The conquest had not sufficed to work this great change; the slow transformation of ideas, the prudent but uninterrupted concessions of the emperors, and the eagerness of individual interests had been necessary. Then all the cities gradually disappeared, and the Roman city, the last one left, was itself so transformed that it became the union of a dozen great nations under a single master. Thus fell the municipal system.

It does not belong to our plan to tell by what system of government this was replaced, or to inquire if this change was at first more advantageous than unfortunate for the nations. We must stop at the moment when the old social forms which antiquity had established were forever effaced.

Chapter III

CHRISTIANITY CHANGES THE CONDITIONS OF GOVERNMENT

THE victory of Christianity marks the end of ancient society. With the new religion this social transformation, which we saw begun six or seven centuries earlier, was completed.

To understand how much the principles and the essential rules of politics were then changed, we need only recollect that ancient society had been established by an old religion whose principal dogma was that every god protected exclusively a single family or a single city, and existed only for that. This was the time of the domestic gods and the city-protecting divinities. This religion had produced laws; the relations among men — property, inheritance, legal proceedings — all were regulated, not by the principles of natural equity, but by the dogmas of this religion, and with a view to the requirements of its worship. It was this religion that had established a government among men; that of the father in the family; that of the king or magistrate in the city. All had come from religion, — that is to say, from the opinion that man had entertained of the divinity. Religion, law, and government were confounded, and had been but a single thing under three different aspects.

We have sought to place in a clear light this social system of the ancients, where religion was absolute master, both in public and private life; where the state was a religious community, the king a pontiff, the magistrate a priest, and the law a sacred formula; where patriotism was piety, and exile excommunication; where individual liberty was unknown; where man was enslaved to the state through his soul, his body, and his property; where the notions of law and of duty, of justice and of affection, were bounded within the limits of the city; where human association was necessarily confined within a certain circumference around a prytaneum; and where men saw no possibility of founding larger societies. Such were the characteristic traits of the Greek and Italian cities during the first period of their history.

But little by little, as we have seen, society became modified. Changes took place in government and in laws at the same time as in religious ideas. Already, in the fifth century which preceded Christianity, the alliance was no longer so close between religion on the one hand and law and politics on the other. The efforts of the oppressed classes, the overthrow of the sacerdotal class, the labors of philosophers, the progress of thought, had unsettled the ancient principles of human association. Men had made incessant efforts to free themselves from the thraldom of this old religion, in which they could no longer believe; law and politics, as well as morals, in the course of time were freed from its fetters.

But this species of divorce came from the disappearance of the ancient religion; if law and politics began to be a little more independent, it was because men ceased to have religious beliefs. If society was no longer governed by religion, it was especially because this religion no longer had any power. But there came a day when the religious sentiment recovered life and vigor, and when, under the Christian form, belief regained its empire over the soul. Were men not then destined to see the reappearance of the ancient confusion of government and the priesthood, of faith and the law?

With Christianity not only was the religious sentiment revived, but it assumed a higher and less material expression. Whilst previously men had made for themselves gods of the human soul, or of the great forces of nature, they now began to look upon God as really foreign by his essence, from human nature on the one hand, and from the world on the other. The divine Being was placed outside and above physical nature. Whilst previously every man had made a god for himself, and there were as many of them as there were families and cities, God now appeared as a unique, immense, universal being, alone animating the worlds, alone able to supply the need of adoration that is in man. Religion, instead of being, as formerly among the nations of Greece and Italy, little more than an assemblage of practices, a series of rites which men repeated without having any idea of them, a succession of formulas which often were no longer understood because the language had grown old, a tradition which had been transmitted from age to age, and which owed its sacred character to its antiquity alone, — was now a collection of doctrines, and a great object proposed to faith. It was no longer exterior; it took up its abode especially in the thoughts of man. It was no longer matter; it became spirit. Christianity changed the nature and the form of adoration. Man no longer offered God food and drink. Prayer was no longer a form of incantation; it was an act of faith and a humble petition. The soul sustained another relation with the divinity; the fear of the gods was replaced by the love of God.

Christianity introduced other new ideas. It was not the domestic religion of any family, the national religion of any city, or of any race. It belonged neither to a caste nor to a corporation. From its first appearance it called to itself the whole human race. Christ said to his disciples, "Go ye into all the world, and preach the gospel to every creature."

This principle was so extraordinary, and so unexpected, that the first disciples hesitated for a moment; we may see in the Acts of the Apostles that several of them refused at first to propagate the new doctrine outside the nation with which it had originated. These disciples thought, like the ancient Jews, that the God of the Jews would not accept adoration from foreigners; like the Romans and the Greeks of ancient times, they believed that every race had its god, that to propagate the name and worship of this god was to give up one's own good and special protector, and that such a work was contrary at the same time to duty and to interest. But Peter replied to these disciples, "God gave the gentiles the like gift as He did unto us." St. Paul loved to repeat this grand principle on all occasions, and in every kind of form. "God had opened the door of faith unto the gentiles." "Is he the God of the Jews, only? Is he not also of the gentiles?" "We are all baptized into one body, whether we be Jews or gentiles."

In all this there was something quite new. For, everywhere, in the first ages of humanity, the divinity had been imagined as attaching himself especially to one race. The Jews had believed in the God of the Jews; the Athenians in the Athenian Pallas; the Romans in Jupiter Capitolinus. The right to practise a worship had been a privilege.

The foreigner had been repulsed from the temple; one not a Jew could not enter the temple of the Jews; the Lacedæmonian had not the right to invoke the Athenian Pallas. It is just to say, that, in the five centuries which preceded Christianity, all who thought were struggling against these narrow rules. Philosophy had often taught, since Anaxagoras, that the god of the universe received the homage of all men, without distinction. The religion of Eleusis had admitted the initiated from all cities. The religion of Cybele, of Serapis, and some others, had accepted, without distinction, worshippers from all nations. The Jews had begun to admit the foreigner to their religion; the Greeks and the Romans had admitted him into their cities. Christianity, coming after all this progress in thought and institutions, presented to the adoration of all men a single God, a universal God, a God who belonged to all, who had no chosen people, and who made no distinction in races, families, or states.

For this God there were no longer strangers. The stranger no longer profaned the temple, no longer tainted the sacrifice by his presence. The temple was open to all who believed in God. The priesthood ceased to be hereditary, because religion was no longer a patrimony. The worship was no longer kept secret; the rites, the prayers, the dogmas were no longer concealed. On the contrary, there was thenceforth religious instruction, which was not only given, but which was offered, which was carried to those who were the farthest away, and which sought out the most indifferent. The spirit of propagandism replaced the law of exclusion.

From this great consequences flowed, as well for the relations between nations as for the government of states.

Between nations religion no longer commanded hatred; it no longer made it the citizen's duty to detest the foreigner; its very essence, on the contrary, was to teach him that towards the stranger, towards the enemy, he owed the duties of justice, and even of benevolence. The barriers between nations or races were thus thrown down; the *pomœrium* disappeared. "Christ," says the apostle, "hath broken down the middle wall of partition between us." "But now are they many members," he also says, "yet but one body." "There is neither Greek nor

Jew, circumcision nor uncircumcision, Barbarian, Scythian, bond nor free: but Christ is all, and in all."

The people were also taught that they were all descended from the same common father. With the unity of God, the unity of the human race also appeared to men's minds; and it was thenceforth a religious necessity to forbid men to hate each other.

As to the government of the state, we cannot say that Christianity essentially altered that, precisely because it did not occupy itself with the state. In the ancient ages, religion and the state made but one; every people adored its own god, and every god governed his own people; the same code regulated the relations among men, and their duties towards the gods of the city. Religion then governed the state, and designated its chiefs by the voice of the lot, or by that of the auspices. The state, in its turn, interfered with the domain of the conscience, and punished every infraction of the rites and the worship of the city. Instead of this, Christ teaches that his kingdom is not of this world. He separates religion from government. Religion, being no longer of the earth, now interferes the least possible in terrestrial affairs. Christ adds, "Render to Cæsar the things that are Cæsar's, and to God the things that are God's." It is the first time that God and the state are so clearly distinguished. For Cæsar at that period was still the *pontifex maximus*, the chief and the principal organ of the Roman religion; he was the guardian and the interpreter of beliefs. He held the worship and the dogmas in his hands. Even his person was sacred and divine, for it was a peculiarity of the policy of the emperors that, wishing to recover the attributes of ancient royalty, they were careful not to forget the divine character which antiquity had attached to the king-pontiffs and to the priest-founders. But now Christ breaks the alliance which paganism and the empire wished to renew. He proclaims that religion is no longer the state, and that to obey Cæsar is no longer the same thing as to obey God.

Christianity completes the overthrow of the local worship; it extinguishes the prytanea, and completely destroys the city-protecting divinities. It does more; it refuses to assume the empire which these worships had exercised over civil society.

It professes that between the state and itself there is nothing in common. It separates what all antiquity had confounded. We may remark, moreover, that during three centuries the new religion lived entirely beyond the action of the state; it knew how to dispense with state protection, and even to struggle against it. These three centuries established an abyss between the domain of the government and the domain of religion; and, as the recollection of this period could not be effaced, it followed that this distinction became a plain and incontestable truth, which the efforts even of a part of the clergy could not eradicate.

This principle was fertile in great results. On one hand, politics became definitively freed from the strict rules which the ancient religion had traced, and could govern men without having to bend to sacred usages, without consulting the auspices or the oracles, without conforming all acts to the beliefs and requirements of a worship. Political action was freer; no other authority than that of the moral law now impeded it. On the other hand, if the state was more completely master in certain things, its action was also more limited. A complete half of man had been freed from its control. Christianity taught that only a part of man belonged to society; that he was bound to it by his body and by his material interests; that when subject to a tyrant, it was his duty to submit; that as a citizen of a republic, he ought to give his life for it, but that, in what related to his soul, he was free, and was bound only to God.

Stoicism had already marked this separation; it had restored man to himself, and had founded liberty of conscience. But that which was merely the effort of the energy of a courageous sect, Christianity made a universal and unchangeable rule for succeeding generations; what was only the consolation of a few, it made the common good of humanity.

If, now, we recollect what has been said above on the omnipotence of the states among the ancients, — if we bear in mind how far the city, in the name of its sacred character and of religion, which was inherent in it, exercised an absolute empire, — we shall see that this new principle was the source whence individual liberty flowed.

The mind once freed, the greatest difficulty was overcome, and liberty was compatible with social order.

Sentiments and manners, as well as politics, were then changed. The idea which men had of the duties of the citizen were modified. The first duty no longer consisted in giving one's time, one's strength, one's life to the state. Politics and war were no longer the whole of man; all the virtues were no longer comprised in patriotism, for the soul no longer had a country. Man felt that he had other obligations besides that of living and dying for the city. Christianity distinguished the private from the public virtues. By giving less honor to the latter, it elevated the former; it placed God, the family, the human individual above country, the neighbor above the city.

Law was also changed in its nature. Among all ancient nations law had been subject to, and had received all its rules from, religion. Among the Persians, the Hindus, the Jews, the Greeks, the Italians, and the Gauls, the law had been contained in the sacred books or in religious traditions, and thus every religion had made laws after its own image. Christianity is the first religion that did not claim to be the source of law. It occupied itself with the duties of men, not with their interests. Men saw it regulate neither the laws of property, nor the order of succession, nor obligations, nor legal proceedings. It placed itself outside the law, and outside all things purely terrestrial. Law was independent; it could draw its rules from nature, from the human conscience, from the powerful idea of the just that is in men's minds. It could develop in complete liberty; could be reformed and improved without obstacle; could follow the progress of morals, and could conform itself to the interests and social needs of every generation.

The happy influence of the new idea is easily seen in the history of Roman law. During several centuries preceding the triumph of Christianity, Roman law had already been striving to disengage itself from religion, and to approach natural equity; but it proceeded only by shifts and devices, which enervated and enfeebled its moral authority. The work of regenerating legislation, announced by the Stoic philosophers, pursued by the noble efforts of Roman jurisconsults, outlined by the artifices and expedients of the pretor, could not completely succeed except by favor of the independence which the new religion allowed to the law. We can see, as Christianity gained ground, that the Roman codes admitted new rules no longer by subterfuges, but openly and without hesitation. The domestic penates having been overthrown, and the sacred fires extinguished, the ancient constitution of the family disappeared forever, and with it the rules that had flowed from this source. The father had lost the absolute authority which his priesthood had formerly given him, and preserved only that which nature itself had conferred upon him for the good of the child. The wife, whom the old religion placed in a position inferior to the husband, became morally his equal. The laws of property were essentially altered; the sacred landmarks disappeared from the fields; the right of property no longer flowed from religion, but from labor; its acquisition became easier, and the formalities of the ancient law were definitively abolished.

Thus, by the single fact that the family no longer had its domestic religion, its constitution and its laws were transformed; so, too, from the single fact that the state no longer had its official religion, the rules for the government of men were forever changed.

Our study must end at this limit, which separates ancient from modern polities. We have written the history of a belief. It was established, and human society was constituted. It was modified, and society underwent a series of revolutions. It disappeared, and society changed its character. Such was the law of ancient times.